W9-CRV-656

From the author of Finale 2011 a Trailblazer Guide ™

FINALE® 2012
A TRAILBLAZER GUIDE™

*Beginner or pro, learn the
essential tips, tricks, and tactics
you need to know to
get the most out of Finale*

MARK JOHNSON

Finale® 2012 *A Trailblazer Guide*™

Copyright ©2011 Penelope Press

All rights reserved. No part of this book may be reproduced without the written permission of the publisher, except for brief passages for review purposes.

All musical examples created with Finale® software.

All copyrights and trademarks used as examples and references in this book are retained by their individual owners.

Cover design by Windmill Design, www.windmilldesign.com.

Cover Photo: "Trail Disappearing Around a Turn" © Corbis. Location: Huesca Province, Spain

Edited for technical accuracy by Kami Johnson, MakeMusic Quality Assurance Engineer.

Technology and the Internet are constantly changing, and by necessity the lapse of time between the writing and distribution of this book, some aspects may be out of date. Accordingly, the author and publisher assume no responsibility for actions taken by readers based upon the contents of this book.

ISBN: 978-0-9814731-6-1

Educational facilities, companies, and organizations interested in multiple copies or licensing of this book should contact the publisher for quantity discount information. Portions of this book are also available individually and can be tailored for specific needs.

Penelope Press

Penelope Press
4515 Xerxes Avenue South
Minneapolis, MN 55410

About the Author

Mark Johnson is an employee at MakeMusic who has worked as a technical support representative, quality assurance technician, and technical writer for Finale and all of MakeMusic's notation products. Building off his degree in music theory and composition from St. Olaf College, Mark has experience composing, arranging, and engraving with Finale. He has authored several Finale books including *Finale Power!*, *Finale 2011-A Trailblazer Guide, and Composing with Finale*. He continues to use and write about Finale on a daily basis.

Dedication

For Kami, and her dedication to a project that could not exist without her.

Acknowledgments

With every revision of this book I am humbled by the nimble accompaniment of virtuosos somehow capable of enduring a performer who is unnecessarily whimsical and always rushing. Thanks to Kami Johnson for once again reminding me why technical editors rightly rule the world (not to mention wives!). To Kathy Mrozek, for your commensurately wonderful and creative design work. And, of course, a special thanks to the wonderful employees at MakeMusic for your continued encouragement and support, and for your contributions to a product that continues to break new ground for musicians year after year. Your skill, hard work, and commitment to professional excellence continues to be an inspiration. Finale exists because of you, and from the trenches it is sometimes easy to forget what a truly great product it is.

Contents

1 Getting Started 1

2 Beginning a New Score 18

3 Note Entry, Articulations, and Expressions 48

5 Clefs, Key Signatures, and Time Signatures 117

6 Slurs, Hairpins, Other Shapes and Repeats 144

11 Measure Numbers, Graphics, Layout, and Printing . . 289

15 Finale, the Web and Other Programs 389

Introduction

So, what does extreme mountain backpacking have to do with music notation software? You launch Finale and before you lies a vast and unknown wilderness. Your feet pound the rocky earth as you advance up the beaten alpine trail, which grows fainter with every step. The sun is high, but the grade is steep, and when the trail ends you will need to make quick, smart decisions to safely reach your destination. You have limited rations, and won't have time to backtrack on your way to the summit. You are in control, you will choose the route, so you reach for your Trailblazer Guide to check for loose rock, glaciers, cliff-dwelling pterodactyls. You will be rounding the next bend any moment, and you do not need any surprises.

Finale 2012—A Trailblazer Guide was designed to pack as much useful knowledge into as few pages as possible using practical, accessible content and by pinpointing the essentials. Finale is huge, and you need useless information like you need an avalanch, so here are the ways this book cuts through the complexity and tells you what you really need to know.

- **Efficient and flexible learning method.** This book is both a conceptual approach and a reference. Carefully organized topics were crafted to transform beginners to power users. But, you can also use it as a reference whenever you need to do something specific.
- **Musical context.** It's organized by musical subject rather than Finale terms wherever possible. You don't need to know a thing about Finale to get the most out of this book!
- **Compatible with Finale's documentation materials.** Use this book along side the Finale User Manual and the other Finale help materials for a comprehensive learning environment.

Whether you want to finish a familiar route faster, take a different path, or blaze a new trail altogether, this book will show you how.

Who This Book is For

This book is for anyone who wants to get the most out of Finale. If you have never used Finale before, you can start at the beginning to develop a comprehensive understanding of Finale's structure while adopting the many important everyday tricks and shortcuts along the way. If you use Finale now, or are learning Finale 2012, you will learn how to take advantage of Finale's exciting new features, boost efficiency, and strengthen your Finale muscle overall.

How This Book is Organized

This book contains 15 chapters:

- **Chapter 1: "Getting Started."** Get acquainted with Finale's framework and learn the important skills crucial to every project.

- **Chapter 2: "Beginning a New Score."** Quickly setup a new score and then learn how to customize any element generated with the Setup Wizard.

- **Chapter 3: "Note Entry, Articulations, and Expressions."** Learn how to use a mouse, computer keyboard, or MIDI keyboard to enter notes efficiently. Then, master the techniques necessary to add articulations, dynamics, tempo markings, rehearsal letters, and other expressions. By the end of this chapter you will be prepared to score an instrumental solo with dynamic markings and articulations.

- **Chapter 4: "Advanced Note Entry, Chords, and Lyrics."** Record your music to the staff in real-time with HyperScribe, then learn the essentials for entering chord symbols and lyrics. By the end of this chapter you will be prepared to create a lead sheet with chord symbols and lyrics.

- **Chapter 5: "Clefs, Key Signatures, and Time Signatures."** Learn how to add clef, meter, or key signature changes at any point in your score. You'll also learn how to manipulate the appearance of these items to suit your needs.

- **Chapter 6: "Slurs, Hairpins, Other Shapes, and Repeats."** Create and customize slurs, crescendos, brackets, lines, glissandos, trill extensions, ottavas, D.S. repeats, codas, and other repeat indications.

- **Chapter 7: "Multiple Staff Scores."** Learn how to properly manage scores of any size. For example, how to work with group brackets, barlines, and even select specific staves for viewing and editing. You'll also learn how to hide empty staves in systems and work with parts.

- **Chapter 8: "Alternate Notation, Staff Styles, and TAB."** Add slash notation, rhythmic notation, percussion, tablature, and guitar markings. You'll learn how to create staves using these styles, or apply them to portions of staves. At the end of this chapter use the skills you have learned to create a guitar part with TAB.

- **Chapter 9: "Editing Your Music."** Learn how to copy, clear, change, transpose, and space your music.

- **Chapter 10: "Fine Tuning: the Details."** Master general alignment and positioning, and then learn to customize beams, stems, noteheads, accidentals, ties, and other elements.

- **Chapter 11: "Measure Numbers, Graphics, Layout, and Printing."** Wrap up your score by finalizing the layout and tailoring the printout.

- **Chapter 12: "Specific Projects and Composing with Finale."** Here, you'll learn techniques for creating specific types of notation including piano scores, figured bass, chant, handbells, cadenzas, and piano reductions. This chapter also includes methods for composing and arranging such as range checking, creating jazz charts, and automatic harmonizing.

- **Chapter 13: "Customizing Finale, Scanning, and Education Tips."** Customize the Finale program to fit your personal working style by managing Finale's Program Options. You'll also learn the best ways to open a scanned score into Finale and how to use Finale as an educational tool.

- **Chapter 14: "Playback, Audio, and the MIDI Tool."** Learn how to use Garritan instruments and Human Playback to get your score sounding great. Here, you will also learn valuable playback techniques, how to customize MIDI, and how to add audio.

- **Chapter 15: "Finale, the Web, and Other Programs."** Here you'll learn how to share files online, transfer files to other programs, create MIDI and audio files, and take advantage of third-party plug-ins.

What's Changed Since 2011?

A lot has changed since the now historic Finale 2011, and some of these things are especially important for upgrading Trailblazers. (If Finale 2012 is your first Finale version, please ignore this section). This isn't a "What's New in Finale 2012" or anything. For that, see the User Manual. This is just a short description of the things you really should know right away, before you even start using Finale 2012. Basically, this section is here to flatten out that 'upgrade speed bump' you may be familiar with.

- **Finale's new "Score Manager" dramatically improves the way Finale handles score instruments and playback sounds, and other score details.** A one-stop-shop for all your score management needs! See...

    "Adding, Removing, and Changing Instruments" on page 26.

    "Changing a Staff's Playback Instrument" on page 30

    "Entering Text Blocks" on page 31

    "Multiple-Instrument Scores" on page 177 (overview)

    "Customizing the Score Order" on page 173

    "Staff Groups" on page 180

    "Managing Playback for Staves with Slash or Rhythmic Notation" on page 204

    "Tablature, Percussion, and Note Shapes Notation Styles" on page 210

    "Instrument Sound Setup" on page 358

    "Using External, Non-General MIDI Sounds" on page 362

    "Using Mute and Solo" on page 377

- **You can now use the new "Add Again" Metatool to add the marking you just entered.** See "Using the "Add Again" Metatool" on page 69.

- **Easily add mid-score instrument changes for instrument doubling.** See "Adding Mid-Score Instrument Changes" on page 206.

- **Finale now supports Unicode fonts,** which probably won't dramatically change your workflow, but means you can add just about any character known to man (and use international keyboard layouts). See "Unicode Fonts" on page 253

- **Export PDFs directly from Finale, and benefit from a few nice Graphics Tool improvements.** See "Working with Graphics" on page 295.

- **Easily create figured bass and harmonic analysis using Finale 2012's new Finale Numeric's font.** See "Figured Bass and Harmonic Analysis" on page 313.

- **Apply letter noteheads to your score instantly with the new AlphaNotes plug-in.** See "AlphaNotes plug-in" on page 351.

What's Changed Since 2010?

Even more has changed since the now ancient Finale 2010. For you trailblazers who have a bit more catching-up to do, and are upgrading from Finale 2010, this section is just for you. (Again, if Finale 2012 is your first Finale version, you can ignore this section).

- **Finale 2011 includes a GREAT new Quick Reference Guide.** Read this resource cover-to-cover and keep it by your side as a helpful memory prod. See "Quick Reference Guide" on page 2.

- **The Finale User Manual is online (if you want it to be).** See **"The User Manual" on page 2.**

- **Different folder and file locations.** Finale installs templates, tutorials, and component files to different places on your hard drive. See **"Where is the Finale 2012 Folder?" on page 4.**

- **Adjusting the staff spacing is now extremely easy.** See **"Changing the Distance Between Staves (for printing)" on page 42.**

- **Moving measures across systems is now CTRL/COMMAND+UP/DOWN ARROW (instead of just up/down arrow).** Well, unless the Selection Tool is selected, in which case it's the same as before, but it's best to just get used to using the CTRL/COMMAND modifier key. See **"Moving Measures Across Systems" on page 44.**

- **You can now add capo chords automatically.** See **"Adding and Removing Capo Chords" on page 104.**

- **A new Lyrics window combines the functionality of the old Edit Lyrics window and the Click Assignment window.** It's almost as simple as that, so no need to worry too much about it. (Lyrics *just work better*.) Check it out to see **"Entering Lyrics" on page 105.**

- **Lyrics can be numbered automatically.** See **"Verse Numbers" on page 113**.

- **Working with staves is generally easier.** For an overview, see **"Adding, Removing, and Changing Instruments" on page 26**.

- **Reordering staves can now done with a dialog box** instead of dragging, sorting, spacing, and all that jazz. As of Finale 2012, this is done in the Score Manager. See "Adding, Removing, and Changing Instruments" on page 26.

- **The Respace Staves dialog box now respects regional selection** instead of always respacing the whole score. See **"Respacing Staves" on page 174**.

- **"Optimization" is gone.** Kaput. Forget it ever existed. The term can be relegated to that dreary place where bad ideas go to die. (Notes never mysteriously disappear anymore. When measures with notes shift across systems to a hidden staff, the staff displays automatically.) To hide an empty staff in a system, you now use the somehow more intuitive command "Hide Empty Staves." See **"Hiding Empty Staves" on page 301**.

- **Staves with notes can be *forced* to hide**, either removed from the system (like the former optimization functionality, now called *collapse*) or hidden without collapsing the adjacent staves (like the former Hide Staff staff style, now referred to as *cutaway*). See **"Hiding Staves with Notes" on page 302**.

- **There's a new Aria Player** with a new look and slightly different controls. See **"Working With Garritan Sounds" on page 359**.

- **Also, see "What's New" and "Finale 2011 Interface Changes" in the Finale 2011 User Manual, and the Finale Read Me** for a complete list of updates, interface changes, and bug fixes.

1
Getting Started

And we're off! And although you'll be able to blaze your own trail soon, for now it's time to properly fasten your hiking boots. The content of this chapter is as integral to learning Finale as it is to using it. These basics apply to any type of user and any project, and some will likely become second nature if they aren't already. Greenhorns, this chapter is absolutely required. Rugged back country roughnecks, there is likely a nugget here for you too. Most importantly, later, when you're gracefully meandering the mountain goats, the basics of navigation will need to be second-nature.

Here's a summary of what you will learn in this chapter:

- How to learn Finale efficiently
- How to get around in Finale
- Other important conventions

Before You Begin

Learning how to learn is a lifelong endeavor; learning how to learn Finale will only take a few minutes. These resources are truly part of everyday life with Finale, and seldom does even the most grizzled power user break free from them entirely.

Your Finale Package

Here's what you've got.

- QuickStart Video Tips
- Quick Reference Guide
- Tutorials
- User Manual

These resources, along with this book, are your faithful companions.

QuickStart Videos

The QuickStart Videos are for both new and experienced users, but if you are somewhat new to Finale, and your computer is available, do this right now. If it isn't, do this at the next opportunity:

1. Launch Finale. Choose **Help** > **QuickStart Videos**.
2. Click **Basic skills** (the top option).
3. Watch each one of these videos.

These concepts are so integral to Finale that it is worth taking a look at these short videos even though I also describe them later in this chapter.

Additionally, whenever you need to perform an unfamiliar task and just want to see a video that covers the basics, check to see if there is a video. For example, if you need to scan a trumpet part:

1. Consider the task and ask yourself: "do a lot of people need to do this?" Scanning is a common one, so you might predict there is a video on the subject - and you'd be right.
2. Choose **Help** > **QuickStart Videos**. Your browser opens and the QuickStart Videos topic appears.
3. Click **getting started** > **scanning** to watch the video.

Glance over all these topics to get an idea of the contents in case you care to view them now or reference them in the future. There is a large amount of info in these collectively, so I do not recommend watching them all at once.

Quick Reference Guide

The Quick Reference Guide is the printed book that accompanies your Finale purchase. This is a fairly new resource deployed by MakeMusic, designed specifically for Finale 2012. It is a visual, accessible overview of Finale's most essential functions. It can be read as either an introduction to the software basics, or as a reference where more experienced users can look for common keyboard shortcuts and other efficiency tips. Reading through the Quick Reference Guide cover-to-cover is an excellent way for new Finale users to scope out the terrain and learn some very useful concepts. Experienced users, it certainly doesn't hurt to keep it nearby.

The Finale Tutorials

Finale 2012 includes a suite of new instructional tutorials including videos and interactive content designed to get you up and running fast. These easy-to-follow tutorials guide you through a single project from start to finish, stopping at just about every common function along the way. I highly recommend completing these as a first step if you are just getting started with Finale, particularly the first 8 chapters. To open the Finale Tutorials, choose **Help** > **Finale Tutorials**.

The User Manual

Refer to the Finale User Manual whenever you have questions not answered by this book. Here's a very quick crash course:

1. Choose **Help** >**User Manual**. The "Finale 2012 User Manual" topic opens in your browser.

2.   Click **How to Use the Finale User Manual** in the navigation pane on the left.

Read through this. I recommend the Index function or Search using one of the Filter.

NOTE:
The Finale User Manual is an online reference, but also installed locally. This allows MakeMusic to offer the most current information, which is always important with constantly changing technology. If your computer is not connected to the Internet, Finale automatically uses a version that was installed to your hard drive. If, you are connected to the Internet, and prefer to use the version of the User Manual on your hard drive, uncheck **Use Online Help when Available** in Program Options-Folders.

If you're ever curious about the functionality of one of Finale's dialog boxes, simply click its Help button. Unlike older Finale versions (before Finale 2008), the help that appears when you click a help button is now the complete User Manual.

Tip:
On Windows, press the **F1** key to open the Finale User Manual at any time.

Read Me Read Me

All the changes and bug fixes are documented in the Read Me as well as that really important thing that didn't make it into the documentation. The Read Me file appears during installation, and on Windows, is also located directly in the Finale folder - best be reading it.

Online Finale Resources

MakeMusic offers plenty of additional resources online, including a robust Knowledge Base, user-to-user forums, and even a blog where various authors contribute their unique and helpful wisdom. See **finalemusic.com/support**.

Your Finale 2012 Trailblazer Online Resource

If you'd like, you can visit trailblazerguides.com to find a list of valuable third-party plug-ins and resources, including the JW plug-ins and TGTools plug-in collection. These are supplemental plug-ins that have been designed to give your Finale package even more power. They make many complicated tasks easy, and include shortcuts for playback, spacing, part extraction and many other tasks. The JW plug-ins are yours for free. TGTools, the Patterson Collection, and Dolet are full-featured demo versions you can use at no cost for a limited time.

Method to the Madness

But how do I know which of these fantastic resources to use when I have a question? Now that is a good question. Here's one practical approach to learning Finale:

1. Buy "Finale 2012: A Trailblazer Guide."
2. Watch the **"Basic Skills" in the QuickStart Videos** (as described earlier). Review the other topics in the QuickStart Videos so you are familiar with them for future reference.
3. (Optional) Read the Finale Tutorials. This will give you a solid footing if you have an hour or two.
4. If it seems like something that should be easy, refer to the **Finale Quick Reference Guide**.
5. If you have additional questions about a topic, check the index at the end of this book. (This book touches on the basics of some subjects before delving into the details in later chapters).
6. If you still can't find the answer, refer to the **Finale User Manual**.
7. If you have a more general question that you suspect might be covered in one of the **main QuickStart Videos**, check there.
8. Then try expanding your search online to the **Finale Knowledge Base** located here: finalemusic.com/support.
9. If it still alludes you, search the **Finale Forums** at http://forum.makemusic.com. If you can't find the answer by searching, you can post your own new question. There are many friendly folks in the Finale community who are happy to help.
10. Under very special circumstances it is appropriate to contact **the muses** in MakeMusic Customer Support. This precious oracle of supreme wisdom is best left undisturbed unless steps 1 through 9 have been attempted without success. (This is for your benefit as much as theirs - they are very busy in there). Contact Customer Support by clicking "Submit" (under "Contact Support") on the finalemusic.com/support website.

Where is the Finale 2012 Folder?

Throughout this book, I refer to various files (tutorial files, etc.) that are included in your Finale 2012 installation. You will usually be able to find these files (or shortcuts to them) by simply choosing **File** > **Open**. The specific path on your computer is usually **<[User]/(My) Documents > Finale Files>**: See "Finale Installation Details" in the User Manual to see where Finale's installer places all the various components.

Getting Around in Finale

Now that you know how to learn Finale let's begin with the hills and valleys - a conceptual overview of Finale's landscape. If you were learning how to plate engrave, these would be your scoring tools.

To prepare for this section, launch Finale. When the Launch Window appears, click Default Document. This will open a single staff document that you can use to experiment with the following subjects.

A Tool-Based Program

At the core of Finale lies the Main Tool Palette (see Figure 1.1). Just about everything you do in Finale is in the context of one of these 26 Main Tools (on Windows, this palette is split into the Main and Advance Tools palettes). For example, to enter an articulation, first click the Articulation Tool 󠀠. To change the key, click the Key Signature Tool 󠀠. As you work on your score, you can usually make a good guess as to which tool you will need to use, but sometimes it isn't completely clear. For example, say the first beat of your piano arrangement requires a pedal marking 󠀠 . To add this you would click the Smart Shape Tool 󠀠, then hold down a modifier key while clicking the Custom Line Tool 󠀠, then choose the marking from a list where it is located between a glissando and rit. marking. Seeing this, the new Finale user says, "Oh, so that's where I add tempo changes like rit." Not usually. For those, you use the Expression Tool, the one that looks like a dynamic marking 󠀠, thus beginning the downward spiral of frustration that has accompanied the novice Finale user for years. Don't worry, that's what this book is for. The chapters are organized by musical subject, so you'll often jump around to different tools to complete similar notation tasks.

Figure 1.1

The Main Tool Palette

When you click a tool in the Main Tool Palette, two things can change on your screen.

- **Another tool palette may appear**, which you can use to specify a certain task. For example, when you click the Simple Entry Tool 󠀠, the Simple Entry Palette appears. You can choose a tool in the Simple Entry Palette to specify a rhythmic value to click into your staff.
- **A new menu item may appear** at the top of your screen. From this menu, you can customize the way the tool works or customize items related to the tool. Click the Staff Tool to see the Staff menu appear at the top of your screen, as shown in Figure 1.2.

Figure 1.2

Some Main Tools, like the Staff Tool, are accompanied by a corresponding menu.

Staff Tool and corresponding Staff Menu

Working with Palettes

You can show or hide any palette with the Window menu. Click the Window menu. The palettes currently visible have a check box to the left of them. Click a checked palette name to hide it from the screen, or click one of the unchecked palettes to display it. In many cases, you won't have to worry about manually turning these palettes on or off because Finale automatically displays them when appropriate.

TIP:
Windows users, right-click on the area surrounding a docked palette (the blank area), or a scroll bar, to easily choose the tool palettes you want to display.

Instead of hiding a palette, you may simply want to move it out of the way. On Mac, the tool palettes are "floating." These palettes can be repositioned and reshaped by dragging with your mouse. On Windows, when you first launch Finale, the tool palettes are "docked" near the top of your screen.

TIP:
Windows users can remove rarely used tools from a palette to save space. On Windows, choose **Window** > **Customize Palettes,** and then select the palette you want to customize.

Message Bar (Mac) or Status Bar (Windows)

Click one of the tools now to see the name of the active tool and its description in the Status/Message bar.

Figure 1.3

On Windows, notice the Status Bar in the lower-left corner of your screen.

STAFF TOOL: Use the menu to add or edit staves (name and transposition); group (name and bracket) selected staves.

Figure 1.4

On Macintosh, notice the Message Bar located just above your score.

STAFF TOOL: Use the menu to add or edit staves (name and transposition); group (name and bracket) selected staves.

Tool Shortcuts

As you work, you will find yourself switching between tools a lot. To easily select tools you use often, program them to function keys.

Windows users:

1. Click the tool you desire to program.
2. Hold down SHIFT and press a function key (**F2-F12**). You have just assigned a function key to the selected tool.

3.   Press the function key you just programmed at any time to return to that tool.

Macintosh users:

4.   Hold down CTRL and OPTION and press a key between **F** and **,** (comma).
5.   Highlight the tool you wish to associate with that key and click **OK**.
6.   To access the tool, press CTRL and the key you programmed (F through comma).

This information is saved with the document, so it will be usable any time you open the document in the future. (Later, you will learn to customize your default files or templates so that new documents will contain your settings.)

The Menus

Notice the menu items at the top of the screen (see Figure 1.5). Each of these is a set of controls that govern the document, the program, or the tool selected. The Help menu, which provides informative resources, is the only exception. Ten of these menus will always be visible; File, Edit, Utilities, View, Document, MIDI/Audio, Plug-ins/ , Tools, Window, and Help. The other menu(s) will appear only if their corresponding tool is chosen (click the Staff Tool and the Staff menu appears). As with the Main Tools, I'll direct you to a menu item when describing a subject that calls for it.

Figure 1.5
The menus

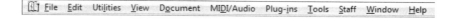

Many menu items can be accessed easily with keyboard shortcuts. There are certain menu items you might find yourself using frequently (in my case Undo is a common one). Click the **Edit** menu and look to the right of the **Undo** command. You will see the keystroke CTRL+**Z** (CMD+**Z** on Mac). Instead of clicking the menu item every time you want to undo, simply use this keyboard shortcut. Refer to the menus for other keyboard shortcuts to save you time as you work.

TIP:
On Windows, you can program any menu item to a keyboard shortcut. To do this, choose **Plug-ins/** **> TG Tools > Menu Shortcuts.**

TIP:
On Windows, you can use keystrokes to open any menu item. Hold down ALT key and type the underlined letter in the menu name (e.g., ALT+**T** to open the Tools menu). Then use the underlined letter of the menu item to select it. The mnemonics are an alternative to clicking the item with your mouse cursor.

Basic Finale Vocabulary

You'll need to know these terms. Some of these are common to other programs, and some are unique to Finale.

Handles

Handles are small boxes that appear near items in your score that are available for editing (see Figure 1.6). Anytime you want to edit an articulation, text block, or expression (for example), click the corresponding tool, or double-click the item with the Selection Tool ▊ , to see its handle appear. You will then be able to click and drag or nudge (with the arrow keys) the handle to move the item.

Figure 1.6
Notice the handle of this expression.

Often handles can be double-clicked to open a dialog box for more editing options.

Context Menus

Handles, markings, notes, and other Finale elements can be *context-clicked* in order to display a menu with additional commands for editing the item. To context-click, Windows users, right-click; Mac users, hold down CTRL and click). A context menu opens containing options specific to that item. You will become more familiar with these procedures as we apply them for certain tasks. With the Selection Tool ▊ selected, you will be able to context-click virtually anything on the screen to see additional options.

TIP:
Mac laptop users: In System Preferences-Trackpad, you can check **Tap trackpad using two fingers for secondary click** (or similar language) for quick access to context menus (instead of CTRL-clicking).

The Cursor

You will find that the state of you mouse cursor can be an informative tool. It can tell you which staff, measure, or note an item will be attached to (e.g. ⭧ or ⭥), the exact item that will be entered (♯○), or whether Finale is processing something. As you work through the program, take note of when the cursor changes and use it to your advantage. There will be descriptions of these cursor changes throughout this book.

The Scroll Bars

On the bottom and right side of your Finale document window you will see vertical and horizontal scroll bars. Click and drag the slider within the scroll bars to adjust the viewable area of your document.

Scroll View

From the View Menu, choose Scroll View to display the music in a continuous horizontal band - a single system that stretches into infinity (or as your computer's memory permits) as shown in Figure 1.7. Alternatively, press CTRL+E (Windows) or CMD+**E** (Mac). (CTRL/CMD+E toggles Page and Scroll View).

Figure 1.7
Scroll View includes many viewing and navigation options.

This is a popular view for composing and entry because it allows bookmarks and Staff Sets, which allow you to display only the staves you are concerned with; more on Staff Sets in Chapter 7.

Studio View

Choose **View** > **Studio View** (or press CTRL/CMD+SHIFT+E). This view is the same as Scroll View, but houses additional features designed exclusively for playback and recording.

Figure 1.8
The TempoTap Staff, Audio Track, and Staff Mixer Controls are only available in Studio View.

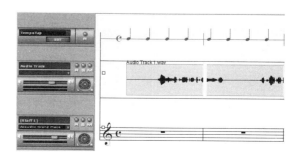

- **TempTap.** This is always the top staff in Studio View and can be used to record, or "conduct," the playback tempo in order to define, for example, and accelerando or ritardando. Recording tempo changes with TempoTap is described in Chapter 14.
- **Audio Track.** Finale 2012 allows you to import or record one audio track that accompanies the other staves during playback. You might use the Audio Track, for example, to import a vocal part into your score. Again, we will discuss the Audio Track more in Chapter 14.
- **Staff Controls.** To the left of every staff rests a collection of mixer controls you can use to adjust the volume, panning, mute/solo, and record settings.

Page View

Choose **View** > **Page View** or press CTRL+E (Windows) or CMD+E (Mac).

Figure 1.9

Page View displays how your music will look on the printed page and allows you to preview and perfect the staff, system, and page layout.

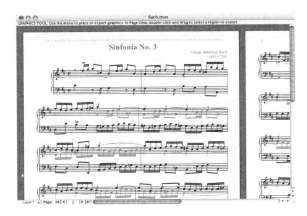

Page View is a representation of how the document will look if printed. Items specific to pages, such as the title, page numbers, and staff systems are now visible. Use the arrows located at the bottom of the screen to move forward or backward through pages. You can also move to a specific page by typing the page number in the entry field and pressing Enter.

TIP:
If you want to set up measures to access quickly in Scroll View or Page View, set up Bookmarks. Choose **View** > **Bookmarks** > **Add Bookmark** (or press CTRL/CMD+B). To navigate to a defined bookmark, choose **View** > **Bookmarks.**

- Press PAGE DOWN multiple times (Laptop: Fn+DOWN ARROW) to advance forward pages.
- Press PAGE UP multiple times (Laptop: Fn+UP ARROW) to advance backward though pages.

- Press CTRL/CMD+PAGE UP or CTRL/CMD+PAGE DOWN (Laptop: Fn+CTRL+UP/DOWN ARROW or Fn+CMD+UP/DOWN ARROW) to navigate forward and backwards through pages while maintaining the same portion of the page visible.

TIP:
The default view is Page View. To change the Default View when opening and starting new documents, choose **Edit** (Mac: **Finale 2012 > Preferences**) > **Program Options** and then choose **New**. Select the desired view and click **OK**.

Display Colors

You may have already noticed the array of colored items in Finale. In addition to contributing to aesthetic appeal, these actually do serve a purpose. The color of an item allows you to see, at a glance, what tool created it. As you work in Finale, note the color of items and which type of item relates to which color. To see a breakdown of all the colors associated with each element in your score, choose **View** > **Select Display Colors**. You can also use this dialog box to modify the display colors as you wish.

If the colors drive you crazy, you can view the music in black and white.

1. Choose **Edit** > **Program Options**. Mac users: Press CMD+, (comma). The Program Options dialog box appears. Choose **Display Colors**.
2. Uncheck **Use Score Colors** and click **OK**.

TIP:
You can easily edit any item on your screen with the Selection Tool . Click an item, drag, nudge (with the arrow keys), or press DELETE to delete it. Press the ESC key to choose the Selection Tool at any time.

Navigation Tools

Quickly navigating around your score is key to working with Finale efficiently. You can easily adjust the viewable area of your score, zoom in and out, move quickly to a specific measure, or even set up bookmarks to common locations. Changing the viewable area your screen has no effect on the printout.

Zooming

You can zoom in to make fine adjustments or zoom out to see more of your score. While in Page View or Scroll View, choose **View** > **Zoom** and select a different view percentage-try **Custom Zoom 2 (200%)**. Notice the staves become larger.

Instead of going all the way to the View menu, you can also use keyboard shortcuts to change your view percentage:

- CTRL/CMD+= ➜ ... Zoom In
- CTRL/CMD+-(minus) ➜ ... Zoom Out
- CTRL/CMD+1 ➜ ... 100%
- CTRL/CMD+2 ➜ ... 200%
- CTRL/CMD+3 ➜ ... 75%
- CTRL/CMD+0 ➜ ... Other (to enter a different percentage)
- CTRL/OPTION+CMD+] ➜ ... Fit Width
- CTRL/OPTION+CMD+[➜ ... Fit In Window

TIP:
"Custom Zoom" refers to the ability to program these keystrokes to a custom view percentage. To do so, choose **View** > **Zoom** > **Define Custom Zooms.**

For more control over viewing various sections of your score, use the Zoom Tool 🔍. Click the Zoom Tool and then click a section of your score to zoom in or CTRL/OPTION-click to zoom out. In Page View, to specify an area to enlarge, click and drag your cursor diagonally. Notice that a dashed box appears. When you release the mouse button, the enclosed area will enlarge to fit the entire viewable area.

TIP:
On Windows, at any time (Zoom Tool does not need to be selected), press the middle mouse button to zoom in; CTRL+middle mouse button to zoom out. On Mac, SHIFT+CMD+click to zoom in and SHIFT+OPTION+CMD-click to zoom out.

Hand Grabber Tool

In addition to zooming in and out, you also need a way to move the viewable region. This is the purpose of the Hand Grabber Tool ✋. Click the Hand Grabber Tool. Now click and drag to move the page or systems around.

TIP:
On Windows, the Hand Grabber can be used at any time regardless of the selected tool by right-clicking and dragging. On Mac, OPTION-CMD-click and drag.

Redrawing Your Screen

If artifacts of items remain on the screen after you delete them, redraw the screen to clean them up. Hold down the CTRL/CMD key and press D. This key command will redraw your screen and restore the integrity of the viewable area.

Other Finale Conventions

Here are a few more things that you should know before we delve into the business of creating some actual sheet music.

Measurement Units

There are many cases where you might be asked to enter a value to specify a certain distance. For example, you may want to place your title an inch, centimeter, or millimeter from the top page margin. To select your unit of measurement, choose **Edit** > **Measurement Units** (Mac: **Finale 2012** > **Measurement Units**) and click one of the available options. Table 1.1 shows an explanation of the relationship between all of the available measurement units.

Table 1.1
Measurement Units Comparison Table

Spaces	EVPUs	Inches	Centimeters	Millimeters	Points	Picas
1	24	.083	.212	2.12	6	.667
.042	1	.0035	.009	.09	.25	.042
12	288	1	2.54	25.4	72	6
4.708	113	.392	1 (.997)	10	28.25	2.3622
.458	11	.038	.1 (.097)	1	2.75	.2362
.167	4	.014	.035	.35	1	.083
2	48	.167	.423	4.23	12	1

In addition to spatial units of measurement, Finale also uses a system of rhythmic or durational measurement. All rhythmic durations (quarter note, eighth note, etc.) can also be expressed in EDUs (ENIGMA Durational Units). Table 1.2 describes the EDU equivalent for each rhythmic duration.

Table 1.2
EDU to Rhythmic Value Equivalents

Rhythmic Value	EDU	Rhythmic Value	EDU	Rhythmic Value	EDU
double whole	8192	quarter	1024	dotted 32nd	192
dotted whole	6144	dotted eighth	768	triplet 16th	171
whole	4096	triplet quarter	683	32nd	128
dotted half	3072	eighth	512	dotted 64th	96
half	2048	dotted sixteenth	384	64th	64
dotted quarter	1536	triplet eighth	341	dotted 128th	48
half note triplet	1365	sixteenth	256	128th	32

Document and Program Options

There are two general types of settings in Finale: document options and program options.

- **Document options** are saved with the document and affect only the document you are working on. They are designed for global changes to your music or layout. Click the Document menu and choose Document Options. Here you will be able to set up a variety of document-wide specifications relating to music spacing, beaming, page format, and many others. I will cover many of these document options throughout this book.
- **Program options** affect the general operation of the program and will not have any effect on the music in a document. Click the **Edit** (Windows) or **Finale 2012** (Mac) menu and choose **Program Options** (see Figure 1.10). Here you can customize how Finale behaves based on your own preferences. Following are some helpful program options that are good to know. You can also find more ways to customize the Finale program using the Program Options in Chapter 13.

Figure 1.10

Make all program-wide settings in the Program
Options dialog box.

Auto Save

Although you will want to get into the habit of saving often, if you want, you can tell Finale to save your
document automatically at regular intervals. This feature adds some insurance in case of a crash, freeze,
power outage, gamma ray burst, etc. (maybe not that last one). In the Program Options dialog box, click
the **Save and Print** option on the left side. Check **Auto Save File(s)** and then enter the number of
minutes. I like to set this to 10 minutes, but you might prefer to save more or less frequently based on the
reliability of your computer and your personal risk tolerance quotient.

Click the **Folders** section of the Program Options dialog box and find the **Auto Save** option. Click the
Browse or **Select** button to the right and specify a folder. If you ever need to find your Auto Save files,
you can look here to find the path. (By default, it's in the Finale Files folder). On Windows, the files
saved by Auto Save are not standard Finale files and will have the extension .ASV. On Macintosh, the
word "copy" is appended to the file name. To open them, launch Finale, click the File menu, choose
Open and navigate to the folder you have chosen for Auto Save. In the Open dialog box, be sure to
display all file types. (To do so: Windows users, from the **Files of Type** drop-down menu, choose **All
Files**. Mac users, from the **Enable** pop-up menu, choose All Readable Files). Then double-click the
Auto Save file to open it.

Make Backups When Saving Files

Each time you save a file, Finale also creates a backup copy of your file. This backup file is the second-t-
last saved version of the file you were working on (not including auto saves). If you save a file and then
find that you have saved undesirable changes, you can rely on your backup file to go back to the previously saved version. Note that you will have only one backup file per Finale file. This file is continually
being overwritten with each Save command. **Make Backups when Saving Files** is turned on by default.
If you would like to turn it off to save space I recommend a larger hard drive, but you can do so by
clicking **Save** on the left side of the Program Options dialog box and unchecking **Make Backups when
Saving Files**.

If you have **Make Backups when Saving Files** turned on, you might want to know where these backup
files are located. Look in the **Folders** section of the Program Options dialog box and find the **Backup**

option. Click the **Browse** or **Select** button to the right and specify a folder. If you ever need to find your backup files, you can look here to find the path. (By default, the folder is the same for auto save and backup files within the "Finale Files" folder). On Windows, the backup files you save are not standard Finale files and will have the extension .BAK. On Macintosh, the word "copy" is appended to the file name. To open them, launch Finale, choose **File** > **Open**, and navigate to the folder you have chosen for Backup files. In the Open dialog box, be sure to display all file types. (To do so: Windows users, from the **Files of Type** drop-down menu, choose **All Files**. Mac users, from the **Enable** pop-up menu, choose **All Readable Files**). Then double-click the Backup file to open it.

Startup Action

Finale automatically opens the Launch Window each time you launch Finale. From here you can choose from several ways to begin or open existing documents. To change the behavior of Finale during startup, click **New** on the left side of the Program Options dialog box, then click the drop-down arrow after Startup Action.

TIP:
To set the initial type of view (Scroll/Page View) and the view percentage for any new document, click **New** in the Program Options dialog box and make your selections.

Your Default Music Folder

Each time you choose to save a new file, Finale automatically prompts you to save in the My Documents (Mac: Documents)/Finale Files folder. When you choose to open a file, Finale automatically directs you to this folder. To keep things simple and convenient, I recommend keeping this setup and using the "Finale Files" folder as your music repository. However, if you would like to designate a different folder for this purpose, do the following:

1. Identify the location of the folder you would like to designate as you Finale files folder. Or, create the folder and name it "My Finale Files" (or whatever you want).
2. In Finale, choose **Edit** (Mac: **Finale 2012** > **Preferences**) > **Program Options** and select **Folders**.
3. To the right of the Music field, click the **Browse** button.
4. Navigate to the "My Finale Files" folder (or the new folder you created) and select it.
5. Click **OK**.

Preferences and the Finale.ini File

All of the settings you make in Program Options are saved to a file on your computer. On Mac, this is the "Finale 2012 Preferences" file, which is located in your Users/Library/Preferences folder. If you want to restore your Finale program back to the way it was when you first installed, quit Finale, navigate to the Preferences folder, and drag the Finale 2012 Preferences file into the Trash.

On Windows, all of your preferences are saved to the Finale.INI file (sometimes it will just say Finale and have a text file icon), which is basically a text file located in your Finale folder. If you want to restore your Finale program back to the way it was when you first installed, exit Finale, navigate to (Windows Vista or 7) <C:\Users\[user]\AppData\Roaming\MakeMusic\Finale 2012>, (Windows XP) <C:\Documents and Settings\[User]\Application Data\MakeMusic\Finale 2012>, and delete the Finale.INI.

2
Beginning a New Score

In this chapter you will learn how Finale's automatic features can be used to quickly begin a new custom score. Then you will learn how to change each of these elements in existing scores manually. You need to know this because while Finale does a great job of setting things up, when you change your mind (e.g. decide your baritone needs a trumpet transposition), identifying the correct setting or procedure to make this change isn't always obvious. Also, the Setup Wizard and templates include all the basic score elements and use the appropriate methods to create them based on your settings, so by reverse engineering them we have a concrete outline for conquering the basics common to almost all documents.

Here's a summary of what you will learn in this chapter:

- How to start a score with the Document Setup Wizard
- How to customize your staves
- How to enter and modify text (title, page number, copyright)
- The fundamentals of working with the Selection Tool
- The basics of Page Layout

Opening a New Document

When you start Finale, the Launch Window appears (Figure 2.1).

Figure 2.1

All options for starting new projects or resuming old ones are available from the Launch Window.

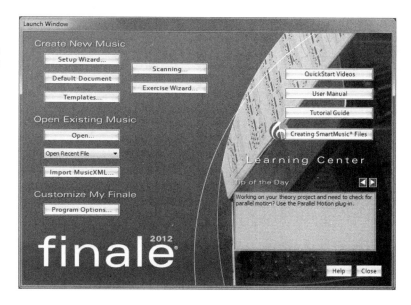

For most projects, I recommend starting with the Document Setup Wizard. You will find this method the easiest for defining all elements critical to a new score, including title, instrument(s), page size, key signature, time signature, and tempo.

Starting a Score with the Document Setup Wizard

The Setup Wizard was designed to require as little explanation as possible, but taking advantage of its potential is important, so let's start it up and take a look. Click **Setup Wizard** in the Launch Window (or, click the **File** > **New** > **Document With Setup Wizard**). You can also hold down the CTRL/CMD key and press N.

Page 1: Ensembles and Document Styles

Any time you start the Setup Wizard you will see this page (see Figure 2.2). You don't have to change anything on this page, but you can save some time if your project closely matches one of these ensembles. If not, you'll be able to add to these lists by defining your own ensembles and Document Styles on the next page for future use.

Figure 2.2
On page 1 of the Setup
Wizard, you can
define the broad
strokes including an
ensemble and
collection of docu-
ment settings.

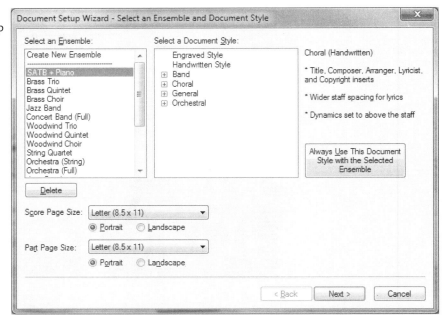

1. From the list on the left, choose the option that most closely matches your project's instrumentation. This is an easy way to populate the list of instruments on the next page, which you will be able to customize. The **Create a New Ensemble** option just means you'll pick each instrument in your ensemble manually on the next page.

2. The list on the right includes "Document Styles" which are basically collections of document settings. Document settings include the default music font, all the settings in the Document Options dialog box, etc. (for a complete list, see "Document Settings and Program Settings" in the Finale User Manual). You can choose a different Document Style here if you wish, but these will be far more useful after you've defined your own custom Document Styles based on your specific needs (See Using Document Styles in Chapter 13).

3. At the bottom you can select the page size and orientation for your score and parts. You can always change this later if you're not sure yet.

4. Click **Next** to move to page 2.

Page 2: Choose Your Parts

Here, you can specify each instrument you want in your piece, or edit the ensemble you selected on the previous page.

Figure 2.3

On page 2 of the Setup Wizard, define the instrumentation.

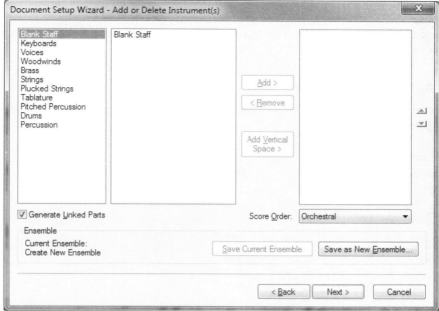

5. Now, add any missing instruments or delete extra ones. To add an instrument, in the left column, choose the instrument family, then double-click the instrument you want to add in the second column. You will see the instrument appear in the third column in orchestral score order regardless of the order in which you choose them (see Figure 2.3). Each instrument you add will become one staff in your Finale score (except in the case of keyboard instruments), so if you want four trumpet staves, add four trumpets. To remove an instrument, click it (rightmost column) and click the **Remove** button.

6. To change the order of your instruments, click the **Score Order** drop-down menu beneath the third column and choose from the available options. To change the order of your instruments manually, highlight the instrument you would like to move (in the third column), then click the up or down arrows on the right to change its positioning. Double-click any instrument in the third column to remove it. When you've defined the instrumentation, click **Next**.

7. If you made changes to an existing ensemble's instrumentation, Finale asks if you would like to update the ensemble definition based on your changes. Click yes if you would like to update the ensemble definition, or no if you would like to leave the ensemble definition as is.

Finale automatically groups staves of similar instrumental sections (with group brackets) in the score upon completing the Setup Wizard. Finale will even number like instruments incrementally, so you need not worry about adding a 1, 2, 3, or 4 to the trumpet names, for example. When you have chosen all of your instruments and placed them in the order you like, click the **Next** button to continue to the next page. You can click the **Back** button at any time to make any changes to the previous page. The Setup Wizard will retain all of your settings.

If you find yourself using the same group of instruments regularly, save an ensemble. When you have chosen the desired instrumentation and order, click **Save As New Ensemble**. Enter a name for your ensemble and click **OK**. Now, you can choose this ensemble on the first page of the Setup Wizard when starting new scores.

Page 3: Score Information

On page three of the Setup Wizard, you can specify the title, composer, and other score information (see Figure 2.4).

Figure 2.4

On page three of the Setup Wizard, enter the score information.

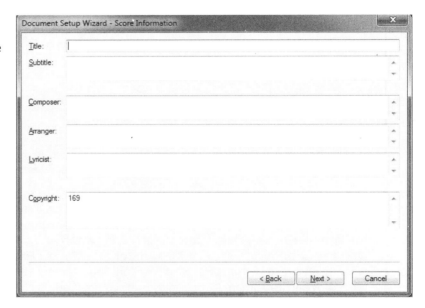

8.   Enter any score information here as required. Some of this information will appear in the score, such as the title and composer. All of these fields are basically variables for text inserts that can be added anywhere in the score. These settings can be referenced and/or changed by choosing **Window** > **Score Manager**, then clicking the File Info tab. When you're done, click Next.

Page 4: Score Settings

These settings are pretty self explanatory.

Figure 2.5

Here, define more score
details.

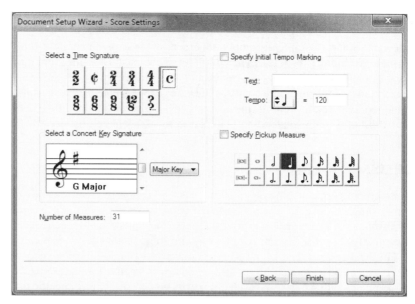

9. Define the meter, key, number of measures, tempo marking, and pickup measure, then
    click **Finish**. Finale opens the new document based on your settings. Of course,
    everything you have just defined can be changed, which will be covered later in this
    chapter (and in greater detail throughout the book).

New Default Document

You can begin a new, basic, single-staff document by choosing **Default Document** in the Launch
Window (or by choosing **File** > **New** > **Default Document**). This will open a treble clef staff in the key
of C, and in 4/4 time. This might be an attractive option for a sketch document. For example, if you are
composing and haven't yet figured out what kind of instrument or key you might be using, a new default
document might be the way to go. Regardless of how you start your document, the ability to change and
manage your score instruments has been significantly improved in Finale 2012, so switching any music
to a different instrument will be a snap when the time is right.

Document from Template

Finale comes with many pre-set templates you can use to get a head-start while starting a new project. If
the score you are working on has a common instrumentation (brass band, SATB chorus, etc.) try starting
with a template. Click **Templates** in the Launch Window (or click **File** > **New** > **Document from
Template**). Then browse through the folders to see the available options. When you open a template, you
are prompted to customize the document with the last two pages of the Setup Wizard.

Document Without Libraries

If you want to start a completely empty document without any presets or libraries, click **File** > **New** > **Document Without Libraries**. (They don't let us choose this option from the Launch Window). You will see a document with a single measure and no text at all (brings back fond memories of Finale 2.0). You will also find that there are no articulations or expressions to choose from. Use this option to start a document only if you feel comfortable setting up your score and loading all libraries entirely from scratch. For information on loading articulation and expression libraries, see Chapter 3.

Exercise Wizard

This feature was built specifically to allow music educators to create customized, technique-building exercises quickly and easily for a rehearsal warm-up (for example). The Exercise Wizard will ask you to choose from a variety of scales, twisters, keys, and articulations for each exercise. Then, you can print the exercise (or number of exercises) for any ensemble while Finale takes care of the transposition and articulation placement. The whole process takes about 10 minutes or so (depending on the speed of your printer) and can be a great utility for any conductor in an educational setting. To start the Exercise Wizard, choose **File** > **New** > **Exercise Wizard**. You can find more specific information on creating exercises with the Exercise Wizard in Chapter 13.

Starting from Printed Sheet Music (Scanning)

Click the Scanning button in the Launch Window to acquire a file from your scanner. You'll learn more about scanning and importing sheet music in Chapter 13.

Customize Your Document

Regardless of the method you used to begin your document, if you decide you need to change the key signature, time signature, or any other basic score element, there is generally a 'correct' way to do it. The following section covers how to quickly and safely change these settings at any point while working on your score, as well as other techniques you should know for any document. Additional details for these subjects will be discussed later in this book (mostly in Chapter 5).

TIP:
Throughout this book you will be prompted to choose the Selection Tool. To do so easily, simply press the ESC key (you may need to press it more than once when using Simple Entry). Also note that several other tools also allow regional selection, and therefore switching to the Selection Tool is often not required.

To Add and Insert Measures

To add a measure to the end of your score:

1. Double-click the Measure Tool  to add a single measure to the end of your document.

2. Or, to add a specific number of measures, choose **Edit** > **Add Measures** (or CTRL/OPTION+click the Measure Tool). You will see the Add Measures dialog box (Figure 2.6).

Figure 2.6

This one's not especially cryptic.

3. Enter the number of measures you would like to add to the end of your score and click **OK**.

To insert measures at the beginning or in the middle of your score:

1. Click a measure to highlight it.
2. Choose **Edit** > **Insert Measure Stack**.
3. Type the number of measures and click **OK**. The number of measures you specify will appear, inserted to the left of the highlighted measure.

Changing the Key Signature

To change the opening key signature:

1. Choose the Selection Tooll 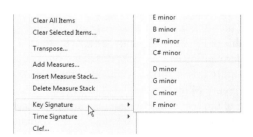, then context-click measure 1 and choose Key Signature to display a submenu with a list of key signatures as shown in Figure 2.7.

2. Select the desired key signature.

Figure 2.7

The key signature is among the many edits possible with the Selection Tool context menu.

3.   If the desired key signature is not in this list, choose **Edit Key Signature** to open the Key
Signature dialog box where you can define one manually.

This will change the concert key signature. (Finale considers transposing staves and assigns the appropriate key signature to each staff automatically.) I'll soon explain how to change the instrument transposition of a staff.

Changing the Time Signature

Changing the time signature of your piece is as easy as changing the key signature:

1.   Choose the Selection Tool , then context-click a measure to display the Selection
Tool context menu.

2.   Choose **Time Signature**, then select the desired time signature.

Choose Edit Time Signature to open the Time Signature dialog box where you can define a custom time signature.

•   For **Number of Beats,** click the left or right arrow to increase or decrease the number
of beats per measure in your time signature.

•   For **Beat Duration,** click the left or right arrow to increase or decrease the rhythmic
value of each beat.

•   Click **OK** to return to your score and see the new time signature. You will find information on more advanced time signature options in Chapter 5.

> **TIP:**
> Press CTRL+Z (Mac users, CMD+Z) at any time to undo the previous
> action. Repeat to undo previous edits as well. CTRL/CMD+Z is your
> friend.

Adding, Removing, and Changing Instruments

Being a Finale user from the dark ages (pre-turn-of-the millennium, in fact), I feel a bit sentimental when looking back at the days of yore; individually adding staves, then changing the clef, transposition, and staff name according to the instrument I am introducing or changing. There will rarely, if ever, be a need for this in Finale 2012, and memory of doing so will likely drift into the vague fog of auld lang syne as modernization chugs away, replacing our enduring traditions with push-button automation. Alas, I'm over it. In this section you'll learn how to instantaneously add and edit instrument staves using Finale's new Score Manager. Note that this type of change pertains to the instrument as it appears at the beginning of the score (starting at measure 1). To learn how to easily add mid-score instrument changes that tell your performers when to switch instruments (and apply appropriate staff changes), see "Adding Mid-Score Instrument Changes" on page 206.

To add and remove instruments

1. Choose **Window** > **Score Manager** (if it's not already open). The Score manager window appears.

2. To add an instrument, click [Add Instrument], then click the category and double-click the instrument you would like to add. Finale adds the instrument to the appropriate instrument section (group), and in the order designated under the Score Order drop-down menu. (You can instantly change the score order at any time using this menu).

3. To remove an instrument, click ❌ for the instrument row on the right side of the Score Manager. Finale deletes the instrument and adjusts the positioning of the other instruments accordingly.

To change instruments

1. **Choose Window** > **Score Manager (if it's not already open).** The Score manager window appears. While the Score Manager allows you to edit the staff name, clef, transposition, and other staff properties, you're probably interested in doing these things in order to change the instrument. Fortunately, Finale can do that in one easy step...

2. In the Score Manager, click the name of the instrument in the Instrument column and select the new instrument as shown in Figure 2.8.

Figure 2.8

To change instruments, along with all staff properties, use the Score Manager. Simply click the instrument name and select the new instrument.

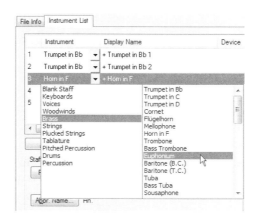

After you have changed the instrument, notice all the staff settings update automatically. This includes most aspects of the staves, including the number of staff lines (for percussion), and even the number of staves (e.g. a piano instrument includes a grand staff with two staves) .The playback sound is also updated (see "Instrument Sound Setup" on page 358 for a description of instrument sound assignments).

A word on instrument transposition. One of the significant changes that may be applied to your music when you change staves is the instrument transposition. Finale automatically calculates and assigns the appropriate key signature for the instrument based on the concert key. For example, if the concert key signature of your piece is C major, a French horn instrument transposition (up a perfect fifth, add one sharp) will automatically display in the key of G (one sharp) and the pitches will be displayed up a perfect fifth. Note that the Staff Transposition affects only the displayed pitches of the music and never the sounding pitches. Finale will always play back any notes in a transposed staff in concert pitch (except during entry, which drives most of us crazy). In the case of a French Horn, the sounding notes are a perfect fifth down from the written pitch, as it would sound if played by a French horn. To view all of your staves back in concert pitch, check **Document** > **Display in Concert Pitch**.

TIP:
See "Alternate Notation, Staff Management, and Tab" on page 201 for more information on editing staves with the Score Manager.

Changing the Clef

You can change the opening clef of any staff with the Selection Tool .

1. Click the Selection Tool and context-click the first measure of the staff.
2. From the Selection Tool context menu, choose **Clef**. The Change Clef dialog box appears.
3. Select the desired clef and click **OK**.

For information on adding a clef change within a staff, see Chapter 5.

Changing the Tempo Marking

Editing an existing tempo marking in your score is easy.

1. Choose the Expression Tool .
2. Right/CTRL+click the tempo marking's handle and select Edit Text Expression Definition. The Expression Designer dialog box appears as shown in Figure 2.9.
3. Type the desired tempo marking into the text box. If you need to add a note character, click the Insert Note button to the lower right.

Figure 2.9
Use the Expression Designer to define or edit tempo markings.

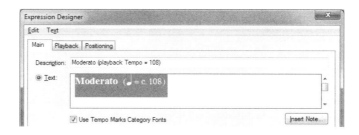

4. If your tempo marking includes a metronome indication (♩ = 120), Finale will automati-
    cally define the playback tempo for you. All tempo markings can be defined for
    playback manually under the Playback tab (see "Creating a Text Expression" in Chapter
    3 for details).

5. Click **OK** to apply your changes and return to the score.

Adding or Removing a Pickup Measure

To add a pickup measure to your score:

1. Choose **Document** > **Pickup Measure**. You should now see the Pickup Measure dialog
    box (see Figure 2.10).

Figure 2.10
Define a pickup in the Pickup Measure dialog box.

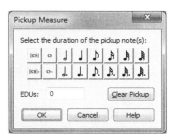

2. Click the box representing the duration of your pickup measure, and then click **OK** to
    return to your score.

Now, Finale will treat the first measure of your score as a pickup measure of the values specified. Replace
the rests that appear with notes as needed. Measure number one will be redefined to the measure after the
pickup.

To remove a pickup measure from your score:

1. Choose **Document** > **Pickup Measure**. You should now see the Pickup Measure dialog
    box (see Figure 2.10).

2. Click **Clear Pickup** and then click **OK.**

NOTE:
To adjust the number of beats in the last measure of your piece (a
common practice in scores with pickup measures), see "Pickup Measures Within a Score" on page 141.

Showing or Hiding Measure Numbers

By default, Finale will display measure numbers at the beginning of each system. To show measure numbers on each measure:

1. Click the Measure Tool , and then choose **Measure** > **Edit Measure Number Regions** (or, from the **Document** Menu, choose **Edit Measure Number Regions**). The Measure Number dialog box appears.

2. In the **Positioning & Display** section, choose **Show on Every...**

3. Leave **Show Measure Numbers at Start of Staff System** checked so that measure numbers at the beginning of each system are nicely aligned with the left edge of the staff.

4. Then, in the fields to the right, enter "1" and "1" to tell Finale to show measure numbers every measure starting with measure one.

5. Use the **Position** button to adjust positioning en masse.

6. Use the **Top Staff** and **Bottom Staff** check boxes, and **Exclude Other Staves,** to show measure numbers only on the top and bottom staff (this overrides Staff Attribute settings).

7. Click **OK** to return to your score. You can now click and drag the measure number handles to position them, or click a handle and press the DELETE key to hide it.

To hide all measure numbers on a staff:

1. Click the Staff Tool and double-click the staff. The Staff Attributes dialog box opens.

2. In the Items to Display section, uncheck **Measure Numbers** and click **OK**. You will find more information on changing the font, style, and enclosure of measure numbers, as well as how to program several measure number regions, in Chapter 11.

Changing a Staff's Playback Instrument

As of Finale 2012, every one of Finale's built-in instrument definitions includes a sound assignment that matches the instrument with its corresponding playback sound whether you are playing through a VST/Audio Units device or using a General MIDI playback device (e.g. General MIDI SoftSynth). Finale does this using Sound Maps. A Sound Map is a list of every sound in the current device, mapped to a Finale instrument. Finale includes a Sound Map for every device installed with Finale (or offered by MakeMusic), so unless you are using a 3rd party VST/Audio Units device, changing instruments will be simple.

1. Choose **Window** > **Score Manager**.

2. Click the **Sound** column for the instrument you want to change and select the desired sound. See Figure 2.11.

Figure 2.11

Use the Score Manager to change the instrument sound.

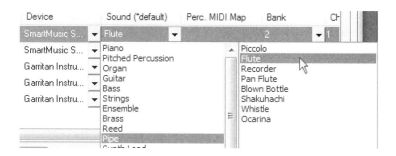

All new documents use Sound Maps by default. In order to use a 3rd party device (VST/AU or MIDI), select it from the **Device** column of the Score Manager, then use the **Sound** column to specify the sound. For more information regarding configuring instrument playback, see "Playback, Audio, and the MIDI Tool" on page 357.

TIP:
For a complete tutorial that explains how to make the most of Finale's included Garritan sounds (and the full version of GPO), see "GPO and HP Tutorial" in the Finale User Manual.

Enter and Modify Text (Title, Composer, Copyright)

When you open a new score, by default you will probably see text blocks on your page including the title, composer, and copyright (depending on the Document Style you are using). These items are page-assigned text blocks, and their placement will remain fixed according to the page margins (or page edge). In other words, as you edit and move measures around, these items will stay in the same place on the page. Page-attached text will always appear black on your screen by default. The use of page-assigned text blocks should generally be restricted to text blocks that have nothing to do with the performance of the music. These includes the title, composer, arranger, lyricist, copyright, and page numbers.

Entering Text Blocks

The best way to enter or modify the title, composer, or copyright text of any piece is to use the Score Manager (Figure 2.12). This is where these entries appear if you entered them with the Setup Wizard. To get there, choose Window > Score Manager, and click the File Info tab.

Figure 2.12

Store the title, composer, description, and other information about the document in the File Info tab of the Score Manager.

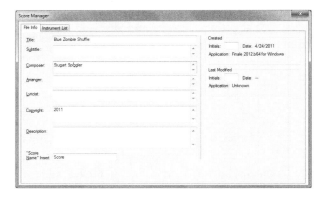

Enter a new title, composer, and copyright in this dialog box, then click **OK**. You will probably see the new text already display in your score in the appropriate place. If not, double-click where you want to place the title. A blinking cursor will appear on your score. Choose **Text** > **Inserts** > **Title**. Now the title appears in the specified location. You can also insert any of the other File Info this way by choosing **Composer**, **Copyright**, etc., from the **Inserts** submenu.

To enter any page-assigned text directly into the score:

1. Choose the Text Tool **A** and then make sure you are in Page View (**View** > **Page View**).
2. Choose **Text** > **Assign to Page**.
3. Double-click in the score.
4. You see a dashed box enclosing a cursor. Type your text here. The box will expand as you type.
5. Click anywhere in the score when you are finished typing to remove the dashed editing frame.

Text blocks can also be assigned to a specific measure. If your measure layout changes, the text block will move with its assigned measure. Any text block entered while working in Scroll View will automatically be measure-assigned. Measure-assigned text blocks are always red by default. In general, if you want to assign text consisting of only a single word, or just a couple of words, to a measure, you will probably want to use a measure-attached expression instead of a measure-assigned text block. You can find more information on measure-attached expressions in Chapters 3 and 7.

If you want to enter a measure-assigned text block in Page View:

1. Make sure the Text Tool **A** is selected and click anywhere in the score so none of the text block handles are selected.
2. Then choose **Text** > **Assign to Measure**. Now any text you enter will be measure-assigned.
3. To revert back to entering page-assigned text, make sure no handle is selected and choose **Text** > **Assign to Page**. Page-assigned text can be entered only in Page View.

TIP:
You can add a hyperlink by selecting text in a text block and then choosing the **Text** > **Hyperlink**. The Hyperlink dialog box appears where you can specify the URL and display text. CTRL/OPTION+click the hyperlink to test it from the Finale document.

Editing a Text Block

You can easily reposition or delete any text block. To move text:

1. Click the Selection Tool ![icon], then click and drag the text anywhere on the page or use the arrow keys to nudge it for fine adjustments.
2. To delete it, click the text block and press the DELETE key.
3. Double-click the text block to select the Text Tool ![A]. When the Text Tool is selected you can double-click a text block to open the editing frame which allows you to edit the text itself. (Text inserts, remember, must be edited elsewhere. For example, some are defined in the File Info dialog box).

Changing the Font, Size, or Style

To change the font, size, or style:

1. Select the Text Tool ![A] and select the text block's handle.
2. From the Text menu, Windows users choose Font, Mac users, Character Settings. This opens the Font/Character Settings dialog box.
3. Select a new font, size, or style for the text block here.
4. Click OK to return to your score.

Alignment and Positioning

If simply dragging text into place isn't precise enough, you can specify the exact location of any text block relative to the page margin, page edge, or assigned measure.

1. With either the Text ![A] or Selection Tool ![icon], right-click (on Mac, CTRL-click) the title, for instance, and choose **Edit Frame Attributes.** This will open the Frame Attributes dialog box (see Figure 2.13).

Figure 2.13
Use the Frame Attributes dialog box for precise positioning of text blocks.

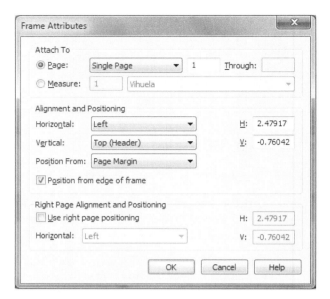

2. In this box, specify the placement of the text block. On the left side of the Alignment and Positioning section, choose the general location of the chosen text block from the drop-down menus. For example, for the title, you would probably choose **Center** for horizontal and **Top (header)** for vertical.
3. Then, you can fine-tune the placement in the **H: (horizontal)** and **V: (vertical)** fields to the right. In this case, to move the title a half inch below the top page margin, enter "-.5" in the V: field.
4. Click **OK** to return to your score and review the placement. Use this method to position any page-assigned text block.

You can also adjust the positioning of measure-assigned text blocks in the Frame Attributes dialog box.

1. With either the Text **A** or Selection Tool ⬚, context-click a measure-assigned text block and choose **Edit Frame Attributes**.
2. Now, use the **H:** and **V:** fields to specify the distance from the beginning of the measure in the **H:** field and the distance above or below the top staff line in the **V:** field. The beginning of a measure in this case relates to the left barline, or just after a displayed key or time signature.
3. Click **OK** to return to your score and review the placement.

Page Numbers

If you started your document with the Setup Wizard, Default Document, or a template, there will already be page numbers on each page starting with page 2. If your document does not have page numbers...

To enter new page numbers into your score:

1. With the Text Tool **A** selected, double-click where you would like to place the page number.
2. Then, choose **Text** > **Inserts** > **Page Numbers** (or press CTRL/CMD+SHIFT+P). You can specify the positioning of your page numbers exactly like page-assigned text blocks (as described above).

To assign the page number to all or multiple pages:

1. Right/CTRL+click the page number handle and choose **Edit Frame Attributes**. The Frame Attributes dialog box appears.
2. In the **Attach To** section, click the drop-down menu to the right of Page and choose **All Pages** (or choose **Page Range** and enter a page range in the text boxes to the right).

Left and Right Pages

Finale places page numbers on alternating sides of each page, as they would appear if you intended your music to end up on left and right pages of a book. If you did not start using a default file or the Setup Wizard, to do this, first move into Page View (**View** > **Page View**) and then follow these steps:

1. Right/CTRL+click the handle on a page number and click **Edit Frame Attributes**.
2. Enter a Page Range in the field to the right. For example "2 through 0," where "0" indicates the end of the piece (odd page numbers are always right pages and even numbers are always left pages).
3. In the **Alignment and Positioning** section, choose **Left** and enter "0" (zero) for horizontal and choose **Top** for vertical. (Use the **H:** and **V:** text boxes to define a specific a position.)
4. Check **Use Right Page Positioning**, then, for Horizontal, choose **Right**.
5. Click **OK** to return to your score.

Other Text Tool Tricks

In this section I have covered the very basics of the Text Tool. There are many other ways to modify text blocks. You can change the tracking, line spacing, baseline, and several other parameters. Many of these other features resemble functionality you may have seen before in word-processing programs. To maintain focus on music notation (and avoid redundancy with the User Manual) I won't go into every one of these features here. There may, however, be a few Text Tool tricks you might want to know about.

Entering Musical Symbols (Sharp, Flat, etc.) in a Text Block

To enter accidentals in a text block:

1. Move the cursor to the desired location within a text block.
2. Choose **Text** > **Inserts** and choose one of the accidentals in this submenu. The accidental will appear in your score.

If you want to add other music characters, such as rhythmic durations, you can change the font of a portion of your text block.

1. Highlight a region of a text block, then choose **Text** > **Font.**
2. Choose one of the music fonts (Maestro, Jazz, etc.) and click **OK.** The characters you type will change to their corresponding music symbol. You will find a chart showing the keystrokes for all characters for every Finale music font under the Help menu (Windows users: **Help** > **Shortcuts & Character Map**; Mac users: **Help** > **Character Sets**).

Finale's Text Editor

If you want to create a large amount of text, or perform more advanced tasks like mixing fonts within a text block, use Finale's text editor. Select a text block handle and choose **Text** > **Edit Text**. You can use this window, shown in Figure 2.14, to enter a large amount of text at once. Use the Text menu in this window to change the font, size, style, or any other attribute of a highlighted region of text.

Figure 2.14
Use the Edit Text dialog box to create larger text blocks.

You can also view any text block in your score using the up and down arrows. Click the up arrow next to ID to view the next text block. This can be particularly helpful while editing large scores with many pages and/or lots of text.

Displaying a Text Block On-Screen Only

If you want a text block to display on your screen but not in the printout:

1. Right/CTRL+click a text block to show the text context menu.
2. Uncheck **Show.**

TIP:
In large documents, you may want to search and change every occurrence of a text block or other text (expression, staff name, etc.). To do this, choose **Edit** > **Text Search & Replace**.

Introduction to Regional Selection and Editing

Selecting regions of music and making changes to several notes and/or measures at once is fundamental to working with Finale efficiently. Finale's mass-editing features eliminate a great deal of redundancy, offering many powerful commands that can be applied to any portion of your score. Easily transpose, move measures around, change beaming, tweak music spacing, and perform a variety of other tasks. For now, I'll cover the most common editing techniques and how to use them most effectively. You will find more information on applying advanced operations in Chapter 9. All of these changes can be accomplished with the Selection Tool (although the Selection Tool is not always required). Click the Selection Tool now. For this section, I'll assume that you already have the Selection Tool selected.

NOTE:
Cut, copy, and paste changed significantly back in Finale 2008. It's now much easier. We'll cover the nitty gritty details in chapter 9.

Selecting Regions

In order to make changes to a region you first must select it. To do so:

1. If you do not have a new default document open, choose **File** > **New** > **Default Document**. Then, choose **View** > **Page View**.

2. Click above measure 1 and drag below the middle of measure 2 (you'll see a dashed box appear). Release the mouse button and measure one and the first part of measure two will be selected as shown in Figure 2.15. You can click and drag over any region of your score to easily select multiple measures. Now, let's say you want to select measures one through five.

Figure 2.15
Click and drag to select any measure region, which can always include partial measures.

3. Double-click the region to extend the selection to include full measures. Notice the highlighted region expands vertically as well. This indicates the measure "stack" is selected, which indicates all measure-specific elements of the region are also selected in addition to the music. (In documents with more than one staff, double-clicking a full measure (or measures) applies a stack selection, selecting the measure(s) for all staves). More on measure stacks later.

4. Hold down SHIFT and click measure three. Or, hold down the SHIFT key and press the right arrow. Either of these methods can be used to expand the region horizontally or vertically (in scores with multiple staves).

5. Hold down SHIFT and press the END key (Laptop: fn+SHIFT+END). Now the selected area extends to the end of the piece. You can also use SHIFT+HOME (fn+SHIFT+HOME) to extend selection to the beginning of the piece.

6. Click anywhere outside the highlighted area to clear the selection.

7. Hold down CTRL/CMD and press A to select the entire document (or choose **Edit** > **Select All**).

TIP:
To move the viewable area of the page while working in the Selection Tool , right-click (Windows)/CMD+OPTION (Macintosh) and drag to temporarily engage the Hand Grabber Tool.

Copying Music

Of course, one of the great beauties of music notation with a computer is the ability to copy music from one place to another. In Finale, this is quite simple to do - very similar to a word processor. Let's start by entering a few notes in the first measure of your document.

1. Click the Simple Entry Tool 🎵 , then click the Quarter Note Tool in the Simple Entry Palette and click four quarter notes on any pitch in the first measure.

2. Now, select the Selection Tool 🖰 .

3. Click the first measure so it is highlighted. (Click in an unpopulated part of the measure to avoid selecting a note).

4. Click on the highlighted area and drag to measure two.

5. When you see a green border surrounding measure two, release the mouse button. The notes appear in measure 2.

6. Now, let's try another technique just as easy. Choose **Edit** > **Undo** (or press CTRL/ CMD+Z) to undo. The notes in measure 2 disappear.

7. With measure 1 still highlighted, hold down the CTRL/CMD key and press C. You have just copied this music to Finale's "clipboard". It can now be pasted anywhere in the score.

8. Click measure 2 to highlight it. Then, hold down CTRL/CMD and press V. The music appears in measure 2. Use this second technique to copy to remote places of the score - different pages for example.

Either of the above techniques can be used interchangeably to copy any region of music from one place to another. (This was not the case in Finale versions older than Finale 2008).

You may want to remove the original music as you copy it to a new location. To do this:

1. Highlight a measure or any region containing music.

2. Hold down the CTRL/CMD key and press X (or choose **Edit** > **Cut**). The music has been cleared and the measure should now be filled with a whole rest.

3. Highlight an empty measure. Hold down the CTRL/CMD key and press V (or choose **Edit** > **Paste**).

4. The music appears in the highlighted measure. Whenever you choose **Paste**, Finale overwrites any existing material with the material you are pasting.

Inserting Music

If you want to insert music between two measures, without replacing any entries (pushing all subsequent music to the right):

1. Click the Selection Tool .

2. Highlight the region you would like to copy. This region can include full or partial measures, but beware, if you insert partial measures the remaining notes in the staff will be nudged to the right, placing downbeats (for example) elsewhere.

NOTE:
"Rebarring music" results when a region of music is displaced from its original beat assignment and barlines are distributed amongst the notes differently. Longer notes, for example, are often split into two notes tied over a barline. Use caution whenever you copy and insert regions including partial measures, particularly in scores with multiple staves.

3. Hold down ALT/CMD, then click and drag the highlighted region until the vertical insertion cursor appears at the beginning of the desired destination. See Figure 2.16.

Figure 2.16

Insert music by holding down
ALT/CMD while drag-copying.

4. The inserted music appears and subsequent music is nudged to the right the duration
    of the inserted material.

Clearing Music

Clear any highlighted region of note or rest entries by pressing the BACKSPACE key on Windows, or
the CLEAR (laptop: fn+6) key on Macintosh. (These keys will always clear and never remove measures.) Alternatively, you can choose **Edit** > **Clear All Items**.

The behavior of the DELETE key depends on the type of selection:

*   If a partial measure or a region of less than a stack is selected, pressing DELETE clears
    the music. (A *stack* is a region of full measures, all staves).

*   If a stack is selected, pressing DELETE removes the selected measures.

Deleting Measures

Deleting measures seems like a simple task, but it's important to recognize the definition of a measure as
a vertical segment, or "stack," of the score. (See "Selecting Music" and "Copying Music" in the User
Manual for exhaustive coverage of selection and measure stacks).

To remove measures (in all staves):

1. Choose the Selection Tool [tool icon], and double-click to select a measure stack, or,
    SHIFT+drag-enclose to select a stack of multiple measures. Highlighting between
    staves indicates the full stack is selected.

2. Hold down CTRL and SHIFT and press the right and left arrow keys to expand the
    selection by full measures.

3. Press the DELETE key, or choose **Edit** > **Delete Measure Stack**.

TIP:
A measure stack can be selected with any tool that allows regional
selection (Staff, Measure, Key Signature, etc.). ALT/CMD+click to
instantly select a measure stack.

Introduction to Page Layout

In general, most Finale users agree that Page Layout should be the last stage in editing a score before printout. There are, however, a few basic principles you should be aware of as you continue to develop a working knowledge of Finale. These concepts should be adequate for finalizing small projects, particularly single staff documents such as lead sheets. I'll cover more advanced page layout topics in Chapter 11.

Figure 2.17

System margins, page margins, and page layout icons appear when you click the Page Layout Tool.

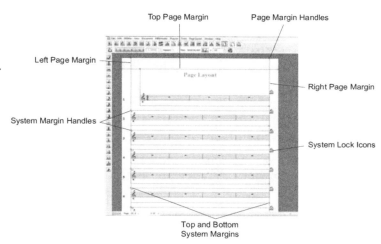

If you have entered music into your score in Page View, you may have noticed measures moving from system to system automatically. This is Finale's way of maintaining consistent music spacing as you enter. Any time you specify a number of measures on a system (by using Fit Measures, or even by manually moving measures between systems), Finale will lock the system, preventing Automatic Music Spacing from shifting the measures. Systems that are locked will be tagged with a System Lock icon that looks like a padlock (see Figure 2.17).

To lock any system, highlight the measures in the system and choose **Utilities** > **Lock Systems** (to unlock systems, choose **Utilities** > **Unlock**). Or, instead of unlocking from the Utilities menu, try using CTRL/CMD+L to lock and SHIFT+CTRL/CMD+L to unlock.

Editing Staff and System Spacing

Now, it's time to learn the basics for editing the layout of staves and systems. Here, I'll cover how to space staves and systems, as well as other techniques that come into play while editing the layout of staves and systems. First, it is important to make the distinction between staves and systems.

When you look at your score in Scroll View (**View** > **Scroll View**), you will see the total number of staves in your document. Think of Scroll View as one really long system that can stretch into eternity. Only when you look at your score in Page View (**View** > **Page View**) will you be able to see your staff systems. In Page View, a system is one or more staves extending across the page that are intended to be played at the same time.

Changing the Distance Between Staves (for viewing/editing)

Move staves in Scroll View to maximize your ease in viewing and editing. (Changes to the staff spacing in Scroll View do not apply to Page View or printing.)

1. First, move to Scroll View. Click the Staff Tool [icon], then choose **Staff** > **New Staves**.
2. In the New Staves dialog box, enter "2" and click **OK**. There are now three staves in your score. Each staff has a handle on the upper-left corner.
3. Click the handle on the middle staff and drag it up or down. For Scroll View, that's all there is to it! Staff spacing in Scroll View is handled separately from staff spacing in Page View. Now, let's talk about staff spacing in Page View.

Changing the Distance Between Staves (for printing)

Position staves in Page View as a means to prepare the layout for printing. Staves can be moved in each system independently, or for all systems at once.

1. Move to Page View (**View** > **Page View**). Note that any staff spacing changes made in Scroll View do not affect Page View.
2. To move a staff **in one system only,** click its handle once and drag (or use the arrow keys to nudge). Subsequent staves in the system move uniformly. Finale displays the space between staves as you drag (see Figure 2.18). Notice the staff is highlighted, but only for that system. To identify the staves/systems you are changing while moving staves, refer to the highlighting. (Any number of staves in as many systems as required can be selected for drag-respacing. See "Introduction to Regional Selection and Editing" on page 37).

Figure 2.18

When you drag staves, Finale shows the distance between the top staff line of each staff and the top staff line of the staff directly above it.

3. To quickly move a staff **in all systems,** double-click its handle and drag (or use the arrow keys to nudge). Subsequent staves *in all systems throughout the score* move

uniformly. Notice that double-clicking a staff handle highlights the entire staff through-out the score.

4. For more staff respacing options, choose **Staff** > **Respace Staves**. The Respace Staves dialog box appears, which allows you to space staves using numerical values, or reset the staff spacing in Page View throughout so that it matches Scroll View.

NOTE:
When you drag the top staff of the first staff system of the score, Finale leaves the top system margin fixed. When you drag the top staff of any other system, Finale instead adjusts the distance between systems. Learn more about system margins under "Page Layout" on page 299.

Changing the Distance Between Systems

You may want to manually adjust the staff systems in your score.

1. Click the Page Layout Tool to see the dashed margins around each system.
2. Then, simply click within any system (not on a handle) and drag. When you drag a system, all systems beneath the one you are dragging will adjust respectively.
3. To drag a system independently (so that systems below are not influenced), hold down the CTRL/OPTION key, then click and drag. You will be able to move a system only until the margin collides with an adjacent system margin or a page margin.
4. To move systems closer together, or closer to the top or bottom page margin, you will need to edit their margins.

TIP:
To move the top staff system closer to the top page margin, simply choose the Staff Tool and drag the top staff handle up. Dragging the top staff handle of other systems moves the whole system (the same as simply clicking and dragging a system with the Page Layout Tool as described above).

To move all systems closer together or farther apart:

1. Click the Page Layout Tool .
2. Click a handle on the lower right of one of your systems and press CTRL/CMD+A to Select All (or choose **Edit** > **Select All**).
3. Now all bottom system margin handles should be highlighted.
4. Drag one handle down to increase the distance between all systems or drag one up to decrease the distance. For more control, you can also use the arrow keys to nudge system handles.

Spacing Systems Evenly

You can easily space all systems evenly on a page so that the top and bottom systems lie against the top and bottom page margins. To do this:

1. Choose **Page Layout** > **Space Systems Evenly** from the Page Layout menu.
2. In the Space Systems Evenly dialog box, choose the page, or a page range, how you want to distribute systems, and click **OK**.
3. All systems will be spaced evenly and will more closely resemble a standard engraving layout (see Figure 2.19).

Figure 2.19

An example of Space Systems Evenly. Notice that the system margins line up with the top and bottom page margins.

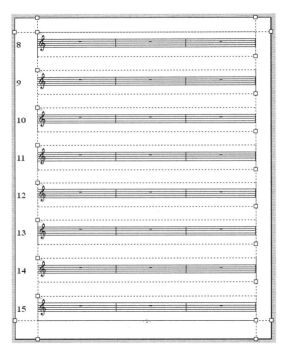

Moving Measures Across Systems

You can easily move measures to different systems.

*   Highlight the last measure in a system and press CTRL/CMD+down arrow to move it to the next system.

*   Highlight the first measure in a system and press CTRL/CMD+up arrow to move it to the prior system.

You can also do this for several measures at once. Also, instead of using the keystrokes, you can use menus to do this: **Utilities** > **Move to Previous System**/**Move to Next System**.

Fitting Selected Measures to a System

You can easily fit any number of measures to a single system.

1. First, make sure you are in Page View (Select **View** > **Page View**).
2. Highlight the measures you want to fit on one system.
3. Choose **Utilities** > **Fit Measures**.
4. Choose **Lock Selected Measures into One System** and click **OK**. The highlighted measures now all appear on one system.

Specifying Number of Measures per System for a Region

To specify a certain number of measures per system for a selected region:

1. Highlight the region you want to change (CTRL/CMD+A to select all).
2. Choose **Utilities** > **Fit Measures**.
3. Choose **Lock Layout with _ Measure(s) per System** and enter a number.
4. Click **OK**. Your selected region will now contain the number of measures per system you specified.

Resizing a Page

If you find all of your music is too large or small on the page, you can use the Resize Tool **%** to reduce or enlarge your music. You can change the size of all the music on your page without changing the margins or page size.

1. Click the Resize Tool **%** and click an empty area of your page (outside any staves or systems). You will see the Resize Page dialog box (Figure 2.20).

Figure 2.20
Reduce or enlarge all elements on a page by choosing a percentage in the Resize Page dialog box.

2. Enter a percentage and choose a page range. You will probably want to keep **Page 1 Through End of Piece** selected so all of your pages appear at the same reduction.
3. Click **OK** to return to your score and review the new sizing. You can also resize individual systems, staves, and even notes with the Resize Tool. You'll find more on the Resize Tool in Chapter 11.

Redefining Pages and Page Format for Score

If you want to revert to Finale's default page format:

1. Choose the Page Layout Tool 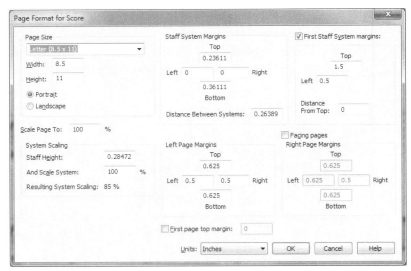.
2. Choose **Page Layout** > **Redefine Pages**.
3. Choose the pages you want to redefine from the **Redefine Pages** submenu. You will see a message warning that all page layout information will be lost.
4. Click **OK** to return to the default page layout settings. Any time you choose to redefine your pages, Finale will draw settings from the Page Format for Score or Page Format for Parts dialog boxes found in **Document** > **Page Format** > **Score** or **Parts**. (See Figure 2.21).

Figure 2.21

Use the Page Format for Score dialog box to specify precise spacing for system and page margins.

Page Size, Orientation, and Printing

When you start a score with the Default Document, for example, Finale will use a standard 8 ½ by 11 page size in portrait orientation. To change the size and orientation of your page:

1. Choose the Page Layout Tool .
2. Choose **Page Layout** > **Page Size**. This will open the Page Size dialog box (see Figure 2.22).

Figure 2.22

Use the Page Size dialog box to specify page size and orientation.

3. In this dialog box, choose a new height and width for your page. You can also change the orientation of the page by choosing **Landscape** or **Portrait**.

4. Choose the page range for which you want to apply the changes, or choose **All Pages**.

5. Click **OK** to return to the score. You should now see the new page size on your screen.

Now that you have set a new page size in Finale, before you print the document you will need to modify your print settings so this information corresponds to the page size and orientation of your document.

1. Choose **File** > **Printer Page Setup**. The Page Setup dialog box appears (see Figure 2.23).

Figure 2.23

In the Page Setup dialog box, choose the page size and orientation for the printed page.

2. Here, choose the paper size for your printer and the same orientation you indicated in the Page Size dialog box.

3. Click the printer driver to open the settings for your print driver.

4. Set up your printer to print the specified page size here. Consult your printer's instruction manual for specific information on how to specify a new page size.

5. Once you have made your print settings, click **OK** in the Page Setup dialog box.

6. Choose **File** > **Print** to open the Print dialog box. Click Print to send your score to the printer.

The above instructions are just the basics to setting up a score for printing. A variety of other options are available in Finale, including left and right pages, tiled pages, and placing many "Finale pages" on a single printed page. Information on more advanced page layout topics can be found in Chapter 11.

3
Note Entry, Articulations, and Expressions

Everything you have learned so far is a fundamental building block, like basic wilderness survival and first aid. Now let's expand the focus to the more diverse practice of entering notes, articulations, and expressions. There is no single method that will accommodate everyone, so this approach is conceptual. After you're done with this chapter you will understand enough about these items to use them in creative and wonderful ways.

Even the order of entry is subject to individual preference. Some find that entering all the notes first, followed by articulations and then expressions works best. Others prefer entering all these items at the same time while progressing from measure to measure. The method you adopt should depend on the size of the project you are working with as well as the materials you have available to you. If you are composing a work from scratch, you may want to include these markings immediately to help you remember a specific phrase or musical idea. If you are copying from an existing score, entering all of your notes and then going back to enter articulations or expressions may be a faster method for you. In some sense, Finale is like a piece of music itself; each of us deriving something unique from the same combination of ones and zeros. It's also important to remember, however, that despite the many possibilities, it's best to keep focus on your composition, which often means using Finale as unimaginatively as possible–the way it was designed to be used. In any case, this chapter will demonstrate acceptable usage of these important tools so that you will be able to most effectively employ them to fit your needs.

Finale offers many ways to enter notes into a staff. In this chapter, I'll cover the two most common: Simple Entry and Speedy Entry. First, I'll define some terminology used in this chapter.

- An *entry* in Finale is a note or rest. Also, notes stacked vertically (as in a chord) are also defined as an entry.
- An *articulation* is a marking attached to a single entry. As you reposition an entry, its articulation(s) will move with it respectively. These include, but are not limited to, standard articulations like accents and staccatos.
- Finally, an *expression* is an item (text or a shape) that affects a region of music and is attached to a measure. Examples of items you will enter with the Expression Tool are dynamic markings, tempo indications, and rehearsal letters.

Here's a summary of what you will learn in this chapter:

- How to enter notes and rests with Simple Entry.
- How to enter notes and rests with Speedy Entry
- How to enter articulations (accents, staccato markings)
- How to enter expressions (dynamics, tempo indications, rehearsal letters)
- How to create a simple arrangement

The Simple Entry Tool

Simple Entry is Finale's most versatile and customizable entry method. You can use the Simple Entry Tool to enter all the basic-notation building blocks including notes, rests, chords, grace notes, tuplets, and ties. In addition, you can use the Entry Caret feature to type-in notes, articulations, expressions, and even clef, key and time signature changes. Simple Entry is also a powerful editing tool. You can modify the pitch of any note, add accidentals and augmentation dots, as well as flip stems, break/join beams, and even hide notes. Though this can be the simplest and most intuitive form of note entry, you can use its incredible versatility to perform the majority of your work. Users of any skill level will benefit greatly by learning how to harness the full potential of this tool. You'll start by getting acquainted with entering notes.

IMPORTANT: If you are using a laptop, switch to Finale's Laptop Shortcut Table, which includes Simple Entry keyboard shortcuts optimized for a smaller keyboard. To do so:

1. Choose the Simple Entry Tool 🎵 .
2. From the Simple Menu, choose Simple Entry Options. The Simple Entry Options dialog box appears.
3. Click Edit Keyboard Shortcuts. The Edit Keyboard Shortcuts dialog box appears.
4. In the Keyboard Shortcut Set section, click the Name drop-down menu and choose Laptop Shortcut Table. You can return to this dialog box to reference all of the keyboard Shortcuts in the Laptop Shortcut Table in the list above.
5. Click OK twice to return to the score.

Entering Notes in Simple Entry with a Mouse

To prepare for this chapter, begin a new document.

1. Choose **File** > **New** > **Default Document**. This provides a good canvas to experiment with basic note entry. The first time you launch Finale, the Simple Entry Tool is already selected by default.
2. Click the Simple Entry Tool 🎵 now if it isn't chosen already. You should see a note and vertical line in measure one. This is called the Simple Entry Caret, and you'll learn about it later.

3. For now, press ESC to hide it. Click the eighth note in the Simple Entry Palette (see Figure 3.1). Notice that when you position your mouse over the staff, your cursor now looks like an eighth note.

4. Now click the half note and the mouse cursor changes to a half note. Your cursor will always reflect the duration chosen in the Simple Entry Palette.

5. Click the quarter note icon, move the cursor to the middle staff line in the first measure, and click to enter a quarter note on middle line B. You can use this method to enter notes of any duration into your staff. Notice your cursor jump between the staff lines and spaces as you slowly drag over a staff.

6. Click to place the note on the desired staff line or space.

Figure 3.1

Choose a rhythmic value, pitch alteration, grace note, tuplet, tie, or combination of these tools from the Simple Entry Palette for entry into the score.

You can specify a great deal of information before entering a note by choosing several items at once in the Simple Entry Palette. Let's say you wanted to enter a dotted eighth note with a tie.

1. From the Simple Palette, double-click the Eighth Note Tool 🎵 (to de-select everything but the eighth note).

2. Click the Dot Tool 🔲 and the Tie Tool 🔲 . You can now see all of these items on your cursor.

3. Click in the score and you will see a dotted eighth with a tie on whatever pitch you click on. To select any one tool independently, just double-click it and all other Simple Entry Tools will deactivate.

Now, let's say you have just entered a note, but it ended up on the wrong pitch. Notice the note just entered is always highlighted in purple (or some seemingly indescribable magenta/red-violet color). This note is now selected (I'll get into this more later on).

1. Press the up and down arrows to change its pitch.

2. You can also click the note, hold down the mouse button, and drag the note up or down to the desired location. These techniques will come in handy anytime you misplace a note or want to change the pitch right away.

3. To deselect a note or rest, press the ESC key.

4. To enter a chord, simply click notes above or below an existing entry. You can stack up to 12 notes vertically on a staff to create thick chords. You will be able to edit the pitches of each note in a chord independently.

TIP:
CTRL/OPTION+click and drag a note to easily change its pitch.

Entering Rests with the Mouse

There are a few ways to enter rests into your score with Simple Entry. You may have already noticed rests added to measures in your score. By default, Simple Entry automatically fills incomplete measures with rests after clicking into a different measure or changing tools in the Main Tool Palette. To see this for yourself, enter a quarter note into an empty measure. Then click a note into a different measure. The first measure fills with rests. If you want to disable this feature and enter all rests manually, choose **Simple** > **Simple Entry Options**, and uncheck **Fill with Rests**. If you turn it off, you will still be able to go back and quickly fill measures with rests later on with the Fill with Rest feature.

To enter rests manually, open the Simple Entry Rests Palette (Figure 3.2) if you don't see it on your screen already. To do so, choose **Window** > **Simple Entry Rests Palette**. Notice the appearance of the new palette filled with rests of different durations.

Figure 3.2
Specify the rhythmic duration of a rest for entry into the score from the Simple Entry Rests Palette.

You can treat this palette the same as the Simple Entry Palette to enter rests. However, there is a better way. Use keyboard shortcuts!

- Press a number key to change the caret to the desired duration, then press 0 (zero) to enter a rest of that value.
- Click in a measure to enter the rest, or on existing notes to change them into rests of the duration you have chosen.
- Press the R key to toggle between notes and rests of the same duration in your cursor. (Careful, if a note is selected pressing R changes the selected note(s) to a rest - press ESC to remove selection).
- To change any note in your score to a rest of the same duration, CTRL/OPTION+click it (it will change color) to select it and press the R key. I'll provide a complete explanation of selection later.

Accidentals

If you enter a note without specifying an accidental, Finale will always assume you want the note entered on the diatonic pitch. Any divergence from the key signature will need to be specified with one of the five alteration tools: Sharp, Flat, Natural, Half Step Up, and Half Step Down.

To 'click-in' a note with an accidental:

1. Click the desired note duration, and then click the Sharp, Flat, or Natural icon in the Simple Palette. Now your cursor tells you the duration and the alteration (sharp/flat/ natural) that will be entered after you click in the score.
2. Click somewhere in the staff to see how this works.
3. Choose the Half Step Up $+\frac{1}{2}$ or Half Step Down Tool $-\frac{1}{2}$ and click a note to raise or lower its pitch in half steps. You can add double sharps or double flats this way as well.
4. To remove the accidental from the cursor, either click its icon again or double-click the desired note duration.

NOTE:
The Sharp, Flat and Natural Tools are "absolute," meaning independent from the key signature. Clicking an F# into a staff with the Sharp Tool will always result in an F#. If you want to ensure that any note you enter will appear one half step above or below the diatonic pitch in any key, choose the Half Step Up or Half Step Down Tool. To clarify, the behavior of the Sharp Tool will differ from that of the Half Step Up Tool only while entering or editing notes already altered by the key signature.

Tuplets

The Simple Entry Tuplet Tool is a bit different than the others. This tool was added in response to many customer requests for an easier method of tuplet entry, particularly, so that tuplets could be added easily on the last beat of a measure (without overfilling the measure). In one click you can add an entire triplet, quintuplet, duplet, or any other type.

Let's start by entering an eighth note triplet.

1. Click the Eighth Note icon ♪ , then the Tuplet icon 🎵 in the Simple Entry Palette.
2. Click in an empty measure. Notice there is now an eighth note, followed by two rests, all within a tuplet bracket. You can leave both tools selected and simply click over the next two rests to finish entering your triplet.
3. To change this figure to a quarter note-eighth note triplet, delete the middle note and change the first entry to a quarter note. You can also change three existing notes into a triplet by clicking on the first of the three with just the Simple Tuplet Tool selected.
4. To specify a tuplet definition other than a triplet (quintuplet, sextuplet, etc.) choose the Simple Tuplet Tool ♪ , hold down SHIFT and click in the score. In the Simple Entry Tuplet Definition dialog box, enter your settings (e.g., 6 in the space of 4 for a sextu- plet, etc.) and click OK. If you will be entering many custom tuplets, check 'Save as default Simple Entry tuplet definition' in the Simple Entry Tuplet Definition dialog box to save your settings. You can find more about tuplets in "Ties and Tuplets" on page 240.

Keyboard Shortcuts

By now you may be wondering, "Am I really going to have to click all these icons before entering each note?" The answer is *no*. Instead of clicking a duration tool, you can choose that tool using the numbers on your computer keyboard. For example, type 3 on your numeric keypad to select a 16th note (use the number row if you've selected the Laptop Shortcut Set). Type 4 for an eighth note, 5 for a quarter, and so on. Now press the + key and the period key (.) to add a sharp and an augmentation dot to the cursor (unless a note is selected, in which case the accidental and dot will be added to the selected note). Choosing durations with your keypad and clicking notes into the score is one way to increase efficiency; however, that's just the tip of the iceberg, as you will see in the next section.

TIP:
To select any single tool in the Simple Palette and de-select all others, double-press any keyboard shortcut (much like a double click).

Editing Notes in Simple Entry

We have learned that it is possible to select any Simple Entry icon by itself (and deselect all others) by simply double-clicking it. This comes in handy when editing existing notes. Double-click the Tie icon (or double-press the letter T), for example, and then click on any note to add or remove a tie. You can edit notes with any Simple Tool by simply selecting the appropriate tool and clicking a note. Keep in mind that all Simple Tools selected will apply to the entry you click. For example, if you have the Sharp and Half Note icons selected, any note you click will become a half note with a sharp. Entering and editing would be far more difficult if there weren't time-saving keyboard shortcuts to make your life easier.

Selecting Notes

Selection is an integral part to making the most of the Simple Entry Tool. The same keyboard shortcuts you used to choose note durations, accidentals, and the like from the Simple Palette can also be used to modify any selected note.

1. Click a series of quarter notes into a measure. After you enter a note, it is highlighted in purple automatically.

2. Press ALT+4 on Windows or OPTION+4 on Mac to change it to an eighth note, or press the + key to raise it by a half step.

3. Use the left and right arrows to move the selection between entries. You can also select any note in your score easily by holding down CTRL/OPTION and clicking an entry.

4. To remove the selection from the note (so that keyboard shortcuts can be used for the mouse cursor again), press the ESC.

Selecting Notes in Chords

You can move the selection between notes in a chord and even select several notes within an entry at once. Enter a chord of seven notes in a measure. Now hold down CTRL/CMD and use the up and down arrows to highlight any one note in the chord for editing. To select multiple notes within a chord, hold down CTRL/OPTION+SHIFT and click each note in the chord you want to select (Figure 3.3).

Figure 3.3
CTRL/OPTION+SHIFT+click to select non-contiguous notes in a chord.

To select all notes in a chord, select one of the notes, press CTRL/CMD+A or CTRL/OPTION+click above or below it. Any keystroke will now affect all highlighted notes. If you change the pitch or duration with any one note of the chord selected, all notes in the chord will change.

TIP:
To see all of the available keystrokes for note selection, click the Simple menu and choose Simple Navigation Commands.

Other Editing Commands for Selected Notes

In addition to note durations, accidentals, and the other commands similar to Tool Selection and Selected Note editing, there are several other commands that were built in specifically for selected notes.

1. Select a note and press the L key to flip its stem, press the R key to change it to a rest, and press the H key to hide an entry.

2. You can also break/join the beam between a note and the previous entry (/ on the QWERTY keyboard) or show/hide a courtesy accidental (Windows: CTRL+SHIFT+-[minus; use the minus key on the QWERTY keyboard] Mac: SHIFT+CMD+-[minus; use the minus key on the QWERTY keyboard]).

3. To see a full list of the possibilities, or apply any command, click the Simple menu and choose Simple Edit Commands (Figure 3.4).

Figure 3.4
Choose Simple Edit Commands from the Simple menu to see a list of keyboard shortcuts.

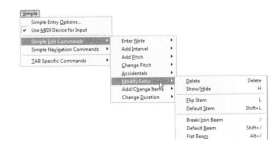

Entering Notes in Simple Entry with your Computer Keyboard

Up to this point I've covered the basic concepts of Simple Entry; now it's time to learn how to do the same stuff faster. Early last decade, MakeMusic implemented a new approach to Simple Entry that allows you to quickly type-in all the musical elements covered so far (and more) using your computer keyboard. In fact, you can even use your MIDI keyboard, or even a wind instrument, to specify pitches in Simple Entry. In this section, you'll learn how to take advantage of these capabilities. To get started, do the following:

1. Laptop users, choose **Simple** > **Simple Entry Options**, then click **Edit Keyboard Short-cuts**. Under Keyboard Shortcut Set, choose **Laptop Shortcut Table**. Then click **OK**.

TIP:
Laptop users: If you have an iPhone or iPod Touch, you can avoid the hassle of using the Laptop Shortcut Table by installing edovia's "NumPad" application (edovia.com/numpad), which turns your device into a wireless numeric keypad. They even have a Finale Simple Entry Layout just for this purpose!

2. Open a new Default Document (**File** > **New** > **Default Document**).

3. Click the Simple Entry Tool ♪. Notice the note with a vertical line through it at the beginning of the first measure (as shown in Figure 3.5). This is called the Simple Entry Caret. The Caret is much like a cursor in a word-processing program. The vertical line tells you where the next note will be entered. The note tells you the currently selected duration.

Figure 3.5
The Simple Entry Caret is like the cursor in a word processor.

4. On the numeric keypad, press 6, then 5, then 4 (laptop users, use the number row for this section). Notice that the Caret changes to a half, then a quarter, then an eighth note. (The mouse cursor and Duration Tool on the Simple Entry Palette change as well). This is how you select the duration for the next entry.

5. Now, press the up arrow and then the down arrow. Notice that the Caret moves up and down on the staff. You can use this method to select the pitch you want to add and press Enter to add the note, but it's faster to do the following.

6. Type the letters A, B, C, D, E, F, and G. These notes appear on the staff. Finale places the pitch you type on the staff position closest to the Caret. Now, for example, if you were to type E, Finale would add a top space E. But say you want to add an E on the bottom staff line.

7. Hold down SHIFT and press DOWN ARROW, and then type E. An E appears on the bottom staff line. Similarly, you can press SHIFT-UP ARROW to move the Caret up an octave. So, thus far you have learned how to specify the duration and pitch. Your first measure should look like Figure 3.6.

Figure 3.6

With the Caret active, use the numeric pad to specify duration and then use letter keys to add pitches.

8. (Notice the last note in measure 1 is selected. You can change this note in many ways using special modifier keystrokes.) Press the + key on the numeric pad to raise the note you just entered a half step. Press - (minus) in the numeric pad to lower it a half step. These keystrokes increment chromatically so you can also easily add double-sharps and flats. Now let's experiment with some other modifiers.

9. Press T to add a tie, \ (backslash) to change the enharmonic spelling, and ALT/OPTION+G to change to a grace note. Press T again to remove the tie and ALT/OPTION+G again to toggle between an unslashed grace note, a slashed grace note and a regular note.

TIP:
Choose **Simple** > **Simple Entry Commands** > **Modify Entry** to see a list of the modifier keystrokes. These Modify Entry keystrokes work on any selected note. (Remember, after you enter a note it is selected automatically).

10. Now let's add a rest. Press 5 on the numeric pad and then 0 (zero) on the numeric pad to enter a quarter rest. (You can also press R to change a selected note to a rest.)

11. Press the F key to add an F. Say we want to create a triad (chord). There are two ways to do this. The easiest: in the QWERTY keyboard (number row), press 3 twice (laptop users, F3). Use the number row to add a note of an interval (unison through ninth) above the selected note (see Figure 3.7. Hold down SHIFT and press a number to add a note below the selected note). You could also hold down SHIFT and type the note letters to create a chord).

Figure 3.7

Use keys in the number row (or SHIFT+letter) to add intervals above or below notes. Laptop users, use the Function keys.

12. Now, if you want to change the pitch of the note you just entered (while the caret is still showing), just hold down ALT/OPTION and press the up or down arrow.

13. To change the duration of a selected note, hold down ALT/OPTION and press a duration key on the numeric pad. For example, press ALT/OPTION+6 to change to a half note.

>
>
> **TIP:**
> All notes on the same beat (chords) change if you change the duration of any note in the chord. To enter notes of different durations (e.g., more than one voice) on the same beat, use a different layer. You'll learn more about layers later in this chapter.

The preceding was a crash course designed to give you a basic idea of how fast and easy entry can be with the Caret. For additional hands-on training, open the file "EntryExercise" in the Finale 2012/Music Files/Tutorials folder (choose **File** > **Open** and click the "Tutorials" shortcut). It's an instructional Finale file that guides you through most of Simple Entry's functionality. Highly recommended! You can also find helpful advice in the QuickStart Videos (**Help** > **QuickStart Videos**).

Navigating with the Caret

If you plan to use the Caret to edit your music, you'll need to know how to get around with it. Here are the keystrokes you need to know:

- CTRL/OPTION+click an empty measure to display the Caret at the beginning of the measure.
- Use the left and right arrow keys to move the Caret (or selection) forward and backward in the staff.
- Press CTRL/CMD+right arrow to advance the Caret to the next measure, CTRL/CMD+left arrow to move the Caret left a measure.
- Press CTRL/CMD+down arrow to move the Caret (or selection) down one staff in the system, CTRL/CMD+up arrow to move the Caret up one staff.
- Select a note (CTRL/OPTION+click) and press Enter to display the Caret to the right of the note.
- Press ESC to hide the Caret (press ESC twice if a note was selected). Press ENTER to redisplay the Caret. (This works well if you want to play around on your MIDI keyboard for experimentation purposes without entering music.)
- Press ESC again to deselect a selected note.
- Pressing ESC (when there's no note selected or caret showing) will also take you into the Selection Tool ▣ .

Adding Articulations and Other Markings with the Caret

Now that you've learned to add notes, you'll also probably want to add other markings such as articulations and dynamic markings to notes as you enter them. Doing so is easy. Let's keep using the document we have open.

1. CTRL/OPTION+click an empty measure to activate the Caret.
2. Enter a note (of any duration).
3. Press the * in the numeric pad (or ` for laptop users). The "Waiting for input" dialog box appears.

4. Press the S key to add a staccato. A staccato marking appears on the note (as shown in Figure 3.8). You just used one of many available "Metatools" to add this articulation. You could have also pressed A to add an accent (>) or pressed Enter to choose from a list of articulations. In the Articulation Selection dialog, the metatool key for each articulation is in the upper right corner.

Figure 3.8

With the Caret, press * and then S to add a staccato, A to add an Accent, or Enter to choose another articulation.

NOTE:
Press X instead of * to add a dynamic marking expression.
You'll learn more about expressions and articulations soon.

5. Now, let's say you want an articulation to appear on the next several notes. To do this, you can use a different keystroke to make the articulation (or expression) "sticky." Hold down CTRL/CMD and press * (laptop users: CTRL/CMD+SHIFT+`). Press a metatool key like A or S (or press ENTER, select a marking and click **OK**). The marking appears on the Caret as shown in Figure 3.9.

6. Enter notes into the score. The articulation appears on each note you enter.

Figure 3.9

Use CTRL/CMD * to specify a "sticky" articulation to appear on several notes.

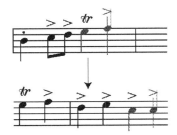

7. Press CTRL/CMD * to remove (or "unstick") the articulation from the Caret.

Using a MIDI Keyboard or Other MIDI Device with the Caret

If you have a MIDI keyboard (or other MIDI device) setup with your computer, you can use it to specify the pitches you want to add while using the Caret. No special setup necessary, just choose the duration from the numeric pad and then play the pitches on your MIDI device. Change the duration at any point from the numeric pad.

Many find using a MIDI keyboard with Simple Entry an easy way to enter music quickly. If you do this, you may need to use the \ (Backslash) key to alter the enharmonic spelling (if, for example, an F sharp appears in the score that should be spelled G flat).

TIP:
Press ESC to experiment on your MIDI keyboard without entering notes.

Entering More Than One Voice Using Layers

It is very common to see more than one melodic line, or voice, entered in the same staff. With layers, you can enter up to four independent voices in any measure (see Figure 3.10). Notice the four boxes (or pop-up menu on Mac) in the lower-left corner of the screen labeled 1, 2, 3, and 4. These are the layer selection controls. Make sure layer 1 is selected and click four quarter notes on the top staff line. Now

select layer 2. Click the Eighth Note Tool , or press the 4 key, and click eighth notes into the same measure on the middle line. They are red so you will always know these notes are in layer 2 in case you want to edit them later.

Figure 3.10
Enter multiple voices in your score using layers.

- The stems on your notes in layer 2 automatically flip down, so if you're using two layers, use layer 2 for the lower voice.
- To flip the stems, select a note and press L, or you can change the default stem direction for each layer of your document in Document Options-Layers (I'll cover this later).
- Use the remaining layers to enter up to two more independent voices in this measure. They will each have their own color so you can distinguish between them (layer 3, green; layer 4, blue).
- You can edit one layer at a time in Simple Entry. For example, if you want to add or edit notes in layer 1, first select layer 1 in the lower-left corner of your screen.

TIP:
You can also use keyboard shortcuts to switch between layers. On Windows, hold down ALT+SHIFT and press the number of the layer you would like to select. On Macintosh, hold down CMD+OPTION and press the number of the layer you would like to select. (See **View** > **Layers** for a reminder of these keystrokes)

To begin entering notes in a new layer somewhere within the measure instead of the first beat:

1. Being entering notes into the measure with the Caret.
2. When you want to switch layers, Windows users type ALT+SHIFT+#, and Mac users type CMD+OPTION+# (where # is the layer number), then continue entering in the new layer. Under the hood, hidden rests are added up until that point in the new layer.

If you want stems extending in both directions on a single note (to indicate two voices in unison), you could enter overlapping notes in layer 1 and layer 2. Do this if you need to enter more than one layer in the measure anyway. To apply beams in both directions in a single layer, use the Double-Split Stem Special Tool 🎼 in the Special Tools Palette (more on the Special Tools in Chapter 10).

Entering Notes and Rests with Speedy Entry

Speedy Entry has been around since the beginning, and many professionals still use it for the majority of their work. Although the Simple Entry Caret now provides the ability to enter notes quickly with a MIDI keyboard (which was the main advantage of Speedy Entry before) it is still a popular choice due to its speed, navigation abilities, and expanded MIDI control. In this section I will cover the various methods of note entry within this tool both with and without a MIDI keyboard.

Click the Speedy Entry Tool 🎵 and notice the Speedy menu that appears at the top of your screen. You will be using the many features in this menu to customize the way Speedy Entry works. These features will be explained throughout this chapter as I cover the methods and tricks they apply to.

If you are using a MIDI keyboard for input, note that the first part of this chapter applies to editing in Speedy Entry with or without a MIDI keyboard. In other words, even in Speedy's MIDI entry mode, all of the non-MIDI features (besides actual note-entry) are available. You may find these techniques useful for editing after entering notes with your MIDI keyboard.

To prepare for this section, launch the Setup Wizard (**File** > **New** > **Setup Wizard**). Click **Next**. On Page 2, add a Piano and complete the wizard. You should now see an empty grand staff score.

Navigation in Speedy Entry

While using Speedy Entry, you will be entering notes within the context of the Speedy Frame as shown in Figure 3.11.

Figure 3.11
Enter notes quickly using the Speedy Frame.

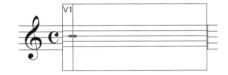

1. Click any measure to activate the Speedy Frame. You can also show or hide the Speedy entry frame by pressing the number 0. When you show it this way, it will appear on the most recently active measure. There are several ways to move the Speedy Entry Frame around your score.

2. Move the horizontal bar left and right using the left and right arrow keys. (I will refer to this horizontal bar as the *Speedy Entry cursor* or just *cursor*). You can also move from measure to measure this way. (The *vertical* line indicates the beat and whether you are entering or inserting - see Figure 3.13).

3. Move the frame horizontally among measures by pressing the left and right bracket keys ([and]) on your computer keyboard.

4. Move the frame between staves in a system (from the top to bottom staff in your piano score): on Windows, hold down SHIFT and use UP and DOWN ARROW; on Mac, press the RETURN key to move down a staff and SHIFT+RETURN to move up.

The Speedy Frame's size will adjust automatically based on your view percentage. To select a fixed size or allow for a greater frame size at low view percentages, click the **Speedy** > **Speedy Options**. You will find these settings in the Frame section.

Speedy Entry Without a MIDI Keyboard

The most basic way to use Speedy Entry is with the computer keyboard. Click **Speedy** and uncheck **Use MIDI Device for Input**. You are now ready to use your computer keyboard for note entry.

1. Press the UP and DOWN ARROWS on your keyboard and notice the small horizontal bar move up and down between the staff lines and spaces.

2. Use the cursor to specify the pitch of the note you want to enter. Move the cursor to the third space C and press the 5 key to enter a quarter note.

3. Use the same keystrokes (1-8) for note durations you used in Simple Entry. After you enter each note, the cursor automatically advances to the right.

4. Press DOWN ARROW twice to move the cursor down to the second space A and press the 4 key twice to enter two eighth notes.

5. Now press the 6 key to enter a half note. Once you have filled a measure, the Speedy Frame automatically jumps to the next measure.

Using the Computer Keyboard to Specify Pitch

There is a faster way to move the cursor between pitches in Speedy Entry–using just your computer keyboard. If you engage CAPS LOCK, all of the letters on your computer keyboard will act differently.

1. Click an empty measure with the Speedy Entry Tool 🎵 chosen.

2. Press CAPS LOCK and press the A key to move the cursor down to middle C. Each letter to the right corresponds to the next highest staff location: S=D, D=E, F=F, and so on.

3. Press the Q key to start from the third space or Z to begin below the staff. Use each adjacent letter to move up or down to different pitches. This can be an effective way to quickly enter notes if you spend some time getting used to the keystrokes.

Entering Rests

- After entering any note, simply press the BACKSPACE/CLEAR key to change it to a rest.
- To change any chord to a rest, position the cursor so that it is not directly over a notehead (otherwise, pressing BACKSPACE/CLEAR will remove an individual note).
- Any time the Speedy Frame leaves a measure, Finale will automatically fill any space at the end with rests. To avoid this, and enter all of your rests manually, choose **Speedy** > **Speedy Options**. In the Frame section, uncheck **Fill With Rests at End of Measure**.

Edit as You Enter

Unlike Simple Entry, in this form of Speedy Entry, you will always add accidentals, dots, ties, etc., after entering the note. There is no "selection" necessary other than placing the cursor on or adjacent to the note.

1. Press 5 to enter a quarter note in an empty measure, then press the + key to add a sharp, press period (.) to add an augmentation dot, or T for a tie.
2. Now enter three more quarter notes (the frame will move to the next measure).
3. Press the S key (make sure CAPS LOCK is Off). Finale will look back across the barline and add the sharp to the last note of the previous measure.
4. Press the T key to begin a tie on the last note of the previous measure. Also use keystrokes during entry to flip stems, break/join beams, change enharmonic spelling, etc. For a complete list of keystrokes, click the Speedy menu and choose Speedy Edit Commands (Figure 3.12).

Figure 3.12

Choose Speedy Edit Commands from the Speedy menu to see a list of keyboard commands for Speedy Entry.

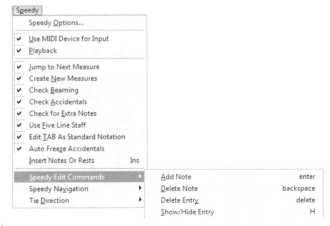

To insert a note between existing entries:

1. Choose **Speedy** > **Insert Notes or Rests** (or on Windows, press the INSERT key, and on Macintosh, press SHIFT+I).

2. Now click an empty measure. You will notice black triangles at the top and bottom of the vertical insertion bar within the Speedy Frame.

3. Enter two quarter notes in the measure.

4. Now, press the left arrow so the cursor is covering the second quarter note. Your measure should look like Figure 3.13.

Figure 3.13
Speedy Entry in Insert mode.

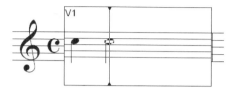

5. Press the 6 key to insert a half note between the two quarter notes. To activate or deactivate Insert Notes or Rests, you can also press the Insert key on Windows or SHIFT+I on Mac.

Accidentals

After you have entered a note, use the + or - keys to raise or lower notes incrementally (by half steps). For instance:

- To change a G to a G#, place the cursor over it and press +.
- To change it back to a G, press -.
- The plus and minus keys act the same as the Half Step Up and Half Step Down keys in Simple Entry.
- To show an accidental on any note, use the A key.
- To hide any accidental, press the * key (you can use these two keystrokes interchangeably in most occasions, though the A key won't hide "real" accidentals, just courtesy accidentals).
- Again, you can also use any of the Simple Entry commands (S, F, N, etc.) to enter accidentals as you would on a selected note in Simple Entry (with Caps lock off).
- Press P to parenthesize an accidental.

Chords

- To enter a chord, simply move the cursor directly above or below a note and press the ENTER key. Finale will automatically enter a note of the same duration as the existing one.
- To remove a single note from a chord, move the cursor directly on top of the notehead and press BACKSPACE/CLEAR.

- To delete an entire chord, use the DELETE key. To change the chord to a rest, move the cursor over the stem (not on top of a notehead) and press the BACKSPACE/CLEAR or R key.

Tuplets

Entering tuplets of any kind is easy in Speedy Entry.

1. With the Speedy Frame active, hold down the CTRL/OPTION key and press the number corresponding to the number of notes you would like to enter in the tuplet (3 for triplet, 6 for sextuplet, etc.).
2. You will see the number appear in the upper-right corner of the Speedy Frame.
3. Now enter these notes (of the same duration for now) and Finale will automatically place them within a tuplet definition.

The first note you enter in the series will contain the information that tells Finale the value of the tuplet. For instance, if you press CTRL/OPTION+3, then enter a quarter note, Finale will assume you want a quarter note triplet. Therefore, always begin the tuplet with the value that represents the crucial subdivision. If you wish to enter a tuplet whose first note does not begin on the crucial subdivision, press CTRL/OPTION+1 to open the Tuplet Definition dialog box for more advanced tuplet settings. You'll find more on defining and editing tuplets in "Ties and Tuplets" on page 240.

Layers in Speedy Entry

The basic concept of layers in Speedy Entry is exactly the same as in Simple Entry. If you need to enter multiple voices or melody lines in the same staff, you will need to use multiple layers. On Windows, click the layer selection boxes in the lower-left of your screen to specify a layer; on Macintosh, click and select the Layer from the pop-up menu. To move between layers on Windows, hold down SHIFT and press the ' (apostrophe) key; and on Macintosh, hold down SHIFT and use the up and down arrows. Choose **View** > **Select Layer** for a reminder of the layer selection keyboard shortcuts.

In the Speedy Frame, non-active layers are grayed out in the background. To hide notes in any layer, use the H or O key. You will also be able to specify multiple note durations on the same beat in Speedy Entry using voices.

NOTE:
You can use ALT+SHIFT+# and OPTION+SHIFT+# to change layers at any time and in any tool.

Voices

To enter multiple melodic lines, I recommend always using layers. However, when working with Speedy Entry, you have the option of using up to two voices in each layer. With voices and layers combined, you can have up to eight independent passages simultaneously in one staff! You may have already noticed the

"V1" located in the upper left of the Speedy Frame. This indicates the voice you are currently working with. At any time, while working in Speedy Entry, press the ' (apostrophe) key to move to voice 2 or back to voice 1. After entering a note in voice 1, press the ' key (notice V1 changes to V2), move your cursor to the desired pitch, and enter a note of any duration. Since notes in voice 2 can be entered anywhere over an existing note in voice 1, they can come in handy for independent lines that begin somewhere other than the first beat (so hidden notes in different layers are not required).

Speedy Entry with a MIDI Keyboard

You can improve the speed of Speedy Entry dramatically with the aid of a MIDI keyboard. In this mode of Speedy, you can use your MIDI keyboard to specify all pitches and use the computer keyboard for durations, ties, etc. You will also have the option to abandon the computer keyboard almost entirely by programming MIDI pitches to durations, ties, and navigation controls. Again, it is important to note that all of the information that pertains to editing existing notes without a MIDI keyboard is still valid and may be useful for adjusting your notes once they have been entered, without changing back to non-MIDI mode.

Using a MIDI keyboard (or any external MIDI device) for input:

As of Finale 2012, your MIDI keyboard should *just work* as soon as you plug it in to your computer's USB port. If something seems amiss, start with this tip...

TIP:
To test if your MIDI keyboard is set up properly, hold down a pitch and press one of the duration numbers while the Speedy Frame is active (make sure Use MIDI Device for Input is checked under the Speedy menu). If you get a note, Finale is receiving the MIDI information from your keyboard. If you get a rest, this information is not getting through. If this is the case, see "Setting up your MIDI system" in the Finale User Manual.

Once your MIDI system is up and running, to enter with Speedy Entry using an external MIDI keyboard:

1. To configure Speedy Entry to use a MIDI keyboard, choose **Speedy** > **Use MIDI Device for Input**.

2. Now click a measure to activate the Speedy Frame. Hold down middle C on your MIDI keyboard and press the 5 key. Finale will place a quarter note into your staff on middle C.

3. While holding down any pitch, use the standard duration keystrokes (1-8) to enter any note duration on that pitch. Finale will add accidentals automatically.

TIP:
To change the enharmonic spelling of any note in Speedy Entry, use the 9 key.

4. Now without pressing down any notes on your MIDI keyboard, press the 5 key. You will see a quarter rest. Any time you press a number without holding down one of the keys on your MIDI keyboard, a rest of the corresponding duration will appear in your score.

5. You can enter several notes at once from your MIDI keyboard. Hold down as many notes as you want (up to 12) and press one of the duration keys to enter a chord into your score.

6. Entering tuplets into your score with MIDI works almost the same way as in Speedy Entry without MIDI. With a Speedy Frame open, hold down CTRL/OPTION and press the 3 key. You will see the number 3 appear in the upper-right corner of the Speedy Frame. Now hold down the first pitch and press a number for the duration of the first note of the triplet. Enter the following two notes as you would normally. Note that triplet duration information is contained in the first note.

Entering Many Notes of the Same Duration

To enter a passage of eighth notes without having to press the 4 key for each note.

1. Press the CAPS LOCK key.

2. Now press the 4 key, and you will see the number 4 appear in the lower-left corner of the Speedy Frame. Now every time you play a note or chord on your MIDI keyboard, Finale will enter an eighth note into your score.

3. To start entering quarter notes, press the 5 key and begin entering notes with your MIDI keyboard. To enter a rest, simply strike three consecutive notes, half steps apart, for instance C, C#, and D. Many Finale users endorse this method as the fastest way to use Speedy Entry, especially in scores containing long strands of notes of similar duration.

NOTE:
The CAPS LOCK method of Speedy Entry is similar to using Simple Entry with the Caret (because the rhythmic durations are specified before the pitch).

Using the Caps Lock mode of Speedy Entry with MIDI also makes entering long strands of tuplets easy.

1. Invoke the Speedy Frame on an empty measure and press CAPS LOCK. Press the 4 key to specify an eighth note duration.

2. Hold down the CTRL/OPTION key and press 3 on your computer keyboard. The number 3 appears in the upper-right corner of the Speedy Frame indicating a triplet.

3. Now enter several notes using your MIDI keyboard. Each new set of three notes will be defined as a triplet (see Figure 3.14).

Figure 3.14

To stop entering tuplets, press any note duration key (the number in the upper-right corner of the Speedy Frame will disappear).

TIP:
 You can also enter a strand of tuplets in Simple Entry with or without a MIDI keyboard. While using the Caret, select the Simple Entry Tuplet Tool. When you are done entering tuplets, disable the Simple Entry Tuplet Tool.

Entry Using Your MIDI Keyboard Exclusively

You do not even need to use your computer keyboard for note entry with Speedy. Instead of using the number keys to specify note duration, you can program them to specific MIDI pitches. To do this, use the MIDI Modifier Key Map.

1. Choose **Speedy** > **Speedy Options**. Click the **Create Key Map** button and the Edit MIDI Modifiers dialog box opens (see Figure 3.15).

Figure 3.15

Assign MIDI notes to Speedy Entry commands with the MIDI Modifier Key Map.

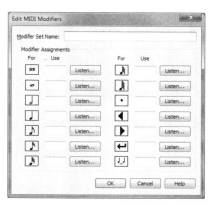

2. To program a MIDI pitch to one of the commands, simply click the corresponding Listen button and press a note on your MIDI keyboard (choose a note used rarely or not at all in the piece you are working on). Do this for any duration or other command you would like to use in this box.

3. Once you have finished programming, click **OK** twice to return to the score.

4. Click a measure and use the notes you programmed to change the rhythmic duration just as you would with the number keys on your computer keyboard.

Entering Articulations

Whether you plan to enter all of your articulations at once or during the note entry process, it is important to make the most of the time-saving tricks Finale has to offer. In this section I will describe how to most efficiently enter staccato markings, accents, fermatas, and any other articulation. I will also cover how to choose from an extended variety of articulations, how to space them properly and also define them for playback. I'll begin with the fastest way to set articulations on individual notes.

To prepare for this section, you need a document containing notes without articulations. You can use the scratch document you used in one of the previous sections or open one of the Finale tutorial files. To open a tutorial, click **File > Open**, double-click the Tutorials shortcut, and then open the file "Tutorial 4a.MUS." This is an arrangement-in-progress of "Auld Lang Syne" that will suit our needs just fine.

Basic Articulation Entry

To get acquainted with the Articulation Tool, start by adding articulations to individual notes.

1. Click the Articulation Tool (if it isn't selected already). Now click a note. The Articulation Selection dialog box appears on your screen, as shown in Figure 3.16. This dialog box shows the items in Finale's default articulation library.

Figure 3.16
Choose articulations for entry in the Articulation Selection dialog box.

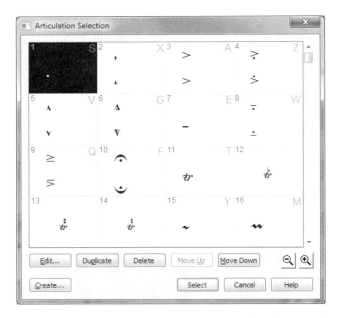

2. For now, click the accent marking and then click the Select button (or, double-click the accent). Notice the accent appears on the note you clicked. You can add any one of the articulations in the Articulation Selection window by simply clicking a note, choosing

the articulation, and clicking the Select button. If you don't like the placement, click its handle and either drag it with your mouse or nudge it using the arrow keys (I'll cover more specific placement techniques later).

3. To delete the articulation, click its handle and press DELETE.

To edit individual articulations:

*   Click and drag to enclose, or SHIFT+click, to select multiple articulation handles.
*   Click an articulation handle and press DELETE to remove it.
*   Right/CTRL+click an articulation handle to open the context menu. From here you can easily access the Articulation Definition dialog box to edit that particular articulation. (Or, simply double-click the handle.) I will cover the usage of this dialog box in this section.

Metatools

Metatools are time-saving shortcuts available in many areas of Finale, and are integral to using the program most effectively. Learning to use articulation metatools is a great introduction to this concept. You will see more discussion of metatools throughout this book.

Usually, while working on a score you will find yourself entering some articulations quite often and others not at all. To click a common articulation into your score without even entering the Articulation Selection dialog box, use a metatool.

1. Click a note in your score to open the Articulation Selection dialog box. Notice the numbers or letters in the upper-right corner on some of the articulation boxes. These are preset metatool assignments. Take note of the staccato marking in the far upper-left, metatool S.
2. Click **Cancel** to close the Articulation Selection dialog box.
3. Hold down the S key and click any note to enter a staccato marking.
4. Hold down the A key and click another note to add an accent. Use these metatools to enter articulations quickly throughout the score. Refer to the Articulation Selection dialog box to reference all of the preset metatool assignments.

Using the "Add Again" Metatool

Once you've added an articulation (or any marking that allows a metatool), from either its selection window or using a Metatool, you can instantly add it again. Just hold down the - (hyphen) key and click the score. If you switch tools, Finale remembers the last marking you entered, so when you switch back, the last marking you last entered in that tool will be available by pressing the - key.

Programming a Metatool

Not all of the articulations in the Articulation Selection dialog box have a preset metatool assignment. There is a simple way to assign any letter or number to any articulation. For instance, let's say you want to use the 2 key to enter accent markings instead of the letter A.

1. Hold down the SHIFT key and press the number 2. The Articulation Selection dialog box opens.
2. Choose the accent marking and click Select. The accent is now assigned to the 2 key.
3. Hold down the 2 key and click any note to add an accent. If you open the Articulation Selection dialog box again, you will notice the number 2 in the upper-right corner of the accent box.

 NOTE:
Metatool assignments are saved with the document.

Entering an Articulation on Several Notes at Once

Finale makes it easy to add articulations to a region of notes.

1. Click and drag to extend the selection rectangle around a region of your staff containing notes. You will notice a black border highlighting part of the staff.
2. Release the mouse button to open the Apply Articulation dialog box.
3. Click the **Select** button and choose the articulation.
4. Click **Select**, then **OK**. Finale adds the articulation you selected to all of the notes in the area you surrounded.

A couple other tips:

*   To enter an articulation to a region of notes faster, hold down a metatool key and drag over the region.
*   To delete all articulations from any region, hold down the DELETE key and drag over the region. Or, select the articulation's handle (or multiple articulation handles) and press DELETE.

Adding New Articulations to the Library

If the articulation you are looking for does not exist in the Articulation Selection dialog box, you can create it. To do this:

1. Click a note in the score to open the Articulation Selection dialog box, and click the **Create** button. This brings us to the Articulation Designer, shown in Figure 3.17. You will notice two buttons in the Symbol section: **Main** and **Flipped**. These refer to the articulation as it will appear above or below the staff, depending on your settings in the Symbol Options section.

Figure 3.17

Specify the visual definition, placement, and playback for an articulation in the Articulation Designer dialog box.

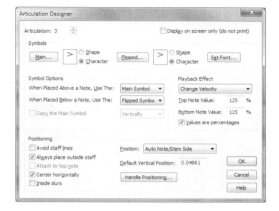

2. To select from a list of font characters, click the **Main** button. Find the character you want to use and click the **Select** button.
3. If you want the same character to appear on the opposite side of the staff, click the **Flipped** button and do the same. If you can't find the character you are looking for, go back to the Articulation Designer dialog and click the **Set Font** button to choose a different font.
4. Once you have selected characters to add to your Articulation Selection, click **OK** and then Select to return to the score.

Finale offers several music fonts that contain articulations you might find useful. For a complete list of characters in all Finale fonts, click **Help** > **Shortcuts & Character Maps (**Mac: click **Help** > **Character Sets)**, and select the Engraver, Jazz, or Maestro character map. Of course, you will be able to select a character from any font that exists on your system in the Articulation Designer dialog box.

Editing Articulations

To modify the size, font, or character of an existing articulation:

1. Click a note in your score to bring up the Articulation Selection dialog box.
2. Highlight the articulation you would like to change and click **Edit**. This brings up the Articulation Designer dialog box.
3. To modify the articulation, click **Set Font**. This launches the Font dialog box (see Figure 3.18).

Figure 3.18
Choose the font, size, and style for an articulation in the Font
dialog box.

4.   Select a new size, style, or font for the articulation here. Click **OK, OK,** and then **Select** to return to your score. Any changes you make to an articulation will apply to every instance of that articulation in your score.

Transferring Articulations from Other Documents

If you have already created or edited articulations in another document or have a document that contains articulations you would like to use, you can transfer these articulations between documents by saving and opening an articulation library.

1.   Open the document containing the existing articulations.
2.   Choose **File** > **Save Library**. You should see the Save Library dialog box shown in Figure 3.19.

Figure 3.19
Save a library of articulations to open in any document by choosing
Articulations in the Save Library dialog box.

3.   Choose Articulations and click **OK.**
4.   Enter a name and save the file to your Libraries folder (Finale 2012/Libraries).
5.   Now open the document you are working on, and choose **File** > **Load Library**. You will now see the Load Library dialog box (Figure 3.20).

Figure 3.20

Add articulations to a document by opening an articulation library from the Load Library dialog box.

6. Double-click the library you saved to open it. Now click a note to open the Articulation Selection dialog box and all of the new articulations will be available. Finale will check for duplicate articulations, so only new ones will appear in the Articulation Selection window.

Articulation Positioning

If an articulation does not appear where you want it to by default, you can change its placement settings in the Articulation Designer dialog box. This will change the placement of the articulation throughout the document.

1. With the Articulation Tool ⟨image⟩ selected, click a note to bring up the Articulation Selection dialog box.
2. Choose the articulation you would like to change and click **Edit**.
3. Use the items in the **Positioning** section to specify the articulation's position in relation to the note.

Defining Articulations for Playback

There are three ways articulations can affect playback of a note or chord: when it starts (attack), how long it is (duration) and how loud it is (key velocity).

1. Click a note to enter the Articulation Selection, choose the articulation you would like to change and click **Edit**.
2. In the playback section, click the drop-down menu to choose the type of effect (see Figure 3.21). An articulation can have more than one effect-for example, an accent with a dot should be played with increased attack and decreased duration. In this case, you would change both the velocity and duration setting.

Figure 3.21
Define an articulation for playback in the Playback
Effect section of the Articulation Designer.

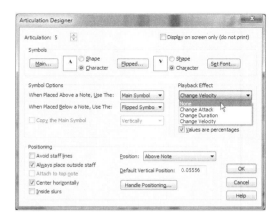

3. Then specify the percentage of change in the box after **Top Note Value**. Most of the
    time you can simply leave **Bottom Note Value** blank. Both the top and bottom note
    value fields will apply only to articulations that you want to scale from the bottom to
    top (or top to bottom) note of a chord—you can use both these settings with the
    Attack function to create a rolled chord.

Copying Articulations Within Your Score

To copy articulations independently, use the Selection Tool.

1. Enter two measures of quarter notes and add some articulations on every note in the
    first of these measures.
2. Choose **Edit** > **Edit Filter**. Click **None** and then check **Articulations**. Click **OK**.
3. Click the Selection Tool ![icon] and highlight the first measure.
4. Drag the highlighted measure to the second measure. Finale will paste the original
    articulations on any note that lines up with the beat placement of the original articula-
    tion.

CAUTION:
After editing the filter, it is common to forget the filter settings continue to apply to subsequent copy and paste actions. To ensure you are
not using the filter, uncheck **Use Filter** under the **Edit** Menu.

Automatically Copy Articulations to Similar Rhythmic Passages

You may have a reoccurring passage in your score that demands the same set of articulations at each occurrence throughout the piece. SmartFind and Paint allows you find and copy articulations to these passages automatically. To demonstrate this:

1. Fill a measure with a combination of eighth and quarter notes on different pitches with the Simple ♪ or Speedy Entry Tool 🎵.

2. Click the Selection Tool 🖰 and highlight this measure. Then hold down (Windows users) CTRL+ALT, (Mac users), CTRL+OPTION and click the next measure. The Paste Multiple dialog box appears.

3. Type "10" and click **OK**. Now there are 11 measures containing the same rhythmic arrangement.

4. Click the Articulation Tool 🎵 and add several various articulations to the original measure.

5. Click the Selection Tool 🖰 again and highlight the measure containing the articulations.

6. Choose **Edit** > **SmartFind and Paint** > **Set SmartFind Source Region** (or press CTRL/CMD+F).

7. Now click **Edit** > **SmartFind and Paint** > **Apply SmartFind and Paint** (or press CTRL/CMD+SHIFT+F). You will see the SmartFind and Paint dialog box shown in Figure 3.22.

Figure 3.22
Choose elements to copy to similar rhythmic passages in the SmartFind and Paint dialog box.

8. Click **Find** and the measure containing the similar passage becomes highlighted.

9. Click **Paint** and the articulations appear on the notes just as they did in the original measure. This is also a great technique for copying Slurs, Smart Shapes and Expressions to identical rhythmic passages throughout your score.

10. To deselect the source region, press CTRL/CMD+F.

Entering Expressions

What exactly is an *expression*? In Finale, expressions are used for:

- Dynamics $\boldsymbol{f}$, $\boldsymbol{pp}$, *really loud*

- Tempo Marks   **Adagio** ♩ = 40

- Tempo Alterations   *accel.*

- Expressive Text   *dolce*

- Technique Text   Con sord.

- Rehearsal Marks   ⏍A⏍

- Some Other Figures   ≡

While expressions generally fall into one of the above categories, any text or shape marking can be added as an expression. Expressions adjust automatically to music spacing changes, can appear on any number of staves and/or parts, and can be set to apply to playback in many ways. The way Finale handles expressions was improved dramatically in both Finale 2009 and 2010, so you may be able to benefit from these valuable updates in Finale 2012. Let's learn how to take advantage of these changes.

To prepare for this section, either use the scratch document from the previous section or open tutorial number 2 (**File** > **Open**, click the Tutorials shortcut, and open the file "Tutorial 4a.MUS.")

Dynamic Markings

Dynamic markings are the most common expressions, let's enter one of those first.

1. Click the Expression Tool 🔲 .
2. Double-click where you would like to add an expression. The Expression Selection dialog box appears (see Figure 3.23).
3. Click the Dynamics category from the list on the left.

Figure 3.23

Choose an expression for entry in the Expression Selection dialog box.

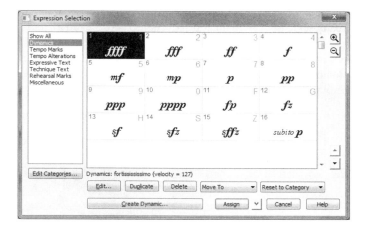

TIP:
Drag the lower right corner of the Expression Selection dialog box to resize it. Use the zoom icons in the upper right to expand or contract the number of expressions visible in the window.

4. Click the *f* expression to highlight it and then click the Assign button (or just double click the forte expression). The expression appears in the score. If you don't like the placement of the expression, click its handle and either drag it with your mouse or nudge it using the arrow keys. (I'll get into more specific placement techniques later.)

5. To delete the expression, click its handle and press DELETE.

6. To edit individual expressions, context-click an expression handle to open the context menu. From here you can easily access the Expression Assignment, Expression Definition, or to edit that particular expression. I'll cover the usage of these dialog boxes throughout this section.

The expression you just entered will adjust accordingly with the *beat* to which it is attached as the music spacing changes. The dashed blue attachment indicator line connects the expression to the attached beat.

Rehearsal Marks

Rehearsal marks in Finale 2012 are easy. If you started your document in Finale 2010 or later, (and used the Maestro Font Default file/Engraved Document Style), use the following steps to add rehearsal marks. (If not, see the note below).

1. Click the Expression Tool *mf* .

2. Hold down the M key and click within a measure to add the rehearsal mark at the beginning of that measure.

They will position and order themselves automatically, update when inserted, added, or deleted, and are already set to appear on the top staff of the score and on all parts.

You can edit the style (letters or numbers), enclosure, and positioning settings in the Expression Designer dialog box. Right/CTRL-click a rehearsal mark's handle and choose Edit Text Expression Definition to edit them.

NOTE:
Finale's nifty rehearsal marks are already setup for you (in most documents started in Finale 2010 and later). If you are using an old document, and would like to benefit from automatic rehearsal marks, do the following:

1. Click the Expression Tool 𝑚𝑓 .
2. Hold down SHIFT and press M.
3. Choose the **Rehearsal Marks** category.
4. Click **Create Rehearsal Mark**.
5. Check **Use Auto-Sequencing** Style.
6. From the Enclosure Shape drop-down, choose the desired enclosure. (Square is Finale 2012's default.)
7. Click **OK**, then **Assign**.
8. Hold down M and click the score to add the marks.

Tempo Marks

To add a tempo mark:

1. Click the Expression Tool 𝑚𝑓 .
2. Double-click within the measure you would like to add the tempo mark. The Expression Selection dialog box appears.
3. Choose the **Tempo Marks** category.
4. If you see the desired tempo mark, double-click it to add it to the score. If not, define one yourself...
5. Click **Create Tempo Mark**. The Expression Designer dialog box appears. Let's create the tempo mark "Allegro ♩ = 120."
6. Type "Allegro" and notice Finale already uses the same text font defined for all the other tempo marks. You can change the font, size, and style for all tempo marks at once using the Category Designer dialog box (which I'll explain soon).
7. Click the **Insert Note** button and choose ♩.
8. Then, type "= 120." Finale is designed to interpret the metronome marking (♩ = 120) automatically for playback. If your tempo mark does not include a metronome

marking, click the **Playback** tab to define the playback tempo manually. (See "Defining an Expression for Playback" on page 83 .)

9. Click **OK** and then **Assign** to add the tempo mark to your score.

Metatools

Like Articulations, you will also be able to enter any expression with a metatool. Again, this is a much faster way to enter them into your score than opening the Selection dialog all the time.

1. Hold down the 4 key and click underneath the second measure. A forte f marking will appear.
2. Now double-click an empty space below the staff to open the Expression Selection dialog box. Notice the numbers and letters in the upper right corner of each expression. These are the preset metatool assignments.
3. While working on your score, hold down one of these numbers or letters and click to quickly enter its associated expression into the score.

Programming an Expression Metatool

You can program your own expression metatools just like articulation metatools with the additional ability to program many at once.

1. Hold down the SHIFT key and press a number or letter key. The Expression Selection dialog box appears.
2. Choose the expression you would like to assign to that key and click **Assign**.
3. Hold down the key you programmed and click in the score to enter the expression you chose.
4. Now, try this. Double-click to open the Expression Selection dialog box.
5. Select any expression, then hold down SHIFT and press a number or letter. You've just assigned a metatool without leaving the dialog box. You can do this whenever the Expression Selection dialog box is open. Repeat for any other expression, selecting a new category if necessary.
6. Click **Cancel** (or **Assign** to add the selected expression). All the metatools you assigned are ready for use.

Creating a Text Expression

If Finale doesn't already include the text figure you need in the Expression Selection dialog box, define a new expression is usually a straightforward process:

1. Click the Expression Tool .

2. Double-click on, above or below a staff to open the Expression Selection dialog box. Choose the desired category for this expression from the list on the left, then click the **Create** button. This opens the Expression Designer dialog box, shown in Figure 3.24.

Figure 3.24
Create or edit text for entry as an expression in the Expression Designer dialog box.

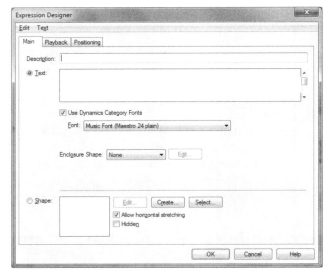

3. Type the desired text into the entry field. Finale uses the font and style defined for the category. See "Changing the appearance of Expression Categories" (next) for details on changing expression categories.
4. When you have finished, click **OK**, then **Assign** to return to your score. You will be able to enter the expression you just created at any time while working on this document.
5. Double-click on, above or below a staff. Choose the category and notice your custom expression at the bottom. If you plan on using this expression often, program a metatool for it.

Changing the Appearance of Expression Categories

Each type of expression listed at the beginning of this section (dynamics, tempo marks, etc.) has its own category. Each expression category is a collection of font, style, positioning, enclosure, and attachment settings that apply to all expressions in its category (for both those that exist in the score and those available for selection). This model is based on the assumption that all dynamics, for example, should use the same font and style within a document, which is standard notation practice.

To change the appearance of all dynamic markings throughout your document:

1. Choose **Document** > **Category Designer**. The Category Designer dialog box appears.

Figure 3.25

Define the appearance for expression types in the Category Designer dialog box.

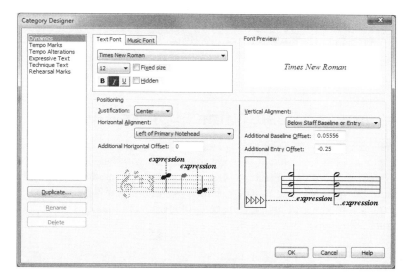

2. Choose the desired category, in this case **Dynamics**, then change the font, style, and positioning settings as required. Here, you can also click **Duplicate** to create a new category.

NOTE:
Tempo Marks, Tempo Alterations, and Rehearsal Marks have an extra *Score List* setting. Since these markings always apply to the entire score, they usually appear only once above the top staff in the score, and also on every part. A Score List allows them to display on specified staves only. See "Score Lists" in the User Manual for more details.

3. Click **OK** to apply your category settings to all expressions in the category.

TIP:
If you want to ensure that an expression will remain the same size, regardless of staff, system, or page resizing, set it to a fixed size.

Aligning and Positioning Expressions

If simply dragging expressions into place isn't consistent enough, you can align and position multiple expressions evenly by selecting several of them or using baselines. For example, drag a box around two or more expressions to select them, then click one of the handles and drag to move them uniformly. Or, to position many expressions at once, use the positioning triangles to adjust the expression baselines. When the Expression Tool is selected, you see four positioning triangles on the left side of the screen as shown in Figure 3.26.

Figure 3.26

Use positioning triangles to position many expressions at once.

If your score has more than one staff, click any staff to display the positioning arrows for that staff. You can use these arrows to move several expressions at once, by staff, system, or score. If you have used Finale's default expression placement (you haven't changed settings under the Positioning tab of the Expression Designer), simply choose the Expression Menu and select whether you want to adjust the above or below staff baselines, and then click a staff containing the expressions you want to position. Now, do the following:

- Drag the left triangle to adjust all expressions in the score.
- Drag the second triangle to adjust all expressions in just that staff (throughout the score).
- Drag the third triangle to adjust expressions for that staff in that system only.
- Drag the fourth triangle to specify a position for the next measure expression added (don't use this one).

NOTE:
You will learn how to assign expressions to several staves at once in chapter 7, under "Expressions and Text Repeats in Multiple-Stave Documents" on page 183

Defining an Expression for Playback

Any expression can be manually defined to affect playback of the score. To define an expression for playback:

1. Double-click above or below a staff to open the Expression Selection dialog box.
2. Click the *f* expression and then click **Edit**.
3. In the Expression Designer, click the **Playback** tab to show the playback options (Figure 3.27).

Figure 3.27
Click the Playback tab to define an expression for playback.

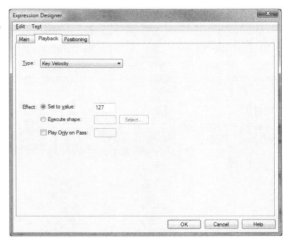

Here you will see that this expression already has a playback definition assigned. This expression, like all the dynamic expressions, has a key velocity assigned to it. Key velocity is basically the volume of the MIDI note (it actually relates to the velocity of a key as it is struck on a MIDI keyboard). To increase the key velocity (make the note play back "louder") enter a higher number into the Set to Value field (0-127). You can define an expression to affect playback in many ways including tempo, pitch, panning, channel, and many others. You will find a more complete description of any text expression's playback capabilities in Chapter 14.

Transferring Expressions Between Documents

Like articulations, you can transfer any expression between documents by saving and loading a library.

1. Open the document containing the existing text or shape expressions that you would like to transfer to another document.
2. Choose **File** > **Save Library**.
3. Check **Text Expressions** or **Shape Expressions** (or both) and click **OK**.
4. Enter a name and save the file to your Libraries folder (Finale 2012/Libraries).
5. Now open the document you are working on, choose **File** > **Load Library**.

6.   Double-click the library you saved to open it. Now these expressions will be available in this document's Expression Selection dialog box.

TIP:
If you want your own custom expressions available in every new document created with the Setup Wizard, **save a Document Style**. See "Using Document Styles" on page 333

Creating a Simple Arrangement

Let's apply the skills we've learned so far to create a simple score. In the following example, we'll begin a new document with the Setup Wizard, enter the notes with Simple or Speedy Entry, program metatools to enter articulations and expressions, finalize layout, and print. For this example, we'll notate an arrangement of Greensleeves. When complete, our arrangement will look like Figure 3.28.

Figure 3.28

Greensleeves Arrangement

1.   Choose **File** > **New** > **Document With Setup Wizard**. Click **Next** to move to page 2. Click **Woodwinds** in the leftmost column. We'll create a part for flute, so double-click **Flute** in the second column. Then click **Next** to move to page 3.

2.   For **Title,** enter "Greensleeves," and for **Composer,** enter "Arr. by" followed by your name. Click **Next** to move to page 4.

3.   Our arrangement will be in 6/4. Notice this isn't one of the available time signatures on page 4 of the Setup Wizard, so we'll have to define it ourselves. Under **Select a Time Signature**, click the $\frac{3}{4}$ button. The Time Signature dialog box appears. After **Number of Beats**, click the right arrow twice, so 6/4 appears in the display window. Then click **OK** to return to the Setup Wizard. Now we'll select the key of the piece. Under **Select a Concert Key Signature**, click the drop-down arrow to the right of the preview window and choose **Minor Key** (notice the preview window updates accordingly). This arrangement will be in A minor.

4.   Check **Specify Initial Tempo Marking**. Then, in the text box to the right of **Tempo**, enter "90." Our arrangement will also have a one beat pickup, so check **Specify Pickup Measure** and make sure the quarter note icon is selected. Click **Finish**. Choose Page View. Your new document appears as shown in Figure 3.29.

Figure 3.29

After competing the Setup Wizard, the score is ready for entry.

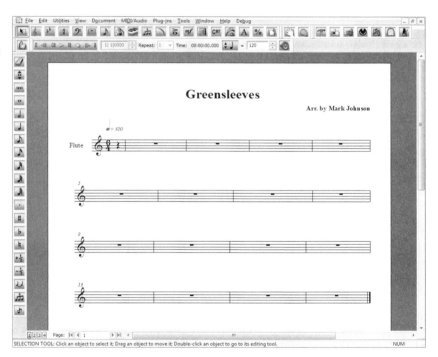

5.   Now, use the Simple or Speedy Entry Tool (as described earlier in this chapter) to enter notes into the first four measures as they appear in Figure 3.28.

6.   Notice that measures five and six are duplicates of measures one and two. Let's save time by copying with the Selection Tool. Click the Selection Tool and then drag over measures one and two so they are highlighted. Then click the highlighted area and drag to measure five (you will see a green border around measures five and six). Release the mouse button.

TIP:
Note the tempo marking copied along with the measure content. Click it with the Selection Tool and press DELETE to remove it. Alternatively, you could have unchecked "Expressions: Tempo Marks, Tempo Alterations..." in the Edit Filter dialog box before you copied.

7. Now use the Simple or Speedy Entry Tool to enter notes into measures seven through twelve.

8. Use the same procedure described in step six to copy measures nine and ten into measure thirteen and fourteen.

9. Enter notes into the final two measures with the Simple or Speedy Entry Tool.

10. To delete the extra measures, click the Selection Tool, and then click to highlight measure seventeen (the first empty measure). Then, while holding down the SHIFT key, press the END key to select every measure to the end of the piece. (Laptop users may have to use the "Fn" key to access the "END" function.") Press DELETE to delete these measures (notice there is now a final barline at the end of the piece).

11. Now that we have entered notes into the score, let's enter the dynamic markings. We'll use the Expression Tool to do this. Click the Expression Tool *mf* , and then double-click beneath the pickup measure. The Expression Selection dialog box appears. Choose the *mf* expression and click **Assign**. Then click **OK**. The *mf* expression appears below the staff. Now, let's use pre-defined metatools to enter the remaining two dynamic markings. While holding down the 4 key, click beneath measure nine to add the *f* marking. Then, while holding down the 5 key, click beneath measure fifteen to enter the *mf* marking. To see all of the metatool assignments, double-click anywhere in the score to open the Expression Selection dialog box. All of the metatool assignments appear to the right of each expression. Click **Cancel** to return to the score.

12. Now, let's enter the articulations. Click the Articulation Tool ⓩ . Click the quarter note in the pickup measure. The Articulation Selection dialog box appears. Choose the tenuto marking (number 7; notice the E in the upper-right corner indicating the metatool assignment) and then click **Select**. The tenuto marking appears beneath the note. To enter the remaining tenuto marking, use a metatool. While holding down the E key, click the last note in measure four. Now, hold down the A key and click each note in measure nine and thirteen to enter the accent articulations. Hold down the F key and click the last note to add the fermata. Click its handle and drag up to move it above the staff.

13. If you wish, click the Play button in the playback controls to hear your piece.

14. Now, let's finalize the layout by fitting four measures to a system. Click the Selection Tool and press CTRL/CMD+A to Select All. Choose **Utilities** > **Fit Measures**. Ensure 4 appears after "Lock Layout... " and click OK. Also, press the 4 key to apply note spacing. Now, the last measure takes up the full system. Click it and press the up arrow to move it to the previous system.

15. Your piece should now look similar to the example in Figure 3.28. To print the score, choose **File** > **Print**. In the Print dialog box, Click **OK/Print** to print the piece.

Congratulations! You have now created a new score from scratch using Finale's entry tools and the Selection Tool, and you've also added expressions and articulations quickly with metatools. These skills can be used whenever you are working on a score and provide a good groundwork for more time-saving concepts you will come across in the following chapters.

4
Advanced Note Entry, Chords, and Lyrics

By this point you've experienced a taste of Finale's power. And, as Peter Parker's uncle once said, "with great power comes great responsibility." In other words...You've learned enough to be dangerous. You will have the potential to become especially sinister in the next few chapters. I will steer clear of the loose gravel, but you can expect some boulders and roots to navigate as we delve deeper into Finale's core.

If Simple or Speedy Entry isn't quick enough for you, there are a few more methods of note entry that could prove very effective, especially if you are a pianist. Here, I'll cover the variety of methods you can use to enter music in real time with either an external MIDI device (MIDI keyboard/MIDI guitar) or even an acoustic wind instrument. You will also learn how to easily create and enter your own chord suffixes as well as enter lyrics. By the end of this Chapter, you will have covered the topics necessary to quickly produce lead sheets and most other single staff documents.

Here's a summary of what you will learn in this Chapter:

- Real-time Entry: HyperScribe
- Entering Chord Symbols
- Entering Lyrics
- Creating a Lead Sheet

Real-Time Entry: HyperScribe

HyperScribe is Finale's tool for translating a live musical performance into sheet music. Recording into Finale with a MIDI keyboard is the most common way to do this. In this section, you will learn how to enter notes in real-time while playing along with a click track or tapping the tempo with the sustain pedal. Since you are entering music without interruption, there is more preparation involved than with Simple or Speedy Entry. However, once you find the settings that work best for you, HyperScribe can really move. While going through this Chapter, you can expect a certain amount of editing needed to make finishing touches on your HyperScribe sessions. Plan on using HyperScribe in conjunction with Simple Entry or Speedy Entry to most effectively enter notes overall. In reality, the key to efficiency is finding the most comfortable combination of note entry tools as you approach each individual project.

To prepare for this Chapter, set your MIDI keyboard to the most basic Piano sound (without any effects). Then open a new Default Document (**File** > **New** > **Default Document**).

> **NOTE:**
> To use a MIDI keyboard (or any external MIDI device) for input, you will need to ensure that it is properly connected to the computer and set up in Finale. For complete instructions on MIDI setup, see "Setting up your MIDI system" in the Finale User Manual (**Help** > **User Manual**).

Playing into the Score Along with a Metronome Click

We'll start by using the most common method of HyperScribe: playing over a click track.

1. Click the HyperScribe Tool , then choose **HyperScribe** > **Beat Source** > **Playback and/or Click** (yes, it's already checked, but click it anyway). You should now see the Playback and/or Click dialog box as shown in Figure 4.1. This is where you will choose the beat subdivision of your score, tempo of the click track, and start signal for recording.

Figure 4.1

Specify a beat duration, tempo, and start signal for your HyperScribe session in the Playback and/or Click dialog box.

2. Choose the **Use This Tempo** radio button (and leave it set to 96). Since we are in 4/4 time, choose the quarter note box. In the future, you might need to select a different note value depending on the time signature of your piece. In cut time, you would choose a half note, in 6/8, probably a dotted quarter note, and so on. Click the drop-down arrow to the right of **Start Signal for Recording**. From this list, choose **Any MIDI Data**. This tells Finale to begin the metronome click on a MIDI note command.

3. Click the **Click and Countoff** button to open the Click and Countoff dialog box (see Figure 4.2). Here, leave both **Countoff** and **Click** fields set to **While Recording**. The Measures field in the upper-right corner controls the number of measures in the countoff. By default, it is set to click for two measures before recording. Leave this at 2 for now. In the future, you may want to set this to 1.

Figure 4.2

Choose the countoff and MIDI attributes for the click in the Click and Countoff dialog box.

NOTE:
Finale 2012 includes a new internal metronome click, which is set by default, and highly recommended.

4. When Finale records your performance, it will round-off the notes you play to the nearest sixteenth note, eighth note, or other rhythmic subdivision depending on your quantization settings. Unlike other MIDI sequencers that use quantization to perfect playback, the quantization settings in Finale are used to accurately translate a performance into notation. As you record, you will find even the most rhythmically accurate performance will vary somewhat with Finale's concrete timing. For example, if you tend to anticipate the beat slightly, a perfectly accurate transcription would result in unwanted sixty-fourth notes or one-hundred twenty-eighth notes. You would probably also see a number of unwanted rests and ties scattered throughout your score. To specify a reasonable rhythmic value for Finale to use as a rounding marker during your HyperScribe session, use the Quantization Settings dialog box (see Figure 4.3).

5. Choose **MIDI/Audio** > **Quantization Settings**.

Figure 4.3

Round your notated rhythms to the nearest eighth note or other rhythmic value by configuring the Quantization Settings dialog box.

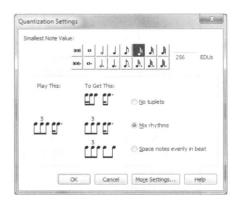

The value you choose for Smallest Note Value should generally depend on the smallest note used most frequently in the piece you are transcribing. If your piece has many small note values, you may consider choosing a slower recording tempo in the Playback and/or Click dialog box. If you intend to enter tuplets, keep in mind the duration of notes in a tuplet is smaller than the base note value. To accurately choose a tuplet duration for the Smallest Note Value, note the number of EDUs for the full duration of the tuplet and divide it by three. For instance, an eighth note tuplet is the same duration as a quarter note, 1024 EDUs. Enter 341 EDUs (one third of 1024) to specify an eight-note tuplet as the smallest note value.

Don't attempt to HyperScribe ornaments more complex than grace notes, such as trills or tremolos, in a HyperScribe session. These should be added afterwards

6.   For now, click the Eighth Note box for Smallest Note Value. Leave **Mix Rhythms** selected and click **More Setting**. You should now see the More Quantization Settings dialog box as shown in Figure 4.4. Here, you can fine-tune your quantization settings.

Figure 4.4

Make settings for playback, treatment of rests and grace notes for a HyperScribe session in the More Quantization Settings dialog box.

7.   If you plan to record a number of syncopated rhythmic passages in your score, you may want Finale to eliminate ties between beats and use larger note durations. If this is the case, leave **Soften Syncopations** checked. If you want notes across beats tied, uncheck Soften Syncopations (see Figure 4.5).

Figure 4.5

HyperScribe results with and without Softened Syncopations.

Tied syncopation   "Softened" syncopation

8.   Click **OK** twice to return to your score. You are now ready to begin.

9.   Click the first measure of your score. You will see the HyperScribe frame appear on the measure you clicked. Finale is now waiting for a signal to start recording.

10. Press a note on your keyboard and Finale will begin to click, giving you two measures before recording. At the completion of the second countoff measure, begin entering quarter notes into your score. After the HyperScribe frame moves on to the subsequent measure, you will see your notes appear.

11. When you are finished, click anywhere in the score to stop recording. To enter music that uses smaller note values, click **MIDI/Audio** > **Quantization Settings**, and choose the eighth or sixteenth note for Smallest Note Value. Then begin your HyperScribe session again. Existing notes are overwritten when you HyperScribe over them.

TIP:
You can specify the enharmonic spelling of accidentals for non-diatonic pitches entered with HyperScribe by editing the spelling tables. Choose **Edit Major and Minor Key Spellings** or **Edit Modal or Chromatic Key Spellings** under the **Edit** Menu on Windows and Finale 2012/Preferences on Macintosh (see ""Changing the Default Enharmonic Spelling" on page 283 for details).

12. After completing a HyperScribe session, you may notice extra rests where notes should be held. You can use TGTools to easily clean up your HyperScribe results with the Modify Rests plug-in. Choose **Plug-ins/** 🔧 > **TGTools** > **Modify Rests**.

TIP:
You probably want Finale to allow ties across barlines as you record. Choose **HyperScribe** > **HyperScribe Options** and check **Tie Across Barlines**, then click **OK**.

Playing into the Score While Tapping the Tempo

You can adjust the tempo of your HyperScribe sessions to conform to your slightest whim using the Tap function. With HyperScribe Tap, the tempo you tap on the sustain pedal is used as the beat source rather than the metronome click, making it adjustable in real-time.

1. Click **HyperScribe** > **Beat Source** > **Tap**. You will now see the Tap Source dialog box as shown in Figure 4.6.

Figure 4.6
Tap to specify the beat for a HyperScribe session by first setting up the Tap Source dialog box.

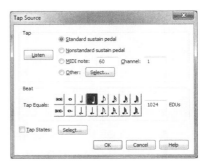

2. At the top, choose the type of MIDI signal you will be using to send the Tap information. The most common is a standard sustain pedal. It should be chosen by default. In the **Beat** section, after **Tap Equals**, choose the rhythmic duration of each beat. Since

we are in 4/4 time, choose the quarter note. For now, click **OK** (I'll talk about Tap States soon).

NOTE:
If your MIDI keyboard does not have a sustain pedal, you can designate a MIDI note instead (although this will occupy one hand while recording). Click **Listen** and play a note to designate it as the tap source.

CAUTION:
Finale will not record MIDI data from the controller you choose to send Tap information, even if it is selected in the Record Continuous Data dialog box. For example, if you want your sustain pedaling to be recorded, you should use Hyperscribe's metronome click, or perhaps use a MIDI note and record with one hand.

3. Click the first measure to see the HyperScribe frame on measure 1. Finale will assume the first tap on the sustain pedal is beat 1.

4. Begin playing while tapping the tempo on the sustain pedal. Feel free to adjust the tempo while you play. After the HyperScribe frame moves on to the subsequent measure, you will see your notes appear. To stop recording click anywhere in the score.

Tap States

If you want to record into a score over a meter change without having to stop and change the beat unit, (for example, record over a time signature change from 4/4 to 6/8), you can instruct the Tap Equals setting to change from a quarter note to a dotted quarter note. To do this, set up Tap States.

1. Choose **HyperScribe** > **Beat Source** > **Tap**. In the Tap Source dialog box, click the **Select** button for Tap States. This will bring up the Tap States dialog box as shown in Figure 4.7.

Figure 4.7
Switch the beat duration per tap on-the-fly by setting up the Tap States dialog box.

2. Here, click the **Select** button to the right of **Tap Equals** to choose a new beat value. You will also need to set up a MIDI trigger to tell Finale to switch to the new Tap State. Then be sure to select a new **Smallest Note Value**.

3. Click the Listen button and then press a MIDI note you won't be using in your notation (perhaps a really high or low note). This will be your trigger for Tap State 1. You can program up to three Tap States.

4. Click the spinner arrows at the top of this box to program any other Tap States you are using.

5. Click **OK** twice to return to your score.

6. Record into the score, and just before the downbeat of the new meter, stop tapping and press the appropriate trigger. Then resume with your performance while tapping along with the tempo.

CAUTION:
Once you trigger a Tap State, you will not be able to go back to your original Beat Equals setting. If you want to return to the original meter during a Tap session, program another Tap State with your original Beat Equals setting.

Recording into Two Staves at Once

Whether you are using a metronome click or are tapping the tempo, you may want to record music directly into a grand staff (both treble and bass clef) in a single HyperScribe session. To do this, choose **HyperScribe** > **Record Mode** > **Split into Two Staves**. You will now see the Fixed Split Point dialog box as shown in Figure 4.8.

Figure 4.8

Tell Finale where to split between the treble and bass clef staves in a grand staff with the Fixed Split Point dialog box.

The split point is the lowest pitch Finale will enter into the upper staff. Any notes entered below the split point will be entered into the lower staff. (MIDI note 60 is middle C.) Click OK to return to your score. Now click on the first measure to begin a new HyperScribe session. Notice the HyperScribe frame surrounding both staves.

TIP:
To easily open a new grand staff document, use the Setup Wizard (**File** > **New** > **Document with Setup Wizard**). Choose Piano from the Keyboards category on page 2. To easily add a grand staff to an existing score, click the Staff Tool and choose **Staff** > **New Staves (with Setup Wizard),** then choose Keyboards and Piano.

Using HyperScribe with a MIDI Guitar

In addition to using a MIDI keyboard for note entry, you can also use a number of other external MIDI devices such as a MIDI guitar. To use a MIDI guitar for entry, follow the same instructions above. You can use a guitar (or other MIDI device) just as you would a MIDI keyboard.

MIDI guitars require an interface between the guitar and the computer to translate the acoustic pitches into MIDI information. As a result of the extra processing necessary, there might be a slight, yet consistent delay in the time it takes from the moment the string is plucked to the time it reaches Finale. This is called latency, and can cause the HyperScribe transcription to lag behind the beat. To compensate for this, you can tell Finale to leave a specific amount of time between clicks/taps and the actual recording tempo. To do this, choose **MIDI/Audio** > **Device Setup** > **MIDI Setup** (**MIDI/Internal Speaker Setup** on Mac). Enter a MIDI Latency value anywhere from 25 to 150 milliseconds (the precise amount of time will depend on your interface and hardware configuration). Once you have established the correct amount of latency, you should be able to use HyperScribe normally.

Finale comes with many features specifically for guitar and notation of other fretted instruments. One of these is the ability to record directly into a tab staff with HyperScribe. When you do this, Finale will even record the actual fret numbers you play during the HyperScribe session. For more information on creating and editing tab staves, see Chapter 8.

Playback (recording playback data)

While HyperScribe is a great way to transcribe notes into your score, it can also be used to record playback data. Finale can capture the subtle nuances of your performance, including the rhythmic feel and sustain pedal and other continuous data. The result is playback that sounds like your original performance. (This is an alternative to Human Playback's interpretation). If you want to playback your HyperScribe recordings as you played them, do the following:

1. Windows users: In the Playback Controls, click the speaker icon. If you don't see the Playback Controls on-screen, select them from the Window menu. The Playback Settings dialog box appears. Macintosh users: Click the expand arrow on the Playback Controls to show the advanced options.

2. Click the Human Playback drop-down menu and choose None. Windows users: Click OK. Macintosh users: Minimize the Playback Controls if desired.

3. Click the HyperScribe Tool .

4. Choose **HyperScribe** > **Record Continuous Data**. The Record Continuous Data dialog box appears. Here, you can choose to record any type of continuous MIDI data (effects applied with various controllers on your MIDI device like pitch wheel, sustain pedal, etc.).

5. You can relieve some of your computer's resources during a recording by specifying up to four controllers. (Click Listen and activate each controller you want to use). Or, just make sure All is selected if you want to retain all of this information.

6. Now, if you want to play back the music exactly as you performed it or exactly as it appears in the score, choose **Document** > **Playback/Record Options**. Here you can specify playback of more individual elements of your recording. Specify whether you want Finale to play back key velocities and note durations as you recorded them or as they appear in the score.

NOTE:
For information on more advanced playback options, such as nifty auditioning features, see "General Playback Techniques" on page 370.

MicNotator

No, you can't hold your microphone up to a stereo blaring your favorite glam rock single and expect an tidy arrangement to materialize in your Finale document (maybe some day). But, if you play a wind instrument, you can carefully produce pitches that Finale can identify and notate using Hyperscribe. Here's how:

1. Choose **MIDI/Audio** > **Device Setup** > **Audio Setup** and check the Enable MicNotator box. Also, use the Mic Level indicator to ensure you are getting a signal from the microphone (which should be plugged into the Mic In port on your computer). If you are using a Mac, there may not be a Mic In port available on your computer. If this is the case, I recommend using a Griffin iMic USB audio interface (store.griffintechnology.com/imic).

2. When you see a signal in the Mic Level indicator, click **OK**.

3. Then use the HyperScribe Tool just as you would with a MIDI keyboard. When you use MicNotator, be sure to play notes as evenly and cleanly as possible for best results. The translation from acoustic pitch to MIDI can be somewhat less accurate than a direct connection to an external MIDI device.

TIP:
MakeMusic sells special microphones designed for use with MicNotator that clip to your instrument or clothing. A MakeMusic customer support representative will send you one for $19.95 for Windows and $29.95 for Mac. Go to finalemusic.com/store/products and see "Finale Instrumental Microphone" for details.

NOTE:
You can apply Finale's Human Playback interpretation to parts of your score, or even mix your recorded MIDI data with Human Playback's using the Apply Human Playback plug-in (**Plug-ins/** ⅀ > **Playback** > **Apply Human Playback**). See "How to Use Human Playback" on page 362.

Working with Chord Symbols

Chord symbols are mostly harmless in Finale, and especially agreeable with the recent design updates in Finale 2010 and also in 2011. You find chord symbols in lead sheets, jazz charts, guitar tablature and many other types of music. Chord symbols in Finale are basically entries of text placed on a baseline above beats or notes in a staff. (Finale no longer requires an entry for each chord symbol, and the benefits are delicious.) Chord symbols consist of three elements: a root, suffix, and alternate bass. The root is simply the root pitch information of the chord (F sharp, B flat, etc.), and the suffix contains the quality of chord (major, minor, etc.). The suffix will also contain higher tertian information (7, 9, etc.) and their pitch alterations. An alternate bass pitch can also be added to any chord symbol. When entering chord symbols, you will always start with the root and then specify a suffix and alternate bass if necessary.

Often, when creating notation for fretted instruments, fretboard diagrams accompany the chord symbols to indicate a specific fingering. You can easily include fretboard diagrams beneath each chord symbol using Finale's default fretboards, or you can define your own custom fretboard diagrams. In addition to adding chord symbols, you will also learn how to enter, and even customize fretboard diagrams.

Entering Chord Symbols

There are several ways to enter and edit chord symbols in Finale. You will be able to type them directly above a staff, define them manually for each entry, or even tell Finale to analyze the music and insert the appropriate chord symbol. You will be able to customize the font, style, and size of chord symbols, suffixes, and fretboards, and even transfer a library of custom chord suffixes between documents. In this section, you will learn how to handle chord symbols efficiently in Finale.

To prepare for this section, open a new Default Document (**File** > **New** > **Default Document**). Unless specified otherwise, assume the Chord Tool ![CM7] is selected.

Type into Score

Typing chords directly into the score is the most basic method of chord entry. It is also perhaps the fastest for entering basic chord symbols. To type-in chord symbols:

1.   Click the Chord Tool ![CM7] .
2.   Choose **Chord** > **Manual Input** (unless it is already checked).
3.   You will see four arrows to the left of the staff. These indicate the vertical positioning of your chords (more about them soon). Click in the first measure.
4.   A blinking cursor appears. Type "CMaj" to indicate a C major chord. When you first type a chord symbol, it will appear as normal text.
5.   Press SPACEBAR. The "CMaj" turns into a chord symbol with Maj as the suffix.
6.   To hide or show fretboards at any time, choose Show Fretboards from the Chord menu. Your cursor is now above the next note. Now, type "Abm7/Db" and press the spacebar. Now you will see an A-flat minor seven chord over D flat (see Figure 4.9).

7. Press SHIFT+SPACEBAR to move backward. Press TAB or SHIFT+TAB to move forward or back by full measures.

Figure 4.9

Elements of Chord symbols

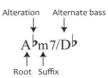

Chord symbols are case sensitive. You can indicate the root of a minor chord by entering a lowercase letter or the root of a major chord by using an uppercase letter. The case of the root letter will affect the playback (major or minor) of the chord symbol.

While typing chords into the score, use the following method:

1. Type the letter representing the root of the chord.
2. Type the alteration of the root of the chord using "b" for flat and "#" for sharp.
3. Type the suffix abbreviation (Maj, min, 7, 9, etc.).
4. Type the Alternate Bass. Precede the alternate bass note with a forward slash (/) to place it to the right of the suffix, a bar symbol (|) to place it below and slightly to the right, and underscore (_) to place the alternate bass directly below the symbol and suffix.

In addition to using "b" for flat and "#" for sharp, you can also use keystrokes for diminished and half-diminished symbols. Use the "o" key (lowercase O, not zero) for a fully diminished symbol and the "%" key (Shift+5) for half diminished.

While typing into the score, you can use keyboard shortcuts to easily select any of the available chord suffixes.

1. After typing the root, type a colon (:) and then the number of the suffix as it appears in the Chord Suffix Selection dialog box. For example, type C:1 to enter CMaj. If you don't remember the number of the suffix, type :0 (colon zero) after the root and then press the spacebar to view the Chord Suffix Selection dialog box.
2. Choose the chord suffix and click the Select button to return to the score with the suffix added.

Defining Chords Symbols Manually

To enter chords with more complicated suffixes, and for more control while entering chords, you may want to use the Chord Definition dialog box.

1. Choose **Chord** > **Manual Input** (unless it is already selected).

2.   Double-click the score, or right/CTRL-click an existing chord and choose Edit Chord Definition (or, select a handle and press ENTER). The Chord Definition dialog box appears (Figure 4.10).

Figure 4.10
Choose the suffix, fretboard, and playback attributes for a chord in the Chord Definition dialog box.

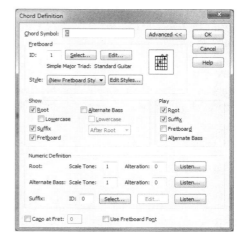

3.   Type the chord just as you would while typing into the score in the Chord Definition text box. You could type the suffix (7, b13, etc.), or, you can also choose from a list of available chord suffixes.
4.   Click **Advanced** and then **Select** in the **Numeric Definition** (Mac: **Definition**) section (at the bottom). You will see a list of available chord suffixes.
5.   Click the one you want to use so it is highlighted and then click **Select** (or double-click it). You will see the suffix to the right of the root in the Chord Definition text box.
6.   Click **OK** to see the chord appear in the score.

TIP:
By default, chords are set to playback. To silence playback for all chords symbols, uncheck **Enable Chord Playback** from the **Chord** menu.

MIDI Input (playing-in chord symbols)

Use MIDI Input to enter chords easily with a MIDI keyboard.

1.   Ensure **Allow MIDI Input** and **Manual Input** are both checked under the Chord menu and click your score. A blinking cursor appears above the staff. This means Finale is listening.
2.   Play a chord on your MIDI keyboard (in any inversion). Finale will analyze the chord you play and enter the corresponding chord suffix into the score. If Finale does not recognize the chord, you will be prompted with the Unknown Chord Suffix dialog box.

3. Click **Let Finale do it** to tell Finale to automatically choose the closest chord symbol. Choose **I'll do it** to teach Finale the chord you played. Finale will take you to the Chord Definition dialog box to define a chord symbol for the chord you played.

You can edit the chord suffix associated with any chord played from the MIDI keyboard. To do this, choose Edit Learned Chords from the Chord menu. You will be prompted with the Edit Learned Chords dialog box as shown in Figure 4.11.

Figure 4.11

Customize the chord to input for a combination of MIDI notes while using MIDI Input in the Edit Learned Chords dialog box.

Choose a key in which the chord is to be learned and click the Learn button. Then play the chord you want to re-assign. Click the **Edit** button to define its associated chord symbol.

TIP:
Play a single note within the octave above middle C to move the cursor forward/backward a beat/note. Play a single note more than an octave above/below middle C to move the cursor by full measures. Press middle C to move the cursor up, above an existing chord symbol.

One/Two/All-Staff Analysis

If you already have music with existing chords in the form of notation, Finale can analyze the music and enter the appropriate chord symbol automatically.

1. Enter a chord (e.g. stacked triads of any note duration) into a staff. Then choose **Chord > One-, Two-,** or **All-Staff Analysis** (depending on the number of staves you want to analyze).

2. Click above a chord to tell Finale to place a chord symbol in the score automatically. If Finale cannot recognize the chord, you will see the Unknown Chord Suffix dialog box.

3. Click **I'll do it** to define a chord symbol manually in the Chord Suffix Selection dialog box or choose **Let Finale do it** to let Finale make its best guess.

Chord Analysis plug-in

To automatically add chord symbols for larger regions, use the Chord Analysis plug-in. This plug-in allows you to analyze the score and specify conditions for adding the chord symbols (e.g. on all down beats).

1.   Select a region of the score.
2.   Choose **Plug-ins/** ✂ **> Scoring and Arranging > Chord Analysis**. The Chord Analysis dialog box appears. Here you can specify on which staff to place the chord symbols, the beats on which you would like to add them, whether or not to repeat them, and other criteria. (Click **Help** for a complete description of these options).
3.   After you have made your setting, click **OK**. Finale adds chord symbols to the selected region based on your settings.

Chord Symbol Metatools

Use chord metatools to quickly enter chords into a score.

1.   Choose **Chord > Manual Input**.
2.   Hold down SHIFT and press any number or letter. You will now see the Chord Definition dialog box.
3.   Enter the chord symbol in the text box at the top (and make any other settings), then click **OK**.

Now, hold down the letter you assigned and click on any note in the score to add the defined chord.

Creating and Editing Chord Suffixes

If you can't find the suffix you want to use in the Chord Suffix Selection dialog box, you can create one yourself.

1.   Choose **Chord** and ensure **Manual Input** is checked.
2.   Double-click the score to bring up the Chord Definition dialog box.
3.   Click **Advanced** (to extend the lower portion), and then click **Select** in the Numeric Definition (Mac: Definition) section to open the Chord Suffix Selection dialog box.
4.   Click **Create** (or, if you see a suffix similar to the one you are looking for, highlight it, click **Duplicate**, and then **Edit**). You will now see the Chord Suffix Editor dialog box as shown in Figure 4.12.

Figure 4.12
Edit or create your own suffix in the Chord Suffix Editor dialog box.

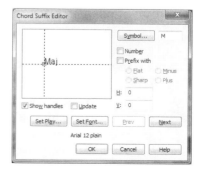

5. Enter a single character in the text box to the upper right (click the **Set Font** button to change the font). If the character is a number, check the **Number** box. To precede the symbol with a sharp, flat, plus, or minus, check **Prefix With** and select the prefix below. Click the Symbol button to browse.

6. If you want another character, click the **Next** button and repeat the process. Use either the handle in the editing window to drag with the mouse or the H: (horizontal) or V: (vertical) text boxes to position each symbol.

To assign playback for the suffix (pitches relative to the defined root):

1. Click the **Set Play** button. This will bring up the Suffix Keynumber Offsets dialog box where you can enter MIDI Note numbers for playback.

2. If you are using an external MIDI device (such as a MIDI keyboard), click the **Listen** button to enter the root and then the chord. Finale will record the MIDI information for you and calculate the offsets.

3. Click **OK, OK, Select,** and **OK** to return to the score and review the suffix.

TIP:
When you play a chord into the Suffix Keynumber Offsets dialog box, Finale will not retain the octave information, only the pitch. To raise or lower an offset an octave for playback, add or subtract 12 from the MIDI Note number (negatives are OK).

Changing Chord Fonts

To change the default fonts of your chord symbols, suffixes, alterations, or fretboards:

1. Choose **Document > Document Options** and click the **Fonts** category.

2. Click the drop-down menu for **Chords** and choose the element you want to change.

3. Click the **Set Font** button to select a new font, size, and style. Do this for all elements of the chord you want to change.

4. Click **OK** to return to the score. Changing the fonts for chord suffixes in the Document Options dialog box will only affect newly created ones, and will not affect suffixes already existing in the score or in your Chord Suffix Selection dialog box.

5. To change the font of existing chord suffixes, select the Chord Tool ![CM7] and choose **Chord > Change Chord Suffix Fonts**.

6. In the Replace With section, click the **Set Font** button. Choose the Font, Size, and Style and click **OK**.

7. Check the Font, Size, and Style boxes (as needed) and click **OK**. Existing suffix fonts will change to the one you specified. If you find that the chords no longer line up on the same baseline, make sure to select Fix Baseline Positioning in the Change Chord Suffix Fonts dialog box.

Chord Symbol Positioning

You can easily move any chord or fretboard diagram by clicking its handle and dragging or using the arrow keys to nudge it around. More than likely, however, you will want all of the chords symbols or fretboards to align to the same distance above the staff along a baseline. You can easily adjust the vertical placement (or baseline) of chord symbols by using the four positioning arrows on the left side of the screen. The arrow you use will depend on the region of chord baselines you want to position. Here is an explanation.

- Use the first arrow (from the left) to adjust the baseline of all chords or fretboards in the *whole document*.
- Use the second arrow to adjust the baseline of all chords or fretboards in *that staff*.
- Use the third arrow to adjust the baseline of all chords or fretboards in a *particular staff in a system* (in Page View).
- Use the fourth arrow to predetermine the baseline of the *next chord or fretboard* you enter. (Don't use this one.)

To use the arrows for chord positioning, choose Position Chords from the Chord menu. To use the arrows for fretboard positioning, choose Position Fretboards from the Chord menu.

To space chords horizontally, or to move individual chords, you can drag them by the handle.

- When you drag the handle of a chord symbol, its fretboard comes along for the ride.
- Drag the fretboard handle to reposition the fretboard relative to the symbol.
- As you drag, the dashed blue attachment indicator links to the attached beat or note.
- Hold down CTRL/CMD and drag a chord symbol to move it without changing the attached beat or note.

If you find your chords and/or fretboards overlap, you can tell Finale to automatically respace your music to avoid collision of chord symbols and fretboards. To do this:

1. Choose **Document > Document Options** and select **Music Spacing**.
2. In the **Avoid Collision Of** section, check **Chords** and click **OK**.
3. Now, select the Selection Tool 🖑 , press CTRL/CMD+A to Select All, and then press the 4 key (to apply Note Spacing). Your music respaces to accommodate the chord symbols. There's more about Music Spacing under "Music Spacing" on page 244.

Fretboard Diagrams

If you are working on a score for guitar, you may want to include fretboard diagrams that display a fingering for the chord. As mentioned earlier, you can activate or deactivate the presence of fretboard diagrams on all chord symbols at once by choosing **Chord** > **Show Fretboards**. If you decide to show fretboards, Finale will display them with a standard fingering for the specified chord. Since there are many ways to finger any given chord, you may want to edit a fretboard diagram so that the chord is played on a different fret (for example).

To customize a fretboard:

1. First ensure **Manual Input** is checked under the **Chord** menu.
2. Double-click the score to open the Chord Definition dialog box.
3. In the Fretboard section, click Select to see any alternate fretboards that already exist for that chord in Finale's default fretboard library.
4. If you see the one you want, click it, then click **Select** and **OK** to return to your score. If you do not see the desired fretboard diagram, create your own.
5. Click **Creat**e to open the Fretboard Editor dialog box as seen in Figure 4.13.

Figure 4.13

Edit or create your own fretboard in the Fretboard Editor dialog box.

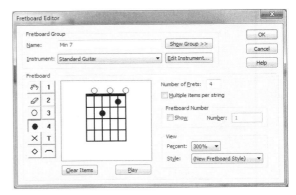

6. Here, make modifications to the existing fretboard using the tools on the left side of the Fretboard section. You can edit the number of strings and string tuning of the fretboard instrument by clicking the **Edit Instrument** button.
7. Once you have finished editing the fretboard diagram, click **OK** and **Select** to return to the Chord Definition dialog box.
8. Click **OK** to return to the score and see the custom fretboard.

If you find that the fretboards are too big or too small, from the Document menu, choose Document Options and select the Chords category. For "Scale All Fretboards By," enter the desired percentage. (the higher the number the bigger the fretboard gets-set it to 100% to see the original size).

Adding and Removing Capo Chords

As you probably already know, guitarists see things differently than most musicians. Instead of referring to the actual chords, guitarists occasionally prefer to put on a capo and read completely different chords because their fingerings are more familiar and easier to play. (This guitarist is no exception.) Finale makes it incredibly easy to add these convenient capo chords to maximize efficiency and performance quality while writing for lazy fretboard instrumentalists.

1. Choose the Selection Tool ▨ and select a region of music that contains chord symbols. (Or, press CTRL/CMD+A to Select All).
2. Choose **Utilities** > **Add/Remove Capo Chords**. The Add/Remove Capo Chords dialog box appears.
3. After Capo at Fret, enter the fret to be capoed. Then, specify the distance above the existing chords in the next text box. (This value will need to be increased to accommodate fretboards).
4. Click **OK**. Finale adds capo chords to the selected region.

To remove capo chords, follow steps 1 and 2 above, check **Remove Existing Capo Chords**, and click **OK**.

Transferring Custom Chord Libraries Between Documents

If you have already created or edited chord symbols or fretboards in another document or have a document that contains chords or fretboards you would like to use, you can transfer these between documents by saving and opening a chord and fretboard library.

1. Open the document containing the existing chords.
2. Choose **File** > **Save Library**. You should see the Save Library dialog box.
3. Choose **Chords and Fretboards** and click **OK**.
4. Enter a name and save the file to your Libraries folder (Finale 2012/Libraries).
5. Now open the document you are working on and choose **File** > **Load Library**.
6. You will now see the Load Library dialog box. Double-click the library you saved to open it. You will now be able to choose these chords and fretboards for entry in the new document.

Entering Lyrics

You will find entering lyrics in Finale is a breeze, as long as you use the right methods. Experimentation can get you into quite a mess if you aren't careful, so don't tread too far from the path. I'll go over the right way to enter lyrics so as to avoid any of these unnecessary hurdles. In this section, you will learn how to type lyrics directly into the score or type the lyrics first and then click them into the score.

To prepare for this section, open any document, and add a single-line melody. Then click the Lyrics Tool. In this section, I assume you have the Lyrics Tool 🎵 chosen unless directed otherwise.

Typing Lyrics into the Score

The easiest and most intuitive way to enter lyrics is to type them directly into the score.

1. Choose **Lyrics** > **Type Into Score**.
2. Now click on a note to see a blinking cursor below the staff.
3. Type a syllable and press SPACEBAR to advance the cursor to the next rhythmic subdivision. If you would like a hyphen between syllables, press the - (dash) key instead of the spacebar.
4. Use the left and right arrow keys to move the cursor between letters and syllables.
5. Click any lyric to highlight it.
6. Use the DELETE/BACKSPACE key to delete syllables like you would in a word processor.

To enter a second verse:

1. Click the first lyric so it is highlighted.
2. Press DOWN ARROW and you will see the cursor shift into position for the second verse. Do this to enter as many verses as you like.
3. Press UP ARROW to move to the previous verse. You can begin a new verse at any time.

TIP:
You may want to change the distance between hyphens in your lyrics. To do this, choose **Document** > **Document Options** > **Lyrics**. Here, change the value in the text box for **Space Between Hyphens**.

Click Assignment

Though typing into the score is adequate for simple scores, you will want to use Click Assignment in any document that contains repeating lyrics. To use this method of lyric entry, you will type all of the lyrics into the Lyrics Window and then click the lyrics into the score accordingly. You will be able to click the same text into the score many times, saving the trouble of retyping the same lyric. Also, you will be able to edit the lyrics once to change a phrase for every occurrence in the document.

1. The Lyrics Window (Figure 4.14) should already be open. This is where you will be entering text. If you don't see the Lyrics Window, choose **Lyrics** > **Lyrics Window**.

Figure 4.14

The Lyrics Window offers control of
most of your lyric entry needs.

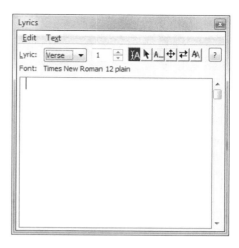

2. Here, enter your lyrics. You can treat this dialog box much like a basic word-processor.
    Finale ignores carriage returns, so you can separate your lyrics into paragraphs if you
    like.

3. Place a hyphen at the end of a syllable to hyphenate it to the next.

4. To enter verse two, click the up arrow to the right of Verse. The editing window will
    appear empty.

5. Enter the second verse just as you did the first. Do this for as many verses as you need.
    If you don't know all the lyrics beforehand, don't worry, you can come back to the
    Lyrics window any time. Now that you have entered some text in the Lyrics Window,
    let's click them into the score.

6. Choose **Lyrics** > **Click Assignment**. You are now ready to start clicking-in syllables.

7. Click the DOWN ARROW next to the verse number to return to verse 1.

8. Click a note and the first syllable appears below the staff. The next lyric to be entered is
    highlighted in the Lyrics Window (see Figure 4.15).

Figure 4.15

Click in the score to enter the highlighted syllable (or the one to
the right of the cursor).

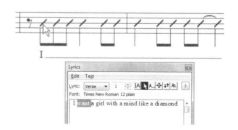

9. Hold down CTRL/OPTION and click a note to enter all lyrics to the end of the verse
    automatically.

TIP:
If you need to shift an entire verse left or right, use the **Lyrics** > **Shift Lyrics.**

You may have noticed that in addition to verses, you can also specify choruses and sections. These are no different than verses, and can be treated the same. They aren't necessary, but can be used for organization. To choose which verse, section, or chorus you would like to enter using **Type into Score** or **Click Assignment**, use drop-down menu in the Lyrics Window. I recommend leaving the Lyrics Window open even when using Type Into Score. It's easy to change verses/choruses/sections and also see which one is currently selected. (There is no preset visual difference between a verse, section, or chorus, and syllables will line up with the verse perfectly.)

TIP:
You can easily copy text from a word-processing program into Finale for lyric entry. Highlight the text in the word-processing program and press CTRL/CMD+C to copy. Then, move to Finale, click inside the Lyrics Window, and press CTRL/CMD+V to paste the lyrics. Then use **Click Assignment** to enter them into the score.

Setting or Changing the Font for Lyrics

To set the font for your lyrics before you have entered them:

1. Choose **Document** > **Document Options**. On the left, click **Fonts** to see the font options.
2. Click the drop-down menu for **Lyrics**, choose **Verse, Section**, or **Chorus**, then click the **Set Font** button.
3. Set the font, size, or style here and click **OK** and then **OK** again to return to the score.

If you want to change the font of existing lyrics, use the Lyrics Window.

1. Choose **Lyrics** > **Lyrics Window** (if it isn't already visible).
2. Move the verse section or chorus you want to change and highlight the text (CTRL/CMD+A to Select All).
3. Choose **Text** > **Font**. You can also select the font, size, or style. Windows users, click **OK**. You will see the lyrics change in the Lyrics Window.

You can change the font of all lyrics at once by using the Change Fonts plug-in.

1. Choose **Plug-ins/** ⅍ > **Miscellaneous** > **Change Fonts**.
2. Click the **Change** button for Lyrics to open the Font dialog box. Here, choose the font, size, and style you would like to change your lyrics to.

3. Click **OK**, and then click **OK** again to return to the score. All existing lyrics will change to the new font, size, or style you specified.

After running the Fonts plug-in, you may find that your verses overlap or that there is too much space between verses due to a new font size or style. To fix this, you can tell Finale to reset your lyric spacing automatically.

1. Choose **Document > Document Options,** and select **Fonts.**
2. From the **Lyric** drop-down menu, select the type of lyric in the score, and then click the **Set Font** button to the right.
3. In the Font dialog box, choose the new font and size you selected with the Change Font plug-in.
4. Click **OK** twice to return to the score.
5. Then, with the Lyrics Tool selected, choose **Lyrics > Adjust baselines.**
6. Click **Set Piece Offsets to Default Font** and click **OK.** The vertical spacing for lyrics are made even for all verses automatically.

Positioning Lyrics

If you change the font of your lyrics, you may want to space them out vertically. You can adjust the baseline (vertical placement) of each verse, section, or chorus independently. These baselines work like those explained for expressions in Chapter 3 and for Chords earlier in this chapter. To choose the lyric you want to move, select it in the Lyrics Window. Choose the lyric type and number, and then click **OK.** Notice the four arrows on the left. You can easily adjust the vertical placement (or baseline) of the chosen lyric by using the four positioning arrows on the left side of the screen just as you would for chords. The arrow you use will depend on the region of lyrics you want to position.

- Use the first arrow (from the left) to adjust the baseline of all lyrics in the *whole document* (all staves).
- Use the second arrow to adjust the baseline of all lyrics in the *staff* (for the whole document).
- Use the third arrow to adjust the baseline of all lyrics in a *system* (in Page View).
- The fourth arrow can be used to predetermine the baseline of the *next lyric you enter.* Don't use this one.

NOTE:
Default lyric spacing was improved in Finale 2011. This means music with lyrics automatically looks better without you having to do anything at all. Yay MakeMusic!

Like chords, to space lyrics horizontally, you will need to reposition the notes to which they are attached. Like chord symbols, avoiding overlapping syllables is most easily done with Finale's Automatic Music Spacing capabilities.

1. Choose **Document** > **Document Options,** and select **Music Spacing.**

2. Under **Avoid Collision Of,** make sure **Lyrics** is checked.

3. Click **OK** to return to the score.

4. Select the Selection Tool 🖼 , press CTRL/CMD+A to Select All, and then press the 4 key (to apply Note Spacing).

5. Your music respaces horizontally to accommodate the lyrics. You'll find more information regarding Music Spacing in "Music Spacing" on page 244.

You can also edit the positioning of lyrics manually.

1. Choose **Lyrics** > **Adjust Syllables**. Handles appear on all syllables.

2. Click to select the handles of the syllables(s) you want to move. Hold down SHIFT and click to select multiple handles.

3. To change the alignment or justification, context click one of the selected handles and choose the desired option (default/left/center/right).

4. Alternatively, you can click and drag, or nudge using the arrow keys, to position the lyric manually. When you move lyrics vertically this way, you are actually separating them from their baselines.

5. After using Adjust Syllables, you can move them back to their original position by selecting them and pressing BACKSPACE/CLEAR or using the Clear Lyric Positioning plug-in. Click the Selection Tool 🖼 .

6. Highlight the region of lyrics you want to reset, then choose **Plug-ins/** ✂ > **Lyrics** > **Remove Lyric Positioning**.

Editing Lyrics

While you enter lyrics, there are a number of editing techniques than can come in handy. In this section I'll cover the common ways you can modify your lyrics while entering or after you have entered them.

Smart Word Extensions and Hyphens

Word extensions and hyphens adjust automatically to spacing changes in the score. You can change the appearance of the offset of word extensions and line thickness, and make a variety of other settings in the Document Options dialog box (Figure 4.16). From the Document menu, choose **Document Options**, and then choose **Lyrics** (or choose **Lyrics** > **Lyric Options**). Here you can control the space between hyphens and turn off Smart Hyphens. Click the Word Extensions button to change the appearance of word extensions in the score.

Figure 4.16

You can change the appearance of hyphens and word extensions in the Document Options dialog box.

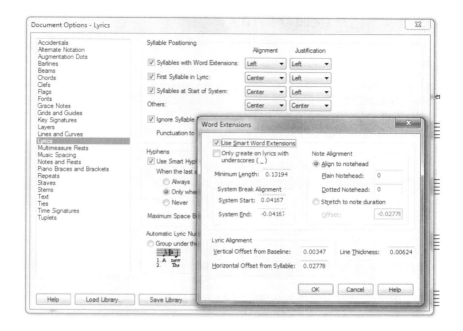

Shifting Lyrics

To shift all or some of your lyrics to the right or left after they have been entered:

1. Choose **Lyrics** > **Shift Lyrics**. You will see the Shift Lyrics dialog box as shown in Figure 4.17.

Figure 4.17

Shift lyrics left or right according to settings in the Shift Lyrics dialog box.

2. Make the desired selections and click **OK**.
3. If you chose to shift lyrics to the left, click the note to the left of the region you want to shift to move the lyrics toward the beginning of the score. If you chose to shift lyrics to the right, click the first note of the region you want to shift to move the region toward the end of the score.

Copying and Deleting Lyrics

Click Assignment, as explained earlier, is the best way to enter repeated lyrics to any location in a document. However, there are some other ways to copy lyrics.

If you want to copy a region of music with lyrics, use the Selection Tool. Click the Selection Tool , highlight the region you want to copy and drag the region to its destination.

If you need to copy music to a region of your score not visible on the screen:

1. Select the measures you want to move.
2. Press CTRL/CMD+C to copy.
3. Navigate to the new section of the piece and highlight the first measure of the desired target region.
4. Press CTRL/CMD+V to paste.

You can also copy lyrics independently with the Lyrics Tool .

1. Choose the Lyrics Tool .
2. Choose **Lyrics** > **Clone Lyrics**.
3. Highlight a region containing lyrics and drag it to another measure containing music. Finale will copy all syllables according to the rhythmic placement of the original lyrics (so you will need the same rhythmic passage in both measures for all lyrics to copy).

Cloned lyrics are linked dynamically - when you edit one copy, all other cloned versions change uniformly.

> **TIP:**
> To copy lyrics only from one region to another, use the Edit Filter dialog box before you copy, selecting only Lyrics. See "Selecting Specific Items to Copy" on page 233.

To delete lyrics from a region of music:

1. Click the Selection Tool .
2. Highlight the region of music containing the unwanted lyrics.
3. Choose **Edit** > **Clear Selected Items**.
4. Click **None**, and then check **Lyrics** and click **OK**.
5. Lyrics in the highlighted region will be deleted. Note that even though you've deleted the lyrics from your score, the lyrics remain in the Lyrics Window.

More Than One Syllable Under a Note (Elisions)

To place more than one syllable on a note:

1. Enter the first syllable, either in the score or in the Lyrics Window.
2. On Windows, type ALT+0160 (type the numbers on the Num Pad - laptop users, use the Fn key to enable the numpad keys). On Macintosh, type OPTION+SPACEBAR. (Or, from the Lyric Tool Text menu, choose **Insert Hard Space.**)
3. Enter the second syllable.
4. You can also enter a "hard hyphen" to place a hyphen between two syllables attached to the same note. To do this follow the same instructions, only use the keystroke ALT+0173 on Windows or OPTION+ - (hyphen) on Macintosh. (Or, from the Lyric Tool Text menu, choose **Add Hard Hyphen.**)

Verse Numbers

Verse numbers in Finale 2012 are automatic. Here's how to use them:

1. Click the Selection Tool 🖊 .
2. Choose **Lyrics** > **Auto-Number** > **Verses**.
3. Start entering verse 1 (by typing or click-assigning). Finale adds a number "1." to the left of the first syllable.
4. Highlight the first syllable and press the DOWN ARROW to move to verse 2.
5. Finale adds "2." to the left of the first syllable in verse 2. Subsequent verses are numbered consecutively.

If your verses don't start at the same note, you can left-justify the lyric numbers so they are aligned above one another in a column. To do this, from the Lyrics menu, choose Lyric Options. You'll see what I mean by looking at the diagrams at the bottom under Automatic Lyric Numbers.

To add a verse number on a syllable other than the first one in the verse:

1. Choose **Lyrics** > **Adjust Syllables.** Handles appear on each syllable.
2. Right/CTRL-click the syllable's handle and choose **Include Lyric Number.** The lyric number appears to the left of the syllable.

Beam to Lyrics

In vocal music, some prefer to coordinate the beaming pattern to the lyrics. Finale can do this automatically with the Selection Tool. Click the Selection Tool 🖊 and select the region of music you want to rebeam (CTRL/CMD+A to Select All). Click **Utilities** > **Rebeam** > **Rebeam to Lyrics**. Click **OK** and Finale will change the beaming of notes according to the lyrics.

TIP:
You can also change the beaming of your score manually by using the Simple Entry ♪ or Speedy Entry Tool 🎵. Use the / (slash) keystroke on the QWERTY keyboard in either of these tools to beam from the previous note. You can also use the / (slash) key to remove a beam from the previous note.

Creating a Lead Sheet

At this point, you have covered all the material necessary for creating a lead sheet with a melody, chord symbols, and lyrics. Now you can apply the skills you have learned to create your own lead sheet, all the way from starting a new document to the final printout. For this example, we'll create a lead sheet arrangement of Amazing Grace, as shown in Figure 4.18.

Figure 4.18
Amazing Grace Arrangement

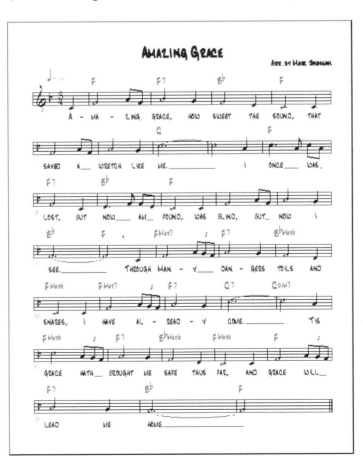

There are a few layout issues that apply specifically to lead sheets (like the left barline on each system, for example). To save the headache of defining these layout changes ourselves, we'll begin this process by opening the Lead Sheet template.

1. Choose **File** > **New** > **Document From Template**. You should now see the contents of the Finale 2012/Music Files/Template folder. Open the General folder, and then double-click **Lead Sheet (Handwritten)** to open the Broadway Copyist Font Lead Sheet Template. The Document Setup Wizard appears.

2. For **Title**, enter "Amazing Grace." Then, for **Composer**, enter "Arr. by" followed by your name. Click **Next**. The Score Settings page appears.

3. In the Score Settings page of the wizard, do the following:

   The meter for this piece is 3/4, so click the ![3/4] button.

   This arrangement is in the key of F Major, so under **Select a Concert Key Signatur**e, click the down arrow (beneath the scroll bar) once.

   The tempo is 90 beats per minute. Check **Specify Initial Tempo Marking**, then in the text box to the right of **Tempo**, enter "90."

   There is a one-beat pickup, so check **Specify Pickup Measure** and select the quarter note icon.

   In the Number of Measures text box, enter "23."

   Click **Finish**. Your piece is now ready for entry (see Figure 4.19).

Figure 4.19
Your template should now look like this.
You are now ready to start entering notes.

4. In this example, the theme is repeated twice. If you have an external MIDI device (a MIDI keyboard for example), you might enter the first sixteen measures using Hyper-Scribe. (Review "Real-Time Entry: HyperScribe" on page 88 if you have any trouble).

5. You could continue and enter the whole piece with HyperScribe, but for practice, use the Simple 🎵 or Speedy Entry Tool 🎵 to enter measures seventeen through twenty-three. In measure seventeen, you will need to enter a triplet on the last beat of the measure. In Speedy Entry, use the CTRL/OPTION+3 method to pre-define the triplet. In Simple Entry, use the Simple Entry Tuplet Tool 🎵 to pre-define the triplet (see "Tuplets" on page 52 (for Simple) and "Tuplets" on page 64 (for Speedy) for help. Continue by entering notes into the remaining measures.

6. Now, let's put five measures on a system. Click the Selection Tool 🖰 , and select all (CTRL/CMD+A). Choose **Utilities** > **Fit Measures,** type "5" and click **OK**. Your piece now has five measures per system (besides the last system which has three).

7. To enter the chord symbols, click the Chord Tool CM7 . Choose **Chord** > **Manual Input** (if it is not already checked). Click the first note in measure one to display a blinking cursor above the staff. Type "F" and then tab to go to the next measure. Then type "F7" and continue entering chord symbols this way until you get to measure seventeen.

8. With the cursor above the half note in measure 17, type "F:0" (colon zero) and then ENTER. The Chord Suffix Selection dialog box appears. Double click **Maj7**. For the remaining chord symbols, when necessary, type ":0" to choose the suffix from the Chord Suffix Selection dialog box. After you have finished entering the chord symbols, move them closer to the staff by dragging the leftmost positioning arrow down closer to the staff. See the information in "Entering Chord Symbols" on page 97 for more chord entry and positioning techniques.

9. Now, enter the lyrics. The easiest way to enter lyrics is to type them directly into the score. Click the Lyrics Tool 🎨 , and then, choose **Lyrics** > **Type Into Score**. Click the first note and type the first syllable "A," then a "-" (hyphen) to move to the next syllable. Continue entering each syllable.

10. Now, let's make all the lyrics a little bigger. Choose **Plug-ins/** ✻ > **Miscellaneous** > **Change Fonts**. After Lyrics, click the **Change** button and then set the size to "16." Click **OK** to return to the score. Your lyrics are now a little larger and more readable (adjust the lyric baseline if you wish by clicking the Lyrics Tool and using the leftmost positioning arrow).

11. Now, let's make the music on the page a little bigger. Choose **View** > **Page View** (if you aren't already in Page View). Click the Resize Tool % , and then click the upper-left corner of the page (away from any staves or notes). In the Resize Page dialog box, enter "112" and click **OK**. Everything on the page is now slightly larger and more readable.

You can use the above procedure as a general guide any time you create a lead sheet. After creating your own piece, you may want to add expressions, articulations, slurs, fretboard diagrams, or any number of other figures not included in the above steps. I'll be touching on most of the common notational possibilities in the remaining chapters (if you haven't seen what you're looking for already).

5
Clefs, Key Signatures, and Time Signatures

Okay, and now we return to a relatively flat clearing where the trail is straight and the insects are managed. There isn't much debate regarding the proper way to handle these items (within the scope of this book anyway). Professional engravers employ these techniques just as you will. If you are already a professional engraver, I hope you are using these techniques and not some arcane method from the dark ages of Finale 2007 or something.

Here's a summary of what you will learn in this chapter:

- How to work with clefs
- How to work with key signatures
- How to work with time signatures

 TIP:
Easily add clef changes, key signature changes, and time signature changes with the Simple Entry Tool. While entering with the Simple Entry Caret, type ALT/Option+Shift+C to change the clef, ALT/Option+Shift+K to change the key, and ALT/Option+Shift+T to change the time signature.

Working with Clefs

In this section you'll learn how to use the Clef Tool to space clefs, enter mid-measure clef changes and even create your own custom clef. In addition, there are a variety of other settings that relate to clefs throughout your document, such as cautionary clef changes. We'll start with the most common, entering clef changes, and then move into how to modify them.

To prepare for this section, open a new Default Document (**File** > **New** > **Default Document**), and then enter a melody with the Simple 🎵 or Speedy Entry Tool 🎵 . Click the Clef Tool 𝄢 .

Changing the Clef at the Beginning of a Measure

Clef changes often appear at the beginning of the measure, just to the left of the barline. These are your standard, run-of-the-mill clef changes.

1. With the Clef Tool selected, double-click the second measure of a staff. You will see the Change Clef dialog box as shown in Figure 5.1.

Figure 5.1

Enter a clef change by choosing from one of the available clefs in the Change Clef dialog box.

2. Choose the new clef from the 18 available options.
3. Once the clef is highlighted, click **OK** to return to the score and review the clef change. It will appear at the beginning of the measure you clicked. All of the music after the clef change will adjust according to the new clef.
4. Now, let's say you only want the clef change to affect a single measure. Double-click measure three to open the Change Clef dialog box.
5. Choose the original clef and then click **OK**. You should now have a clef change back to the opening clef of the staff.

NOTE:
If you have an instrument with a "Set to Clef" transposition (in the Staff Transpositions dialog box), and you need to change the clef, you will first need to uncheck Set to Clef in the Staff Transposition dialog box. Choose **Window > Score Manager, select the instrument** and then click the **Settings** button next to **Transposition**. Uncheck **Set to Clef** and click **OK** and close the Score Manager.

You can also highlight measures to apply a clef change to a region.

1. Choose the Clef Tool 𝄢 and drag-select a few measures.
2. Double+click the highlighted region. The Clef Selection dialog box appears.
3. Double-click the clef you want to apply to that region. Finale adds the clef change at the beginning of the selected region, and then a clef change back to the original clef in the measure following the region.

You can also indicate a return to the original clef by specifying a region in the Change Clef dialog box. If you would like the clef to appear to the right of the barline, check **Place Clef After Barline** in the Change Clef dialog box.

Entering Mid-Measure Clefs

Sometimes clefs appear in the middle of a measure, most of the time at a slightly reduced size. To enter a mid-measure clef change:

1. With the Clef Tool 𝄢 selected, drag-select the region to which you want to apply the new clef (as shown in Figure 5.2).

Figure 5.2

Enter mid-measure clefs by first selecting a partial measure region.

Before

After

2. Double-click the highlighted region. The Change Clef dialog box appears.
3. Choose the desired clef.
4. Click **OK** and you will see the new clef appear within the measure.
5. To delete any mid-measure clef, click its handle and press DELETE, or right/OPTION+click the handle and choose DELETE.

Editing Mid-Measure Clefs

You can easily edit mid-measure clefs, or change any mid-measure clef to a regular clef change in the Mid-Measure Clef dialog box (Figure 5.3). CTRL/OPTION-click the handle on the mid-measure clef to open this dialog box.

Figure 5.3

Specify the size and placement of a mid-measure clef in the Mid-Measure Clef dialog box.

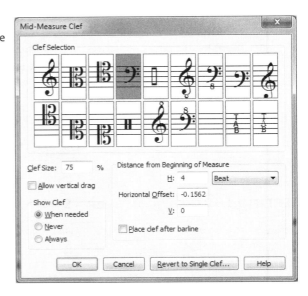

Here, choose a new clef in the clef selection, or resize the clef by entering a different percentage in the Clef Size text box. In the Show Clef section, specify when you want Finale to display the clef in the score, and pinpoint the positioning of the mid-measure clef on the right under Distance from Beginning of Measure (more about these settings soon). If you want to be able to drag the clef vertically, check Allow Vertical Drag.

CAUTION:

With **Allow Vertical Drag** checked you will be able to drag or nudge clefs up or down in the staff. When you do this, notes will not reposition according to the vertical staff placement. To enter a clef that accurately repositions notes in a staff according to standard notation rules, choose one of the existing clefs from the clef selection or design your own clef with the Clef Designer. See "Creating a Custom Clef (the Clef Designer)" on page 123.

If you like, you can also change the clef back to a regular clef change at the beginning of the measure. To do this, choose **Revert to Single Clef**. You will be taken back to the Change Clef dialog box. Make any desired settings and click **OK** to return to the score.

Clef Metatools

Like articulations and expressions, you can also enter mid-measure clef changes easily by using metatools.

1. With the Clef Tool ![clef tool icon] selected, hold down the SHIFT key and press 1 to open the Clef Selection dialog box (Figure 5.4). In the upper-left corner, you will see the preset metatool assignments for each type of clef. For example, note the "4" in the bass clef box.

Figure 5.4

The Clef Selection dialog box.

2. Click **OK** to return to the score.
3. Hold down the 4 key and click in the staff to enter a mid-measure bass clef.

You may want to program your own clef metatools. For instance, let's say you want to use the T key to enter a treble clef instead of the number 1.

1. Hold down the SHIFT key and press the letter T. The Clef Selection dialog box opens.
2. Now choose the treble clef and click **OK**. The treble clef is now assigned to the T key.
3. Hold down the T key and click anywhere in a staff to enter a mid-measure treble clef. If you open the Clef Selection dialog box again (by holding down Shift and pressing a number or letter), you will notice the letter T in the upper-left corner of the treble clef box.
4. You can also apply a clef change to a selected region. Highlight a few measures and then press the T key (or any clef metatool) to apply a clef change for the region.

Clef Spacing and Placement

In addition to dragging or nudging mid-measure clefs, there are a number of ways to specify placement of clefs in a staff, globally or individually.

You may want to change the default positioning of clef changes relative to the barline. Choose **Document > Document Options**. Choose Clefs from the column on the left to display the Clef options (see Figure 5.5).

Figure 5.5

In the Clef portion of the Document Options dialog box, make document-wide settings for the appearance and spacing of clefs.

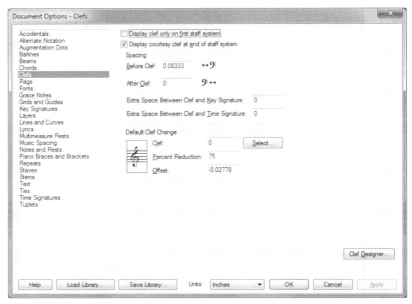

For example, specify the space "Before Clef" (between the clef and left barline) or "After Clef" (between the clef and first note) and click **OK** to apply these settings to the entire document.

TIP:
Use the **Extra Space Between Clef and Key Signature** and **Extra Space Between Clef and Time Signature** to space clefs relative to the key or time signature.

To choose the measurement unit (inches, points, EVPUs, etc.) for any parameter in Document Options, click the drop-down menu to the right of **Units** and make a selection. You can find a description of all the measurement units in Table 1.1 (in Chapter 1).

Showing or Hiding Clefs and Courtesy Clefs

To show the clef at the beginning of the first measure only (which is common practice in certain types of documents such as lead sheets):

1. Choose **Document** > **Document Options**.
2. Click the **Clefs** category on the left and check **Display Clef Only on First Staff System**.
3. Click **OK** to apply your settings and return to the score.

If there is a clef change at the beginning of a system, it is customary to place a "courtesy" clef at the end of the previous system to warn the performer of the upcoming change in clef. Courtesy clefs are turned on by default. To hide or show courtesy clefs (globally for the whole document):

1. Choose **Document** > **Document Options**.
2. Click the **Clefs** category on the left and check or uncheck **Display Courtesy Clef at End of Staff System**.
3. Click **OK** to apply your settings and return to the score.

You can also hide cautionary clefs, key signatures and time signatures for an individual measure, or region of measures, with the Measure Tool.

1. Choose the Measure Tool 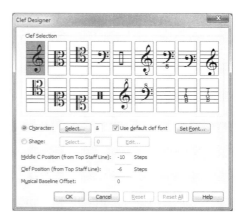 .
2. Double-click the measure prior to the courtesy clef change to open the Measure Attributes dialog box.
3. Check **Hide Cautionary Clefs, Key and Time Signatures** and click **OK**.

Creating a Custom Clef (the Clef Designer)

There may be a clef you want to use that doesn't exist among the 18 available clefs in the Clef Selection dialog box. In this case, you can actually create your own clef that will contain all the properties of a legitimate clef pre-defined in Finale. To design a custom clef:

1. Choose **Document** > **Document Options**. Select the **Clefs** category on the left and click the **Clef Designer** button among the options on the right. This will open the Clef Designer dialog box as seen in Figure 5.6.

Figure 5.6
Create a custom clef definition in the Clef Designer dialog box.

2. Choose the clef you want to edit from the selection boxes at the top. You will be redefining one of these clefs, so make sure you choose one you do not plan on using in this document.
3. To change the appearance of the clef, click the **Select** button to the right of Character. This will take you into the Symbol Selection window. Choose the character you want to

use for your new clef and click Select. If you can't find the character for the clef you want to use, you could try selecting a character from a different font. To do this, click the **Set Font** button in the Clef Designer. This will open the Font dialog box where you can choose the new font, size, and style for your clef.

NOTE:
Finale offers several music fonts that contain clef symbols you might find useful. For a complete list of characters in all Finale fonts, click the **Help** menu on Mac (or on Windows, click **Help**, then User Manual) and select the Engraver, Jazz, or Maestro character map. Of course, you can also select a character from any font that exists on your computer in the Font dialog box.

4. If you cannot find a font with the clef you want, you can design your own. In the Clef Designer, click the **Shape** radio button, then click **Select**. Click **Create**. You will now see the Shape Designer window. Use this editor to create a custom shape for your clef. You can even import existing graphics with the Graphics Tool available in this window. Click **OK** and then **Select** to return to the Shape Designer. Now it's time to configure the functional clef characteristics (how the clef will affect the notation).

5. For Middle C Position (from Top Staff Line), indicate the staff position of middle C in the clef you are defining. Enter 0 to place middle C on the top staff line. Subtract one for each line and space below the top staff line or add one for each line and space above the top staff line. (For example, enter -4 to set the middle C position of your clef to the middle staff line.)

6. In the **Clef Position** (from Top Staff Line), use the same parameters to position the clef in the staff. You may need to adjust the Musical Baseline Offset for mid-measure (reduced) clef changes after defining a custom clef, particularly if you created a custom shape for the clef.

7. Click **OK** to return to your score to see your new custom clef.

Transferring Custom Clefs Between Documents

Like articulations and expressions, you can transfer custom clefs (created in the Clef Designer) between documents by saving and opening a library.

1. Open the document containing the existing clefs.
2. Choose **File** > **Save Library**.
3. Choose **Clefs** and click **OK**. Enter a name and save the file to your Libraries folder (Finale 2012/Libraries).
4. Open the document you are working on, then choose **File** > **Load Library**.
5. Double-click the library you saved to open it. Now your custom clefs will be available in this document's Clef Selection window.

Key Signatures

Chapter 2 touched on the basics for changing the key signature at the beginning of a document. Here you will learn how to make key changes at any measure or even create a customized key signature. Keep in mind the instructions in this section refer to changing the concert pitch of a score, therefore a transposed staff may appear in a different key. To view your score in concert pitch at any time, select **Document** > **Display in Concert Pitch** (choose the same option again to display the transposed staves).

To prepare for this section, either continue using the document from the previous section, or open a new Default Document (**File** > **New** > **Default Document**). Also use the Simple or Speedy Entry Tool to enter a simple melody into the document for the purpose of demonstration.

Entering and Changing the Key Signature

Unlike clefs, key signatures generally affect all staves in a system, so at any given measure you will only need to make one key change. Let's say you want to change to the key of A major in measure three.

1. Choose the Selection Tool 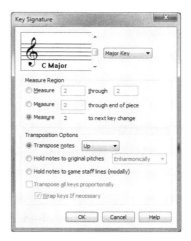. Then, right/CTRL+click measure 3. Choose **Key Signature**, then select the desired key signature from the submenu and you're done!

2. If you do not see the desired key signature, choose **Edit Key Signature** to open the Key Signature dialog box as shown in Figure 5.7.

Figure 5.7
Define a key change in the Key Signature dialog box.

3. Next to the key signature preview window is a vertical scroll bar. Click the up arrow three times to add three sharps to the key signature. The display now indicates a key of A major. Since any notes in your score will transpose into the new key, you will need to choose which direction to move them.

4. In the Transposition Options, for **Transpose Notes**, click the drop-down menu to transpose them up or down. At this point, if you want to change the key signature without moving the notes, you have three options. Check **Hold Notes to Original**

Pitches and select **Enharmonically** to respell the notes based on the new key signature. See "Managing Notes while Changing the Key" on page 127.

5.   Click **OK** to return to your score and review the key change.

In the Key Signature dialog box, you can also:

- Click the down arrow next to the display window to add flats or remove sharps from a key signature.
- Click the drop-down menu to the right of the preview window to specify a major, minor, or nonstandard key (I'll discuss nonstandard key signatures soon). By specifying a major or minor key from the drop-down menu, you tell Finale how to assign accidentals accurately when entering notes via MIDI.
- Specify a region for the key signature change in the Measure Region section. Note that every time you enter the Key signature dialog box, the setting for Measure Region will reset to Measure _ To Next Key Change, so you will need to make adjustments to this setting when necessary.

If you want to change the key of a region of your score that already contains a key change, and you want the existing key change (or any number of key changes) to adjust accordingly, check **Transpose All Keys Proportionally** (note that this option is not available if **Measure_To Next Key Change** is selected). When you do this, all affected key changes will transpose proportionally from the new key you specify (see Figure 5.8).

Figure 5.8

Transposing keys proportionally

Original

Transposed up a whole step proportionally

Key Signature Metatools

If you intend to enter many key changes in a document, you may want to program Key Signature metatools.

1.   Choose the Key Signature Tool ![icon] .
2.   Hold down the SHIFT key and press the 1 key to open the Key Signature dialog box.
3.   Specify the new key here and click **OK** to return to the score.
4.   Hold down the 1 key and double-click a measure to enter the specified key change to a measure.
5.   Program a key signature metatool to any number or letter key on your QWERTY keyboard.

Managing Notes while Changing the Key

To change the key of a region without transposing the music:

1. Double-click the measure of the key change to open the Key Signature dialog box.
2. Select the key signature you wish to use.
3. Under **Transposition Options**, select **Hold Notes to Original Pitches**.
4. From the drop-down menu, choose **Enharmonically** to respell the notes according to the new key.
5. Choose **Chromatically** to leave the spelling the same.
6. To leave all notes at the same staff position and change only the pitches affected by the change of key, choose **Hold Notes to Same Staff Lines Modally**.

TIP:
If you want to transpose notes without changing the key signature, choose the Selection Tool and select the region of notes you want to transpose. Choose **Utilities** > **Transpose**. Select an interval and click **OK**. There will be more information on transposition in Chapter 9.

Changing the Key on Individual Staves

If you are working on a bitonal score (one that oversteps traditional key signature usage), you may need to specify a concert key signature change on one staff without affecting the concert key of the other staves. To do this:

1. Click the Staff Tool ![icon] and double-click the staff you want to change.
2. In the **Independent Elements** section, check **Key Signature** and click **OK**.
3. Use the Key Signature Tool ![icon] to change the key on that staff. Key changes to this staff will not affect the key of other staves, and key changes in other staves will not affect this staff.

Selecting the Default Font for Key Signatures

You may want to change the font of your key signatures to one of the other available Finale fonts or a different music font installed on your computer. To do this:

1. Choose **Document** > **Document Options** and select **Fonts**.
2. Click the drop-down menu for **Notation** and select **Key**.
3. Click the **Set Font** button to open the Font dialog box where you can specify the font, size, and style for your key signatures.
4. Click **OK** to return to the Document Options dialog box and click the **Apply** button to apply the change in font.

Since Finale expects the accidental characters to be in one of the Finale music fonts, you may need to re-assign the accidental characters for your key signatures if you are using a third party music font. To do this:

1. Choose **Document** > **Document Options** > **Key Signatures**.
2. Click the drop-down menu for Music Characters and choose the type of accidental you want to assign. Then, click **Select** to open the Symbol Selection dialog box.
3. Choose the matching font character and click **Select** to return to the Document Options dialog box.
4. Choose any other character you need to assign and click the **Apply** button to apply your new character settings.

Spacing Key Signatures

There are a couple ways to adjust the spacing of key signatures in a document. You may want to increase or decrease the space between the key signature and the barline or the following entry.

To do this on a document-wide basis:

1. Choose **Document** > **Document Options** and click **Key Signatures** (see Figure 5.9).
2. Enter a value in the **Space Before Key Signature** text box to indicate the distance between the barline and the key signature.
3. Enter a value in the **Space After Key Signature** text box to indicate the distance between the key signature and the following entry.
4. Use the **Extra Space Between Key and Time Signature** to space key signatures relative to the time signature.

Figure 5.9

Make document-wide settings for key signature spacing, characters, and appearance in Document Options-Key Signatures.

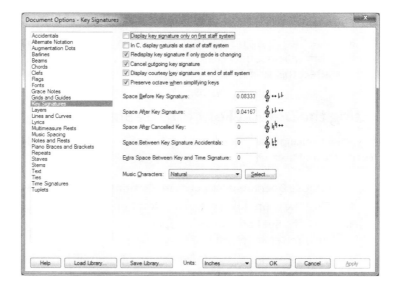

In the Document Options dialog box, you can also change the distance between the accidentals within a key signature:

1. Enter a new value for **Space Between Key Signature Accidentals**.
2. Click **OK** to apply changes and return to the score.

To choose the measurement unit (inches, points, EVPUs, etc.) for any parameter in the Document Options, click the drop-down menu at the bottom of the dialog box, to the right of Units, and make a selection. You can find a description of all the measurement units in Table 1.1 (in Chapter 1).

Showing and Hiding a Key Signature in Staves and Measures

To show the key signature at the beginning of the first measure only:

1. Choose **Document** > **Document Options** and click **Key Signature**.
2. Check **Display Key Signature Only on First Staff System**.
3. Click **OK** to apply your settings and return to the score.

To hide all key signatures in a staff:

1. Click the Staff Tool ![icon] and double-click a staff to display the Staff Attributes.
2. Under **Items to Display**, uncheck **Key Signature**s.
3. Click **OK** to return to the score.
4. All key signatures in the specified staff will be hidden. Hidden key signatures apply to the music even though they are not visible.

CAUTION:
Hiding the key signature will not automatically make accidentals appear on diatonic notes. To do this, change the key to C and select **Hold Notes to Original Pitches Enharmonically** in the Key Signature dialog box.

You can also force a key signature to show or hide at the beginning of any measure with the Measure Tool.

1. Click the Measure Tool ![icon] and double-click a measure.
2. Click the drop-down menu to the right of **Key Signature** and choose **Always Show** to show the key signature in that measure.
3. Choose **Always Hide** to hide the key signature in that measure.
4. Click **OK** to return to the score and review your changes.

TIP:
To show or hide key signatures or time signatures for a region of measures, select the region with the Measure Tool and double-click the highlighted area. Changes you make in the Measure Attributes will apply to all selected measures.

Showing or Hiding Courtesy Key Signatures

If there is a key change at the beginning of a system, it is customary to place a "courtesy" key signature at the end of the previous system to warn the performer of the upcoming change in key. Courtesy key signatures are turned on by default.

To show or hide courtesy key signatures:

1. Choose **Document** > **Document Options**.
2. Click the **Key Signature**s category on the left and check or uncheck **Display Courtesy Key Signature at End of Staff System.**
3. Click **OK** to apply your settings and return to the score.

To hide a courtesy key signature individually:

1. Select the Measure Tool ▦ .
2. Double-click the measure prior to the courtesy key signature to open the Measure Attributes dialog box.
3. Check **Hide Cautionary Clefs, Key, and Time Signatures** and click **OK.**

Outgoing Key Signatures

While changing key signatures in a score, it is common to indicate changes from the previous key signature to the left of the new key. For instance, in a key change from F Major (one flat), to G major (one sharp), you may see a natural to the left of the new key "canceling" the B flat in the key of F Major (see Figure 5.10).

Figure 5.10
Canceling the Outgoing Key Signature

Outgoing key signature cancelation

To show or hide the canceled key signature for the whole document:

1. Choose **Document** > **Document Options** and select **Key Signatures** from the list on the left.

2. Check **Cancel Outgoing Key Signature** to show the canceled key signature, or uncheck this box to hide the canceled key signature.

3. Click **OK**.

You can also adjust the spacing of the canceled key signature indication in the Document Options by entering a value in the **Space After Canceled Key** text box.

Nonstandard Key Signatures

In addition to major and minor keys, you can also create your own custom key signatures with any combination of accidentals on any staff position. Although a thorough exploration is squarely outside the scope of this book, this feature does warrant a word or two. To define a nonstandard key signature:

1. Double-click a measure to open the Key Signature dialog box.

2. To the right of the preview display, click the drop-down menu and choose **Nonstandard**.

3. This will open the Nonstandard Key Signature dialog box as shown in Figure 5.11.

Figure 5.11
Define a custom key signature in the Nonstandard Key Signature dialog box.

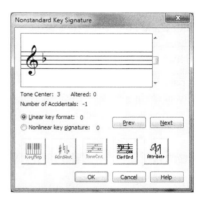

4. There are two types of nonstandard key signatures: linear and non-linear. Choose the **Linear Key Format** to define a key signature with a reoccurring sequence of whole and half steps. All linear key signatures will cycle through a "circle of fifths" type of relationship (though your key signature may cycle through sixths, fourths, or another interval). Major and minor key signatures both fall into the linear category, and are already defined as Format 0 (Major) and 1 (minor). So, click **Next** twice to get to **Linear Format 2** and the buttons become available. While defining a linear key signature, use the scroll bar to the right of the preview display to add sharps, flats, double-sharps, double-flats, etc.

5. Non-linear key signatures are not based on a system of related keys. Choose **Nonlinear Key Signature** to define a key with any number of accidentals in any order. The scroll bar in the preview display will not be available while defining a nonlinear key. You will need to use the options below.

The five buttons at the bottom of the Nonstandard Key Signature dialog box can be used to define linear or non-linear key signatures (though some parameters will be limited with linear keys).

- Choose **KeyMap** to define the number of steps in an octave and the sequence of whole and half steps.
- Click **AOrdAmt** to specify where you want to place the accidentals in the staff.
- Click **ClefOrd** to assign the octave to place each accidental.
- Click the **ToneCnt** button to specify a root for your key signature.
- Click **Attributes** for more options, such as assigning special characters to accidentals for quarter-tone key signatures.
- Whether you are creating a linear or non-linear key signature, click the **Next** button to move to the next format or **Prev** to move back to the previous one.

Time Signatures

Like clefs and key signatures, there are many ways to enter and edit time signatures beyond the options available in the Setup Wizard. Here you will learn how to enter meter changes at any measure, create compound and composite meters, specify beaming patterns, and make other settings related to time signatures on an individual or global basis. Since time signatures and key signatures exhibit many of the same characteristics in Finale, some of these instructions will look familiar.

To prepare for this section, use the same document you have been working with, or open a new Default Document (**File** > **New** > **Default Document**). Use the Simple or Speedy Entry Tool to enter a simple melody into the document for the purpose of demonstration.

Entering and Changing the Time Signature

Like key signatures, time signatures usually affect all staves in a system, so at any given measure you will only need to make one meter change (we will cover independent meters later in this section). Since the document you have open is in 4/4 time, we'll start by creating a time change to 11/8.

1. Choose the Selection Tool . Then, right/CTRL+click measure 3. Choose Time Signature, then select the desired time signature from the submenu.
2. If you do not see the desired time signature, as is the case in this example, choose **Edit Time Signature** to open the Time Signature dialog box as shown in Figure 5.12.

Figure 5.12
Define a meter change in the Time Signature dialog box.

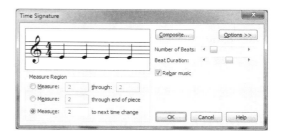

3. Click **Composite**. The Composite Time Signature dialog box appears.
4. After **Beat Groups**, IN THE FIRST BOX, type "3+3+3+2" and then type "8" in the box below after **Beat Durations**, then click **OK**. Since you still want the time signature to display as simply 11/8, click **Options** (Mac: **More Choices**) to expand the dialog box and check **Use Different Time Signature for Display**.
5. Use the scroll bars to define 11/8 in the bottom half of the dialog box and click **OK** review the change in meter.

In the Time Signature dialog box, you can also specify a region for the time signature change in the Measure Region section. Note that every time you enter the Time Signature dialog box, the setting for Measure Region will reset to Measure _ To Next Time Change, so you may need to make adjustments from this setting as needed.

Hiding the Time Signature

To hide the time signature completely for an entire staff:

1. Click the Staff Tool and double-click a measure in a staff. The Staff Attributes dialog box opens.
2. In the **Items to Display** section, uncheck **Time Signature**.
3. Click **OK** to return to your score. Do this for any other staves as necessary.

Shortcuts: Context Menu and Metatools

If you intend to enter many time signature changes in a document, you may want to program Time Signature metatools.

1. Select the Time Signature Tool .
2. Hold down the SHIFT key and press the 1 key to open the Time Signature dialog box.
3. Specify a meter here and click **OK** to return to the score.
4. Highlight a region of measures, hold down the 1 key, and double-click the region to apply the time change to the selected measures. You can program a time signature metatool to any number or letter key on your QWERTY keyboard.

Abbreviated Time Signatures

You may or may not want to abbreviate 4/4 as 𝄴, and 2/2 as 𝄵. To change these settings:

1. Choose **Document** > **Document Options** and select **Time Signatures**.
2. **Check** or uncheck **Abbreviate Cut** or **Common Time**.

Selecting the Default Font for Time Signatures

To change the font of your time signatures to one of the other available Finale fonts or a different music font installed on your computer:

1. Choose **Document** > **Document Options** and select **Fonts**.
2. Click the drop-down menu for **Notation** and select **Time (Score)** or **Time (Parts)**, depending on which you want to change.
3. Click the **Set Font** button for Notation to open the Font dialog box where you can specify the font, size, and style for your time signatures (regular and abbreviated).
4. Click **OK** to return to the Document Options dialog box. Click **Apply** to apply the change in font
5. Now, choose **Time Signatures** to adjust the positions of the top and bottom time signature characters as needed. Click **Apply** or **OK** to apply the change in time signature character positioning.

TIP:
Try using the EngraverFontSet or Engraver Time font for an alternative style for your time signatures. For a complete list of characters in all Finale fonts, click the **Help** menu on Mac and choose **Character Maps** (or on Windows, click **Help** > **Shortcuts & Character Maps** and select the character map).

Using a Different Time Signature for Display

For a number of reasons, you may need to display a different time signature than the actual one defined in the Time Signature dialog box (pickup measures, measures across systems, beaming, cadenzas etc.). (We used this technique earlier while defining beams for our 11/8 time signature.) To do this:

1. Select the Time Signature Tool 🕮 and double-click a measure to open the Time Signature dialog box and specify the beat duration and number of beat. Click the **Options** button (Mac: **More Choices**) in the upper right to expand the lower section of the dialog box (see Figure 5.13).

Figure 5.13

Click **Options** (Mac: **More Choices**) to expand the Time Signature dialog box where you can create a separate time signature for display.

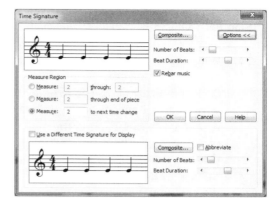

2. Set up the time signature as you want it to display in the lower section, then check **Use a Different Time Signature for Display.**
3. Click **OK** to return to the score.

The time signature you choose to display will be visible only if it is different than the time signature of the previous measure.

Beaming Patterns and Time Signatures

Beaming patterns are stored in time signatures (as we saw earlier in our 11/8 example). When you specify a time signature, Finale will apply a beaming pattern for the music based on the duration of the main beat. For example, in 6/8 time, with a dotted quarter note as the main beat, Finale will automatically beam six eighth notes in two groups of three as seen in Figure 5.14.

Figure 5.14

Beaming for a 6/8 time signature is usually in groups of three eighth notes.

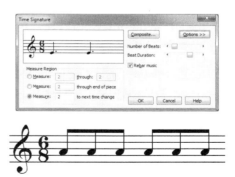

You can specify a custom beaming pattern for any time signature manually, and even apply a new beaming pattern without changing the time signature. To demonstrate this, here are steps for creating a custom beaming pattern for a 7/8 measure. Note that the Time Signature context menu already includes

2+2+3 and 3+2+2. So, in this example, you will create a beaming pattern with eighth notes in groups of 2+3+2. Start fresh with a new Default Document (**File** > **New** > **Default Document**).

1. With the Time Signature Tool ⌶ selected, double-click a measure to display the Time Signature dialog box.
2. Click **Composite** at the top to open the Composite Key Signature dialog box. This is where you will specify the beats/beaming pattern.
3. After **Beat Duration**, enter the rhythmic value that represents the smallest subdivision of notes you will be beaming. In this case, enter 8. This value will usually be the same as the bottom number in your key signature.
4. Now, after **Beat Groups**, in the first box, specify the number of notes in each group. In this case you'll enter 2+3+2 (see Figure 5.15). Notice the preview display indicates the beamed groups.

Figure 5.15
Specify beat groups for beams in irregular meters in the Composite Time Signature dialog box.

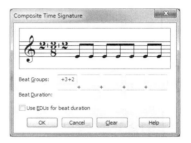

5. Click **OK**. You will now see the composite time signature in the preview display, though you will probably just want to display 7/8 in the score.
6. Click the **Options** (Mac: **More Choices**) button to expand the lower section.
7. Adjust the **Number of Beats** and **Beat Duration** in the lower section of the Time Signature dialog to indicate a time signature of 7/8. For **Number of Beats**, click the right arrow until 7 appears as the top number in the preview display. For beat duration, click the left arrow until 8 appears as the bottom number in the preview display, indicating a key signature of 7/8.
8. Check **Use a Different Time Signature for Display**. By checking this box, you tell Finale to use the time signature in the lower section for display, but the actual time signature and beaming pattern that will be used is in the upper display of the Time Signature dialog.
9. Click **OK** to return to the score.
10. Enter eighth notes into the staff with the Simple ♪ or Speedy Entry Tool ♫. You will see the notes beamed to the pattern specified in the Composite Time Signature dialog box.

TIP:
To beam this way ♪♪♪♪♪♪♪ instead of this way ♪♪♪♪♪♪♪ , choose **Document** > **Document Options** and select **Beams**. Uncheck **Beam Four Notes Together in Common Time**. Then, to update existing music, select the music, and choose **Utilities** > **Rebeam** > **Rebeam Music.**

TIP:
To apply beaming settings for any region of your score without changing the time signature, see "Rebeaming to Time Signature" on page 267.

Changing the Time Signature on a Single Staff Only

To specify a meter change on one staff without affecting the meter of the other staves:

1. Click the Staff Tool 🎼 and double-click the staff you want to change.
2. In the **Independent Elements** section, check **Time Signature** and click **OK**.
3. Now use the Time Signature Tool 🎼 to change the meter on that staff. Meter changes to this staff will not affect the meter of other staves, and meter changes in other staves will not affect this staff. Finale will continue to line up all barlines regardless of the meters being used. You will find a more in-depth discussion of under "Isorhythmic Notation" on page 142.

Spacing Time Signatures

You may want to increase or decrease the space between the time signature and the barline or the following entry. To do this on a document-wide basis:

1. Choose **Document** > **Document Options** and select **Time Signatures**.
2. Enter a value in the **Space Before Time Signature** text box to indicate the distance between the barline or clef and the time signature. Enter a value in the **Space After Time Signature** text box to indicate the distance between the time signature and the following entry.
3. You can also move any time signature vertically.
4. In the **Vertical Adjustment** section, specify a value for the bottom and top number in your time signature. To move a 4/4 time signature (in the default font and size) above the staff, enter 100 EVPUs, for example, for both **Top Symbol** and **Bottom Symbol**. Then make any fine adjustments. If you are using an abbreviated time signature, you need only modify the Abbreviated Value text box.

Showing and Hiding Time Signatures in Staves or Measures

To hide all time signatures in a staff:

1. Click the Staff Tool ▦ and double-click a staff to display the Staff Attributes.
2. Under **Items to Display** uncheck **Time Signatures**.
3. Click **OK** to return to the score. All time signatures in the specified staff will be hidden.
4. Recheck this box in the Staff Attributes to show time signatures in the staff.

You can also show or hide a time signature at the beginning of any measure with the Measure Tool.

1. Click the Measure Tool ▦ and double-click a measure.
2. Click the drop-down menu to the right of Time Signature and choose **Always Show** to show the time signature in that measure. Choose **Always Hide** to hide the time signature in that measure.
3. Click **OK** to return to the score and review your changes.

Showing or Hiding Courtesy Time Signatures

If there is a time change at the beginning of a system, it is customary to place a "courtesy" time signature at the end of the previous system to warn the performer of the upcoming change in meter. To show or hide courtesy time signatures for the whole document.

1. Choose **Document** > **Document Options** and click Time Signatures.
2. Check or uncheck **Display Courtesy Time Signature at End of Staff System**.
3. Click **OK** to apply your settings and return to the score.

To hide a courtesy time signature in an individual measure:

1. Select the Measure Tool ▦ .
2. Click the measure prior to the courtesy time signature to open the Measure Attributes dialog box.
3. Check **Hide Cautionary Clefs, Key, and Time Signatures** and click **OK**.

Multiple Time Signatures

You may want to enter a time signature followed by a second time signature in parentheses, indicating an alternate subdivision as shown in Figure 5.16.

Figure 5.16

Multiple Time Signatures

To enter multiple time signatures:

1. Choose the Time Signature Tool ⟋ and double-click a measure to display the Time Signature dialog box.
2. Use the scroll bars to specify the "real" time signature (enough beats to accommodate the notes you want to place in the measure.)
3. Click **Options** (Mac: **More Choices**) to display the lower portion of the dialog box.
4. Check **Use a Different Time Signature for Display**.
5. Click the **Composite** button in the lower section.
6. Enter the first time signature in the first set of boxes and the second in the second set of boxes (with the top number in the Beat Groups row and the bottom number in the Beat Duration row).
7. Click **OK** to return to the Time Signature dialog box, then click **OK** again to return to the score. You should now see the multiple time signatures separated with a + sign.
8. If you want to remove the + sign, choose **Document** > **Document Options** and select **Time Signatures**. Click the **Composite Time Signature Plus Sign Character** (**Score** or **Parts**) button and choose the blank character (#9 on Mac and #32 on Windows). Click **Select** and **OK** to return to the score.
9. Now, you may want to increase the distance between the two time signatures. To do this, choose **Document** > **Document Options** and select **Fonts**. For **Notation**, click the drop-down menu and choose **Time Signature Plus Sign** and click the **Set Font** button. Choose a larger font size, like 96, and click **Apply**. If this is too much space, adjust the font size of the blank character accordingly and click **Apply**. Click **OK** to return to the score.
10. You may want to surround one of the time signatures with parentheses. To do this you'll need to create an expression. Click the Expression Tool *mf* . Then, double-click the first measure to open the Expression Selection window.
11. Choose the **Miscellaneous** category and click **Create**.
12. In the Text Expression Designer, enter "( )" (with a space).
13. Highlight the parentheses then choose **Text** > **Size** > **Other**. Enter "28" and click **OK**.
14. Click **OK** then **Assign** to return to the score.
15. Drag the parentheses into place around the time signature.

Large Time Signatures

It is not uncommon to see large time signatures in a score placed between staves as shown in Figure 5.17.

Figure 5.17
Large Time Signatures

Here is a method for creating large time signatures that allows you to easily customize the size and positioning. This process involves creating hidden staves that display the time signature only, without interfering with time signatures in parts.

First, hide all time signatures in the score and add a new invisible staff:

1. Choose the Staff Tool ![icon], and choose **Staff** > **Define Staff Style**. The Staff Styles dialog box appears.
2. Click **New** in the upper right. Then, in the **Available Styles** text box, click "(New Staff Style)" and enter "Hide Time Signature."
3. Under **Items to Display**, click **Time Signatures** so it is unchecked. Then click **OK**.
4. In your score, select the first measure then press SHIFT+DOWN ARROW until the first measure is selected in all staves.
5. Choose **Staff** > **Apply Staff Styles To** > **Current Score/Part**. Then select **Hide Time Signature** and click **OK**. Your opening time signature is now hidden in all score staves.
6. Move to Page View (**View** > **Page View**).
7. Locate the position that you wish to specify as the vertical center of one of the score's time signatures. Choose **Window** > **Score Manager** and select the staff above the desired center location.
8. Click the **Score Order** drop-down menu and choose **Custom**.
9. Choose **Add Instrument** and choose **Blank Staff** > **Blank Staff**. A new staff appears below the staff you selected (and it is highlighted in the Score Manager).
10. In the Score Manager, click the **Staff** drop-down menu and choose **0-line with Full Barline**.
11. Double-click the staff (in the score) to open the Staff Attributes dialog box. Under **Items to Display**, uncheck **Barlines**, **Clefs**, **Key Signatures** and **Measure Numbers**. Under Options, uncheck **Display Rests in Empty Measures**, then click **OK**.
12. Double-click and drag the staff handle on your instrument staff up or down so that the time signature appears centered appropriately. (Do the same for the staff below, as necessary). Repeat the above steps to add the additional staves where you would like the center of the time signatures to appear.

Next, define the large time signature:

1. Choose **Document** > **Document Options** and select **Fonts**.

2. Click the **Notation** drop-down menu and choose **Time (Score)**. Then click the Set Font button to the right. Change the font to **EngraverTime** and the size to **48**. Then click **OK**.

3. Click the **Time Signatures** category on the left side of the Document Options dialog box.

4. At the bottom, for **Units**, click the drop-down menu and choose **EVPUs**.

5. In the **Vertical Adjustment** section, under **Score**, for **Top Symbol**, enter "400." For **Bottom Symbol**, enter "0." Click **OK**. The large time signature appears in the score and extends over several staves.

6. With the Staff Tool Selected, double-click and drag the handle to adjust the vertical positioning.

7. Now, you can resize the staff to change the time signature's size to your specifications. To do so, choose the Resize Tool %, click the invisible staff. In the Resize Staff Dialog box, enter a percentage and click **OK**.

TIP:
This method is designed to allow you to easily size the time signatures. Instead of creating a new staff specifically for each large time signature, and hiding all its elements, you could alternatively remove the "Hide Time Signature" Staff Style in a few of the existing score staves, and then adjust the Vertical Adjustment and character size to meet your sizing needs.

Pickup Measures Within a Score

Often, pickup measures appear somewhere within a score instead of at the beginning (see Figure 5.18). This is typical, for example, in hymnal music.

Figure 5.18
Pickup measures within a score.

Here are steps for creating a pickup measure at any point in a document in cases such as the figure above.

1. Click the Selection Tool [ ]. Then, identify and select the measure to be split, in this case, measure 9.

2. Choose **Plug-ins/** ✕ **> Measures > Split Measure**. The Split Measure dialog box appears.

3. In the text box, specify the beat prior to the measure split. In this example, beat 3.

4. Uncheck **Move second part of split measure to next system**. Then click **OK**.

5. Click the Measure Tool [ ]. Then, double-click the first part of the measure to open the Measure Attributes dialog box. In the Barline row, click the Double or Normal icon (whichever is needed) and click **OK**.

6. Enter the music as you would normally. The measure numbering is configured for you automatically.

Isorhythmic Notation

Isorhythmic notation is the practice of using several different time signatures at once. When you do this, each staff will be in a completely independent meter, so barlines for each staff will not line up vertically most of the time (see Figure 5.19).

Figure 5.19

Isorhythmic notation

This is a particularly unconventional notation practice, so getting it to work in Finale is a bit of a rigma-role. Nonetheless, it can be done, and here's how:

1. You will need to set all of your staves to use time signatures independently. Click the Staff Tool ![staff tool icon], and double-click the top staff to open the Staff Attributes. Then, in the **Independent Elements** section, check **Time Signatures**. To view the attributes for a different staff, select the staff name from the drop-down menu at the top of Staff Attributes and then, under Independent Elements, check **Time Signature**. Click **OK** when you have done so for all staves in your score.

2. Now you will need to create a time signature that will encompass all of the time signatures you wish to use. To do this, you basically need to determine the lowest common denominator for the multiple meters. For example, if you want to use 3/4 in one staff and 2/4 in another, use 6/4. This is the shortest measure that will encompass both a 3/4 and 2/4 meter.

3. Click the Time Signature Tool ![time signature tool icon] and double-click the first measure in the top staff to open the Time Signature dialog box.

4. Enter the time signature that represents the lowest common denominator (as calcu-lated above), then click the **Options** button (Mac: **More Choices**) to expand the lower portion of this dialog box.

5. Check **Use a Different Time Signature for Display**.

6. In the lower portion, set the time signature you want to display for the staff.

7. Click **OK**. Then repeat steps 3 through 6 for all staves in the score. Remember, if you will be doing this frequently, set up appropriate metatools for each time signature needed to save yourself the trouble of going to the dialog box every time. You can also save time by using the Time Signature context menu.

8. Now, add additional barlines manually using one of the barline Shape Expressions. Choose the Expression Tool *mf* and double click where you would like to add a barline. The Expression Selection dialog box appears.

9. Choose the **Miscellaneous** category. Notice the barline options. Double-click the barline you want to add (7 is a regular barline). The barline appears in the score. It is really just a vertical line defined to match the default staff height, but should work fine for this purpose. Assign it to a metatool for faster entry.

6

Slurs, Hairpins, Other Shapes and Repeats

Okay, now that you've had quite enough of staff-related figures and settings, let's move on to something completely different; Smart Shapes. Smart Shapes are not particularly dangerous, nor are they exhilarating, but it is important to use them properly or time can be wasted.

You can use the Smart Shape Tool to enter slurs, hairpins, trill extensions, brackets, bend shapes, glissandi, and other markings. Like Expressions, Smart Shapes are designed to adjust intelligently while you work. As you edit and adjust the layout of your score, each Smart Shape moves with the measure or note it is attached to, and can even adjust automatically to avoid collision with notes, accidentals, and other items. In this chapter you'll learn when to use Smart Shapes and how to enter, edit, and copy them. You'll also learn how to make global changes and create your own custom Smart Shapes.

The end of this chapter will be devoted to Repeats, which can be somewhat dangerous, but only when used recklessly. Repeats are represented by both text and barline figures. You will learn how to safely and easily enter repeat barlines and text repeats, edit their appearance, and get them to play back.

Here's a summary of what you will learn in this chapter:

- How to work with Smart Shapes, slurs, and hairpins
- How to enter glissandi, guitar bends, lines, and other Smart Shapes
- How to define Repeats

Introduction to Smart Shapes

When you click the Smart Shape Tool, you will see the Smart Shape palette appear (see Figure 6.1).

Figure 6.1

Choose a shape from the Smart Shape palette for entry into the score.

Use the Smart Shape palette to choose the shape you'd like to enter. To enter a slur:

1. Click the Smart Shape Tool 🖌, then choose the Slur Tool from the Smart Shape palette 🖌 (yes, both tools look the same).
2. Double-click a note to extend a slur to the next note.
3. Double-click and drag, holding down the mouse button on the second click, to extend a slur between two notes (I'll cover more about entering other shapes soon). By default, any Smart Shape you enter will appear red in the score (to distinguish them from text blocks, expressions, and other items). In addition to the Smart Shape palette, you will also see the SmartShape menu appear at the top of your screen (see Figure 6.2).

Figure 6.2

Customize the appearance, placement, and other attributes of Smart Shapes by choosing an item from the SmartShape menu.

Each Smart Shape has its own properties relating to how it can be edited and what it can be attached to (notes, noteheads, or measures). In addition, there are a number of placement and graphical changes you can make from the SmartShape menu at a document-wide level. Throughout this chapter I will refer to this menu to apply some of these changes.

Hold down one of the following metatool keys (see Table 6.1) and double-click and drag to enter its corresponding Smart Shape.

Table 6.1
Smart Shape Metatools

Tool	Metatool	Tool	Metatool
Slur	S	Double-Ended Bracket Tool	O
Dashed curve	V	Dashed Double-Ended Bracket Tool	Z
Decrescendo	>	Bracket Tool	K
Crescendo	<	Line	L
Trill	T	Dashed Line	D
Trill Extension	E	Glissando Tool	G
8va/8vb	8	Guitar Bend	B
15ma/15mb	1	Custom Line	C

NOTE:
Human Playback automatically interprets several Smart Shapes during playback, including hairpins, trills, glissandos, and ottavas (e.g., 8va). To hear these effects, select a Human Playback style in the Playback Settings dialog box on Windows or Playback Controls on Mac.

General Smart Shape Editing

Before beginning to explore the various Smart Shape types, you should understand some editing techniques common to many Smart Shapes. Whenever the Smart Shape Tool is selected you will see a handle appear on every Smart Shape in the score. I will refer to this handle as the *primary handle*. Click and drag this handle to move the Smart Shape around. Use the arrow keys to nudge it for fine positioning adjustments. Click and drag over several primary Smart Shape handles to move several of them at once. Press the DELETE key to delete all selected Smart Shapes.

Secondary diamond handles available for editing the shape or contour of a Smart Shape. These will be referred to as *diamond handles*.

Measure, Note, and Notehead-Attached Smart Shapes

Many Smart Shapes can be set to attach to either a measure or a note. Before entering a Smart Shape, from the Smart Shape menu, you can choose Attach to Measures, Attach to Notes, or Attach to Note-heads depending on the role of the Smart Shape you are about to enter (note that some of these options are limited to certain Smart Shapes). Note the default attachment settings are usually appropriate.

- **Measure-attached** Smart Shapes can be entered anywhere in the score and will attach to the measure closest to the point of entry. They will adjust to their corresponding measure like a measure-attached expression. Hairpins, trills, and ottavas are examples of measure attached Smart Shapes.
- **Note-attached** Smart Shapes will adjust according their corresponding notes much like a note-attached expression. Their position is determined by settings in the Smart Shape Placement dialog box (**SmartShape** > **Smart Shape Placement**). Slurs are an example of note-attached Smart Shapes.
- The **Attach to Notehead** option is used for the Tab Slide and Glissando Smart Shape.

The default setting for Measure/Note/Notehead-Attached is usually adequate for the common usage of each Smart Shape, so you may never need to change this setting. However, making the distinction between these three Smart Shape types is fundamental to the way Smart Shapes are organized in Finale.

Other Techniques

There are some other tricks that apply to all Smart Shapes.

- Drag-enclose to select several Smart Shapes. You may also select several Smart Shapes by holding down the SHIFT key and clicking in each handle. Then use the mouse to drag all selected Smart Shapes uniformly, or use the arrow keys to nudge them.
- Hold down the SHIFT key while creating or editing a Smart Shape to "constrain" dragging to either vertical or horizontal movement. For example, do this to draw a vertical or horizontal line.
- Hold down the DELETE key and drag over as many Smart Shapes as you like to delete them.
- When a Smart Shape's primary handle is selected, press the TAB key to cycle selection through the diamond editing handles of any Smart Shape. Pressing ESC will select the primary handle again and hide the diamond editing handles. When there are no editing handles showing, the Tab key will cycle through the primary handles of the various Shapes in the document.
- ALT/OPTION+click a primary SmartShape handle to see its source measure.
- Pay attention to the direction of the arrow on the mouse cursor when adding measure-attached Smart Shapes like hairpins to ensure they are attached to the intended staff (and not the one above or below).

The Smart Shape Context Menu

Any Smart Shape can be edited in the score with a context menu. Right/CTRL+click any Smart Shape handle to invoke the Smart Shape context menu as seen in Figure 6.3.

Figure 6.3

Quickly edit Smart Shapes in the score with the Smart Shape context menu.

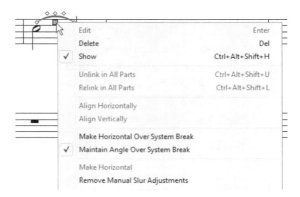

This menu can be used to quickly make a number of adjustments to individual Smart Shapes including direction and alignment. The available options in this context menu will depend on the type of Smart Shape (certain options will be grayed out with some smart shapes). To save time, learn to use the context menu frequently while editing Smart Shapes.

Context Menu-Aligning Smart Shapes

You can easily align any number of measure-attached Smart Shapes, such as hairpin crescendo or decrescendos, vertically or horizontally.

1. Click and drag to select several measure-attached Smart Shape handles.
2. Right/CTRL+click one of the highlighted handles to open the context menu.
3. Click Align Horizontally/Vertically to align all selected Smart Shapes. Then, press the UP or DOWN ARROW keys, or click one of the highlighted handles to position all of the aligned Smart Shapes at once.

Context Menu-Extending Smart Shapes Over System Breaks

Many Smart Shapes can be extended over a system break. When this is done, Finale basically generates a new Smart Shape at the beginning of the second system (and any subsequent system as necessary). If you would like to "flatten" the Smart Shape as it is moved over a system break, from the context menu, choose **Make Horizontal Over System Break**. This option can also apply to existing Smart Shapes. To allow Smart Shapes to retain their angle across system breaks, choose **Maintain Angle Over System Break** from the context menu.

Slurs

Slurs can be used to indicate a legato, uninterrupted performance style, or to indicate a musical phrase. To enter a slur:

1. Click the Slur Tool ◥ in the Smart Shape palette.
2. Double-click the first note of the slur and drag to the destination note.
3. When you release the mouse button, the slur will adjust automatically to avoid collision of notes and accidentals. As you drag the cursor over subsequent notes, refer to the highlighted note to specify the endpoint of the slur (see Figure 6.4).

Figure 6.4
Specify the Slur Endpoint by referring to the highlighted note.

After you have entered the slur, you will notice a surrounding pentagon with small diamonds at each corner. You can use these diamond editing handles to manually edit the shape of the slur. Click and drag them, or click a handle and use the arrow keys to make fine adjustments. Use these reshaping handles to edit the arc and endpoints

If you want to remove all manual changes you have made to a slur, press the BACKSPACE/CLEAR key with the handle selected. Or, context-click the slur's handle and choose Remove Manual Slur Adjustments.

Flipping Slurs Over or Under a Staff

After you have entered a slur, you might want to move it to the other side of the staff. To do this:

1. Select the slur's primary handle.
2. Press F.

Editing the Slur Contour Globally

If you are not satisfied with Finale's default slur contour settings, you can adjust them for an entire document. To do this:

1. From the SmartShape menu, choose Slur Contour. This will open the Slur Contour dialog box as seen in Figure 6.5.

Figure 6.5
Edit the default contour of slurs in the Slur Contour dialog box.

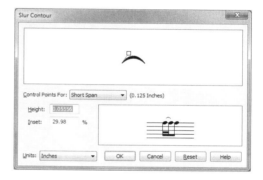

2. Click the drop-down menu and choose from the four available slur lengths. Since no one contour will work for every slur length, Finale divides the contour settings into four different lengths.
3. Choose the length that most closely compares to the slurs you want to change.
4. Use the handle in the editable preview window to adjust the default slur contour. Notice the preview window at the bottom will update to display any changes you make.
5. Hold down the SHIFT key to constrain dragging to vertical or horizontal movement only. If you prefer, enter values in the Height and Inset text boxes for more precise control over slur contour.
6. Click **Reset** to revert to the default settings for the chosen length.
7. Click **OK** to apply any changes and return to the score. Contour settings will affect existing slurs in the score.

Editing the Slur Width

You can edit the thickness of slurs in the Smart Shape Options dialog box.

1. With the Smart Shape Tool 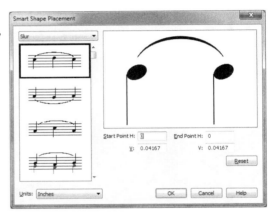 selected choose **SmartShape** > **Smart Slur Options.**
2. On the right side of the Smart Slur Options dialog box, use the **Thickness Left, Thickness Right**, and **Tip Width** parameters to adjust the thickness of slurs and slur tips.

Editing Default Slur Placement

Finale offers a great deal more flexibility for editing slurs globally. You can change the default placement for any slur based on the surrounding notation.

1. From the SmartShape menu, choose Smart Shape Placement. You will see the Smart Shape Placement dialog box as shown in Figure 6.6.

Figure 6.6

Edit the default placement of slurs, tab slides, glissandi, and guitar bends in the Smart Shape Placement dialog box.

2. Choose the general type of slur from the list on the left. Use the scroll bar to view all the options. Notice the placement of the slur related to the stem settings to determine which type of slur to adjust.
3. In the large, editable preview window, make adjustments to the slur manually. Click the left and right endpoints to adjust the slant and length of the slur. Click the middle of the slur and drag to adjust the vertical placement. You can also enter specific values for the start and end point in the H: (Horizontal) and V: (Vertical) text boxes. Click **Reset** to revert back to the original default settings.
4. Click **OK** to return to the score and review your changes. (Note they will not change if they have been manually adjusted).

Changes made in the Smart Shape Placement dialog box will affect any new slurs you create, as well as existing slurs in the score, provided that they have not been adjusted manually.

S-Slurs

Sometimes slurs need to extend from one staff to another, requiring an "S" shape as shown in Figure 6.7 instead of a simple curve. This type of slur is quite simple to create in Finale.

1. Enter the slur as you normally would, between notes in two adjacent staves (a grand staff for example).
2. Then, drag the endpoints of the slur to the desired location.
3. Drag the editing handles to create the S shape as seen in Figure 6.7.

Figure 6.7

Creating an S-Slur

Dashed Curves

Dashed curves behave just like slurs. Click the Dashed Curve Tool in the Smart Shape palette, and then double-click in the score to create a dashed curve/slur. Most settings made in the Smart Slur Options dialog box will apply to dashed slurs as well as regular slurs.

The width of dashed slurs/curves is customizable. Dashed slurs/curves are not tapered, unlike regular slurs, and are basically just curved lines. To change the width of a dashed slur, the dash length, or the space between dashes, use the Smart Shape Options dialog box.

1. Choose **SmartShape** > **Smart Shape Options**.
2. In the right side of this dialog box, specify a value for **Line Thickness**, **Dash Length** and/ or **Dash Space**.
3. Then, click **OK** to return to the score. Note that these changes will also apply to Line and Bracket Smart Shapes as well.

Avoiding Collisions with Articulations (TGTools)

If you find that some of your slurs collide with articulation markings, you can use TGTools to tell Finale to automatically reposition the endpoints of slurs to avoid this collision. Here's how:

> **NOTE:**
> This feature is available with the full version of TGTools available at tgtools.de.

1. Click the Selection Tool .

2. Select a region of your score containing slurs that collide with articulations, or CTRL/CMD+A to Select All.

3. Choose **TGTools** > **Modify** > **Modify Slurs**.

4. Click the **Resolve Collisions** tab.

5. Here, you can specify the offset for slurs that collide with articulations. The default values usually work fine.

6. Click **Go**. Slurs in the selected region adjust to avoid collision with articulations. Depending on the musical passage, you may want to adjust slurs colliding with certain articulations only. Select the **Articulation Types** tab in the TGTools Slurs dialog box to choose specific articulations to avoid.

> **TIP:**
> You can define an articulation to be placed inside a slur by default in the Articulation Designer dialog box. This is already the case for Finale's included staccato and tenuto articulations.

Engraver Slurs

Finale's *Engraver Slurs* automatically avoid collision with notes, accidentals, and beams, and are used by default whenever you enter a slur. These will even update as you edit notes in the score. This is one of those things that will really save you time. There are a number of parameters available that help control the behavior of engraver slurs. From the SmartShape menu, choose Smart Slur Options. On the left side of this box, make adjustments to the way Finale configures engraver slurs.

Any time you edit a slur manually, it will change into a normal slur, meaning, its shape will no longer automatically adjust with the changes you make to your document. Essentially, the slur will be frozen into position and will no longer automatically adjust its shape to avoid collisions. To convert it back to an engraver slur, highlight its handle and press BACKSPACE/CLEAR.

To set all slurs in a converted document (or selected region) to engraver slurs:

1. Click the Selection Tool .

2. Select a region of your score, or CTRL/CMD+A to Select All.

3. Choose **Utilities** > **Check Notation** > **Remove Manual Slur Adjustments**.

4. Click the Smart Shape Tool .

5. Choose **SmartShape** > **Smart Slur Options**.

6. Check **Use Engraver Slurs.**

7. Click **OK**. Slurs in the selected region are now set to adjust to avoid collision with notes, accidentals and beams.

Hairpins (Crescendos and Decrescendos)

Hairpins in music notation are used to indicate a gradual dynamic contrast. They are also referred to as crescendos and decrescendos, an increase or decrease in dynamics, respectively. In Finale, hairpins generally appear as measure-attached Smart Shapes, and can be entered with either the Crescendo or Decrescendo Tool in the Smart Shape palette.

- With the Crescendo Tool ◿ selected (or while holding down the < key), double-click below a staff and drag to the right. (Make sure the arrow on the cursor is pointed to the correct staff).

- Release the mouse button to create the crescendo. You will notice three diamond editing handles on the crescendo in addition to the main handle (if not, click the main handle to display the diamond handles).

- Click and drag the right-most diamond handle to adjust the placement of the end of the hairpin.

- Click the left-most handle to adjust the placement of the beginning of the hairpin.

- Move your cursor over the diamond handle on the right side of the hairpin (on the line) to adjust the width of the opening (see Figure 6.8).

Figure 6.8

Use handles to edit the length and opening width of hairpins.

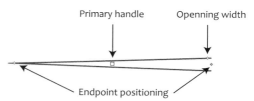

Decrescendos can be entered and edited the same way as crescendos (use the > keystroke for a decrescendo). Press Backspace/Clear to revert a hairpin back to the way it looked when originally entered.

With either hairpin tool selected, you can create both shapes. For example, Click the Crescendo tool ◿, double-click and drag to the left. Instead of a crescendo, you get a decrescendo.

To specify the line thickness and opening width for all hairpins you create:

1. Choose **SmartShape** > **Smart Shape Options**.
2. In the Crescendo/Decrescendo section, specify a value for Line Thickness and Opening Width and click **OK**.
3. All hairpins that have not been edited manually will change to the values you specified. Also, new hairpins will use these values.

> **TIP:**
> If you want to indicate a crescendo simply as text (e.g., "cresc."),
> create a text expression (as described in Chapter 3). To create the text
> "Cresc." followed by an adjustable dashed horizontal line, create a
> Custom Smart Shape. You can find information on how to create
> custom shapes later in this chapter.

Aligning Hairpins

Aligning hairpins horizontally or vertically is easy.

1. Drag to select the handle(s) of the hairpins you want to align (or SHIFT+click to select the desired hairpins).
2. Right/CTRL+click one of the selected handles and choose **Align Horizontally** or **Align Vertically.** They all become aligned with the one you context-clicked.

You may want to align all hairpins horizontally at a certain position above or below the staff. You can do this with the Align/Move Dynamics plug-in.

1. Choose the Selection Tool 🔧.
2. Highlight the region of your score containing hairpins (CTRL/CMD+A to Select All).
3. Choose **Plug-ins/** ✂ > **TGTools** > **Align/Move Dynamics.** You will see the Align/Move Dynamics dialog box.
4. On the right, make sure **Hairpins** is checked (and uncheck any other items if you do not want them to align). Choose the appropriate option on the left. If you choose **Set To Value**, enter an offset from the bottom staff line in the Move Vertically text box.
5. Click **Go** to align your hairpins.

Hairpins Over System Breaks

To create a crescendo or decrescendo over a system break (from the end of one system to the beginning of the next):

1. Simply double-click where you want the hairpin to begin, and drag it down to the next system.
2. When you release the mouse button, there will be a break in the hairpin lines at the beginning of the second system as shown in Figure 6.9.

Figure 6.9

Drag the right editing handle of a hairpin down to extend it across a system break.

3.   You can drag a hairpin over as many systems as there are on a page. The width of the opening on each one can be adjusted independently.

Angled Hairpins

All hairpins are automatically constrained when created so that they are perfectly horizontal. To create angled hairpins:

1.   Right/CTRL+click a hairpin handle and uncheck Make Horizontal.
2.   Click the hairpin's primary handle and then drag the rightmost or leftmost diamond editing handle up or down.

Generating Hairpins Between Expressions Automatically (TGTools)

If you have already entered dynamic expressions into your score, you can use TGTools to easily extend crescendos or decrescendos between them automatically. Here's how:

NOTE:
This feature is available with the full version of TGTools available at tgtools.de.

1.   Click the Selection Tool .
2.   Select a region of your score containing dynamic expressions you want to extend hairpins between.
3.   Choose **TGTools** > **Music** > **Create Hairpins**. The Create Hairpins dialog box appears.
4.   Click **Go**. A hairpin extends between dynamic markings in the selected region. If you do not like the results, press CTRL+Z to undo. Then try again and specify values for Offset and Opening Width in the Create Hairpins dialog box. You can also choose to add hairpins between specific dynamic expressions in the dialog box.

Other Smart Shapes

There are a number of other Smart Shapes you can use for a variety of other purposes. These include trills, ottavas (8va/8vb), glissandos, bend hats and curves, brackets, lines, and custom shapes. These will all have the note- or measure-attached properties as described earlier in this chapter, as well as many of the same editing capabilities.

Trills and Trill Extensions

Trills can be entered with the Smart Shape Tool as well as the Articulation Tool ![tr], although with the Smart Shape Tool ![icon] you will be able to create an adjustable extension.

1. Click the Trill Tool **tr** in the Smart Shape palette. Then, double-click and drag to the right to create a trill indication with an extension.
2. Use the primary handle to move the whole figure around. Use the left and right handles to adjust the endpoints individually.

The Trill Extension Tool ![icon] in the Smart Shape palette can be used to indicate guitar tremolos as well as trill extensions. They can be edited just like regular trill Smart Shapes. To add an accidental at the beginning of a trill figure to indicate the pitch variation, use an articulation (already included in Finale's articulation library) or a Custom Smart Shape. You'll find more information on creating Custom Smart Shapes later in this section.

Ottavas (8va/8vb) and 15va/15vb

To tell the performer to transpose a section of music up or down an octave, an 8va or 8vb symbol is often used (see Figure 6.10). Both of these can be created with the Smart Shape 8va Tool. Simply double-click above a staff to enter an 8va, or below the staff to enter an 8vb. Take note of your mouse cursor because the arrow points to the staff to which the shape will be attached. You can extend the dash line over system breaks, and Finale will place the 8va or 8vb symbol in parentheses automatically at the beginning of each subsequent system. 8va and 8vb figures will always be measure-attached and apply to playback.

Figure 6.10
Click above the staff to enter an 8va; click below the staff to enter an 8vb.

Use the 15va Tool the same way as the 8va Tool. This figure is used to indicate a two-octave transposition from the written pitches.

If you are not satisfied with the text attached to default ottava or 15va/vb figures, you can choose your own. To change the attached text:

1. Choose **Smart Shape** > **SmartShape Options.** This opens the Smart Shape Options dialog box as seen in Figure 6.11.

Figure 6.11

Choose the font, character, style, and other Smart Shape attributes in the Smart Shape Options dialog box.

2. In the **Symbols** drop-down menu, choose the marking you want to edit. Then, click the **Set Font** button to choose the font of your new character.

3. Once you have chosen the font, size, and style, click **OK**.

4. Click the **Select** button to open the Symbol Selection dialog box.

5. Choose the character you would like to use, and click **Select**.

6. Click **OK** to return to the score. Create the Smart Shape you edited to review your changes.

Glissandi and Tab Slides

Glissandi are used to indicate a rapid slide through ascending or descending pitches. They appear as wavy lines between adjacent notes (see Figure 6.12). Creating these in Finale is easy. Click the Glissando Tool in the Smart Shape palette and double-click a note. Finale will automatically extend a glissando to the next note.

Tab slides are generally used in tablature notation to indicate a pitch change by sliding up or down the fretboard of a fretted instrument (see Figure 6.12). Enter these the same as you would a glissando.

Figure 6.12

Double-click to extend a glissando or tab slide to the next note.

When a glissando reaches a certain length, you will see the text "Gliss" or "Glissando" attached to the Smart Shape (depending on its length). To enter a glissando without this text

1. CTRL/OPTION+click the Glissando Tool in the Smart Shape palette to open the Smart Line Style selection dialog box.

2. Choose the regular wavy line (without text) and click Select. Now any glissando you enter will not include the attached text.

The endpoints of glissandos and tab slides can be adjusted relative to the noteheads to which they are attached on a document-wide scale. To specify placement of these items throughout your document.

1.   Select the SmartShape menu and choose Smart Shape Placement (see Figure 6.6).

2.   From the drop-down menu, choose either **Tab Slide** or **Glissando**. For tab slides, specify the type of tab slide from the list box on the left (depending on whether the notes are on staff lines or spaces, ascending or descending).

3.   Click the left and right endpoints to adjust the slant and length of glissandi and tab slides. Click the middle of the glissando or tab slide and drag to adjust the vertical placement.

4.   You can also enter specific values for the start and end point in the H: (Horizontal) and V: (Vertical) text boxes. Click **Reset** to revert back to the original default settings.

5.   Click **OK** to return to the score.

Changes made to tab slides and glissandi in the Smart Shape Placement dialog box apply to new Smart Shapes and existing Smart Shapes in the score that have not been edited (Finale will not make changes to tab slides or glissandi you have already adjusted manually). You can find more information on Tab Slide Smart Shapes in Chapter 8.

Bend Hats and Guitar Bends

Bend hats and curves are used to indicate a bend in pitch. To enter a bend hat:

1.   Click the Bend Hat Smart Shape, and double-click a note. Finale will extend the bend hat to the next note automatically (see Figure 6.13). You will see three diamond editing handles attached to the bend hat in addition to the primary handle.

2.   Drag the diamond handles on the ends of the bend hat to adjust the placement of the endpoints and drag the handle at the joint to adjust the angle.

3.   To create a bend hat that isn't bound to two notes, click the SmartShape menu and choose Attach to Measures. Then double-click and drag anywhere in the score.

Figure 6.13
Use bend hats to indicate a pitch bend.

The Guitar Bend Smart Shape was introduced in Finale 2003 and is used primarily for bend and release figures in guitar tablature notation. This is perhaps the smartest Smart Shape due to its ability to analyze the notation and create the appropriate pitch-change text for the existing notes as well as hide unnecessary notes. To enter a guitar bend in a tab staff, simply choose the Guitar Bend Smart Shape and double-click a fret number to create the guitar bend. (Learn more about entering tablature in Chapter 8). Finale will hide the following fret number and indicate the appropriate pitch change in text (see Figure 6.14).

Figure 6.14

Use the Guitar Bend Tool to create bend curves with text automatically generated to indicate the pitch variation.

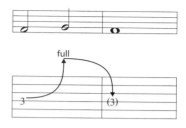

You can customize Finale's handling of guitar bends (generated text, font, etc.) with the Guitar Bend Options. Choose **SmartShape** > **Guitar Bend Options**. There is a more complete discussion of how to enter and edit guitar bends and how to create guitar tablature in Chapter 8.

Brackets and Lines

There are six remaining Smart Shape Tools for creating brackets and lines.

- The four bracket Smart Shapes (Bracket, Dashed Bracket, Double-ended bracket, and Dashed double-ended bracket) behave almost the same. With one of them selected, double-click and drag to create a horizontal bracket. Use the diamond editing handles to adjust the length and the primary handle to move it around.

- To create a line, click the Line ▬ or Dashed Line Tool ▦ , then double-click and drag anywhere in the score. Unlike brackets, lines can be drawn at any slope. Bracket and Line Smart Shapes are always measure-attached.

- Hold down SHIFT to constrain dragging in order to create a perfectly horizontal or vertical line.

There are several ways to customize brackets and lines throughout your document. Change the width, dash length, dash space, and length of bracket hooks in the Smart Shape Options dialog box.

1. Choose **Smart Shape** > **Smart Shape Options**. The Smart Shape Options dialog box appears (see Figure 6.11).

2. In the four text boxes on the right, you can specify line thickness, dash length, and dash space. These parameters affect both Bracket and Line Smart Shapes, as well as dashed curves. To change the length of the bracket hooks (the vertical lines on the ends of brackets), enter a new value in the Hook Length text box (of course, the Hook Length setting applies only to brackets).

3. Click **OK** to review changes in your score.

Custom Smart Shapes

There are a number of other available Smart Shapes that do not exist in the Smart Shape palette. To see a list of other Smart Shapes, CTRL/OPTION+click the Custom Line Tool 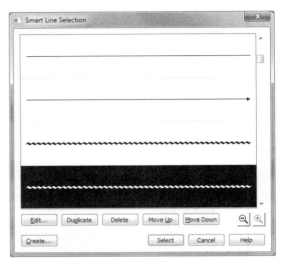 in the Smart Shape Palette. You will see the Smart Line Style Selection dialog box as seen in Figure 6.15.

Figure 6.15
Edit or create a smart line in the Smart Line Style Selection dialog box.

Here, there are a number of other Smart Shape Line styles available for you to choose from. They are basically specialized lines for figures not available in the Smart Shape palette. To use any of the following, click to highlight it, and then click the Select button. Double-click and drag in the score to create the figure you chose.

- Glissando: Choose a glissando with or without text. These are the same as regular glissandi.
- ℘ℯ𝒹. and ✳ (sustain): These figures are generally used to indicate the beginning and end of a sustained section of piano music. Many Custom Smart Lines, such as this one, do not contain a line at all, but displays a figure at the beginning and end of an "invisible" line. Also, notice the graphical pedal markings available here.
- Lines with arrowheads: These are just like regular lines, except with an arrowhead attached.
- Ritardando: Often, ritardandos are indicated with "rit." followed by a dashed horizontal line.
- Trills: Choose from a number of trill markings, set to indicate possible pitch variations with accidentals.
- Figures for Guitar Notation: Choose from a variety of figures for guitar notation, including harmonics (A.H., N.H.), mute indications (P.M.) and picking symbols, hammer-ons, and pull-offs. There will be more information on guitar notation in Chapter 8.

Like regular lines, custom lines are measure-attached. As the name of the tool suggests, you can edit any of the available lines, or create your own from scratch.

Creating Custom Smart Shapes

Create a custom Smart Shape for any type of line you need. Perhaps the most common Smart Shape is cresc. text followed by a dashed line. Below are steps. Before you begin, from the **Edit** menu (Mac: **Finale 2012** > **Preferences**), choose **Measurement Units** and then **Inches**.

1. Hold down the CTRL/OPTION key and click the Custom Line Tool [?] . The Smart Line Style Selection dialog box appears.

2. Click **Create**. You should now see the Smart Line Designer dialog box as shown in Figure 6.16.

Figure 6.16

Define the appearance and add text to a smart line in the Smart Line Designer dialog box.

3. Click the **Line Style** drop-down menu and choose **Dashed**. Notice the updated preview in the lower right.

4. Check **Horizontal**. You'll want to constrain to horizontal dragging while entering the crescendo markings in the score.

5. Now, increase the frequency of the dashes. Some find the default dashes a bit too long. For **Dash Length**, enter .04. For Space, enter .04 (inches). Notice that the preview in the lower right updates after leaving each text box.

6. Now, add the text. In the text section, at the bottom of this dialog box, click the **Edit** button for **Left Start** (since you'll want the text at the beginning of the line). The Edit Text box opens.

7. Type "Cresc.".

8. Most often, this type of marking is italicized. Hold down CTRL/CMD and press A to Select All.
9. Choose **Text** > **Style** > **Italic**. The text becomes italicized.
10. Click **OK**. You return to the Smart Line Style dialog box.
11. In the upper right, for Start H, check **After Text**.
12. Click **OK** and **Select** to return to the score.
13. Double-click and drag to create the marking anywhere in the score.

You can edit custom lines in the score just as you would a regular line. If you want to change the text, line thickness, dash length, etc.

1. CTRL/OPTION+click the Smart Line Tool. Your custom Smart Shape will now always appear in the Smart Line Style Selection dialog box for this document.
2. Click it and choose **Edit** to make any edits to the line.

If there is a custom line similar to the one you would like to create, you can save time by duplicating and then editing the smart line.

1. In the Smart Line Style Selection dialog box, click the Smart Line similar to the one you want to create and click the **Duplicate** button. A duplicate of the Smart Line will appear at the bottom of the list.
2. Click the duplicate Smart Line, and then click the **Edit** button to make the adjustments.

One additional benefit to Custom Smart Shapes is the ability to rotate text. If you need text to appear vertically, for example, create a Custom Smart Shape line and then create the shape vertically.

Copying Smart Shapes

When you copy music with the Selection Tool, Finale will copy all Smart Shapes along with the notation. You can, however, copy Smart Shapes independently from one area of your score to another.

1. Click the Selection Tool .
2. Choose **Edit** > **Edit Filter**. Click **None**.
3. Check **Smart Shapes** (Attached to Notes or Attached to Measures).
4. Click **OK**.
5. Select the region of your score containing the Smart Shapes you want to copy, and drag to the new measures (or CTRL/OPTION-click the first measure in the destination region, or CTRL/CMD+C the source region then CTRL/CMD+V the target).
6. The Smart Shapes copy to the new location.

Automatically Copy Smart Shapes to Rhythmically Identical Passages

You may have a recurring rhythms in your score that demands the same set of smart shapes at each occurrence throughout the piece. SmartFind and Paint allows you find and copy smart shapes to these passages automatically. To demonstrate this:

1. Fill a measure with a combination of eighth and quarter notes on different pitches with the Simple or Speedy Entry Tool.
2. Click the Selection Tool 🔣 and highlight this measure. Then hold down CTRL+ALT (Windows users), CTRL+OPTION (Mac users) and click the next measure. The Paste Multiple dialog box appears.
3. Type "10" and click **OK**. Now there are 11 measures containing the same rhythmic arrangement.
4. Click the Smart Shape Tool 🎵 and add some slurs to the original measure.
5. Click the Selection Tool again and highlight the measure containing the slurs.
6. Choose **Edit** > **SmartFind and Paint** > **Set SmartFind Source** (or press CTRL/CMD+F).
7. Now choose **Edit** > **SmartFind and Paint** > **Apply SmartFind and Paint** (or press CTRL/CMD+SHIFT+F). You will see the SmartFind and Paint dialog box shown in Figure 6.17.

Figure 6.17
Choose elements to copy to similar rhythmic passages in the Smart-Find and Paint dialog box.

8. Click the Find button and the measure containing the similar passage becomes highlighted.
9. Click **Paint** and the Smart Shapes appear on the notes just as they did in the original measure. This is also a great technique for copying Articulations and Expressions to identical rhythmic passages throughout your score.

Defining Repeats

Repeats are a common way to tell the performer to go back and play a section of music once, twice, or several more times. Often, a new ending is specified for each run through the same section of music. In notation, repeat barlines and text are used to indicate these repeated sections.

Basic Repeat Creation and Editing

Defining basic repeats in Finale is easy. To create a simple repeat with two repeat barlines, one at the beginning, and one at the end:

1. Click the Repeat Tool .
2. Highlight the region of your score that will be the repeated section (click the first measure, then SHIFT+click the last measure of the desired region).
3. Right/CTRL+click the region and choose **Create Simple Repeat**.

The selected region now begins and ends with a repeat barline and will play back correctly. To create a repeat with a first and second ending is almost as easy:

1. Click the Repeat Tool .
2. Highlight the measure (or measures) you would like to include in the first ending.
3. Right/CTRL+click the highlighted area and choose **Create First and Second Ending** (see Figure 6.18).

Figure 6.18
Create a first and second ending easily using a context menu.

4. Now, context-click a measure and choose **Create Forward Repeat Bar** to add a forward repeat. This first and second repeat will play back correctly. If you do not add a forward repeat prior to the endings, Finale will automatically skip back to the beginning of the score after playing the first ending.

NOTE:
Feel free to add or delete measures within repeated sections. Finale updates the playback definitions for you automatically.

To see the playback route, choose **Repeat** > **Check Repeats**. The Check Repeats dialog box appears as shown in Figure 6.19.

Figure 6.19
To see the playback route of your score after adding repeats, use the Check Repeats dialog box.

Deleting Repeats

To delete repeat indications from any region of your score:

1. Click the Repeat Tool ▤ .
2. Highlight the handles on the repeat text or brackets you want to remove.
3. Right/CTRL-click the highlighted repeats and choose DELETE.

Repeat definitions in the highlighted area of your score are removed along with any playback information.

Assigning Repeat Brackets and Text to Staves

It is common to display the repeat brackets and text on the top staff, and not on subsequent staves (in a piano grand staff for example). Before you assign your repeats, assign these repeat items to appear on one staff and not others (or any number of staves) in the Document Options dialog box. For example, to display the ending brackets you just created on the top staff only, do the following:

1. Choose **Document** > **Document Options** > **Repeats**. (Or, **Repeat** > **Repeat Options**.) Document Options-Repeats appears as shown in Figure 6.20.

Figure 6.20

Assign ending brackets to staves in the Edit Ending dialog box.

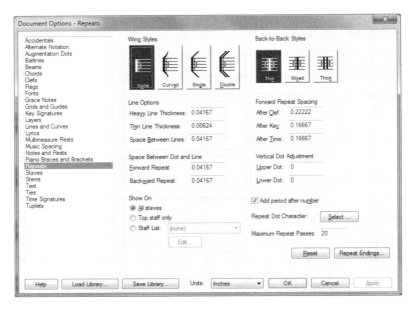

2. Under **Show On**, select **Top Staff Only**. (Note that here you can also choose **Staff List** and select a staff list to assign the ending brackets to certain staves (or click edit to modify or create a staff list).

3. Click **OK** to return to the score. The ending bracket will appear on the top staff only for any future repeats you add to the score.

TIP:
You can also choose to hide all repeat endings and text for a specific staff. Click the Staff Tool and double-click a staff. Under Items to Display, uncheck **Endings and Text Repeats** and click **OK**. These settings can also be applied for individual repeats in the Edit Ending dialog box.

Assigning Text Repeats and Repeat Endings to Specific Staves

You can choose to assign repeat markings to specific staves using *Staff Lists*, which are virtually identical to Score Lists in function.

Before adding any repeats:

1. Choose **Document** > **Document Options** and then choose **Repeats**.
2. Under **Show On**, choose **Staff List**.
3. Either choose and existing staff list or click **Edit** to define your own.

Click **OK**. Now, all repeats you will enter will use this staff list automatically.

Assigning Multiple Endings

Assigning second, third, fourth, or more endings could not be easier. For this example, we'll create a repeat with three endings like the one shown in Figure 6.21.

Figure 6.21

Use context menus to easily create multiple endings.

1. Start a new default document (**File** > **New** > **Default Document**) then click the Repeat Tool ▤ .
2. Right/CTRL+click the desired first ending measure (or selected measure region) and choose Create Ending. The Create Ending dialog box appears. Click **OK** to add the first ending.
3. Right/CTRL+click the measure following the first ending and choose **Create Ending**.
4. Click **OK**. The second ending appears and a "2." is placed in the ending bracket automatically. Click **OK**.
5. Right/CTRL+click the measure following the second ending and choose **Create Ending**.
6. Since this is the third and final ending of our repeat, we'll remove the backward repeat bar. Uncheck **Create Backward Repeat Bar** and click **OK**. The third ending appears in the score. Finale adds a "3." in the ending bracket automatically. Add as many endings as you like using the same method, Finale configures playback for you automatically. (Choose **Repeat** > **Check Repeats** to review the playback route).

Assigning Multiple Passes

When an ending is intended to be repeated multiple times, the passes are numbered beneath the bracket as shown in Figure 6.22.

Figure 6.22

Specify multiple passes of the same ending in the Edit Ending dialog box.

To create an ending with multiple passes:

1. Click the Repeat Tool ▤ .
2. Right/CTRL+click the desired first ending measure (or selected measure region) and choose **Create Ending**. The Create Ending dialog box appears.

3.   Type the passes in the Ending Number(s) text box at the top separated by commas (e.g. 1,2,3).

4.   Click **OK**. The passes appear beneath the ending bracket. If you wanted to place alternate text, such as *Fine*, you could use the Alternate Text in Ending instead.

D.S. al Coda/Fine

It is common for repeat markings to indicate a return back to a sign (D.S. and Segno) and then jump to a Coda. Use the following steps to quickly enter the D.S., Segno, and Coda. After following these steps you will be able to create a score containing all of the repeat symbols in the following musical example (see Figure 6.23).

Figure 6.23

First and second ending repeat example with D.S. al Coda.

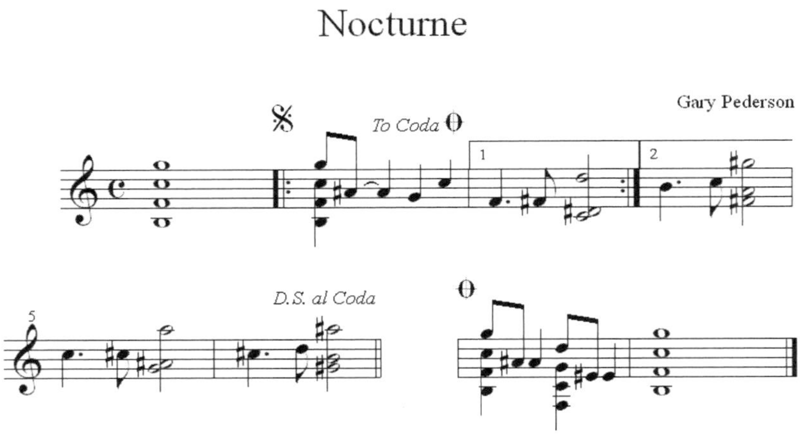

I recommend using the following steps after the measure layout of the score has been finalized. (The Create Coda System plug-in does some things behind the scenes that can be a pain to undo manually.)

1.   Highlight the desired coda measure(s). (In the above example, this would be measures 7 and 8). Then, note the measure numbers of the segno, the *To Coda*, and *D.S./D.C.* markings - where you would like them to appear.

2.   Choose **Plug-ins/** ✂ **> Measures > Create Coda System**. The Create Coda System dialog box appears as shown in Figure 6.24.

Figure 6.24
Use the Create Coda System plug-in to quickly create a coda system, to coda, and segno.

3. Enter the values you recorded in this dialog box. Figure 6.24 is configured to result in the Figure 6.23 example (measures 7 and 8 highlighted).
4. Click **OK**. The markings appear in the score and the coda system is separated from the previous measure. (If something doesn't look right, press CTRL/CMD-Z to undo).

Creating Custom Text Repeats

In addition to using the available text repeats, you can create your own or edit the already available ones.

1. Click the Repeat Tool ▦ , and then double-click a measure.
2. Click **Create** to open the Repeat Designer dialog box.
3. Enter the text of your repeat marking here (click **Set Font** to change the font, size, or style). You can use the # character to indicate a customizable measure number or symbol for the text repeat, depending on settings you will make in the Text Repeat Assignment dialog box.
4. Click **OK** to return to the Repeat Selection dialog box. From now on, the repeat text you created will appear in this dialog box. Like articulations, expressions, and other items, you can transfer text repeats between documents by saving and opening a library (**File** > **Save/Load Library**).

Resolving Infinite Loops

After defining the repeats as described in this chapter, they will play correctly. However, playback of text repeats added to the score individually need to be defined manually (see "Repeats (barlines and text indications)" in the Finale User Manual). If you do this, it is quite possible to unintentionally define infinite loops, which must be resolved for playback to function properly. If you find your score containing repeats that play the same section many times (more than intended), your repeats have been defined to loop infinitely. To identify and fix this problem:

1. Click the Repeat Tool .

2. Choose **Repeats** > **Check Repeats**. The Check Repeats dialog box appears. Any infinite loops will be listed several times. Note the final measure of any infinite loops, then click Done.

3. Double-click the backward repeat text or barline in the measure(s).

4. In the Backward Repeat Bar assignment or Text Repeat Assignment dialog box, you can edit the Target repeat or Measure number as well as the Repeat Action and number of Total Passes.

> **TIP:**
> Note that there is a limit to the number of times repeats are allowed to loop (to prevent infinite loops). Choose **Repeat** > **Repeat Options**. The value entered for **Multiple Repeat Passes** specifies the greatest number of times a section is allowed to repeat.

Play Nth Time Only

You can tell Finale to play back at a specific volume, tempo, or even patch number (sound) for the first, second, or third pass only. To do this:

1. Click the Expression Tool *mf* and double-click at the beginning of a repeated section. The Expression Selection dialog box opens.

2. Choose the **Technique** category. Click **Create** to open the Expression Designer.

3. In the text box, enter a description of the playback definition you are entering ("Play 1st time only," for example).

4. If you don't want this expression to print, highlight the text, and choose **Text** > **Style** > **Hidden**.

5. Click the **Playback** tab.

6. For **Type**, click the drop-down menu and choose **Key Velocity**.

7. For **Effect**, enter the value of change. For this example, enter 0 (zero - for silence).

8. For **Play Only on Pass**, enter the number of the pass for which you want this expression to affect playback. In this example, enter 2. The second time these measures are played, the notes will be silent.

9. Click **OK** then **Assign** to return to the score.

10. You will notice that on the second time through the repeated area, the notes do not sound on this staff. The playback definitions of expressions affect channels. To make sure that this expression affects only the staff you intend, make sure all of your staves are set to their own channel in the Score Manager. You'll also notice this staff will

continue to be silent after that point, which is why you need to add another expression that contains a key velocity greater than 0.

11. Double-click a measure after the repeated area or in your second ending. When the Expression Selection appears, choose the **Technique** category and click **Create**. Choose **Text** > **Style** > **Hidden,** and type the desired text. Then click the **Playback** tab.

12. For **Type**, choose **Key Velocity** and enter a value greater than 0 and less than 127, such as 64. Note that the dynamic markings in your document are already assigned a key velocity, so you may use a dynamic instead. Click **OK** then **Assign** to return to the score.

Click the Play button in the playback controls to hear your results. You'll find a more complete discussion of the playback capabilities of the Expression Tool in Chapter 14.

7
Multiple-Instrument Scores

In a previous edition of this book, I introduced this chapter as one that "demonstrates the skills you would need to effectively scramble your score beyond all recognition." I am pleased to report that this is no longer the case. Because of updates made last year to Finale 2011, empty staves can be hidden with impunity and moving or reordering staves is accomplished with far more ease and almost no fear. Power users upgrading from Fianle 2010: if you're afraid that MakeMusic removed your crafty and ingenious workarounds, there is nothing to worry about. You can still do all the crazy stuff you did before (hide staves with notes, etc.). It's just harder to do these things *accidentally*.

In the most recent chapter of staff drama, the Score Manager was introduced in 2012, which again revolutionizes the way staves are handled. The Score Manager is kind of like a spreadsheet that lists your score instruments, all their visual properties (clef, transposition, style), and also their playback properties (VST/AU or MIDI sound, channel, bank, etc.), integrating functions previously available in the Instrument List. In other words, Finale now knows what an "instrument" is (vs. loose staves set to channels), and this will mean very good things for your workflow.

While working with scores containing multiple instruments is easier than ever, it will still require the exploration of several tools, including the Staff, Measure, Page Layout, and Expression Tools. You will learn how to position, view, and reorder staves, manage barlines, group staves in brackets, remove empty staves from systems, add expressions to any number of selected staves, and perform a variety of other tricks that apply specifically to multiple-instrument documents. Then, you will learn how to manage an inevitable result of the multiple-instrument score: parts.

Finale aficionados, working with instrument staves in Finale 2012 will feel like a walk in the park. New Finale users: your progress will move along swiftly without any idea what all the cheering is about, and that is exactly as it should be.

Here's a summary of what you will learn in this chapter:

- How to work with multiple staves
- How to work with staff groups
- How to enter expressions in documents with multiple staves
- Other tricks for multiple stave scores

Working with Multiple Staves

A Finale document can contain any number of instrument staves. Finale handles new scores and the addition of new instruments automatically as long as they are added with the Setup Wizard or the Score Manager. Refer back to "Starting a Score with the Document Setup Wizard" on page 178 for information on starting a new document, and "Adding, Removing, and Changing Instruments" on page 178 for information on accomplishing these basic tasks with the Score Manager. This section focuses on tasks like inserting and reordering staves in any existing document, as well as viewing and editing them most efficiently.

To prepare for this section:

1. Open a new Default Document (**File** > **New** > **Default Document**).
2. Choose **View** > **Page View**. Page View works best for demonstrating staff handling in Finale 2012. In Scroll View, staves can be dragged (using the staff handles) to whatever position works best for viewing and editing, but staff spacing in Scroll View does not affect staff spacing in Page View or for printing.

TIP:
Staff spacing in Page View can be reset to the spacing defined in Scroll View using the "Set to Scroll View Spacing" command in the Respace Staves dialog box (**Staff** > **Respace Staves**).

Customizing the Score Order

Finale 2012 is designed to handle the score order automatically with the help of a few commands in the Score Manager (**Window** > **Score Manager**). At any point, you can instantly reconfigure the order of all score instruments from, say, a Marching Band order to a Concert Band order, using the Score Order drop-down menu. Simply choose the desired order and your staves update instantly. If you haven't changed Finale's default Score Manager settings, as you add or delete instruments, Finale magically renumbers the instruments in sections and adjusts the group brackets accordingly. For example, in a concert band score with three trombones, add a trombone and you will see "Trombone 4" added to the trombone section. With all this automation, let's focus on a few of the cases that require you to actually do something. For example, let's say you actually wanted to add "Trombone 2" to the section instead of "Trombone 4." In this case you need to shuffle things around a bit.

To manually reorder staves:

1. Choose **Window** > **Score Manager**. Take note of the current Score Order.
2. Click to the left of the instrument name and drag the instrument into place. Release the mouse button when the indicator line appears in the desired spot.

Figure 7.1

Reorder staves manually by dragging them in the Score manager.

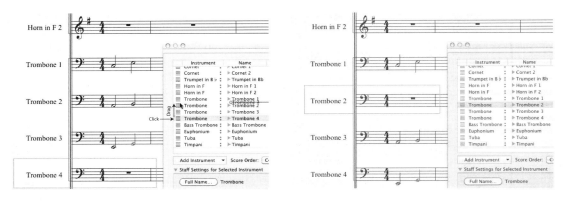

3. Notice the Score Order has changed to **Custom**, which means you now have complete control of the score order. If you would like Finale to handle the score order (for adding instruments etc.), you can always click the **Score Order** drop-down and choose one of the available orders.

NOTE:

For information on manually repositioning staves, see "Changing the Distance Between Staves (for printing)" on page 179.

Respacing Staves

You may want to increase or decrease the space between all your staves to make more room for music on ledger lines, slurs, expressions, or other score elements.

1. To respace specific staves, select a potion of all staves in the system(s) you want to respace. To respace all staves, select nothing and move to step 2.

2. Choose **Staff** > **Respace Staves** to invoke the Respace Staves dialog box (see Figure 7.2).

Figure 7.2

Set the distance between staves in the Respace Staves dialog box.

3. Click **Scale To** and type "90" in the text box to tell Finale to respace the staves at 90 percent of their original spacing.

4. Click **OK** to return to the score. Notice the staves respace proportionally bringing them closer together.

To increase the space, follow the same instructions except, in the Respace Staves dialog box, enter a value over 100 in the Scale To text box. If you know a precise value, choose Set To and enter the space between each staff in the corresponding text box (the default is 1.111 inches). To change the unit of measurement, choose **Edit** (Mac: **Finale 2012** > **Preferences**) > **Measurement Units**.

Resizing Staff Systems

In Page View, if you add many staves to your score, they may end up running beyond the lower page margin. If this is the case, first try respacing the staves so the system takes up less vertical space. If you do this, and find that after all staves fit on the page, there is not enough space between the staves to fit music and/or expressions and other markings, you will need to resize the systems (reduce them). To do this:

1. Respace the staves so there is an adequate amount of space between them.

2. Click the Resize Tool , and then click an area between two staves in the system. (Or, context-click a staff and choose **Resize System**). The Resize Staff System dialog box appears as shown in Figure 7.3.

Figure 7.3

Resize systems and/or staff heights in the Resize Staff System dialog box.

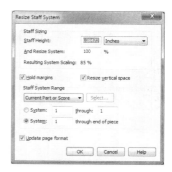

3. After **And Resize System,** enter a new percentage. For example, type "80" in this box to reduce the system to 80 percent of its original size.

TIP:
If you change the staff height in the Resize Staff System dialog box, it will be further adjusted by the system resize percentage. The cumulative system scaling is listed below after **Resulting System Scaling**. Use a staff height of .33333 inches or 96 EVPUs if you want to enter the percentage directly.

4. You will probably want to resize all systems in your score at once. In the **Staff System Range** section, select **System 1 Through End of Piece**.

5.   Click **OK** to return to the score and review the system reduction. You may need to experiment with several different system reductions to find the one that fits best on the page.

NOTE:
When you choose to scale the spacing percentage in the Resize Staff System dialog box, Finale will retain the original proportions of the space between staves. To space the staves evenly, choose **Staff** > **Respace Staves** and enter a value (in your current measurement unit) in the **Set To** field. Once your staves are evenly spaced, you may find it more convenient to fine tune your staff spacing within systems by scaling to a percentage.

Working with Barlines

When you edit the appearance of barlines, the changes you make automatically apply to affected measures for all staves in the system. They can also have implications on parts extracted from the score, such as breaking multi-measure rests. To create double, dashed, solid, or other barline styles, use the Measure or Selection Tool context menu. Right/CTRL+click a measure to open the context menu. Choose Barline > [barline style] to edit the barline instantly. To make more advanced barline changes:

1.   First click the Measure Tool , then double-click a measure to open the Measure Attributes dialog box as seen in Figure 7.4.

Figure 7.4
Choose a barline style in the Measure Attributes dialog box.

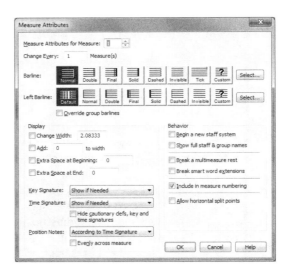

2.   Choose the barline (top row) and click **OK** to return to the score. The new barline appears at the end of the measure you clicked.

Creating and Editing Barlines

If you can't find the barline you want to use, create your own.

1. With the Measure Tool 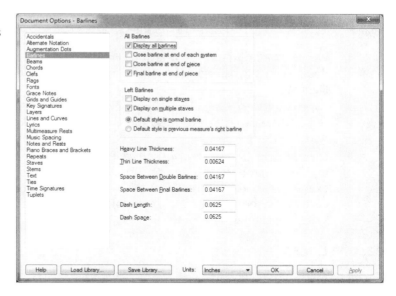 selected, double-click a measure. The Measure Attributes dialog box appears.

2. In the top row of barline icons, click the rightmost option (the Custom Barline icon). The Shape Selection dialog box appears.

3. Click the **Create** button. The Shape Designer dialog box appears. Use the tools in this window to design your own custom barline.

4. Once you have finished, click **OK, Select,** and **OK** to return to the score. Your custom barline now appears on every staff in that measure.

To manage barlines throughout your document, use the Barlines portion of the Document Options dialog box. Choose **Document** > **Document Options** and select **Barlines**. The Barline options appear as seen in Figure 7.5.

Figure 7.5

Make document-wide settings for barlines in the Barlines category of the Document Options.

Here are some common ways to edit barlines using the Document Options. These settings apply to barlines throughout the document:

- Uncheck **Display All Barlines** to hide all barlines in the score.
- By default there is usually a final barline at the end of the document. To remove this, uncheck **Final Barline at End of Piece**.
- Check **Display on Single Staves** to place a barline on the left edge of each single-staff system. This is particularly useful for lead sheets.
- Use the text boxes to control the thickness of barlines, distance between double barlines and the length and frequency of dashes on dashed barlines.

Adjusting Measure Width Manually

You can use the Measure Tool to increase or decrease the width of measures.

1. Select the Measure Tool.

2. Click and drag or use the arrow keys to nudge a barline handle horizontally. Notice music in the measure respaces proportionally in all staves as the width of the measure changes. Also note that note-attached items will also respace along with the notes. You can use this method to give a measure more space for chord symbols, lyrics, and expressions.

NOTE:
You may notice two handles on some barlines. The lower one can be used to assign spacing for beats in the measure with a "Beat Chart." You can find more information on Beat Chart Spacing under "The Beat Chart and Spacing with the Measure Tool" on page 248.

You can also set the width of measures to a specific value.

1. With the Measure Tool ▦ selected, highlight a measure or region of measures. Then, double-click the highlighted region to open the Measure Attributes dialog box (see Figure 7.5).

2. For **Change Width**, enter the amount of space you would like between barlines in the selected measures. You can also add space between barlines by entering a value for **Add_to Width**.

3. Click **OK** to return to the score and review changes. If you don't see a change, your measures may be *locked* (see below) so that they will not reflow across systems (for example, if there are three measures in a system, and you set the measure width for each to .5 inches, Finale needs to be able to reconfigure the number of measures per system to compensate for the extra space).

Measure Locks

Whenever measures are arranged into systems manually, the system is "locked" from any Automatic Music Spacing changes. To view system locks, choose **View** > **Show** > **Page Layout Icons**. A padlock icon appears to the right of locked systems.

1. To unlock a system, choose the Selection Tool ▨ .

2. Highlight the system and adjacent systems. Choose **Utilities** > **Unlock Systems**. (Then you can go back and change the measure width with the Measure Tool ▦ as described in the steps above.)

TIP:
Use the Page Layout Tool 🗋 to view and adjust system margins. See "Customizing Systems" on page 304.

Adding Double Barlines at Key Changes Automatically

In conventional notation, you will usually find a double barline at every key change. In Finale, instead of using the Measure Attributes to add these double barlines for each key change, you can do it for your whole score automatically with the Automatic Barlines plug-in.

To apply these changes to a region of your score:

1. Choose the Selection Tool 🔲 , and select a region of your score (for the whole document, no selection is necessary).
2. Choose **Plug-ins/** ✗ **> Measures > Automatic Barlines**.
3. Double barlines appear at key changes in the region you selected, or throughout the document.

Customizing Staff Viewing: Staff Sets

With large scores, you may not be able to see all staves at the same time while entering or editing your music. Or, to see all your staves, the view percentage needs to be too small to effectively work with them. With Staff Sets, you can specify certain staves for viewing and hide staves you don't need to see.

To demonstrate this, let's start a new score:

1. **Choose File > New > Document with Setup Wizard.**
2. Under **Select an Ensemble**, choose **Brass Choir.**
3. Click **Next, Next, Next,** then **Finish** to complete the setup wizard and open the new score.

Let's say you are beginning the piece with a trumpet and tuba duet. Depending on your screen resolution, monitor size, and view percentage, both of these staves may not appear on your screen at the same time (if they do, let's pretend they are spaced too far apart). To isolate the trumpet and tuba staves for viewing:

1. Move to Scroll View (if you are in Page View). Choose **View > Scroll View.**
2. With the Staff Tool 🔲 selected, hold down SHIFT and click the handles of the staves you want to isolate. In this case, the "Trumpet in Bb 1" and "Tuba" staves. If you can't see the Tuba staff, use the scroll bar on the right to move the score vertically.
3. While holding down the CTRL/OPTION key, click the View menu.
4. Continue holding down CTRL/OPTION and choose **Program Staff Set > Staff Set 1.**

The display now shows the trumpet and tuba staves only. You can use this Staff Set to enter and edit music as you would normally. To see the full score again, choose **View** > **Select Staff Set** > **All Staves**. You can program up to eight staff sets, each with any number of staves. Select any staff set you program by choosing **View** > **Select Staff Set**.

TIP:
For even greater control over staff viewing (including the ability to define a view percentage for your staff sets), try the Patterson Staff Sets plug-in. This plug-in is part of the Patterson Plug-in Collection available for download from Robert Patterson's Web site at robertgpatterson.com. You can find more information regarding the Staff Sets plug-in under "Patterson Beams Plug-In" on page 274.

Staff Groups

Staves in large scores are generally divided into groups of instrumental families (see Figure 7.6). All staves in a group are enclosed by a bracket to the left of the score that usually extend through all staves of a group throughout the score.

Figure 7.6
Group Brackets

Often, within each group there are also secondary groups, such as the secondary Violin group in Figure 7.6. Whenever you use the Setup Wizard to begin a new score or use the Score Manager to add instruments, Finale enters these group indications for you automatically. In this section, you will learn how to create your own group definitions and edit the ones Finale creates for you.

Start by defining groups for a score from scratch. To prepare for this section:

1. Open a new Default Document (**File** > **New** > **Default Document**).
2. Move to Page View (**View** > **Page View**). Then, choose **Window** > **Score Manager** and add 3 Blank Staves.
3. Close the Score Manager.
4. Choose the Selection Tool 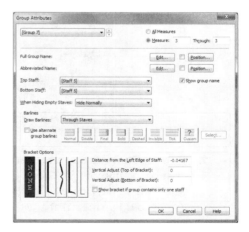, then click the blue bracket to the left of the first system and press DELETE. The bracket disappears. We now have a clean bracket-free canvas to work with.
5. Change your view percentage so all staves are visible. Try 75%: **View** > **Zoom** > **Custom Zoom 3 (75%)**.

Adding Groups

To add a group:

1. Choose the Staff Tool .
2. Choose **Staff** > **Groups and Brackets** > **Add**. The Group Attributes dialog box appears as shown in Figure 7.7.

Figure 7.7
Define the enclosed staves, group name, and bracket style for a group in the Group Attributes dialog box.

From this dialog box, you will be able to create and manage all group definitions. Let's say you need to create a "Strings" group containing the top four staves.

3. In the Group Attributes, click the **Edit** button for **Full Group Name**. The Edit Text dialog box appears. Type the name of the group here. Type "Strings." In the future, you may want to highlight the text and use the Text menu to edit the font size and style of the group name.
4. Click **OK** to return to the **Group Attributes**.
5. Click the **Edit** button for **Abbreviated Group Name**. Type "Str."

6.   Click **OK** to return to the Group Attributes.

7.   For Staff:, leave the setting [Staff 1] since the top staff in the score is the top staff of the group.

8.   For **Through,** leave the setting [Staff 4] since it is the bottom staff in the group.

9.   For **Draw Barlines,** leave the setting at **Through Staves** (this is most common). Use this setting in the future to specify barlines only on staves (for choral music) or Mensur-striche (only between staves) barlines.

10. In the **Bracket Options** section, choose the style of your bracket. For now, choose the bracket second from the right (the straight bracket with curved hooks).

11. Place a checkmark on **Show Group Name.**

12. Click **OK** to return to the score.

You will see a bracket (blue by default) to the left of the four staves, and barlines through them. You should also see the text "Strings" to the left of the group bracket on the first system and "Str." to the left of the second system. The abbreviated group name you define in Group Attributes will appear on the second and all subsequent systems.

Now, let's say you want to add a secondary bracket to the top two staves as if they were both violins.

1.   With the Staff Tool selected, hold down SHIFT and click to the left of both staves (so they are both selected).

CAUTION:
As of Finale 2011, groups are assigned to measure regions, which is especially helpful for multiple movements. Be sure to check the measure region in the Measure Attributes dialog box to verify you are adding measures to the desired systems.

2.   Choose **Staff > Group and Bracket > Add.** The Group Attributes dialog box appears. Notice the number for **Group ID:.** Whenever you choose **Add Group and Bracket** from the Staff menu, Finale will begin a new group definition. You can use the arrows here (or drop-down menu) at any time to move between group definitions. Text is often unnecessary for secondary group brackets, so you can leave the **Name** and **Abbreviated Name** alone.

3.   For **Staff,** [Staff 1] should be selected, and for **Through,** [Staff 2] (based on your selection earlier).

4.   In the **Bracket Options** section, choose the rightmost bracket (the thin one with perpendicular hooks). This is the most common secondary bracket figure.

5.   Finale will always leave the same amount of space between the left edge of the system and the group bracket by default. Since you want this bracket to the left of the existing one, enter a greater value in the Distance from Left Edge of Staff text box. You can also

adjust the bracket length in this section if necessary, though the defaults should be fine.

6. Click **OK** to return to the score. Click and drag the bracket to reposition if necessary using one of the two bracket handles.

The secondary group bracket appears to the left of the main group bracket. You can use the above methods to enter any number of group and secondary group definitions into a score, specifying the appropriate text, top and bottom staff, bracket style, and positioning for each group.

In the score, drag or nudge text and bracket handles to position them manually. To further edit any group bracket, double-click a group handle The Group Attributes dialog box will open, where you can modify its definition.

To delete a group, as well as the barline settings of the group, click its handle in the score and press the DELETE key.

Removing Barlines Between Staves

You can break barlines between any two staves, regardless of the group definition. To do this:

1. Double-click the lower of two staves connected by barlines. The Staff Attributes dialog box appears.
2. Check **Break Barlines Between Staves,** and click **OK** to return to the score. Barlines will no longer connect the two staves.

Expressions and Text Repeats in Multiple-Stave Documents

Working with multiple-staff scores requires some additional decisions; for example, do I place this marking on all staves, the top staff, or the top staff of each instrumental group? But I definitely want this marking on all my parts...When this series of thoughts crosses your mind, think assignment lists and score lists; both designed for this.

To demonstrate the need for both of these, it is important to remember there are essentially two types of expressions: Expressions that apply to a single staff (dynamics, expressive text, technique text), and expressions that apply to the full score (tempo marks, tempo alterations, and rehearsal marks). Tempo markings and rehearsal marks are universal, affect the performance of the whole ensemble, and (almost) always appear on every part. It is a rare composition that designates one tempo for the flute part and another for the tuba. And, while a f may appear on every staff of the score at a certain measure, each dynamic marking always applies only to its staff, and always appears on both the full score and the part. Therefore, while Finale allows you to easily assign both of these expression types to multiple staves, it offers two paradigms, each considering the nature of one these two expression functions.

- **Score Lists** (called Staff Lists pre-Finale 2011) are available for tempo indications and rehearsal marks, and used to hide expressions that apply to the full score from certain staves. Often, these expressions appear on the top staff of the score and on all parts.
- **Assignment Lists** (added in Finale 2009) are used for dynamics, expressive text, and technique text, and are used to identify the staves to which an expression should be added, such as all the staves of an instrumental section.

To prepare for this section, use the same multiple-staff document you have been working with. You could also begin a new document and add several staves.

Assigning Expressions to Multiple Staves

Use the following techniques to assign dynamics, expressive text, and technique text to multiple staves:

1. Choose the Expression Tool ![mf] .
2. Hold down the expression's metatool key, we'll use 4 (for f), and click a measure in the top staff. A f appears below the staff and its handle is selected.
3. Hold down CTRL/OPTION and press the down arrow a couple times. Finale adds the expression to the subsequent staves. Use the up arrow to add a selected expression to the previous staff.

Use the above procedure to easily add any dynamic, expressive text, or technique text expression to adjacent staves. You can quickly add an expression to many staves this way and then go back and delete the ones you don't need. Or, if you would like to designate specific groups of staves for expression entry, use assignment lists, explained next.

Assigning Expressions to Multiple Staves with Assignment Lists

Assignment lists are simply lists of staves you can choose from while adding expressions. For example, if your brass section generally plays at the same dynamic level, you might setup an assignment list that includes all of your brass instruments to easily apply dynamics to these staves at once. Remember, assignment lists are only used for dynamics, expressive text and technique text (as well as the Misc. category and others you may add duplicated from these categories).

To define and use Assignment lists:

1. Choose the Expression Tool ![mf] .
2. Double-click a measure in the top staff. The Expression Selection dialog box appears.
3. Choose the **Dynamics** category and click the f expression once to select it.
4. Click the drop-down arrow to the right of the **Assign** button and choose **Assign to Staves**. The Assign to Staves dialog box appears. (See Figure 7.8).

Figure 7.8

Use the Assign to Staves dialog box to specify staves for expression entry.

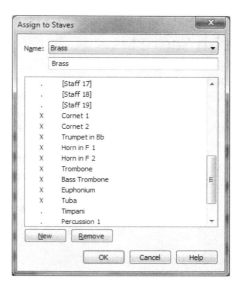

5. Type a descriptive name to replace "(New Assignment List)," in this case, we'll use "Brass."
6. Click to the left of each instrument staff you would like to designate for expression entry.
7. Click **OK** to assign the f expression to the staves you selected. This assignment list has also been saved for future use.
8. Double-click the score again to open the Expression Selection dialog box.
9. Click the drop-down arrow next to the **Assign** button. Notice the new Assignment List is available at the bottom of this menu. Use it any time you want to assign the selected expression to the designated (in this case, brass) staves.

There are two ways to apply assignment lists. You can either:

- Choose the Assignment List in the Expression Selection dialog box. Or,
- Context-click an existing expression and choose Assign to Staves to open the Assign to Staves dialog box where you can choose any Assignment list.

NOTE:
Assignment lists are exclusively for quickly adding expressions to multiple staves. Changes to assignment lists do not apply to expressions thathave already been entered into the score.

Assigning Tempo and Rehearsal Marks to Specific Staves with Score Lists

Although it wasn't mentioned, we used score lists in Chapter 3 when you learned how to add rehearsal letters and tempo markings to the top staff only. Now, let's say you want to enter your tempo marks on the top staff of the score, and on the top staff of your brass section. In order to do this, we must change the Score List setting for the entire Tempo Marks category.

1. Choose **Document** > **Category Designer**. The Category Designer dialog box appears.
2. Choose the **Tempo Marks** category and click **Edit Category**. Score List options appear at the bottom of this dialog box. Finale allows you to define up to 8 Score Lists.
3. Click the **Score List** drop-down menu and choose **Score List 2** and click **Edit**. The Score Lists dialog box appears. See Figure 7.9.

Figure 7.9

Use the Score List dialog box to specify staves for tempo and rehearsal mark entry.

4. Give the Score List a descriptive name, I'll call it "My Tempo Marks." It is already set to appear on the top staff of the score and all the parts. But, I also want my tempo marks to appear on the top staff of the brass section, so, under score, I'll click the Trumpet staff.
5. Click **OK**. "My Tempo Marks" appears in the Score List drop-down menu.
6. Click **OK** to return to the score. Now, all tempo marks appear both on the top staff of the score, on the Trumpet in Bb staff of the score, and on all parts. Also note that if the "Cornet 1" staff is hidden due to optimization, the tempo mark will automatically appear on the next visible staff in the score.

Score List Expression Positioning

Drag the top expression to reposition all expressions in a score list uniformly, or drag the lower expressions to position them independently.

Copying Expressions

If you want to copy expressions to another area of your score, but not the notation, do this:

1. Click the Selection Tool .
2. Choose **Edit** > **Edit Filter**.
3. Click **None** then check one of the two expression check boxes (depending on the ones you want to copy) and click **OK**. (Score list expressions require a full stack selection to be copied.)
4. Select the measures (in any staff) containing the expressions and drag to the new location (or CTRL/OPTION+click). Or, select the source and press CTRL/CMD+C, then the destination and press CTRL/CMD+V. The expressions will appear in the new measures, and all score list information continues to apply.

Other Tricks for Multiple-Stave Scores

Here are some other tricks you can use while working with large scores.

Viewing Several Regions of Your Score on the Screen

If you are copying music between remote areas of your score, or referencing a different area during entry, you can avoid having to scroll back and forth between sections by using multiple windows.

1. Choose **Window** > **New Window**. Then, choose **Window** > **Tile Windows** (Windows: **Vertically** or **Horizontally**). A new window appears on your screen with the same score visible. Any changes you make to the score in one of these windows will apply to the other as well. These are just two views of the same score.
2. You can scroll to any region of the score independently, or even set one view to Scroll View and the other to Page View (see Figure 7.10).

Figure 7.10

Use multiple windows to see any combination of views for the same score, or to view more than one document at the same time.

You can use as many windows as you like to view your score on-screen.

Adding Cue Notes Automatically

While working on a score with many staves, you may want to add cue notes of existing music in another staff. Add cue notes to any number of staves in your score automatically with the Create Cue Notes plug-in.

1. Press ESC to choose the Selection Tool, and highlight the region of your score containing the original notes.

2. Choose **Plug-ins/** > **Scoring and Arranging** > **Add Cue Notes**. The Add Cue Notes dialog box appears as shown in Figure 7.11.

Figure 7.11

Assign cue notes to staves and edit their appearance in the Add Cue Notes dialog box.

3. From the drop-down menu, choose the layer of the original music. Then, hold down the CTRL/CMD key and click each staff you want to add cue notes to.

4. Type the name of the cue notes (the part/staff name of the original notes).

5. Choose the layer you wish Finale to place the cue notes into and click **OK**. They will also be reduced to 75% of their original size (or the percentage specified).

TIP:
The Add Cue Notes plug-in will be unable to write cue notes over existing notes in the same layer. In the Add Cue Notes window, be sure **Write the Cue In** is set to a layer that is not being used.

To scan your entire score and let Finale propose possible cue note locations, and then add them automatically, use the Smart Cue Notes plug-in.

1. Choose **Plug-ins/** ✗ > **Scoring and Arranging** > **Smart Cue Notes**.

2. Here, you can specify the length of cue notes and choose the number of seconds/measures required before a cue note is necessary. You can also choose the layer and percentage of the cue notes you are about to generate.

3. Click **Start Search** to scan the score. When the plug-in finds a stretch of rests that meet the requirements you have specified, you are prompted to create cue notes (see Figure 7.12).

Figure 7.12

Use the Smart Cue Notes plug-in to find appropriate cue note locations and add them automatically.

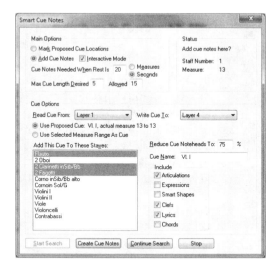

4. Note that the proposed cue note measures are highlighted. (Drag the dialog box to get a better look at the score). To specify destination staves, CTRL/CMD+click staves in the **Add this cue to these staves** section.

5. Click **Create Cue Notes**. Cue notes appear in the score and the plug-in searches for the next applicable region. (Click **Continue Search** to advance to the next region without creating cue notes).

Global Staff Attributes Plug-in

This plug-in is particularly useful while working with large scores.

1. Choose **Plug-ins/**  > **Scoring and Arranging** > **Global Staff Attributes** to display the Global Staff Attributes plug-in as seen in Figure 7.13. Here, you see many of the options available in the Staff Attributes dialog box. Apply these attributes to many or all staves of your document at once.

Figure 7.13

Assign staff attributes to several staves at once by using the Global Staff Attributes plug-in.

2. In the list of staves, select all staves you want to affect (CTRL/CMD+click to choose non-contiguous staves). Then make any desired changes in the **Options** and **Items to Display** sections to modify all selected staves.

3. In the Group Attributes portion of this dialog box, you can apply settings for groups on a global basis as well. Select the group(s) you want to change, and use the check boxes to show/hide brackets on single staves and show/hide group names for the selected groups. Click the **Set Font** button to select the font, size, and style for staff names or group names.

4. Click **Apply** to update your score without leaving the Global Staff Attributes, or click **OK** to apply settings and return to the score.

Working with Linked Parts

Along with multiple-staff scores comes the distinct possibility that parts will need to be prepared and printed. Fortunately, one of Finale's greatest time-savers it its ability to update parts automatically as you edit the score (or vise versa). This mechanism is called "Linked Parts" and was introduced back in Finale 2007.

Here are the basic principles:

- **A part is simply a representation of an instrument from the main score.** It is usually a single staff, but can be multiple staves (for piano, etc.). Parts can be created, deleted, or redefined at any time and are always embedded in the score document (available from the Document Menu).
- **The notation of the part always matches the score.** Changes to notation in either the score or its part change both in uniform.
- **The page layout of the part is autonomous**, and unrelated to the page layout of the score. Changes to page layout in a part has no effect on the score and vise versa.
- **Markings (expressions, articulations, etc.) in the part adjust automatically to changes made in the score (generally).**
- **Markings (expressions, articulations, etc.) in the score are unaffected by changes made in a part (generally).** Once a marking is edited in a part, its link is "broken" and all subsequent edits to that marking apply only to the part or score and not both.

So, basically, the notes are always the same, the page layout is always independent, and almost everything else is linked until adjusted in a part. The Finale User Manual details the minutia of each element that differs from this rule, so there is no need to go into such detail here. Instead, in this section we will focus on the most common stumbling blocks and methods you can use to resolve them.

Generating Linked Parts

In Finale 2012, linked parts are always created when you start a new document with the Setup Wizard or add new staves with the Score Manager. Your score will only be missing parts if you have converted the file from an old version of Finale or created your score with a default document or document without libraries. Nonetheless, you might decide to generate parts in a score that already has parts if you want to omit all manual changes made to those parts and relink all items in parts back to the score.

CAUTION:
After you create multimeasure rests in a part, they will break automatically as new notes are entered in the score. However, you may need to re-apply them as you wrap up the part editing process. To do so, choose the Selection Tool, press CTRL/CMD+A to Select all, and choose **Edit** > **Multimeasure Rests** > **Create.**

1. Choose **Document** > **Manage Parts**. The Manage Parts dialog box appears as shown in Figure 7.14.

Figure 7.14

Use the Manage Parts dialog box to add and edit linked parts.

2. Click **Part Creation Preferences** (see Figure 7.15). Click **Multimeasure Rests** to open Document Options - Multimeasure Rests. Ensure the **Update Automatically** check box is checked and click **OK**. You may also want to review the Music Spacing settings - best changed before creating parts than after. Click **OK** when you are ready to continue.

Figure 7.15

Review the options in the Part Creations Preferences dialog box before you generate parts.

3. Click **Generate Parts**. The parts appear in the list box in the same order as the score. Finale recognizes multiple-staff instruments, such as piano, and automatically puts both staves in the same part.

4. Click **Edit Part Definition**. The dialog box expands to show additional options. You can edit the staff (or staves) assigned to each part and even the voicing in order to create two or more parts from the same score staff (more on that later). In the **Staves and Groups in Parts** list box of Figure 7.16, notice the Harp part consists of two staves.

Figure 7.16

Use the "Part Definition" options in the expanded Manage Parts dialog box to define the part name, staff assignment for the part, and part voicing.

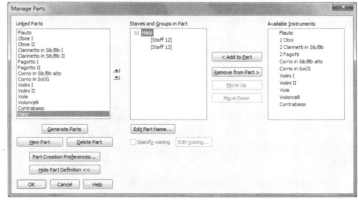

5. Select the parts from the left list box to review the part definitions. Again, the middle list box displays the staff assigned to the part and the right list box displays all staves in the score. Any part can contain any staff or combination of staves, even if they have been added to other parts. (This flexibility allows for some creative uses of linked parts which we will discuss later).

6. Click **OK** to return to the score. If everything looks the same, don't worry, it should. Next you'll learn how to navigate to and from the linked parts.

Navigating Linked Parts

Moving from one part to the next or choosing a specific part is fast and easy:

- Windows users, press CTRL+Alt+> to move to the next part. Macintosh users, CMD+OPTION+>. Use CTRL+Alt+< or CMD+OPTION+< to move to the previous part. (> is also the . (period) key and < is also the , (comma key). Get used to using these keystrokes, they are a big time-saver. You can reference them under the **Document** > **Edit Part** submenu.

- To toggle between the score and most recently viewed part, Windows users, press CTRL+Alt+/ (Mac: CMD+OPTION+/).

- To move to a specific part, choose **Document** > **Edit Part**.

Markings in Linked Parts

It is important to be familiar with the way Finale handles expressions, text, text repeats, most smart shapes, and other markings in linked parts. Since expressions are common, we'll focus on them (but most other markings work the same way). Here is a summary:

- When an expression is moved or hidden in the *score*, its corresponding expression in the part(s) change uniformly.

- Once an expression is moved or hidden in the *part*, its color changes to orange, indicating its link has been broken. This expression is now independent. Future changes to the positioning or show/hide setting of its twin in the score do not apply to the part. (Deleting or changing other attributes applies to both).

- Whenever a link has been broken, the marking changes color in both the part and the score. An orange marking in the score means the link has been broken in at least one part. (Remember, the same staff can be included in several parts). Changes to the marking in the score will continue to apply to the corresponding marking in all other parts containing that marking (if they are still linked).

- Expressions that have been broken can be "relinked" at any time. Simply context-click the broken expression and choose **Relink to Score**.

Figure 7.17

This expression was moved in the *part*. The marking in the *score* remains stationary and the marking changes color indicating the positioning link between the two has been broken.

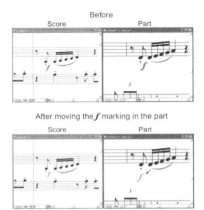

- Hold down CTRL/CMD to reverse the linking behavior. For example, hold down CTRL/CMD and move an expression in the score to break the expression's link to all parts. Alternatively, hold down CTRL/CMD while moving an expression in a part to retain the link, moving the expression in score (and any other parts containing the expression).

Setting the Page Format for Linked Parts

To edit the page margins, system margins, page size, and other attributes for all the parts at once:

1. Choose **Document** > **Page Format** > **Parts**. The Page Format for Parts dialog box appears.
2. Set the page size, margins and orientation here. For details, see "Editing the Overall Page Format for Your Score or Parts" on page 299.
3. When you are done, click **OK**. If you haven't generated parts, future parts will respect these settings. If the parts have already been generated, you must now redefine all pages of all the parts.
4. Click the Page Layout Tool ⬚ . Choose **Page Layout** > **Redefine Pages** > **Selected Pages of Selected Parts/Score**. The Redefine Selected Pages dialog box appears as shown in Figure 7.18.

Figure 7.18
Choose All Parts to redefine all pages of all parts in the score.

5. From the **Redefine** drop-down menu, choose **All Parts.** (If you would like to redefine certain parts, choose **Selected Parts/Score**).

6. Click **OK**. A redefine warning appears reminding you that by redefining pages, all other page layout information is lost.

7. Click **OK**. Finale redefines pages of your parts based on your Page Format for Parts settings.

Now, review your parts. If you find problems with this general format, repeat the above steps until all the parts are as close as possible to ideal. Any smaller-scale page layout changes you make will be overwritten if you need to redefine pages again.

TIP:
For layout of systems in linked parts, use **Page Layout** > **Space Systems Evenly.**

Part Voicing

Often, more than one instrument is notated on a single staff of the score to maximize page real estate (e.g. "Flutes 1 & 2"). When this is the case, it is often preferable to separate the staff into two (or more) parts, one for each voice. If each voice is fully notated in its own layer, Finale can handle the translation easily:

1. Choose **Document** > **Manage Parts**. The Manage Parts dialog box appears. Click **Edit Part Definition** to expand the dialog.

2. Click **New Part**. A new part appears in the Linked Parts list box.

3. Click **Edit Part Name** and type the name of the part (e.g. Flute 1).

4. In the **Available Instruments** list box on the right, select the staff containing the flute 1 & 2 staff, for example, and click the **Add to Part** button.

5. Click **Edit Voicing**. The "Voicing for _ Staff in _ Part" dialog box appears as shown in figure 7.19.

Figure 7.19

Assign a layer from a multi-voice score staff (or use the more advanced options) to produce a single-voice part.

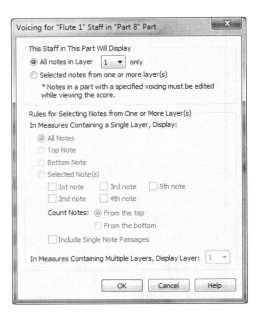

6. From the drop-down menu at the top, choose the layer of the voice you would like to include. Here, you would choose **Selected Notes** from **One or More Layers** if both voices were in, for example, layer 1 (using the parameters in the lower section to appropriate them).

7. Click **OK**. Now, repeat steps 2-6 for the other part(s).

8. Click **OK** to return to the score.

If each layer contains each part in full, your work is basically done. Treat these like any other part, and continue using the prescribed layer for additional notes.

 NOTE:
Once voicing is applied to a part, its notes can only be edited from the score.

Unfortunately, voices in a multi-voice staff are seldom notated completely in their own layer. Instead, there are various indicators that communicate how a multi-part staff is to be performed (split stems, a2, tutti, etc.). A simple example is illustrated in Figure 7.20.

Figure 7.20

Multiple voices are often notated in the same layer with expressions informing the performers when to play.

For this situation, Finale includes a staff style you can use to hide the extra notes. Simply apply the "Blank Notation with Rests" staff style over the necessary regions. See chapter 8 for more information on Staff Styles. (This is also described in the Finale User Manual under "Part Voicing").

For more complicated multi-voice parts you will simply find it easier to avoid using Finale's Linked Parts voicing mechanism. In these cases, extract parts (**File** > **Extract Parts**), and then use the Process Extracted Parts plug-in (**Plug-ins/** ✂ > **TGTools** > **Process Extracted Part**) to parse the individual voices at the very end of the editorial process. You can find more information regarding this plug-in in chapter 15.

Other Linked Part Details

There are many specialized relationships between elements of the score and its parts, and not all of them can be covered here. When there is a question, reference the thorough "Linked Parts" chapter of the Finale User Manual. The following are important concepts that apply to many projects that contain linked parts.

Staff Styles in Linked Parts

Staff styles are handled differently than most other elements with regards to linked parts. Here are a few tips worth remembering:

- Applying or clearing a staff style applies to both the score and part unless context menus are used to specify otherwise.
- Right/CTRL+click a selected region of a part and choose "Use Selected Staff Style for Score and Parts" to automatically apply/clear staff styles in parts so that the region matches that of the score.

Staff Groups in Linked Parts

In the **Available Instruments** (rightmost) pane of the Manage Parts dialog box, you may see a + (plus) sign next to an instrument choice like this: ⊞ Piano . This indicates a staff group, and is generally used for instruments that require a grand staff (i.e. piano, harp, etc.).

- Click the ⊞ to expand the group and display its individual staves.

- For a group to appear in the Available Instruments pane, the staff name (in the Score Manager) of the top staff in the group must be empty.

Measure-Attached Smart Shapes in Linked Parts

- The vertical positioning of measure-attached smart shapes can be different/unlinked between the part and score.
- The horizontal placement of all measure-attached smart shapes is permanently linked.

Adding Linked Parts to Old Files

If you need to add linked parts to a file created in Finale 2006 or earlier, the process is almost completely automatic. All you have to do is generate them in the Manage Parts dialog box (see "Generating Linked Parts" on page 191), then define the part names and add the file information text inserts. Then, set multimeasure rests to update automatically. Here's how:

1. Choose **Document** > **Manage Parts** to open the Manage Parts dialog box. Click **Edit Part Definition** to expand the dialog box. Now, to create parts, click **Generate Parts**.

2. Verify each linked part is named properly. (They are based on the staff name by default). To change a part name, select it from the **Linked Parts** (left) window and click **Edit Part Name**. Rename the part and click **OK**. When all the parts are named properly, click **OK** to return to the score.

3. Choose **Window** > **Score Manager**, and click the **File Info** tab.

4. For **Score Name Insert**, enter the name of the score (like "Score" or "Conductor's Score"). Enter additional information as necessary. Click **OK**. You can now use text inserts to add this information.

5. Move to Page View (**View** > **Page View**). Click the Text tool **A** , double-click the page to display the text window.

6. Choose **Text** > **Inserts**, and then **Part/Score Name**. View a part and see that its part name is now displayed on the page.

7. Choose **Document** > **Document Options** > **Multimeasure Rests**. Under **Options**, ensure **Update Automatically** is checked and click **OK**. Now, any notes added in the score over multimeasure rest region will automatically break the appropriate multimeasure rest in the part.

Extracting Parts

Extract parts whenever you need to save a part as an independent file. For example, you might do this if you need to send a student his band part without including the full score.

There are other reasons you may need to do this. If you find yourself spending a disproportional amount of time tweaking the score and parts in order to uphold an appropriate appearance for both while retaining the linked relationships, you might consider breaking the parts off and managing them independently. After all, the linked parts mechanism is only beneficial as much as it saves you time and effort, and complicated scores sometimes reach the point at which this is no longer the case. Extracting parts allows you to save each part as its own document unrelated to the original score document.

TIP:
To manage a large score with many complicated, multi-part staves, some prefer editing two copies of the document; one focused on the score, the other focused on all the parts. This method isn't perfect, but beats a separate file for each part. Just save your document under a new name and manage the 2 files separately.

To extract parts:

1. Choose **File** > **Extract Parts**. The Extract Parts dialog box appears as shown in Figure 7.21.

Figure 7.21
Save parts into separate documents using Extract Parts.

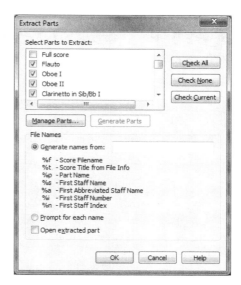

2. Check the parts.
3. In the **File Names** section of the Extract Parts dialog box, choose **Generate Names From** if you want to use one of the available naming conventions for your extracted parts. If you let Finale generate your extracted part names, you must use at least one, preferable two, of the naming conventions. They are listed below the text box (for example, type "%f%s.MUS" to tell Finale to name each new file with the score file name followed by the staff or group name). Choose **Prompt for Each Name** to name each extracted part yourself during the extraction process.

CAUTION:
If you get the warning message, "This file already exists. Replace Existing File?", and you have chosen **Prompt for Each Name** in the Extract Parts dialog box, be absolutely sure that you name each part with a unique file name to avoid overwriting your score.

4.   Check **Open Extracted Part** to tell Finale to open each part immediately after extraction.

5.   Click **OK** to begin part extraction. Finale will generate new separate files for each linked part.

TIP:
For lead sheets, generate a repository of parts in different transpositions so they are readily available to extract and distribute to any instrument. Or, create several ensembles from the same score - a linked part can contain any number of instruments.

8
Alternate Notation, Staff Management, and Tab

Don't let the terminology fool you; if you are a percussionist, guitarist, or early musician, "alternate notation" may be the only type of notation you care to use. That's okay, this book is for all you fringe outcasts too! It's like Revenge of the Dirge Chanting Rhythm Lutists. But unfortunately, all you non-alternate individuals need to pay attention; some of this stuff applies to you too.

These concepts are actually very important; particularly Alternate Notation and Staff Styles. Basically, this chapter returns to staff settings again, but demonstrates how to handle more advanced types like specialized percussion and guitar notation. These settings, in addition to the staff settings covered in Chapter 2 (staff names, clefs, transposition, etc.), can be applied to either a whole staff, or individual regions within a staff. Some figures in this chapter, like one-bar repeats, are common to any style of western music.

Don't fear the alt crowd, you may find you share more in common with them than you thought.

Here's a summary of what you will learn in this chapter:

- How to set up a staff for slash, rhythmic, and other alternate notation
- How to apply alternate notation to part of a staff only: Staff Styles
- How to create tablature, percussion, and other notation styles
- How to create a guitar part with tab

Staff Setup for Slash, Rhythmic, and Other Notation Styles

Whenever you want to create notation with slashes, enter one or two bar repeats, or hide the existing music in a staff, apply alternate notation to the staff. First, you will learn how to apply alternate notation to a full staff, and then to specific regions using Staff Styles.

To prepare for this section, open a new Default Document (**File** > **New** > **Default Document**).

Slash and Rhythmic Notation

Slash and rhythmic notation are often used in conjunction with chord symbols to indicate comping, or the background harmonic progression of a piece. This type of notation is particularly common in guitar and piano parts in Jazz ensembles, for example, where rhythm and style take precedence over exact pitches.

In slash notation, there is one slash for each beat of the measure, and chord symbols usually appear above the staff (see Figure 8.1). The precise rhythm is left up to the performer.

Figure 8.1

Apply alternate notation in the Staff Attributes to create slash notation.

NOTE:

Finale 2012 makes it easy to add chords above slash notation. Just click the Chord Tool and click a measure to display the blinking entry cursor above the staff. (Be sure Manual Input is checked under the Chord Menu). See Chapter 4 for details.

To set up a staff for slash notation:

1. Click the Staff Tool and double-click the staff. The Staff Attributes dialog box appears.

2. Click the **Settings** button next to **Alternate Notation**. The Alternate Notation dialog box appears as shown in Figure 8.2.

Figure 8.2

Choose a type of alternate notation in the Alternate Notation dialog box.

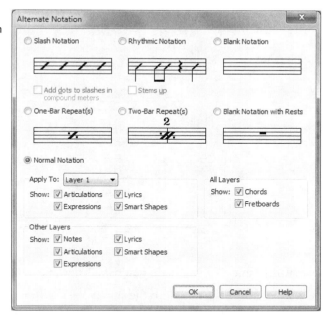

3. Select **Slash Notation**. If your piece is in a compound meter, such as 6/8, and you want to add dots to your slashes, check Add Dots to Slashes in Compound Meters. For now, leave this box unchecked.

4. Click **OK** to return to the Staff Attributes. Notice the **Alternate Notation** check box is now checked.

5. Click **OK** to return to the score. You should now see slashes throughout your staff.

Rhythmic notation is similar to slash notation but more closely resembles regular notes and indicates the specific rhythmic pattern (see Figure 8.3). The slashed notes in rhythmic notation are often used to notate strumming patterns for guitar.

Figure 8.3
Apply alternate notation in the Staff Attributes to create rhythmic notation.

To demonstrate rhythmic notation, start a new default document (**File** > **New** > **Default Document**):

1. Enter notes and rests into the staff in the rhythmic pattern you want - the pitch of any notes you enter will convert to standard slashes. Rests will remain rests (consult Chapter 3 for information on entering notes and rests in Simple or Speedy Entry).

2. Click the Staff Tool [image] and double-click the staff to open the Staff Attributes dialog box.

3. Click the **Settings** button next to **Alternate Notation** to open the Alternate Notation dialog box.

4. Select **Rhythmic Notation.**

5. By default, Finale will place stems down on rhythmic notation. If you want to change the stem direction, check **Stems Up In Rhythmic Notation.**

6. Click **OK** to return to the Staff Attributes and **OK** again to return to the score. You should now see slashes with stems for each note you entered in the staff.

Since there are underlying notes or rests in the slash and rhythmic notation you applied, you can enter note-attached Smart Shapes or expressions to your slashes as needed. If you only want to apply slash or rhythmic notation to a portion of your staff, apply a Staff Style (more about Staff Styles soon).

Managing Playback for Staves with Slash or Rhythmic Notation

You will notice that Finale will play back any underlying notes that exist beneath the alternate notation. To eliminate playback of these notes from rhythmic or slash notation (for the whole staff):

1. Choose **Window** > **Score Manager.**
2. Click the expand triangle/+ to the left of the staff with alternate notation. Now, layers, chords, and expressions are available.

3. If the **M** column is not visible, click the **Customize View** drop-down menu and choose **Mute & Solo**.

4. Under the **M (Mute)** column, click to mute the whole staff or any layer.

5. Do the same for chords or expressions to remove them from playback.

TIP:
To disable chord playback for all staves, from the Chord Menu, uncheck **Enable Chord Playback**.

Managing Layers in Rhythmic and Slash Notation

If there is more than one layer in the staff to which you want to apply alternate notation, you may want to show the notes in other layers, or items attached to them. For example, you may have a staff that has slash notation throughout, but in a couple of measures you want standard notation in a different layer to appear as well. To do this:

1. Double-click a staff and click **Settings** next to **Alternate Notation**.

2. In the Alternate Notation dialog box, choose the layer you want the alternate notation to occupy from the **Apply to:** drop-down menu (any notes in this layer will be overwritten with the alternate notation, but they will still play back).

3. Then, in the **other layers** section, from the check boxes, check **Notes** and any other object you want to show.

4. Click **OK** twice to return to the score.

Blank Notation

Blank notation can be used any time you want to hide a layer of notation. This type of alternate notation is often used to hide notes in a layer that you want to use exclusively for playback. For example, you may have notated a special ornament in layer one and entered the notes as you want it to playback in layer four. Use Blank Notation to hide the notes in layer four.

1. With the Staff Tool ![icon] selected, double-click the staff to open the Staff Attributes.

2. Click the **Settings** button next to **Alternate Notation** to open the Alternate Notation dialog box.

3. Choose **Blank Notation**.

4. From the **Apply to:** drop-down menu, choose the layer you want to hide-in this case, layer four.

5. Click **OK** to return to the Staff Attributes, then **OK** to return to the score.

Notes in the layer you specified are hidden in the staff, and will play back. To hide notes and eliminate them from playback instead, use the H key command in Speedy or Simple Entry (see Chapter 3 for details). You can also eliminate playback for any layer of a staff (even one hidden by blank alternate notation) with the Score Manager. (See the earlier section, "Managing Playback for Staves with Slash or Rhythmic Notation," for steps to remove a layer from playback.)

NOTE:
When you hide notes, they will appear in a lighter color onscreen but will not appear in the printout. To hide the hidden notes on-screen as well, from the View menu, choose **Show** and uncheck **Hidden Notes and Rests**.

Adding Mid-Score Instrument Changes

If you are writing a part for an instrumentalists who will be switching instruments at some point during the piece (e.g. putting down an flute and picking up a piccolo), you will need to add one or more instrument changes to the staff. An instrument change might require several staff adjustments including a different transposition or clef, and also a change in playback sound. Fortunately, Finale 2012 pretty much does all this for you. To add an instrument change:

1. Choose the Selection Tool .
2. Select the region of measures to be performed with the new instrument.
3. Choose **Utilities** > **Change Instrument**. The Change Instrument dialog box appears, which includes a two-tiered list much like the one in the Setup Wizard.
4. Select the new instrument from the list.
5. Click **OK**. Finale adds the instrument change, making all the required staff adjustments for the region you selected.
6. You can add the marking (e.g. "To Flute") as an expression. See "Creating a Text Expression" on page 79.

Choose **Window** > **Score Manager** and click to the left of the Name to display the instrument changes (among the layers, expressions, and chords). You'll notice another instrument change, back to the original, is also required. If you would like to make adjustments to any of these instruments (e.g. change the Staff Name), you can do so using the Score Manager settings just as you would any other instrument.

Applying Staff Attributes to Part of a Staff Only: Staff Styles

The alternate notation types discussed earlier, such as slash and rhythmic notation, can be applied to any part of a staff using Staff Styles. A Staff Style is a collection of staff attributes you can apply to any region of your score. Hide portions of a staff, change the notehead font, or define any set of attributes for any region using Staff Styles. You can apply one of Finale's preset Staff Styles or create your own.

Continuing with the file you've been working with, double-click the staff to open Staff Attributes, uncheck **Alternate Notation**, and click **OK** to return to the score.

Applying a Staff Style

First, apply rhythmic notation to a portion of a staff using Staff Styles. This happens to be one of the styles that already exists in Finale's default Staff Style library.

1. With the Staff Tool selected ![icon], highlight any region of measures. Context-click to expand the context menu and choose a Staff Style. Alternatively, choose **Staff** > **Apply Staff Style To** > **Score and Parts** (or > **Current Part/Score**). The Apply Staff Style dialog box appears as shown in Figure 8.4.

Figure 8.4
Choose a collection of staff attributes (Staff Style) to apply to a portion of a staff in the Apply Staff Style dialog box.

2. Select Rhythmic Notation and click **OK**. The highlighted region of your staff converts to rhythmic notation. A (non-printing) gray line will appear above every region of a staff containing a Staff Style whenever the Staff Tool is selected.

To easily assign a Staff Style:

1. Choose the Staff Tool ![icon].
2. Highlight a region of your staff and press the metatool key of the desired Staff Style. If you do not know the metatool key, context-click the highlighted region and choose the Staff Style you want to apply from the list. Choosing a Staff Style from the context menu, or using a metatool, will add to both the score and parts.

Apply as many Staff Styles as you like to the same region of a staff. You will see a new gray line appear above the staff for each new Staff Style you apply. If you find yourself applying several Staff Styles to the same region, define your own Staff Style that includes all of the desired attributes. I'll talk about defining your own Staff Style soon.

One- and Two-Bar Repeats

One- and two-bar repeats tell the performer to repeat the previous one- or two-bar segment of music (see Figure 8.5). In Finale, one- and two-bar repeats are handled with Staff Styles.

Figure 8.5

Use Staff Styles to create one- and two-bar repeats.

To enter one- or two-bar repeats.

1.   Highlight a region of the staff.
2.   Right/CTRL+click the highlighted region and choose One-Bar Repeat or Two-Bar Repeat. The staff automatically updates to reflect the selection you made. You can also use the metatool "O" to apply a one-bar repeat or the metatool "T" to apply a two-bar repeat Staff Style to the selected region of a staff.

The Staff Style Library

There are many Staff Styles already included in Finale's default Staff Style library. You can use these any time you begin a document with the Setup Wizard, the Default Document file, or one of Finale's templates. If the file you are working on does not contain these preset Staff Styles (such as an older Finale file), you can import them by saving and opening a library. To import the default Staff Style library, from the File menu, choose Load Library. Navigate to your Finale 2012/Libraries folder. Double-click the file "Staff Styles.lib." Now the default Staff Styles will appear in the context menu and in the Apply Staff Styles dialog box.

Like articulations and expressions, all Staff Styles in a document can be transferred to another by saving and loading a library.

Clearing Staff Styles

To clear a Staff Style:

1.   Choose the Staff Tool ![icon] . All Staff Styles are indicated with gray bars above the staff.
2.   Click a gray bar and press DELETE. (This deletes in both the score and parts).

To clear a Staff Style from a measure region:

1.   Choose the Staff Tool ![icon] . All Staff Styles are indicated with gray bars above the staff.
2.   Highlight the region of measures.
3.   Right/CTRL+click the region and choose **Clear Staff Style From** > **Score and Parts** (or > **Score Only** or > **Parts Only**) . Alternatively, you can choose this option from the Staff menu.

Defining a New Staff Style

If the staff attributes you want to apply to a staff do not exist in the default Staff Style library, create your own. To create your own Staff Style:

1. With the Staff Tool ![icon] selected, choose **Staff** > **Define Staff Styles**. The Staff Styles dialog box appears as shown in Figure 8.6. This dialog box is almost identical to the Staff Attributes.

Figure 8.6

Define a custom Staff Style in the Staff Styles dialog box.

2. Click the **New** button in the upper-right corner.
3. Click in the text box to the right of **Available Styles** and type a name for your Staff Style.
4. Make sure **Display in Context Menu** is checked if you want this definition to appear in the Staff Styles context menu.
5. Make any setting you would like to apply to a region of a staff. Change the number of staff lines, the transposition, the clef, or adjust any other parameter. Gray checks (Mac: dashes) in the check boxes tell Finale to leave the setting alone in the applied region of the staff.
6. Make sure **Copyable** is checked if you want to be able to copy this Staff Style.
7. Click **OK** to return to the score.
8. Highlight a region of your staff, then context-click the highlighted area to open the Staff Styles context menu. The Staff Style you just defined will appear at the bottom. Choose it to apply your Staff Style to the highlighted region of the staff.

To assign a metatool to any Staff Style:

1. Hold down the SHIFT key and press any number or letter on the QWERTY keyboard. The Apply Staff Styles dialog box appears.

2. Choose the Staff Style you want to assign to the number or letter you pressed and click **OK**.

3. Now, highlight a region of measures and press the metatool number or letter to apply the Staff Style.

Viewing Staff Styles

You have already seen that any Staff Style applied to a region of your staff is indicated with a gray line. To tell Finale to include the name of each Staff Style within this gray line.

1. Choose **Staff** > **Show Staff Style Names**. Now, each gray Staff Style indicator line includes the name of the applied Staff Style.

2. Zoom in using the Zoom Tool 🔍 (or the view menu) to see these Staff Style names more clearly.

3. To remove Staff Style names from the gray indicator line, uncheck **Show Staff Style Names** from the Staff menu.

While working with the Staff Tool ![icon], if you want to remove the gray indicator lines altogether, choose **Staff** > **Show Staff Styles**. Check **Show Staff Styles** again from the Staff menu to display them.

Tablature, Percussion, and Note Shapes Notation Styles

In addition to alternate notation, there are a few other notation styles you may want to use throughout a staff or in a Staff Style. Choose **Window** > **Score Manager**. Click the drop-down menu to the right of Notation Style. There are three options here: Standard, Percussion, and Tablature (see Figure 8.7).

Figure 8.7
Choose a notation style for a staff from the Notation Styles drop-down menu of the Score Manager.

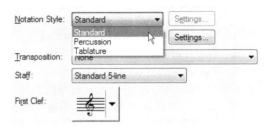

Most staves in Finale are in the standard notation style, so this option is usually selected by default. If you chose an instrument from either the **Tablature** or **Percussion** category in the Setup Wizard or Score Manager, the instrument will be set to the respective Notation Style. The Note Shapes Notation Style is available in the Staff Attributes dialog box, and allows you to set each staff position to its own character in a chosen font. Most Finale Trailblazers do not need to customize Finale's default Tablature, Percussion, or Note Shapes Notation Styles, but just in case you are doing something kind of crazy, we'll discuss these Notation Styles and related features in this section.

Percussion

If you are notating for a non-pitched percussion instrument, all of the special parameters, including music font, number of staff lines, and the percussion clef can be set in the Score Manager. Again, always, always, always use one of Finale's available percussion instruments (by choosing it from the Setup Wizard or Score Manager) to add percussion staves. Then, if you need to change the appearance of a percussion staff, in some fundamental way you can do so using one of the following methods.

Changing the Number of Staff Lines

Many percussion parts contain staves with only one line. To change the number of lines in the staff.

1. Choose **Window** > **Score Manager**.
2. Click the drop-down menu for **Staff:** and choose **1-Line with Short Barline**. This setting will remove all but the middle staff line from the score. Of course, choose any of the other options depending on the part you are defining. If you want, you can set up a staff to include any number of staff lines. To do this, from the **Staff:** drop-down menu, choose **Other**. The Staff Setup dialog box appears as shown in Figure 8.8.

Figure 8.8

Customize the number and placement of staff lines in the Staff Setup dialog box.

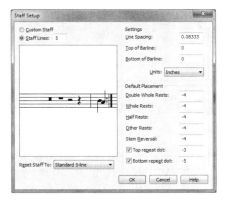

3. Click the **Custom Staff** radio button. Then, click the handles to the left of the staff in the preview window to add or remove staves from the custom staff.
4. Adjust the length of the barlines for the staff in the **Settings** section. For **Top Barline**, enter the length you want your barlines extended above the top staff line. For **Bottom Barline**, enter the length you want your barlines extended below the bottom staff line.
5. Click **OK** to return to the Score Manager.

Specifying a Notehead Font

If you would like to use a different font for percussion notation, you can set an independent percussion font for any percussion staff. (If you used one of Finale's instruments this is done for you already.)

1. Click the Staff Tool and double-click a staff to open the Staff Attributes dialog box.

1. In the **Independent Elements** section, click the **Select** button for **Notehead Font**. The Font dialog box appears.

2. To use Finale's standard percussion font, choose Maestro Percussion. You may also want to choose the Tamburo font (an older percussion font), which is also included with Finale. Of course, you can choose any font on your computer from this dialog box if there is an alternative percussion font you want to use.

3. Click **OK** to return to the Staff Attributes dialog box.

Percussion Layouts

Finale is designed to make percussion entry as easy and straightforward as possible. If you have tried to enter percussion in an earlier Finale version (before Finale 2010), and were frustrated that you could not simply click to get a snare drum, your worries are over. Now, as long as you use one of Finale's available percussion instruments, notating percussion is so easy that I will only say a word about it here. (Search for "Percussion" in the User Manual for details on entering percussion with Simple Entry).

> **NOTE:**
> *Those familiar with percussion in Finale 2009 or earlier:* As of Finale 2010, the functionality from Finale's old Percussion Map Designer dialog box was split into two parts, 1) the Percussion Layout Designer dialog box, which allows you to assign the notehead character and staff position for each percussion instrument, and 2) Percussion MIDI Maps, which allow you to specify appropriate MIDI mapping for input and playback. Percussion entry is way easier now because you can see visual feedback of the instrument you are entering, and, rather than setting up a different percussion map for each input/playback device, you can simply select its Percussion MIDI Map when needed (in the Percussion MIDI Maps dialog box for input and in the Instrument List for playback). Percussion MIDI Maps can be customized or defined for any input/playback device in the Percussion MIDI Map Editor dialog box.

The staff position and notehead character for each percussion instrument on a percussion staff is defined as a *Percussion layout*. You will need to change Finale's percussion layout if:

- You want to add or remove percussion instrument choices to/from the staff.
- You want to change the staff position and/or notehead of percussion instruments.

To do these things:

1. Choose **Window** > **Score Manager**.

2. For **Notation Style**, choose **Percussion** and click the adjacent **Settings** button. The Percussion Layout Selection dialog box appears.

3. Click **Edit**. The Percussion Layout Designer appears as shown in Figure 8.9.

Figure 8.9

Define the staff placement and noteheads for percussion instruments in the Percussion Layout Designer dialog box.

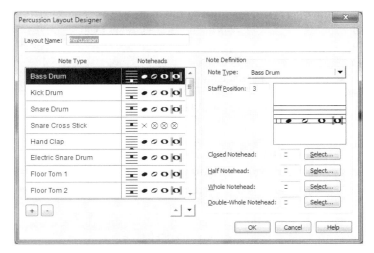

4. If you want to add a percussion instrument, click the + (plus) button in the lower left corner. A new instrument appears. Otherwise, select the instrument you want to change. (To delete a percussion instrument, select it and click the - (minus) button).

5. Click the **Note Type** drop-down list and specify the desired percussion instrument.

6. Click the handle next to the staff display and drag the notes to the desired staff position.

7. Use the following **Select** buttons to define a notehead for the various note durations.

8. That's it. Click **OK, Select** to return to the score. When you enter notes onto your percussion staff, these instruments will be available.

Transfer percussion layouts between documents by saving and loading a percussion layout library. To do so:

1. Choose **File** > **Save Library**.

2. In the Save Library dialog box, choose **Percussion Layouts** and click **OK**, and save the library file.

3. Open the destination document, and choose **File** > **Load Library**. Then navigate to the library file you saved and double-click it. The new percussion layouts will appear in the Percussion Layout Selection dialog box. Apply the layout to staves as required.

Note Shapes

Some notation like chant and medieval music uses note shapes for scale degrees . Additionally, educational notation may require special noteheads, like pitch letters on each notehead ◑/ ◉ (Kidnotes and Finale AlphaNotes fonts).

You can assign a particular note shape or font character to either a particular scale degree or notehead type (open, closed, etc.) using *note shapes*. Note shapes can be applied to either the full document or to a particular staff.

First, the desired notehead characters may not be in your current notehead font. You may need to select a notehead font for the full document or a particular staff. (If the desired notehead characters exist in the current default music font, you can skip the next two sets of steps).

To select the notehead font for all staves in the document:

1.   Choose **Document** > **Document Options** and select **Fonts.**
2.   Click the drop-down menu next to **Notation** and choose **Noteheads.**
3.   Click the **Set Font** button to the right, choose the desired font, and click **OK**. Click **OK** again to return to the score.

To select the notehead font for a particular staff:

1.   Choose the Staff Tool and double-click the staff. The Staff Attributes dialog box appears.
2.   In the lower right, under **Independent Elements**, next to **Notehead Font**, click **Select.**
3.   Choose the desired font, and click **OK**. Click **OK** again to return to the score.

Now, to select note shape characters for specific scale degrees and/or noteheads, do the following:

1.   **To apply note shapes to all staves in a document**, choose **Document** > **Document Options**, then click **Notes and Rests.** Check **Use Note Shapes** (at the top). Then skip to step 3. Or,

2.   **To apply note shapes to a particular staff**, with the Staff Tool selected, double-click a staff to open the Staff Attributes dialog box. Click the **Settings** button next to **Use Note Shapes.** The Note Shapes dialog box appears as shown in Figure 8.10. (These settings are the same as those in Document Options).

Figure 8.10

Assign a notehead character for rhythmic values and/or scale degrees in the Note Shapes dialog box.

3. Click the drop-down menu for **Replace,** and choose the notehead type you would like to replace with a shape.

4. Choose the scale degree with the up and down arrows for **on Scale Degree**. Or click and enter a scale degree in this text box manually. Finale will use the key signature of the piece to discern the appropriate note for each scale degree.

5. Click the **Select** button to choose a shape from the list of characters.

6. Repeat steps 3 through 5 for each notehead type and scale degree you want to assign to a shape character.

7. When you have finished assigning note shapes, click **OK** back to the score.

8. If you plan on using this notation often, save this file as a template.

Now, any notes you add in the staff will use the note shapes you assigned.

Guitar Notation and Tablature

Modern science has proved that notation that looks like the fretboard of the instrument you are playing, with fingerings, offers a statistically higher chance of your performer playing the correct pitch. Fortunately, the Finale stewards were aware of this, and integrated a tablature notation model that is delightfully accessible to users of all skill levels, from classical to hair band. In this section you will learn how to begin a new score for guitar with tablature, and create one from scratch. Also, I'll cover how to enter fret numbers, bends, hammer-ons, pull-offs, and other items specific to tablature notation, each making your composition more mathematically achievable to eager performers and listeners alike.

Setting up a Tablature Staff

If you are beginning a new document, and plan to include any fretted instrument with tablature (guitar, lute, dulcimer, etc.), add one of Finale's **Tablature** instruments using either the Document Setup Wizard for new scores (see "Starting a Score with the Document Setup Wizard" on page 19) or the Score Manager for existing scores (see "Adding, Removing, and Changing Instruments" on page 26). When you do this you will be presented with a plethora of fretted instruments to choose from, such as those shown in Figure 8.11.

Figure 8.11

The Tablature options in the Score Manager should be used for adding tab staves to existing scores.

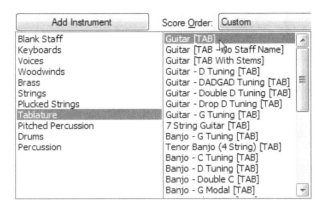

Fretted instrument parts often include both a tab staff and a standard notation staff. Add the standard notation staff using one of the **Plucked Strings** category. The standard notation staff generally appears above the tab staff, and will do so using any of Finale's pre-set Score Orders. (For information on reordering staves, see "Customizing the Score Order" on page 173.)

Entering Tablature

There are a number of ways to enter tablature into a tab staff. You can copy music from a notation staff, enter directly into a tab staff with Simple or Speedy Entry, or use a MIDI guitar for entry into a tab staff. I'll start by demonstrating the easiest: copying notation directly into a tablature staff from a standard notation staff.

Copying Music to a tab Staff

I'll assume you have a score with both standard and tablature notation open. If not, go back to the previous section and create a new score with the Setup Wizard containing a notation and tablature staff. For the remainder of this section, I'll refer to the regular five-line staff as the "notation staff" and the tablature staff as the "tab staff."

1. Select the Simple Entry Tool 🎵 .
2. Enter the melody seen in Figure 8.12 into the first three measures of the notation staff (you can find information on Simple Entry in Chapter 3).

Figure 8.12

Use the Selection Tool to copy notation to a tab staff and vice versa.

3. Click the Selection Tool  .
4. Highlight measures 1-3 in the notation staff.
5. Click within the highlighted area and drag down over the first three measures of the tab staff. When you see black border around the first three measures of the tab staff, release the mouse button. The Change Lowest Fret dialog box appears.
6. Click **OK**. The tab staff now contains fret numbers that correspond to the above notation.

You can also copy tablature into a notation staff. To demonstrate, highlight measure one in the tab staff. Then drag the highlighted area to measure four of the notation staff. You will see the notes appear in the notation staff.

Now, while copying to a tab staff, you may want to indicate that the notes should be played higher on the fretboard. For this reason, the Change Lowest Fret dialog box appears (as seen in Figure 8.13) any time you copy from a notation staff into a tab staff (as you saw in the previous steps).

Figure 8.13

Specify the lowest fret for music copied to a tab staff in the Change Lowest Fret dialog box.

In this dialog box, you can specify the lowest fret, and Finale will distribute the fret numbers to the appropriate strings. Now use the same document you've been working with to try this.

1. Select the Selection Tool  .
2. Click to the left of the notation staff to highlight the entire staff.
3. Click within the highlighted area and drag down over the tab staff (yes, right over the existing tab). The Change Lowest Fret dialog box appears.
4. For **Lowest Fret**, enter "5."
5. Click **OK**. The tablature now recalculates with fret numbers on new strings, all on fret five or above.

As we saw in this example, you can copy over existing tablature or an empty tab staff. Finale will recalculate the tablature each time you do this to account for any changes in the notation staff and the value you set in the Change Lowest Fret dialog box.

You can also change the lowest fret of any region of a tab staff independently. To do this:

1. Click the Selection Tool and highlight a region of the tab staff.
2. Choose **Utilities** > **Change** > **Lowest Fret**. The Change Lowest Fret dialog box opens.
3. Enter the new lowest fret and click **OK** to modify the highlighted region of the tab staff.

Entering tab with Simple Entry

To enter tab using the mouse and keyboard:

1. Select a note duration from the Simple Entry palette and click in the tab staff. By default, you will see a "0" appear in the score, and it will be selected.
2. Type the fret number using the number keys on your numeric keyboard (laptop: CTRL/OPTION+SHIFT+#).
3. Press UP ARROW and DOWN ARROW to move the fret number up or down a string, and the number will adjust accordingly (to represent the same pitch).
4. Use the left and right arrows to move the selection horizontally between fret numbers. CTRL/OPTION+click any fret number to select it.

TIP:
To see a list of Simple Entry keystrokes for tablature, choose **Simple** > **Tab Specific Commands.**

You can also easily enter tab with the Caret.

1. With the caret active, type UP ARROW and DOWN ARROW (or press a number, 1-6, in the QWERTY keyboard) to choose the string.
2. Hold down CTRL+ALT+SHIFT/CMD+OPTION+SHIFT and press the duration key in the QWERTY keyboard to specify the duration.
3. Press ENTER to add a 0.
4. Type the fret number on the number pad (laptop users CTRL/OPTION+SHIFT+#). You can continue entering on the same string and duration by typing with the number pad.
5. To add an additional fret number above or below the one you just entered, hold down ALT/OPTION and press the string number on the QWERTY keyboard. A "0" appears on the string. Hold Down ALT/OPTION and type the fret number on the number pad (laptop: CTRL/OPTION+SHIFT+#).

TIP:
While entering tab, Finale will warn you if a fret number is beyond the range of a string by turning it orange. If it is below the range of the string, you will also see a "-" (minus sign) preceding the fret number. If a fret number is orange, try moving it to a different string, changing the string tuning, changing the default lowest fret of the staff, or the number of frets in the staff.

Entering tab with a MIDI Guitar and HyperScribe

Chapter 4 covered the basics for entering music into Finale with a MIDI guitar. You can enter into a tab staff just as you would a standard notation staff by using the HyperScribe Tool 🖎 . When you do this,

Finale can even record the correct string you play and place fret numbers on the appropriate tab line. Finale can distinguish between strings because each string is set to a different MIDI channel. Your guitar-to-MIDI interface will send the MIDI data to Finale on specified channels. You can coordinate the MIDI string channels assigned on your guitar to MIDI interface with Finale by editing the Tablature MIDI Channels dialog box (see Figure 8.14).

Figure 8.14

Coordinate MIDI notes to strings in the Tablature MIDI Channels dialog box.

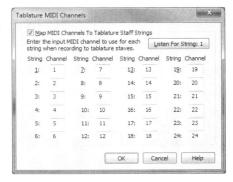

First, check the guitar-to-MIDI interface device to see which channel is assigned to each string. Consult the MIDI interface's instruction manual for information on how to assign and view the string channels. Then, assign the corresponding channel for each string in the Tablature MIDI Channels dialog box (located under **MIDI/Audio** > **Device Setup** > **Tablature MIDI Channels**). Now, Finale will be able to translate your performance properly into a tab staff.

Adding Tablature Markings

Beyond fret numbers, there are several other figures standard in tablature notation. These include bends, releases, tremolos, hammer-ons, hammer-offs, and tab slides.

Entering Bends and Releases

In tablature, bends are usually indicated with a curved line pointing up and text indicating the pitch variation from the original note. A bend can be followed up by a release, telling the performer to "bend back down" to the original pitch. You can see an example of a bend and release in Figure 8.15.

Figure 8.15

Easily create a bend and release with the Guitar Bend Tool.

Creating these in Finale is easy with the Guitar Bend Smart Shape:

1. First enter three fret numbers on a string, "5," "6," then "5" again (as in the "Before" example in Figure 8.15). Then click the Smart Shape Tool .

2. In the Smart Shape palette, choose the Guitar Bend Tool .

3. Double-click the first "5" you entered (then press CTRL/CMD+D to redraw). Notice Finale creates the bend, adds the "½" text and hides the second fret number. Any time you create a new guitar bend, Finale will add text corresponding to the pitch variation of the fret numbers (whole step=1, minor third= 1-½, etc.).

4. Now, double-click on the hidden fret number and redraw the screen (it should be on the same tab line directly under the ½ text). Finale creates a release for you automatically, and parenthesizes the destination fret number.

> **TIP:**
> To create a quarter bend, CTRL/OPTION+double-click on any fret number.

You can also generate bends and releases automatically by copying any music from a standard notation staff into a tab staff that contains a Bend Hat Smart Shape. Finale automatically takes into account the pitch variation.

Use the primary handle to reposition the entire Guitar Bend, or use the small diamond arrows to reposition the end points.

You can set the default placement for your bends in the Smart Shape Placement dialog box. Choose **SmartShape** > **Smart Shape Placement**. From the drop-down menu on the upper left, choose **Guitar Bend**. You will see a list of options for default placement of guitar bends (see Figure 8.16).

Figure 8.16

Edit the default placement of guitar bend smart shapes in the Smart Shape Placement dialog box.

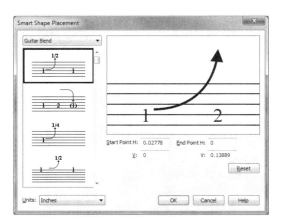

Drag the figure in the preview window to reposition the default appearance of bends, releases, and quarter bends. Changes here will apply to all new guitar bends you enter as well as all existing guitar bends that have not been repositioned manually.

In addition to placement, you can also manipulate other default characteristics of the Guitar Bend Smart Shapes with the Guitar Bends Options.

1.   Choose **SmartShape** > **Guitar Bend Options**. The Guitar Bend Options dialog box appears as shown in Figure 8.17.

Figure 8.17

Make settings for default text, parentheses, and other attributes of guitar bends in the Guitar Bend Options dialog box.

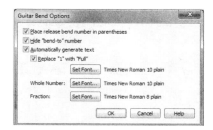

2.   You can tell Finale to place release bend numbers in parentheses, hide the "Bend-to" number, and automatically generate text. You saw Finale do all of these things in the above example. They are all turned on by default. Changes here apply to all guitar bends in the score as well as newly created ones. Sometimes the text "Full" is used to indicate a bend of a whole step instead of the number "1." Check **Replace "1" with "Full"** to use "Full" for any guitar bend of a whole step. Then, click the **Set Font** button if you want to modify its font, size, or style. Also, set the font, size, and style for whole numbers and fractions by clicking the corresponding **Set Font** button at the bottom of this dialog box.

Tremolos and Tab Slides

Like guitar bends, tremolos and tab slides can be entered as Smart Shapes. Tab slides tell the performer to slide to a note without leaving the string. Tremolos are used to tell the performer to add vibrato to the pitch. You can see an example of a tremolo and tab slide in Figure 8.18.

Figure 8.18

Create tab slides with the Tab Slide Tool and tremolos with the Trill Extension Tool .

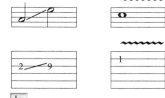

Simply double-click a note or fret number with the Tab Slide Tool selected to extend a tab slide to the next note or fret number. When you copy regular notation that contains tab slides into a tablature staff, the tab slides copy with it. In the tablature staff, tab slides will always begin near the bottom of the first fret number and slant upwards to end near the top of the second fret number (since tab slides will always appear between fret numbers on the same tab line).

To enter a tremolo above a staff, use the Trill Extension Smart Shape.

1.   Click the Trill Extension Tool in the Smart Shape palette.
2.   Double-click and drag to create the tremolo.

Entering Hammer-Ons and Pull-Offs

Hammer-ons tell the performer of a fretted instrument to temporarily "capo" a string with one finger, and use another for the next fret number. A pull-off tells the performer to release the top fret position to sound the lower of the two pitches. You can see an example of a hammer-on and pull-off in Figure 8.19.

Figure 8.19
Add hammer-ons and pull-offs with the Custom Line Tool.

To enter a basic hammer-on or pull-off requires a regular Smart Shape Slur.

1. Click the Slur Tool ◥ in the Smart Shape palette.
2. Double-click a fret number to extend the slur to the next fret number. You now have a basic hammer-on or pull-off figure.

To add accompanying text for hammer-ons ("H") or pull-offs ("P"), as shown in Figure 8.19, use one of Finale's preset custom shapes. To do this:

1. CTRL/OPTION+click the Custom Line Tool **?** to open the Smart Line Style Selection dialog box
2. Scroll down and click to highlight the "H" or "P" custom line. These are basically hidden Smart Shape Lines with attached text.
3. Click **Select** to return to the score.
4. Double-click on the first of two fret numbers and drag to the right until the "H" or "P" appears in the desired location.

TIP:
You can also add several guitar markings with Smart Shape metatools. Hold down the H key, and then click and drag to add a hammer-on. Use the A key for an "A.H." or the N key for a "N.H.".

Entering Picking or Bowing Figures

It's common to see picking indicators in tablature that tell the performer which direction to pluck the string or strings (see Figure 8.20). These figures are also used for bowing indications.

Figure 8.20
Use articulations to specify picking or bowing.

For these, use articulations.

1. Click the Articulation Tool , hold down D (down) or U (up), and click a note. Or, click the note to open the Articulation Selection dialog box appears.

2. Choose either the up pick marking (#19) or the down pick marking (#20) and click Select.

3. You return to the score with the marking above the staff directly above the fret number or note you clicked. For more information regarding adding articulations, see "Entering Articulations" on page 68.

Entering Guitar Fingerings

Left hand (fretting-hand) fingerings appear as numbers; 1=index, 2=middle, 3=ring, and 4=pinky; T is used for the thumb. Picking-hand fingerings appear as letters; i=index, m=middle, a=ring, c=pinky, and p=thumb (see Figure 8.21).

Figure 8.21
Use articulations to enter guitar fingerings.

To create and add guitar fingerings, first load the guitar articulation library, and then add the articulations.

1. Choose **File** > **Load Library**. Open the "Tablature Libraries" folder and double-click **Guitar Articulations**. This step is not necessary if you began using one of Finale's guitar templates.

2. Choose the Articulation Tool .

3. Click a note to open the Articulation Selection dialog box. Scroll down to find the fingering articulations. If you don't see the letter "c," it needs to be added. (If you see the "c," skip to step 6.)

4. Click the "a" articulation and click duplicate. Then click **Edit**.

5. Click **Main**, double-click "c" and click **OK**. Now, your document contains all the necessary fingering articulations. You can use the options in the Articulation Designer to adjust the default positioning of any of these articulations, for example, to place them above or below the staff by default (using the **Always place outside staff** check box).

6.   Double-click to add the desired fingering.

Remember to assign and use metatools to add these articulations quickly.

Editing tab Staff Settings

There are a number of ways to modify existing tablature staves in a document. You can add stems and beams to fret numbers in a staff, change the default lowest fret for a specific fretted instrument, change the string tuning, or even customize the pitch variation between frets for diatonic fretted instruments such as dulcimer.

To make general settings for any tab staff, choose **Window** > **Score Manager**, and select the tab staff. Click the **Settings** button next to **Notation Style** to open the Tablature Staff Attributes dialog box as seen in Figure 8.22.

Figure 8.22

Set up a tab staff for use with any fretted instrument in the Tablature Staff Attributes dialog box.

Here, click the **Instrument** drop-down menu to choose from a number of pre-defined fretted instruments. Each one contains a different string tuning. Choose the instrument you are writing for here so fret numbers will display properly. You can also create your own custom instrument (we'll explain how to do that soon).

- The **Default Lowest Fret** and **Capo** settings dictate the lowest fret number you want to allow in the tab staff you are working with.

- In the **Fret Numbers** section, you can change the font and vertical placement of your fret numbers.

- If you want to use Finale's default tab settings in its Staff Attributes, make sure **On "OK", Reset Staff Attributes To Tablature Defaults** is checked before clicking **OK**. If this box is checked, when you click **OK**, all of the settings in the Score Manager and Staff Attributes (number of staff lines, staff line spacing, items to display, etc.) will reset so your tab staff will appear as it would after creating it with the Setup Wizard. If you have changed settings in the Staff Attributes and do not want these settings to be reset, leave this box unchecked and click **OK**. If you have changed any settings in your Tablature Staff Attributes that affect the number of strings in your tab staff, then you must check **On "OK" Reset Staff's Attributes To Tablature Defaults** to see the changes in your document (as the number of lines on the staff is directly linked to Score Manager.) This includes selecting a different instrument that contains a different number of strings in the Tablature Staff Attributes or editing the number of strings of the current instrument by clicking Edit Instrument.

Adding Stems and Beams to a tab Staff

To add stems and beams to fret numbers in a tablature staff, do the following:

1. Click the Staff Tool 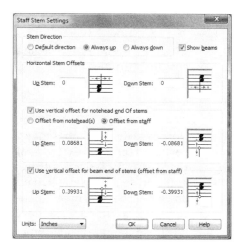.
2. Double-click the tab staff to open Staff Attributes.
3. In the **Items to Display** section, click the **Stem Settings** button to the right of Stems. The Staff Stem Settings dialog box appears as shown in Figure 8.23.

Figure 8.23

Customize stems for a specific staff in the Staff Stem Settings dialog box.

4. Here, specify how you want your stems to appear in the score. Choose the stem direction, placement, and whether or not to show beams. If you want to use Finale's default tab stem settings, you can leave these parameters as they are.
5. Click **OK** to return to the Staff Attributes.
6. Click **OK** to return to the score. Stems and beams appear in the tab staff, reflecting the settings in the Staff Stem Settings dialog box.

Creating a Custom Fretted Instrument Definition for tab

If you're using an instrument in your score that requires a special number of strings or string tuning, you can define your own fretted instrument. To do this:

1. Choose **Window** > **Score Manager**.
2. Select the tab staff.
3. Click the **Settings** button next to **Notation Style** to open the Tablature Staff Attributes.

4. Click **Edit Instruments** in the upper right to open the Fretboard Instrument Definition dialog box as seen in Figure 8.24.

Figure 8.24

Specify tuning, number of strings, and number of frets for a fretted instrument in the Fretboard Instrument Definition dialog box.

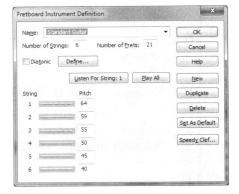

5. Click the **New** button to begin a new instrument definition. Then type a name for your custom instrument.
6. Enter the number of strings on your fretted instrument in the **Number of Strings** text box.
7. Enter the number of frets on your fretted instrument in the **Number of Frets** text box.
8. Now, specify the pitches for each open string as MIDI notes. If you are using a MIDI keyboard (or other external MIDI device), simply click in the text box for a string, click the "Listen for String" button, and then play the open string pitch. Repeat for each string on your instrument. If you do not have a MIDI keyboard, click in each text box and enter the MIDI note number that corresponds to each open string (60 = middle C, 61 = C#, 62 = D, etc.). Click the **Play All** button to hear the pitches you've assigned.
9. If you are creating an instrument with a non-chromatic fretboard (dulcimer, for example), click the **Define** button to open the Diatonic Instrument Definition dialog box as seen in Figure 8.25. If you are not creating an instrument with a diatonic fretboard, skip to step 12.

Figure 8.25

Specify fret tuning for a non-chromatic fretboard in the Diatonic Instrument Definition dialog box.

10. Enter the pitch variation between each fret here. Enter "1" for a half-step, "2" for a whole step, "3" for a minor third, etc. For example, if you want a note played on the first fret to sound a whole step higher than the open string, enter "2" as the first number. Separate each entry with a comma.
11. Click **OK** to return to the Fretted Instrument Definition dialog box.

12. Click **OK**. In the Tablature Staff Attributes box, be sure to check **On "OK", Reset Staff's Attributes to Tablature Default**. Click **OK** to return to your score. Your tab staff now contains the number of strings you specified. Any music you copy to the tab staff will accurately reflect the string tuning, fret tuning, and number of frets for the instrument you defined.

Creating a Guitar Part with tab

Now use the skills you have learned in this chapter (and previous chapters) to create a guitar part with tab, chord symbols, and custom fretboard diagrams.

Finale comes with some nice guitar templates. We'll use one of these to start with. In the future, if you are creating a score for another fretted instrument, use the Document Setup Wizard to choose from a variety of fretted instruments with other string tunings.

Use the following steps to create a short guitar score with tab. After following these steps, your document should look like this (see Figure 8.26):

Figure 8.26

Guitar notation example
with tab

Guitar Example *Mark Johnson*

1. Choose **File** > **New** > **Document from Template**. In the Templates folder, open the Guitar folder. Then double-click the file "House Style 3." The Document Setup Wizard appears.

2. Enter "Guitar Example" for the **Title**. For **Composer**, you can enter "Arr. by" and then your name if you like. Click **Next**.

3. Under **Select a Concert Key Signature**, click the up arrow three times to change the key to A major. The other settings are already correct, so click **Finish**.

4. Now, enter the notation into the standard (top) staff using any of the available entry methods. Use the Smart Shape Tool 🖊 to enter the slurs and tab slides.

5. If you own a MIDI guitar, you could also use HyperScribe to enter the music into the standard or tab staff (see "Entering tab with a MIDI Guitar and HyperScribe" on page 218). When you get to measure 8, 9, 12, and 13, use the Tab Slide Smart Shape to add the tab slides.

6. After you have entered the notation, slurs, and tab slides, click the Selection Tool . Click to the left of the standard (top) staff so the entire staff is highlighted. Now, click in the highlighted area and drag down into the tab staff. Release the mouse button. The Lowest Fret dialog box appears. Click **OK**. Fret numbers for each note now appear in the tab staff.

7. In this template, you may want to move the fret numbers down a bit so they are more centered on the line. To do this, choose **Window** > **Score Manager**, click the **Settings** button to the right of **Tablature**. The Tablature Staff Attributes dialog box appears. In the **Fret Numbers** section, for Vertical Offset, enter "-0.05" inches. Then click **OK** twice to return to the score.

8. Click the Selection Tool and press CTRL/CMD+A to Select All. Then choose **Utilities** > **Fit Measures**. Type "4" and click **OK**. Now there are four measures per system. To delete the extra measures, highlight them and press DELETE.

9. Click the Simple Entry Tool . Notice the third beat of measure three contains fret numbers on the B and E strings. CTRL/OPTION+click and drag these down a string. Notice the numbers update accordingly. Also, do this to modify the fret numbers in measure 7, 10, 13, and 15 so they appear as shown in Figure 8.26.

10. Click the Smart Shape Tool . To enter the "Let Ring" indications, CTRL/
    OPTION+click the Custom Line Tool in the Smart Shape palette. The Smart Line Style Selection dialog box appears. Scroll down and click to highlight the "Let Ring" smart line. Click **Select**. Now, double-click and drag in the score to enter the Let Ring indications.

11. Now, enter the hammer-ons and pull-offs.

    a. Click the Smart Shape Tool, and then click the Slur Tool in the Smart Shape palette.

    b. In measure 4, beat 3 and 4, notice the slurs didn't carry over from the standard staff.

    c. Double-click the lower "2" on the third beat. The slur is now actually overlapping the slur above. Click the handle on the slur attached to the top "2" on the third beat. Then, press and hold DOWN ARROW to nudge it over the lower fret numbers. Do the same for the fret numbers on the fourth beat. To place the letter "H" above the slur, hold down the H key, click the left side of the slur and drag to the right. Notice the H appears above and between the two fret numbers. Now, you need to enter pull-offs in measures 8 and 12.

    d. Click the Slur Tool again and double-click the fret number on the "and of two" in measures 8 and 12.

e. Now, to add the P, hold down the O key, click the fret number on the "and of two" in measure eight and drag to the next fret number. Do the same in measure 12.

NOTE:
If O doesn't add a pull-off, it's a mistake in the template. Press SHIFT+O (letter O) and choose the "P" option in the Smart Line Selection dialog box to define the metatool. Click **OK** and repeat letter e.

12. Enter the chord symbols (as described in Chapter 4). Then, to show fretboard diagrams, choose **Chord** > **Show Fretboards**. When you get to measure three, notice the fretboard diagrams shown in Figure 8.26 are slightly different. To add the thumb indication on the low E string, create a custom fretboard diagram.

a. With the Chord Tool ⬛ selected, context-click the chord symbol handle and choose **Edit Chord Definition.**

b. In the **Fretboard** section, click **Select**, and then click **Create**. The Fretboard Editor appears.

c. Click the T tool and then click the second fret E string to place the T on the fretboard diagram.

d. Click **OK, Select** and **OK** to return to the score. Now, the second fretboard diagram in measure 3 is quite different than the default fretboard.

e. Right/+click the second chord symbol handle in measure 3 and choose **Edit Chord Definition.**

f. In the **Fretboard** section, click **Select**, and then click **Create**.

g. Use the available tools to create the new fretboard (as shown in Figure 8.27). This chord will need to be fingered higher on the fretboard, so in the **Fretboard Number** section, check **Show**, and then for **Number**, enter "4." The Fretboard Editor dialog box should now look like Figure 8.27.

h. Click **OK, Select** and **OK** to return to the score. Your custom fretboard now appears above the staff. Use the same method to create custom fretboards as necessary for the remaining measures (you won't have to create the same fretboard twice for the same chord, just choose the one already created in the Fretboard Selection dialog box by clicking Select in the Fretboard section of the Chord Definition dialog box).

Figure 7.27

Use the Fretboard Editor to quickly edit fretboard diagrams in your score.

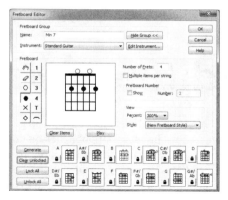

13. Now, you may notice the chord symbols overlap, particularly in measure fifteen. To resolve this, choose **Document > Document Options**, and then select **Music Spacing**. Under **Avoid Collision Of**, check **Chords** and click **OK**. Your music adjusts to avoid collision of chord symbols. (To apply music spacing manually, choose the Selection Tool [image], highlight the region and press 4).

14. Now, click the Page Layout Tool [image]. Choose **Page Layout > Space Systems Evenly** and click **OK**. Make any other changes to the layout as necessary.

If you like, play back the piece for review. If you want to disable chord playback, click the Chord Tool, and then, choose **Chord**, and uncheck **Enable Chord Playback**. You can use the general method above at any time while creating a guitar part with tab. If a guitar part you are writing requires slash or rhythmic notation, see "Slash and Rhythmic Notation" on page 202 for more information.

9
Editing Your Music

Now let's put your Finale machine in top gear. After learning some key efficiency tricks you'll scarcely even notice the hundreds of publisher-quality manuscripts flying from your desktop to music stands across the globe.[1] This chapter is full of broad-scope features like advanced copying, merging documents, and music spacing. Hold on tight, because the thrill of manipulating massive quantities of music notation in the blink of an eye does tend to breech the limits of modesty for some. But, there is no need to panic. The Undo command (CTRL/CMD+Z) shall remedy any fits of irrational exuberance you might encounter when getting acquainted with Finale's more brazen functions.

Here's a summary of what you will learn in this chapter:

- How to specify what, how, and where to copy
- How to change music en masse (transpose, edit entry items, move pitches, etc.)
- How to space your music
- How to change and manage fonts

Specifying What, How, and Where to Copy

You learned the basics of copying and pasting in Chapter 2. This chapter covers the more advanced ways you can copy based on:

- What you want to move (everything, just notes, just expressions, etc.)
- How you want to copy (merge, append, using clip files, etc.)
- Where you want to move it (across staves, across documents, across programs)

You may also need to perform more advanced operations, like search-and-replace for specific pitches, or find similar rhythmic passages to apply articulations and expressions consistently. In this section I'll cover a variety of ways to move and change music.

The first step to copying will always include selecting a region. For information on selecting regions of measures, see "Selecting Regions" on page 37.

---

1   Results may vary.

Methods of Copying

In this section, you'll use the same methods described previously to select measure regions and copy music (drag-copy, CTRL/OPTION+click copy, etc.). You'll learn how these methods also apply to copying specific items from any selected region and copying across documents.

To prepare for the following instructions, open a new Default Document (**File** > **New** > **Default Document**).

Copying Single Layers

You can isolate any layer for copying by showing the active layer only.

1. First, choose the layer you want to copy from the Layer selection buttons/pop-up menu in the lower-left corner of the screen.
2. Choose **Document** > **Show Active Layer Only**.

Now copy the music as you would normally. Only the layer that displays will be copied. Also, music in other layers in the destination measures will not be affected.

> **TIP:**
> Move music from one layer to another with the Move/Copy Layers dialog box under the Edit Menu.

Selecting Specific Items to Copy

Identify specific musical elements for pasting with the Edit Filter dialog box. It's fastest to do this on the fly as you paste using a modifier keystroke. Remember in Chapter 2 you learned how to CTRL/OPTION+click a target measure to paste; this is the same idea with an additional step:

1. Click the Selection Tool ▣ .
2. Highlight a region of your score containing the items you want to copy.
3. CTRL/OPTION+SHIFT+Click the first measure of the destination region. The Edit Filter dialog box appears as shown in Figure 9.1.

Figure 9.1

Specify measure-attached items to copy in the Edit Filter dialog box.

4. Check each item you want to paste. Click **All** if you want to copy all items.
5. Click **OK.** The selected items appear in the target region.

Now, click the Edit menu. Notice Use Filter is checked. Next time you copy and paste, Finale will respect these settings. You can continue to copy the items you selected for other areas of your score (by simply drag- or clipboard-copying). When you want to go back to copying everything, uncheck Use Filter from the Edit menu.

- Press CTRL+ALT+F (Mac: CMD+OPTION+F) at any time to activate/deactivate the **Use Filter** setting under the Edit Menu.
- Press CTRL+ALT+SHIFT+F (Mac: CMD+OPTION+SHIFT+F) at any time to display the Edit Filter dialog box.

Copying Between Documents

You can copy notation between documents just as you would within the same document using the clipboard. To view both documents while copying, try the following:

1. Open both the source and destination document.
2. From the Window menu, choose Tile Horizontally or Tile Vertically (Mac: Time Windows) so you can see both documents simultaneously on your screen.

3. Now, drag-copy or use the clipboard to move music between documents. Remember, in order to copy measure settings, the source region needs to be a stack (full measure(s)/all staves).

TIP:
If you want to view documents on the entire screen while copying, switch between documents by choosing the file name at the bottom of the Window menu. Press CTRL+TAB (Mac: CMD+' (that button way on the upper left of your keyboard)) to quickly switch back and forth between documents.

Merging Documents

The procedures used for appending one file onto the end of another (e.g. for multiple movements) or consolidating many parts into a score have been greatly simplified by Finale's ScoreMerger utility. ScoreMerger is particularly useful when combining files that have different number of staves/instruments, which was particularly difficult in previous Finale versions.

To append one file to the end of another (for multiple movements, etc.):

1. Choose **File** > **ScoreMerger**. The ScoreMerger dialog box appears as shown in Figure 9.2.
2. Click **Add Files**. The Select the Files to Merge dialog box appears, prompting you to select one or more files. (Hold down the CTRL/CMD key to select multiple files).
3. Click **Open**/**Choose**. The files are added to the file display window of the Score Merger dialog box. Add additional files if necessary, then use the **Move Up** and **Move Down** buttons to change the file order.

Figure 9.2
Score Merger allows you to easily consolidate multiple movements into a single file.

4. Be sure **Merge These Files into One File** is selected. There are some options here for handling left and right pages and numbering (see ScoreMerger in the User Manual for details).

5. Click **Merge**. Name and save the file when prompted. The Instrument Junction dialog box appears as shown in figure 9.3.

Figure 9.3

The Instrument Junction dialog box displays how ScoreMerger will join and add staves.

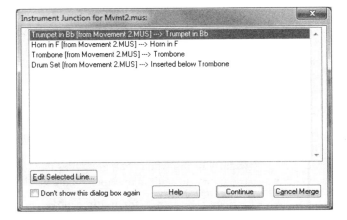

ScoreMerger works by joining staves. This dialog box displays the staves that will be joined and any additional staves that will be added. (The resulting score will house at least the number of staves of the merged file containing the greatest number of staves - any extra staves will be hidden automatically.)

Notice in this merge a Drum Set staff will be added beneath the Trombone staff in Movement 2 of this brass trio. Note that at this point you can double-click a staff (or click Edit Selected Line) to open the Choose Junction dialog box which allows you to edit all aspects of this configuration.

6. Click **Continue**. ScoreMerger joins the staves and displays a report detailing its operations.

7. Click **Close** to view the merged document.

Consolidating several parts into a score is much easier. Simply follow steps 1 through 3 above, choose **Merge These Parts into One Score** and click **Merge**.

Clearing Items

You can clear any type of musical item from a selected region of your score.

1. Highlight a region of your score. Then, choose **Edit** > **Clear Selected Items**. The Clear Selected Items dialog box appears (which resembles the Edit Filter dialog box shown in Figure 9.1).

2. Check the items you would like to clear. Measure Settings are only available for clearing if a stack is selected.

3. Click **OK** to clear the items you have selected and return to the score.

Changing Music

Anything you enter in Finale can be changed, moved, or deleted. This section focuses on the many ways to edit existing notes, expressions, chords, tuplets, and other items for any region of your score or for the whole document. Many of the following steps require a selected region of measures. Remember, many tools allow measure selection (see "Selecting Regions" on page 37 or "Selecting Music" in the User Manual for details).

Changing Notes: Search and Replace

There may be a reoccurring passage of music in a score, or even a short motif, that you want to edit for every occurrence. You can change the pitch or enharmonic spelling of individual notes in a reoccurring musical passage with the Note Mover Tool's Search and Replace function.

1. Choose the Note Mover Tool ![] (on Windows, first choose **Window** > **Advanced Tools**; then, choose the Note Mover Tool from the Advanced Tools Palette).
2. Click a measure containing an arrangement of notes that you want to change for another, or all other occurrences in the score. You will see a handle on every note as shown in Figure 9.4.

Figure 9.4
Selecting a region for search and replace

3. Drag over a region of handles to choose the notes in your source region. SHIFT+click to select non-consecutive notes.
4. Choose **Note Mover** > **Search and Replace**. The Search and Replace dialog box appears as shown in Figure 9.5. Mac users, you will first see the "Do you want to search..." dialog box also shown in Figure 9.5. Choose the desired option to open the Search and Replace dialog box.

Figure 9.5
Customize your search in the Search and Replace dialog box.

5. Here, choose **In All Octaves** if you want Finale to search for the selected notes in every octave of your score. Choose **In Selected Octave Only** to isolate the search to the

octave of the selected notes. Check **Match Durations** if you only want Finale to search for the selected arrangement of notes in their rhythm only.

6. Click **OK.** The Alteration for Slot dialog box appears.

7. Each "slot" is a selected note. The first selected note is slot 1, the second, slot 2, etc. Move to the slot of a selected note you want to change by clicking Next. If you want to change the enharmonic of the slot, select **Enharmonic.** If you want to change the pitch, select **Transposition.** If you select Transposition, the Transposition dialog box appears. Choose an interval to transpose the note in the specified slot. If you wish to apply the same transposition to each selected note, set your transposition first and then click **Set All.** Click **OK.**

8. Once you have finished specifying the changes, click **OK** to return to the score. You will now see a new menu at the top of the screen-the Search menu.

9. Choose **Search** > **Find.** Finale will look for a matching arrangement of notes and will highlight their handles.

10. Choose **Search** > **Replace Then Find** to apply the changes you specified to the region, and automatically select the next occurrence. To go to the next occurrence without changing it, choose **Find** again. To find and replace all occurrences at once, choose **Search** > **Replace All.**

Changing Entry Items En Masse

In addition to changing notes with the Note Mover Tool , Finale can also modify the appearance of several other items in any region of the score using options under the Utilities Menu.

Swapping Articulations and Expressions

You can swap an expression or articulation for another in any selected region of your score with the Change Articulation Assignments and Change Expression Assignments features. If you would like to swap an expression or articulation, first make sure the new figure exists in the Expression Selection or Articulation Selection dialog box (you can find information on creating and editing expressions and articulations in Chapter 3). Use the following steps to change articulations in a selected region of your score:

1. Select a region of your score containing articulations you want to change.

2. Choose **Utilities** > **Change** > **Articulations.** The Change Articulation Assignments dialog box appears as shown in Figure 9.6.

Figure 9.6
Swap articulations with the Change Articulation Assignments dialog box.

3. If you want to change all articulations in the selected region to the same one, leave **Position All Articulations** chosen and move to step 6. To change specific articulations, select **Position Selected Articulation** and continue to the next step.

4. Click the **Select** button to the right of Position Selected Articulation. The Articulation Selection dialog box appears.

5. Choose the existing articulation that you would like to change from the list and click **Select**. You return to the Change Articulation Assignment dialog box and the number of the articulation you selected appears in the top text box.

6. Check **Change All Articulations** (or **Selected Articulation**).

7. Click the **Select** button next to "to articulation." The Articulation Selection dialog box appears.

8. Choose the new articulation from the list and click **Select**. You return to the Change Articulation Assignment dialog box and the number of the articulation you selected appears in the middle text box.

9. For **H:** and **V:**, enter a value if you wish to adjust the default positioning of the new articulations. Or, click the drop-down menu and choose **Add to Current Position** to make adjustments from where they are currently positioned. (Even if you are not swapping, this can be used to change articulation positioning en masse).

10. Click **OK** to return to the score and review your changes. The articulations you specified (or all articulations) change and reposition accordingly.

To change a specific expression assignment, or all expressions in a region, follow the same steps but choose Expressions from the Utilities > Change submenu.

Editing Chord Symbols

Like articulations and expressions, every chord symbol in a selected region can be changed at once. You can edit their transposition, playback, and visual definition. To do this:

1. Select a region of your score containing chord symbols you want to change.

2. Choose **Utilities** > **Change** > **Chords.** The Change Chord Assignments dialog box appears as shown in Figure 9.7.

Figure 9.7
Change the visual definition, playback, or transposition of an existing
chord symbol in the Change Chord Assignments dialog box.

3. Here, choose how you want to change the selected chord symbols (any check boxes in gray (Mac: with a - (dash)) mean the settings will be unaltered). In the **Show** section, choose chord components to show or hide. In the **Play** section, assign components of the chords for playback. Click the **Transpose** button to open the Transpose dialog box where you can choose a new transposition for the selected chord symbols. Transposition will apply to fretboard diagrams as well as chord symbols.

NOTE:
When you change the key of a piece using the Key Signature Tool, all chord symbols will also transpose accordingly. Use the Change Chord Assignments dialog box only to transpose chord symbols independently from the key signature.

4. When you have finished specifying changes, click **OK** to return to the score. All chords and fretboards in the selected region change according to the settings you made.

To make global changes to the appearance of accidental characters on chord symbols, choose **Document > Document Options**, and then select **Chords**. In the Chords portion of the Document Options, you can set the baseline (vertical placement) and change font characters for accidentals in chord symbols. Note that any changes you make in Document Options apply only to the document you are working on.

Ties and Tuplets

The placement and visual definition of ties and tuplets can be altered in a selected region like expressions, articulations, and chords.

1. With a region of the score selected, choose **Utilities** > **Change** > **Ties** or **Tuplets** to do so. However, you will most likely want these items to remain consistent throughout an entire document.

2. To edit the placement, visual definition, and other attributes of ties and tuplets throughout a document, choose **Document** > **Document Options.** In the Document Options dialog box, choose the **Ties** or **Tuplets** category to make global changes to ties and tuplets.

Changes applied in the Document Options dialog box only apply to future tuplets you add to the score. To modify existing tuplets, highlight the region containing the tuplets you want to change and choose **Utilities** > **Change** > **Tuplets**.

TIP:
Tuplets were improved in Finale 2005 so that they slope according to the angle of notes and beams. They also avoid notes and stems automatically. These are called "Enhanced Tuplets" and only apply to tuplets added in Finale 2005 or later. If you want to update tuplets in a document converted from an ancient Finale version, use **Utilities** > **Change Tuplets** described above. (Refer to the Finale 2005 default tuplet settings (in the default file) to convert old tuplets so they appear exactly the same as native 2005 tuplets.)

TIP:
To alter tie and tuplet definitions and placement for a region of music, try the Patterson Tuplet Mover and Tie Mover plug-ins.

Changing Note Durations and Appearance

You can easily change the note duration, notehead character, and note size for any selected region of music. Like the previous features, these can be found in the **Utilities** > **Change** submenu.

Changing Note Durations

You have a great deal of control over the duration of notes in a selected region. You may need to change note durations if you decide to change the time signature (doubling note durations while changing from common time to cut time, for example). To modify the duration of notes in any region, use the following steps.

1. Select a region of your score containing notes you want to change. (If you want to change note durations in a specific layer, choose the layer and, then, choose **Document** > **Show Active Layer Only**.)

2. Choose **Utilities** > **Change** > **Note Durations**. The Change Note Durations dialog box appears as shown in Figure 9.8.

Figure 9.8
Edit the duration of a region of notes according to settings in the Change
Note Durations dialog box.

3.   To change all note durations, ensure **Change All Note Durations By** is selected. Then
     click the drop-down menu and choose the new percentage (200 percent doubles the
     note values, 50 percent reduces durations by half, etc.). If there is a specific note
     duration within the selected region you want to change, choose **Change Selected
     Note Duration**. In the From row, click the duration of the note you want to change (use
     the dot on the right to indicate a dotted note). In the To row, click the new duration
     you want to assign.

4.   Check **Rebar Measures** if you want the resulting notes to flow into different measures
     as dictated by the time signature. If this box is not checked, Finale will leave the
     resulting notes in their original measures (likely creating overfilled or incomplete
     measures).

5.   Click **OK** to return to the score and review changes to note durations.

CAUTION:
When you use these steps, all notes and rests in the selected region
change except default whole rests. If you would like to include default
whole rests while changing note durations with this method, first run
the Change To Real Whole Rests plug-in. Highlight the region of your
score you want to change. Then, choose **Plug-ins/** > **Note, Beam and
Rest Editing** > **Change to Real Whole Rests**. Now rests in the selected
region are "real" and will be affected by note duration changes with
the Utilities Menu.

Changing Notehead Characters

You can change the notehead character in any selected region of your score. If the character of the
notehead you want to use is in your existing default Notehead font, use the Change Noteheads plug-in in
the Notes, Beams and Rests submenu of the Plug-ins menu. You can see your current default music font
by choosing **Document** > **Set Default Music Font**.

NOTE:
If you are creating percussion notation, use the Percussion Layout
Designer to assign notehead characters to staff lines (see Chapter 8).

Changing the Note Size (cue notes)

You may want to change the size of notes in a region (to create cue notes for example). Before using this method for cue notes, however, be sure to try the Add Cue Notes and Smart Cue Notes plug-ins under **Plug-ins/** ✂ > **Scoring and Arranging**. To change the size of notes, and their corresponding stems and beams:

1. Select a region of your score containing notes you want to resize. If you want to change note size in a specific layer, choose the layer, and then **Document** > **Show Active Layer Only**.
2. Choose **Utilities** > **Change** > **Note Size**. The Change Note Size dialog box appears as shown in Figure 9.9

Figure 9.9
Change the size for a region of notes according to settings in the Change Note Size dialog box.

3. Enter a new percentage for notes in the selected region (200% doubles the note size, 50% reduces the size by half, etc.).
4. Click **OK** to return to the score. All visible notes in the selected region are resized.

TIP:
You can also change the size of notes individually by clicking them with the Resize Tool %️ . Notice that when you click on the stem you get the Resize Note dialog, and when you click directly on the notehead, you get the Resize Notehead dialog box.

Transposing

We have already seen how to transpose music by changing the key signature (in Chapters 2 and 5). You may, however, need to transpose music without changing the key. To transpose notes diatonically or chromatically in any region of your score within the key:

1. Click the Selection Tool 🖱 , select a region of your score containing music you want to transpose, and then press 6 or 7 to transpose up or down by whole steps, 8 or 9 to transpose up or down an octave. If you need additional control, continue with the following steps.
2. Choose **Utilities** > **Transpose**. The Transpose dialog box appears as shown in Figure 9.10.

Figure 9.10

Specify an interval to transpose a selected region in the Transposition dialog box.

3. For Transpose, choose the direction you want to transpose the music (Up or Down). Then choose **Chromatically** to transpose any number of half-steps, or choose **Diatonically** to transpose within the key.

4. Click the drop-down menu for **Interval** and choose an interval to transpose the notes. The options you have here depend on the Diatonic/Chromatic setting above.

5. In the text box for **Plus_Octaves**, enter the octave displacement. "1" = up one octave, "-1" = down one octave, etc.

6. Choose **Preserve Original Notes** if you want to leave the existing notes in the score and make copies of them at the specified transposition. This works well for quickly creating octave doubling in a staff or doubling at the third, etc.

7. Click **OK** to return to the score. Music in the selected region is now transposed to the interval you specified.

As alluded to in step one above, with the Selection Tool selected, the 6, 7, 8, and 9 keys are transposition keyboard shortcuts. These are metatools which can be programmed to any transposition.

To program a transposition metatool:

1. With the Selection Tool selected, hold down the SHIFT key and press the 6, 7, 8, or 9 key on the QWERTY keyboard. The Transposition dialog box appears.

2. Define a transposition and click **OK**.

3. Now, highlight a region of music and press the number key you assigned to transpose it.

> **TIP:**
> If you want to transpose the music for an instrument doubling, add a mid-score instrument change. Select a region and choose **Utilities** > **Change Instrument**. See "Adding Mid-Score Instrument Changes" on page 206 for details.

Music Spacing

Finale does most of the music spacing for you. You may have noticed notes shifting after you enter them. This is Finale's attempt to space music proportionally during entry. If you are not satisfied with the default spacing, or want to make manual adjustments on your own, Finale offers you plenty of power to do so. Manipulating the automatic music spacing settings, moving measures across systems, stretching measures by moving barlines, or moving notes around individually are just a few ways to adjust the spacing of your music in Finale. In this section you'll learn how to use several of Finale's most effective music spacing methods.

Music spacing is largely affected by the width of systems, so for the following instruction, it is best to be working in Page View (remember there is one continuous system in Scroll View). Choose View > Page View.

Automatic Music Spacing and Music Spacing Libraries

Automatic Music Spacing is turned on by default, so it is likely you have put it to use without even knowing it. It affects the spacing of your music after entering notes with any of the available entry methods. It can automatically adjust the space between notes and the width of measures. It can also make fine adjustments to your music to avoid collisions. Automatic Music Spacing can be turned on or off in Program Options-Edit.

TIP:
Highlight a region of measures and press CTRL/CMD+4 to easily apply Note Spacing to the region.

You can modify the parameters Finale uses for spacing in the Music Spacing category of the Document Options dialog box (see Figure 9.11). From the Document menu, choose Document Options, and then select Music Spacing from the list on the left.

Figure 9.11

Make changes to document-wide settings for music spacing in the Music Spacing portion of the Document Options dialog box.

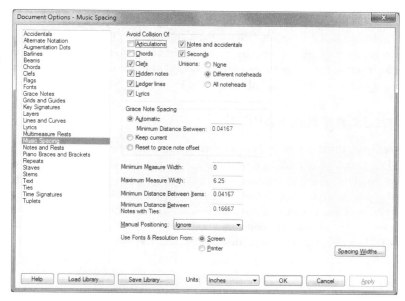

In this dialog box, you can make adjustments to Finale's default music spacing settings. Here, tell Finale to:

- Avoid collision of certain items
- Choose a minimum and maximum measure width, and specify the minimum and maximum space between notes.
- Ignore, clear, or incorporate spacing of notes you have positioned manually by choosing one of these items from the Manual Positioning drop-down menu. For example, if you have manually positioned some notes and later you decide that you want to space your music using Finale's spacing, select Clear for Manual Positioning and then apply Note Spacing to your document. You can then set Manual Position back to Ignore so that future manual adjustments you make will be retained unless you specify otherwise.

You can have further control over Finale's automatic spacing by modifying the spacing widths. Click the Spacing Widths button to specify a number of EDUs allotted to each rhythmic duration. The process of adjusting spacing widths manually and reviewing the score can be quite time consuming and tedious. Instead, choose from a number of preset spacing width configurations by loading one of Finale's available Music Spacing Libraries. (The Fibonacci Spacing library is already loaded into Finale's default documents.)

To load a music spacing library:

1. Click **Load Library** in the Document Options dialog box (or, choose **File** > **Load Library**). The Open Library dialog box appears.
2. Double-click the "Music Spacing" folder.
3. Double-click one of the available music spacing libraries to open it (then click **OK** to return to the score if necessary).

Now, Finale will use the spacing widths defined by the library you opened. One of the five music spacing libraries should meet your needs. If not, configure custom music spacing settings in the Spacing Widths dialog box, and save your own music spacing library to use with any document. After customizing the spacing widths, click **Save Library** in the Document Options to save a Music Spacing library.

Updating the Layout

By default, Finale updates the page format and number of measures per system during entry, while adding measures or making other changes that have an effect on the page layout (in Page View only). You may have seen measures jumping between systems while entering music. This is a result of Automatic Update Layout (found in Program Options-Edit), Finale's attempt to create evenly spaced measures within systems. Updating the layout also brings together other elements of the page format, such as the number of systems per page while resizing systems, staves, or pages. Press CTRL+U on Windows or CMD+U on Mac (or choose **Utilities** > **Update Layout**) to update the layout at any time.

Locking Measures Per System

To tell Finale how to handle the number of measures per systems while updating the layout, use the Update Layout Options.

1. Choose **Edit** > **Program Options** (Mac: **Finale 2012** > **Preferences** > **Program Options**). Click **Edit**. Program Options-Edit appears as shown in Figure 9.12.

Figure 9.12

Tell Finale how to reconfigure systems and pages while updating the layout in Program Options-Edit.

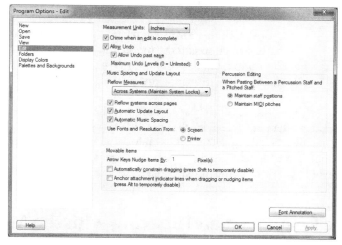

2. Make sure **Across Systems (Maintain System Locks)** is selected. This is Finale's default setting and perhaps the most flexible setting. Click **OK** to return to the score.
3. Choose **View** > **Show** and make sure **Show Page Layout Icons** is checked so that any system locks will be visible.
4. To lock a system or systems, highlight measures in the systems you want to lock. Choose **Utilities**> **Lock Systems.** You will notice a padlock icon to the right of the selected systems. This icon indicates that the number of measures in the system and will not be changed while updating the layout.
5. To remove system locks, highlight a region and choose **Utilities** > **Unlock Systems.**

While moving measures between systems manually, or using the Fit Measures command (under the Utilities menu) to fit a number of measures to systems (see "Moving Measures Across Systems" on page 44), Finale locks these systems automatically. To demonstrate this, clear system locks from a (select the region and press CTRL/CMD+L). Then, click the last measure of a system, and press CTRL/CMD+DOWN ARROW to move it to the next system. Notice a lock appears to the right of both modified systems.

Spacing Regions of Measures

To apply spacing changes to a certain region of the score without affecting any other region, apply music spacing to any desired region with the Utilities Menu.

1. First, turn off **Automatic Music Spacing** in Program Options-Edit (Win: under the Edit Menu, Mac: **Finale 2012 Menu** > **Preferences**).

2. Click the Selection Tool ![icon] and highlight a region of measures containing music you want to respace.

3. Choose **Utilities** > **Music Spacing** > **Apply Note, Beat, or Time Signature Spacing**. Or, instead of choosing the menu item, simply press CTRL/CMD+4 to apply Note Spacing to a region, or press CTRL/CMD+5 to apply Beat Spacing to a region. You will typically want to use Note Spacing.

Beat Spacing will space each beat according to the table of widths and will space notes between beats linearly (quarter note gets twice the space of an eighth note, and so on). Note Spacing provides more precision by using the spacing widths table for each note (Note Spacing is also used for Automatic Music Spacing). Time Signature Spacing will use linear spacing throughout the measure. For example, a half note would get twice as much space as a quarter note. This is how your music looks directly after entering it into the score with Automatic Music Spacing off.

The Beat Chart and Spacing with the Measure Tool

Chapter 7 showed how to increase or decrease the width of measures by dragging barlines with the Measure Tool . When dragging the barlines, the entries in the measures will respace proportionally. There are some other music spacing techniques possible with the Measure Tool.

Occasionally, you may want to respace all notes on a certain beat for all staves in a measure. You can manually adjust the placement of each beat using the Measure Tool's Beat Chart. To space your music using a Beat Chart:

1. Click the Measure Tool ![icon] . You will now see two handles on each barline in the selected region. If you do not see two handles, be sure there are notes in the measure(s) and turn on **Automatic Music Spacing** (Program Options-Edit) or apply music spacing to the region.

2. Click the lower barline handle. The Beat Chart appears above the top staff in the system as shown in Figure 9.13.

Figure 9.13
Specify the placement of beats for a
measure in all staves of a system with the
Beat Chart.

3. Drag the bottom handle to position all notes on the beat in all staves of the system.
4. Double-click the top beat chart handle to open the Beat Chart dialog box as shown in Figure 9.14.

Figure 9.14
You can specify the precise placement of beats using the Beat Chart dialog box.

5. Click **OK** to close the Beat Chart dialog box and click anywhere in the score to hide the Beat Chart handles.

TIP:
You can use measure spacing handles (added in Finale 2005) to manually adjust the space before and after music in each measure. Choose the Measure Tool. Choose **Measure** > **Show Measure Spacing Handles**. Now, two handles appear on the bottom staff line in each measure. Drag these handles to adjust the spacing.

Spacing Notes Individually

You can use the Speedy Entry Tool or the Special Tools to space notes individually.

1. Click the Speedy Entry Tool and click a measure containing notes to open the Speedy frame.
2. Click and drag notes in the active layer to move them horizontally.

To use the Special Tools for spacing:

1. Click the Special Tools Tool (on Windows, first choose **Window** > **Advanced Tools Palette**, then click the Special Tools Tool). You will see the Special Tools Palette appear on the screen.

2. From this palette, choose the Note Position Tool.

3. Click in a measure to see positioning handles appear above the measure. Click and drag these handles to move the corresponding notes left or right in the measure.

To incorporate your manual note spacing into all future music spacing applied to the region:

1. choose **Document** > **Document Options**, then select **Music Spacing**.

2. Click the drop-down menu for **Manual Positioning** and choose **Incorporate**. Or, choose **Ignore** to tell Finale to reapply your manual positioning after spacing the music. You can also choose **Clear** to remove manual spacing adjustments while spacing.

Positioning Notes Evenly in a Measure

With the Measure Tool , you can also tell Finale to position notes evenly in a measure regardless of the time signature, measure width, or number of notes in the measure. This is sometimes used for chant notation where a measure takes up an entire staff system or a long cadenza in a solo. Also, use this method when you want to space a measure containing too many beats relative to the time signature-for example, in a cadenza passage.

1. Click the Measure Tool .

2. Double-click a measure to open the Measure Attributes dialog box.

3. In the **Display** section, under **Position Notes**, check **Evenly Across Measure**.

4. Click **OK** to return to the score. Notes in the measure are now positioned evenly. Any notes you add to this measure will also be positioned evenly.

Setting a Measure to Begin a Staff System

If you know you want a specific measure to always begin a new staff system, you can mark the measure with the Measure Tool .

1. With the Measure Tool Selected, double-click a measure to open the Measure Attributes dialog box.

2. In the **Behavior** section, check **Begin a New Staff System**.

3. Click **OK** to return to the score. Now, the measure will always mark the beginning of a new system. Notice the resulting arrow icon in the left margin as a reminder to you.

CAUTION:
The above setting also applies to linked parts. If you intend to use linked parts, limit the use of the above to measures that should begin a system in both the score and parts, like the first measure in a movement, for example.

Changing and Managing Fonts

Just about everything you enter into a score—music, text expressions, articulations, and other items—are font characters. Just as you can change the font, size, or style of your letters in a word-processing program, you can do the same for most items in a score. All font settings are document-specific, so they are saved along with each document. You can see the fonts currently selected in an open document by looking in the Document Options. Choose **Document** > **Document Options** and select **Fonts** from the list on the left. The Font options appear as shown in Figure 9.15.

Figure 9.15

Set the default font for any item in the Fonts portion of the Document Options dialog box.

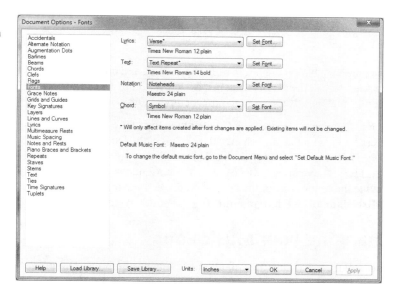

Here you can choose any font on your system for each option under the four drop-down menus. The fonts on your system include the Finale music fonts that were added when you installed Finale. (You can find a list of the Finale fonts and their characters under the Help menu—on Windows, choose **Help** > **Shortcuts & Character Maps**. On Mac, choose **Help** > **Character Sets**.) Let's say you want to set the font of your lyric verses to Arial. First, click the drop-down menu for Lyrics and choose Verses. Then click the Set Font button to the right. The Font dialog box opens as shown in Figure 9.16.

Figure 9.16
Specify the font, size, and style for an item in the
Font dialog box.

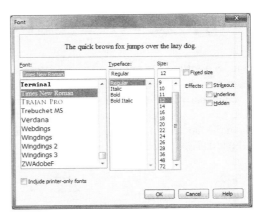

Use the scroll bar on the left to move up the list, and click Arial to select it. Notice that you can change the point size and style of a font just as you would in a word-processing program. When you have set up your font, click **OK** to return to the Document Options dialog box.

Notice that there is an asterisk (*) next to many of the items listed under the four drop-down menus. The asterisk tells you that any change to the font in the Document Options will apply only to new items added to the score (or to selection dialogs) and will not apply to existing items already in the score. For example, if lyrics have already been entered, your font change here will not apply to them. If you want to change the font of one of the asterisked fonts, try using the Change Fonts plug-in under **Plug-ins/** ✂ >**Miscellaneous > Change Fonts** (more about how to do this soon).

Changing Your Music Font

Finale makes changing the default music font easy. Choose **Document** > **Set Default Music Font**. The Finale music fonts include Maestro, Maestro Percussion, Maestro Wide, Finale Copyist, Broadway Copyist, Jazz, Jazz Perc, FinaleAlphaNotes, FinalePerc, FinaleMallets, Finale Numerics, and Engraver fonts.

Remember, you can see a list of all of Finale's fonts and their characters under the Help menu. Remember also that Finale gives you the ability to change different elements of music, as mentioned above. The Default Music font changes all of these elements at once.

Swapping and Checking Fonts

You can change all characters in a certain font to another font by using Finale's Font Swapping utility. Choose **Document** > **Data Check** > **Font Utilities**. The Swap One Font for Another dialog box appears as shown in Figure 9.17.

Figure 9.17

The Swap One Font for Another dialog box

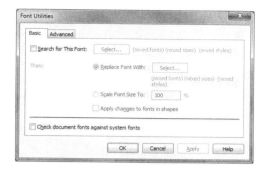

1. Under the **Basic** tab, check **Search for This Font** and click **Select** to open the Font dialog box.
2. Select the font you want to change and click **OK**.
3. After **Replace Font With**, click the **Select** button. The Font dialog box appears again.
4. Select the new font, size, and style for your font and click **OK**.
5. Click **OK** to return to your score and review the appearance of items in the new font.

Keep in mind that changing the font this way will apply to all items in the selected font in this file. Consult the Fonts category of the Document Options to see all items that use any given font.

Unicode Fonts

One of Finale 2012's big advantages is Unicode font support. Unicode is an international standard for handling of text and consolidates all the world's languages into a consistent coding system. With regards to your work with Finale, Unicode means less hoops to jump through to get your scores looking right, especially if you are working with projects in languages other than English. In fact, it may require no work on your end at all. When you think Finale and Unicode, think of a disheveled software engineer burning the midnight fluorescent lighting for months on end to make your life easier, knowing you probably won't notice anything changed. When you think "how do I get this foreign document to look right?" or "how do I get that strange character placed in my score?" Consider the advice in this section. (The word "Unicode" doesn't even need to enter into the equation.)

TIP:
Mac users: If you want the greatest chance of displaying a character pending the possibility its font isn't installed on your computer, choose **Finale 2012 > Preferences > Program Options** and select **Edit**. Ensure **Substitute Font for Missing Unicode Characters** is checked. If you are a stickler for every character being displayed in its intended font, you might not want this box checked.

Inserting a Unicode Character

If you have memorized the hex values of all the characters you would like to use, there is apparently some way to enter Unicode characters by setting up your operating system to allow for hex entry and then use an elaborate combination of keystrokes while wearing a lamp shade on your head. If you discover that this process is possible in Finale, please let me know. As an alternative, I recommend choosing the character you would like to add from a convenient visual display. Fortunately, Finale includes one known as the Symbol Selection dialog box, which is available wherever text can be entered (Expression Designer, Lyrics Window, Smart Line Designer, etc.).

To add a Unicode character into a text block:

1. First, we'll select the font. Choose **Document** > **Document Options** and select **Fonts**.
2. Click the **Text** drop down and choose **Text Blocks,** then click the adjacent **Set Font** button. If you would like to add the character as another type of Finale element, you would choose that element (e.g. for an articulation, you would choose **Notation** > **Articulation**).
3. Choose the desired font, then click **OK**, and **OK** again to return to the score.
4. Choose the Text Tool [A].
5. Double-click the score to display a bounding box.
6. Choose **Text** > **Inserts** > **Symbol** to open the Symbol Selection dialog box as shown in Figure 9.18.

Figure 9.18

Select Unicode characters from the Symbol Selection dialog box.

7. Double-click the desired character to add it to the text block.

TIP:
If you are using a Unicode keyboard layout, adding Unicode characters will happen seamlessly with every keystroke. For information on Unicode keyboard layouts, see unicode.org/resources/keyboards.html.

Adding characters using the Character Viewer/Map

To quickly search for all Unicode and other characters on your computer, and copy and paste them to your heart's content, you can always use your operating system's Character Viewer/Map.

Macintosh users:

1. Choose ⌘ > **System Preferences** > **Language & Text** > **Input Sources**.
2. Check **Keyboard and Character Viewer**.
3. Close System Preferences.
4. Click ▦ (or the flag icon) in the upper right corner of your screen and choose **Show Character Viewer** to open the Character Viewer where you can navigate to the desired character. See your OS X documentation for details explaining how to use this dialog box.
5. In Finale, ensure the text cursor is ready to accept an entry, and set to the same font as the character you are about to add. (Or, you could highlight the character after it has been added and choose the font).
6. With the desired character selected, click **Insert with Font** to add the character.

Windows users:

1. Choose **Start** > **All Programs** > **Accessories** > **System Tools** > **Character Map**.
2. Click the **Font** drop-down menu and choose the font that includes the character you would like to add.
3. Double-click the desired character so it appears in the text box and click **Copy**.
4. In Finale, activate the text cursor, and press CTRL+V to paste the character. (Highlight the character and select the font if it was not already selected in Finale).

The Change Fonts Plug-In

You can change the font for existing items in the score with the Change Fonts plug-in. Choose **Plug-ins/** ✄ > **Miscellaneous** > **Change Fonts**. The Change Fonts dialog box appears as shown in Figure 9.19.

Figure 9.19
Change the font for existing staff names, group names, text blocks, and lyrics in the Change Fonts dialog box.

Click the Change button for any of the available items to open the Font dialog box where you can set a new font for the item. If Finale does not detect any existing entries for one of these categories, the selection will not be available.

Checking Document Fonts Against System Fonts

Finale remembers the fonts you use in any document after saving. When you open a file, Finale finds each font used in the document on your computer and displays it. If Finale cannot find a font on your computer that it needs to properly display one or more elements, you may end up seeing incorrect-looking music or markings in your score. This can happen when you use a third-party music font, or any uncommon font, and open the file on a different computer that does not have the font installed. To check a document to ensure that all fonts used in the document exist on the computer, and to substitute missing fonts, use the Check Document Fonts Against System Fonts utility. Choose **Document** > **Data Check** > **Font Utilities**, then check **Check Document Fonts Against System Fonts** and click **OK**. If Finale finds any fonts used in your document that do not exist on your computer, the Font dialog box appears as shown in Figure 9.20.

Figure 9.20

Checking document fonts against system fonts.

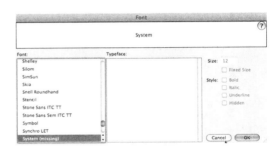

Here, choose a substitute for any missing fonts that Finale finds. Choose a new font, and click **OK** to tell Finale to display the next missing font, or return to the score (if there are no more missing fonts).

Everything Looks Funny: Reinstalling Your Finale Music Fonts

If all music in a document looks completely messed up–for example, you see funny symbols or letters instead of note and clefs–you probably just need to reinstall your Finale music fonts. You may have uninstalled an old version of Finale, thus removing your music fonts. The easiest way to fix this is to simply reinstall fonts from the original Finale installation disc using a Typical (Macintosh: Easy) install when prompted to do so. You can also download the fonts from MakeMusic's Web site, which, as of the printing of this book is finalemusic.com/finale/announcement. (If that doesn't work, Google "MakeMusic Font Pack.") Follow instructions on the site for installing these fonts.

10
Fine Tuning: the Details

Enough with all these sweeping changes, let's zoom into the nitty gritty details. I like everything to be easy and automatic as much as anyone, but translating a musical idea through paper often requires some careful finagling. (Hmm, "finagle" is one letter away from "Finale"...coincidence?) Anyway, to bridge the gap between the composer and performer we need to deal with some wacky musical ideas, and also make everything as easy to read as possible.

The following instructions apply primarily to fine-tuning the appearance of markings and notation rather than creating, editing, and moving pitches and rhythms. I'll focus on details that can make any score look neat, clean, and professional. Many prefer to use the techniques described below after all markings and notation have been entered into a score, though the method you adopt for using any editing technique will depend on the project you are working on and your own work style. In this chapter, I'll describe how to align and position a variety of items on the page, as well as make global and individual changes to beams, stems, accidentals, dots, and ties.

The main conceptual portion of this chapter is the "Alignment and Positioning Techniques" section. For some of you, the remainder can be referred to as necessary as you work, and perhaps skipped for now if you want to salvage some vestige of sanity. The hardened notation control freak masochist will be delighted with every word.

Here's a summary of what you will learn in this chapter:

- Techniques for alignment and positioning
- How to edit beams
- How to edit stems
- How to edit notes and noteheads
- How to edit accidentals
- How to edit dots and ties

Alignment and Positioning Techniques

After creating a page of music, you may want to specify precise placement for text, chords, graphics, or other marking in your score relative to the page edge and/or each other. Here, I'll show you how to easily position items using a ruler, grid, or guide as a reference.

Since we are only concerned with adjusting the placement of items as they will appear after printing, move to Page View (**View** > **Page View**). Remember, only in Page View can you see the score as it will appear in the printout.

NOTE:
Use the following alignment and positioning techniques in Page View to place various markings before finalizing your page layout. See "Page Layout" on page 299 for more information on laying out your staff, system, and page margins for printing.

The Selection Tool

The Selection Tool ![icon] is Finale's universal selection and editing utility. You've already used the Selection Tool for measure selection throughout this book. In addition to measures, you can also use this tool to select virtually any item in the score including expressions, text, smart shapes, and so forth. Context-clicking with the Selection Tool offers a menagerie of editing options. (see Figure 10.1).

Figure 10.1

Context-clicking a measure selection reveals some of the Selection Tool's capabilities.

After you click an item, it will be surrounded with a rectangle. Then, you can either click and drag or use the arrow keys to nudge the item into place. Press the DELETE key to delete an item. Double-click any item with the Selection Tool to select the item's corresponding tool for further editing. Use the Selection Tool in conjunction with the following positioning techniques to specify precise placement of just about any item in your score.

As shown in Figure 10.1, you can also invoke context menus for many items or measures with the Selection Tool, and make edits without leaving the Selection Tool. For example, with the Selection Tool chosen, right/CTRL+click an unoccupied portion of a measure. The measure context menu appears; note the various options. Choose **Insert Measure Stack** to insert a measure. While editing existing scores, make a habit of using the Selection Tool as much as possible to avoid the hassle of switching tools frequently.

NOTE:
Press ESC at any time to select the Selection Tool . (If a note is selected in Simple Entry, you will need to press ESC multiple times.)

Rulers and Margins

By default, in Page View, page edges and staves are the only visual references when positioning text and other items. For greater control over the exact placement of an item as it will appear on the printed page, use rulers. Choose **View** > **Show** > **Rulers**. You will now see two rulers appear, one across the top of the screen and one on the left side (see Figure 10.2).

Figure 10.2

Use rulers and margins for precision placement

As you click and drag any item, you will notice dashed lines extending vertically and horizontally. Use these lines to position items in your score relative to the distance from the top and left page edge. To specify inches, centimeters, EVPUs, or another measurement unit to display on the rulers, choose **Edit** (Mac: **Finale 2012**) > **Measurement Units**, and then select the desired unit of measurement.

TIP:
For more precision, try zooming in. Press CTRL/CMD+= to zoom in or CTRL/CMD+-(minus) to zoom out. Right/CMD+OPTION+click and drag to move the viewable region of the page. As you change the view percentage and viewable area of the page, the rulers will adjust accordingly.

If you would like to position items relative to the system or page margins, choose **View** > **Show** > **Margins**. Now, the system and page margins appear in a light gray line (see Figure 10.2). With Show Margins selected, you can also see two vertical lines-one marks the midpoint of the page, and the other marks the midpoint of the page margins. There are two horizontal lines marking the page and page margin midpoint as well. You can hide rulers and margins by unchecking **Show** > **Rulers** or **Show** > **Margins** under the View menu.

Grids and Guides

Like rulers and margins, grids and guides can also be used as a reference to position a variety of items in your score. Grids and guides are both basically reference lines that extend through the page at specified points along a vertical or horizontal axis. A key advantage to both grids and guides is the ability to snap items to them.

Positioning with Grids

Instead of manually dragging or nudging expressions, text, Smart Shapes, and other items into place, Finale contains a powerful utility for snapping items to a grid automatically. To do this:

1. Choose **View** > **Show** > **Grid.** There is now a grid covering your page (with a quarter inch between each line by default). Each intersection of the grid displays as a + on your page.
2. To tell Finale to snap specific items to the closest intersection, choose **View** > **Grid/Guide** > **Grid/Guide Options**. Document Options-Grids and Guides displays as shown in Figure 10.3.

Figure 10.3

Make document-wide settings for grids and guides in the Grids and Guides category of the Document Options.

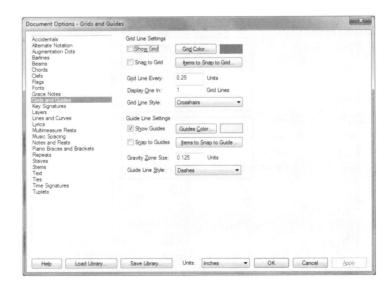

3. In the Grid Line Settings section, click **Items to Snap To Grid**. The Items to Snap To Grid dialog box appears. Here, check any items you want to position in the score using the grid and click **OK**.

4. Check **Snap to Grid** and click **OK** to return to the score. Now, any time you drag one of items checked in the Items to Snap To Grid dialog box, it will snap to the nearest intersection. See Figure 10.4 for an example of a score with the grid visible.

Figure 10.4

Viewing the grid

To increase or decrease the distance between each grid intersection:

1. Choose **View > Grid/Guide > Grid/Guide Options**.

2. Specify a value in the Grid Line Every field. In this section, you can also choose to display fewer grid lines and, using the **Grid Line Style** drop-down menu, change the grid line style from crosshairs to dots, dashes, or a solid line.

Positioning with Guides

A guide is basically a vertical or horizontal line that you can add as a reference point. To create a guide, double-click in the ruler. Notice the triangle appear on the ruler with a line extending through the score. Click and drag the triangle to reposition the guide if needed. You can context-click the guide and choose **Reposition Guide** for more settings. If you do so, the New Horizontal/Vertical Guide dialog box appears as shown in Figure 10.5.

Figure 10.5
Specify the guide location in the New Horizontal/Vertical Guide dialog box.

Here, you can specify the distance you want to position the guide from the top or left edge of the page and click **OK**.

Like the grid, you can also snap items to this guide:

1. Choose **View** > **Grid/Guide** > **Grid/Guide Options**.
2. In the **Grid Line** Settings section, click **Items To Snap To Guide**.
3. Make sure the items you want to position using the guide are checked, and click **OK** to return to the Grid/Guide Options.
4. Check **Snap To Guides**. For Gravity Zone Size, enter the region to either side of the guide you want the Snap To setting to affect. For example, enter ".25" inches if you want any item dragged within an quarter inch of the guide to snap to it.
5. Click **OK** to return to the score. Now, use guides to align markings vertically or horizontally. You can use grids and guides simultaneously or independently.

To see the "gravity zone" of your guides (the region in which an object will snap to the guide), context-click on an existing guide in the ruler and choose **Show Gravity Zone** (see Figure 10.6).

Figure 10.6

Specified items will snap to a guide if they are dragged within the gravity zone.

TIP:

Remember, you can align expressions vertically above or below the score using the expression positioning triangles. Refer to "Aligning and Positioning Expressions" on page 82 for details.

Positioning Rests

By default, Finale places rests according to standard notation conventions. In measures with a single layer, rest placement generally lies in the middle of the staff (the precise placement depends on the rest's duration). As long as you are using one of Finale's music fonts, placement of rests should look fine. However, if you are using a third-party music font, the rest characters may be offset. Or, you may be creating notation that calls for rests in a document to be repositioned vertically. You can change the default placement of rests in the Document Options dialog box. Choose **Document** > **Document Options** and select **Notes and Rests**. The Notes and Rests options appear as shown in Figure 10.7.

Figure 10.7

Make document-
wide settings for
rests in the Notes and
Rests category of the
Document Options.

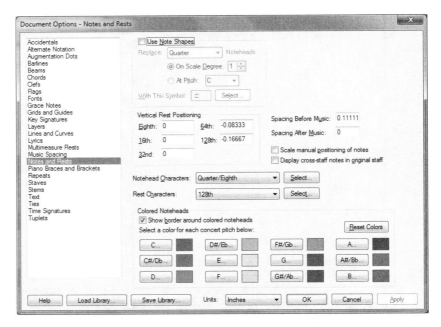

In the **Vertical Rest Positioning** section, set the offset for any rest duration of an eighth or less from the middle staff line. Click **OK** to apply changes and return to the score.

In measures with more than one layer, Finale automatically offsets rests higher or lower in the staff to distinguish between multiple voices. These are called "Floating Rests." For example, enter a quarter rest in layer 1, and then in the same measure, enter a quarter rest in layer 2. Notice that as you enter the rest in layer 2, the rest in layer 1 jumps up, and the rest in layer 2 appears lower in the staff. You can tell Finale how to treat the placement of rests while working in multiple layers in the Layer options. Choose **Document** > **Document Options** and select **Layers**. The Layer options appear as shown in Figure 10.8.

Figure 10.8

Make document-wide settings for layers in the Layers category of the Document Options.

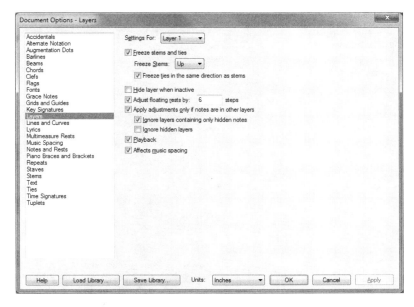

From the drop-down menu at the top, choose the layer of the rests you want to change. Then, enter the offset in steps for **Adjust Floating Rests by_** (a step is a line or space in the staff). The default value is 6 for layer 1 and -6 for layer 2, so floating rests appear centered on the first ledger line above the staff for layer 1 and below the staff for layer 2. Uncheck this option to tell Finale to use the positioning for rests as specified in Document Options-Notes and Rests for all rests in the selected layer.

If you want to use the vertical rest positioning specified in the Layer options even when there are no notes in other layers, uncheck **Apply Adjustments Only if Notes Are in Other Layers**. With this box unchecked, all rests in the layer will position themselves according to the floating rest setting. Click **OK** to return to the score and review your settings. Changes made will apply to all existing music and all new music added to the document.

Editing Beams

By default, Finale beams together all notes in a beat (with the exception of eighth notes in common time, which, by default, are beamed in groups of four). You can find general beaming settings for a document in the Document Options dialog box. Choose **Document** > **Document Options** and select **Beams**. The Beam options appear as shown in Figure 10.9.

Figure 10.9

Make document-wide settings for beams in the Beams category of the Document Options.

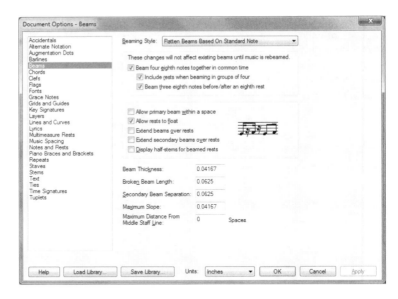

Use these options to adjust the default appearance of beams throughout your document. Here you can use Flat beams (under the Beaming Style drop-down menu), beam over rests, modify the maximum slope of beams, and make other document-wide adjustments. Here are some common ways to edit beams throughout your document in the Document Option's Beam settings:

- By default, Finale beams groups of four eighth notes together in common time. In other words, it breaks eighth note beams only on beat three. To break eighth note beams on every beat in common time (in groups of two), uncheck **Beam Four Eighth Notes Together in Common Time**.

TIP:
As noted beneath these beaming options, changes will not affect existing beams. To rebeam, select the region, then choose **Utilities** > **Rebeam** > **Rebeam Music**.

- Note the section containing five check boxes and a preview example. This short musical example updates to display the appearance of beams based on the combination of check boxes selected. For example, check **Allow Rests to Float** and **Extend Beams over Rests**. Notice the figure updates as you check or uncheck these options. Use this preview as a guide to customize the default appearance of beams for your document.
- In the lower portion, enter values to specify beam thickness, broken beam length, secondary beam separation, and max slope for beams. To change the measurement unit to use for these settings (inches, centimeters, etc.), click the drop-down menu for **Units** at the bottom of this dialog box.

Besides settings for treatment of eighth note beams in common time, the beam settings in the Document Options do not apply to the default beam grouping (i.e. 2+2+3 for 7/8 time etc.). To specify default beam groups to use as you enter music into the score, use the Time Signature Tool. See "Beaming Patterns and Time Signatures" on page 135.

Rebeaming a Selected Region

At any time, you can reset the beaming for a region of music back to the settings specified in the time signature and Document Options.

Most often you would use this feature if you wanted to return to the default beaming after having manually changed the beaming with Simple or Speedy Entry (i.e. with the / (slash) key). For more control over the beaming of a selected region, you can rebeam to a time signature with the Utilities Menu as well. To do this:

1. Highlight a region of your score.
2. Choose **Utilities** > **Rebeam** > **Rebeam Music**. Beaming in the selected region reverts back to the region's time signature settings, and updates the region to your settings in Document Options-Beams (see Figure 10.9).

Rebeaming to Time Signature

You can also apply beaming settings for any region of your score without changing the time signature, or even going into the Time Signature Tool. To do this:

1. Select a region of music. Choose **Utilities** > **Rebeam** > **Rebeam to Time Signature**. The Rebeam to Time Signature dialog box appears as shown in Figure 10.10.

Figure 10.10
Edit beamed groups in the Rebeam to Time Signature dialog box.

2. Here, edit the beat groups for the region as you would by changing the time signature.
3. Click the **Composite** button to open the Composite Time Signature dialog box where you can specify beaming groups for each beat (see "Beaming Patterns and Time Signatures" on page 135 for details).

Rebeaming to Lyrics

In some vocal music, beams appear only over melismas (when more than one note is sung for a syllable). In Finale, you can rebeam music to lyrics automatically to fit this paradigm.

1. Select a region of a score with lyrics.
2. Choose **Utilities** > **Rebeam** > **Rebeam to Lyrics**.
3. The Rebeam to Lyrics dialog box appears as shown in Figure 10.11.

Figure 10.11

Specify a lyric to rebeam to in the Rebeam to Lyrics dialog box.

4. Here, after **Break Beams at Each Syllable In**, click the drop-down menu and specify the type of lyric you want Finale to take into account while beaming to syllables. If you have only one line of lyrics, choose **All Lyrics** here.
5. From the lower drop-down menu, choose a specific verse, section, or chorus to beam to. If you want Finale to break beams over melismas that carry over a beat, check **Also Break Beams at Each Beat in the Time Signature**.
6. Click **OK** to apply lyric beaming to the selected region. See Figure 10.12 for an example of music before and after running Rebeam to Lyrics.

Figure 10.12

Beaming before and after applying Rebeam to Lyrics

Breaking and Joining Beams Individually

Finale lets you edit the appearance of individual beams in several ways. You can add or remove beams between notes with the Simple or Speedy Entry Tool, or modify the appearance of beams using several tools in the Special Tools Palette.

To add or remove beams in Simple Entry:

1. Click the Simple Entry Tool ♪ .

2. CTRL/OPTION+click the second of two beamed notes.

3. Press the / key on the QWERTY keyboard to break or join a beam from the previous note. To revert to the default beaming, in Simple Entry, press Shift+/.

To add or remove beaming in Speedy Entry:

1. Click the Speedy Entry Tool .

2. Move the cursor over the second of two beamed notes.

3. Press the / (or B) key to break or join a beam from the previous note.

More beaming tricks:

*   In Simple Entry, press ALT/OPTION+/, to flatten an angled beam. In Speedy Entry, press the M key.

*   To view all Simple Entry and Speedy Entry commands, from the Simple (or Speedy) Menu, choose Simple (or Speedy) Edit Commands.

> **TIP:**
> To flatten all beams in a region, use the Flat Beams plug-in. Select a region of measures, then choose **Plug-ins/** ✂ **> Note, Beam and Rest Editing > Flat Beams.** Choose **Flat Beams (Remove)** to remove flat beams in a region.

Changing the Beam Angle

You can edit the angle of any beam individually with the Beam Angle Tool.

1. Click the Special Tools Tool 🔨 to display the Special Tools Palette. (On Windows, choose **Window > Advanced Tools palette**, then select the Special Tools Tool from the Advanced Tools palette).

2. Click the Beam Angle Tool 📐 in the Special Tools Palette.

3. Click a measure to display a handle on the end of each beam in the measure.

4. Click the right handle to adjust the angle of the beam and the left handle to adjust the vertical placement of the beam (see Figure 10.13).

Figure 10.13
Adjusting beams with the Beam Angle Tool

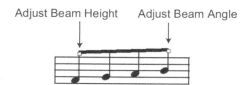

Feathered Beaming

Editing beams with the Beam Angle Tool will adjust all beams in the group (eighth, sixteenth, etc.) evenly. You can also adjust the height and angle of secondary beams individually, to create feathered beaming for example (see Figure 10.14). To create feathered beaming:

1. Enter a string of consecutive 32nd notes (or notes of any duration that are connected with multiple beams).

2. Click the Special Tools Tool to display the Special Tools Palette. (On Windows, choose **Window > Advanced Tools palette,** then select the Special Tools Tool from the Advanced Tools palette).

3. Click the Secondary Beam Angle Tool in the Special Tools Palette.

4. Click the measure containing the 32nd notes so there is a handle on each end of all secondary beams.

5. Drag the left handle to position the placement of the start point for each secondary beam, and drag the right handle to adjust the angle and endpoint for each secondary beam as you would with the Beam Angle Tool. Using these positioning handles, you can create feathered beaming in both directions as shown in Figure 10.14. Use the up and down arrow keys to nudge handles for fine adjustments.

Figure 10.14
Feathered beaming

6. Now, if you want to adjust the angle of all beams, click the Beam Angle Tool and adjust the left handle to change the height, and the right handle to adjust the angle of all beams in the group evenly. This way, you can slant the primary beam as well, as shown in Figure 10.15.

Figure 10.15
Feathered beaming adjusted with the Beam Angle Tool

TIP:
If you have trouble seeing the transparent handles while working with the Special Tools, turn them off. Go to Program Options-View and uncheck **Transparent Handles.**

Extending Beams

In addition to adjusting the beam angle, you can also change the length of any beam.

1. Click the Beam Extension Tool  in the Special Tools Palette.
2. Click a measure containing beamed notes. You will see a handle appear on each end of primary beams.
3. Click and drag or use the arrow keys to nudge the start or endpoint of the beam.
4. If you want to extend a secondary beam, double-click one of the handles to open the Beam Extension Selection dialog box as shown in Figure 10.16.

Figure 10.16
Select the beams you want to extend in the Beam Extension Selection dialog box.

5. Here, check the beam type you want to extend (8th = primary beam, 16th = first secondary beam, 32nd = second secondary beam, etc.). Then click **OK**.
6. Drag a handle to adjust the beams you selected in the Beam Extension Selection dialog box. You might use this technique to beam over rests individually.
7. If you find yourself making many changes to your score with the Beam Extension Tool, try adjusting the default beaming settings in the Document Options (choose **Document Options** > **Beams**–see Figure 10.9).

Flipping Broken Beams Across Stems

Broken beams can appear when a beamed group contains different rhythmic durations. Any broken beam can be flipped to the other side of the stem with the Broken Beam Tool. To see this, enter a dotted eighth note followed by a sixteenth note and then another eighth note in a measure. Beam the second eighth note to the previous sixteenth with the Simple Entry Tool. Your measure should look like the top example in Figure 10.17.

Figure 10.17
Flipping broken beams across stems

Click the Broken Beam Tool [icon] in the Special Tools Palette. Then, click the measure. You will see a handle appear above and below the broken beam. Click the bottom handle to flip the broken beam across the stem as shown in Figure 10.17.

Breaking Through Secondary Beams

Sometimes secondary beams are broken within beamed groups, as shown in Figure 10.18.

Figure 10.18
Breaking through secondary beams

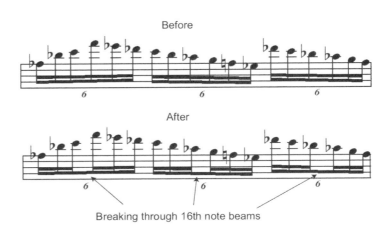

To break secondary beams, click the Secondary Beam Break Tool [icon] in the Special Tools Palette. Click a measure containing secondary beams. You will see a handle appear above each note. Double-click the handle on the second of two notes (you will be editing the beams to the left of the note you double-click). The Secondary Beam Break Selection dialog box appears as shown in Figure 10.19.

Figure 10.19
Specify the beams you want to break in the Secondary Beam Break
Selection dialog box.

Here, check the beams you want to break. To break all beams up to the primary beam, choose Break
Through, and check all boxes in the Beam Durations section. Click OK to return to the score. All
secondary beams to the left of the note disappear.

You can also specify individual beams to break. Follow the same instructions as described above, but in
the Secondary Beam Break dialog box, choose Break Only. Then, in the Beam Durations section, check
all beams you want to break.

Beaming Over Barlines

Sometimes beams extend across barlines into the next measure as shown in Figure 10.20.

Figure 10.20
Beaming across barlines

Up until Finale 2004, beaming across barlines was no fun at all. Now, Patterson's Beam Over Barlines
plug-in makes this easy. To extend a beam across a barline:

1. Enter the notes on either side of the barline as you would normally.
2. Highlight the region you want to beam over barlines. This plug-in will connect the full
   beamed group before and after each barline.
3. Choose **Plug-ins/** ✂ > **Note, Beam, and Rest Editing** > **Patterson Plug-ins Lite** > **Beam
   Over Barlines**.
4. Beams extend over barlines automatically. You will see hidden notes (that will not
   print) to the right of the barline. These are "placeholder notes" to maintain correct
   spacing.
5. To remove these beams, highlight the region and choose **Plug-ins/** ✂ > **Note, Beam,
   and Rest Editing** > **Patterson Plug-ins Lite** > **Beam Over Barlines (Remove)**.

TIP:
The beamed notes to the right of the barline are actually a part of the
previous measure. To edit these notes, select a note in the previous
measure in Simple Entry and press the right arrow until the selection
moves across the barline.

Patterson Beams Plug-In

The Patterson Beams plug-in can make adjustments to beam angles, widths, and stems automatically to produce a publisher-specific look to beaming for a region of measures or for the entire score. To use this plug-in:

1. Choose **Document** > **Document Options** and select **Beams**.
2. Check **Allow Primary Beam Within a Space**, uncheck **Extend Beams Over Rests** and set the **Max Slope** to 6 EVPUs.
3. Click **OK** to return to the score.
4. Highlight a region of the score (or, if you want to apply the plug-in to the entire score, no selection in necessary).
5. Choose **Plug-ins/**  > **Note, Beam, and Rest Editing** > **Patterson Plug-Ins Lite** > **Patterson Beams**. The Patterson Beams dialog box appears as shown in Figure 10.21.

Figure 10.21

Use the Patterson Beams plug-in to specify the appearance of beams for a region or for your entire document.

6. Here, you can choose from a variety of options for beam and stem adjustment. Robert Patterson, the third-party plug-in developer responsible for the Patterson Beams plug-in, explains each parameter in the Patterson Beams dialog box at his Web site, robertgpatterson.com. Also, refer to this Web site for specific settings you can use that meet professional publishing standards.
7. After making your settings, click **OK** to return to the score and review your results. Note that the Patterson Beams plug-in makes static adjustments based on note position, measure width, and page layout. It is recommend that you make these adjustments when your score is nearing completion.

Editing Stems

As you enter notes, Finale determines stem direction and length based on a number of factors. The default settings are based on standard notation practice. Stems on notes below the middle staff line go up; stems on notes on or above the middle staff line go down; stems on notes above and below the staff always extend to the middle staff line. You can adjust several default stem settings in the Document Options dialog box. Choose **Document** > **Document Options** and select **Stems**. The Stem options appear as shown in Figure 10.22.

Figure 10.22

Make document-wide settings for stems in the Stems category of the Document Options.

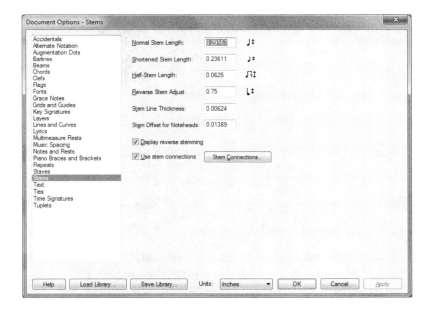

Use these options to adjust the default appearance of stems throughout your document. Change the default stem length, flipped stem length, or even modify the placement of stems relative to notes by selecting Stem Connections (more about stem connections in the next section). In addition to the Stem Options, you can also modify the default direction of stems in measures with multiple layers in the Layer Options.

Without leaving the Document Options, click the **Layers** category on the left. The Layer Options appear (see Figure 10.8). In the Layer options, you can set the default stem direction for each layer. From the drop-down menu at the top, choose the layer you want to change. Check **Freeze Stems and Ties**, and then choose the default direction from the **Freeze Stems** drop-down menu. This setting also affects the default direction of ties. Click OK to apply all settings you have made in the Document Options dialog box and return to the score.

Stem Connections

You can modify Finale's default placement of stems relative to any notehead character for any document. Setting up stem connections may be necessary if you are using custom noteheads, or noteheads in a third-party music font. To edit stem connections for a notehead character, use the Stem Connection Editor.

1.   Choose **Document** > **Document Options** > **Stems** and click **Stem Connections**. The Stem Connections dialog box appears as shown in Figure 10.23.

Figure 10.23

All custom stem connections are visible in the Stem Connections dialog box.

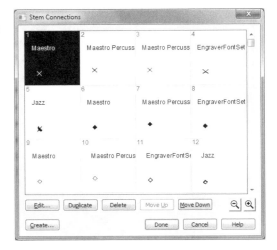

2.   Here you see a list of custom noteheads that require specialized stem connections. In the upper left of each selection you will see the name of the font for each notehead character. You will not see the default noteheads here, because they use default stem connection settings (and need no adjustments, though they can be edited).

3.   To edit any of the existing stem connections, click one of the notehead characters and then click **Edit**. To create a stem connection for a character not available in the Stem Connections dialog box, click **Create**.

4.   After choosing either **Edit** or **Create**, the Stem Connection Editor dialog box appears as shown in Figure 10.24.

Figure 10.24

Edit the placement of a stem for a specific notehead character in the Stem Connections Editor dialog box.

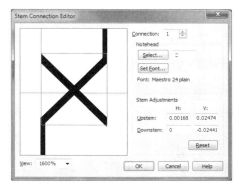

5. Here, make adjustments to the placement of the stem relative to the notehead. If you clicked **Create,** use the **Set Font** button to open the Font dialog box where you can choose the font for a notehead.

6. Click **Select** to open the Symbol Selection dialog box where you can choose a specific character. Use the following tricks to adjust the stem connection to the selected character in the Stem Connection Editor dialog box:

   • Click and drag the stems to move them around manually. Hold down SHIFT to constrain dragging vertically or horizontally. Notice the values change in the Stem Adjustments section as you move the stem. You can also enter specific values for the stem connections placement offset from the default placement in the Stem Adjustments section.

   • Use the **View** drop-down menu to zoom in for fine adjustments, or zoom out to see the complete figure.

   • Right/OPTION+CMD+click and drag in the preview window to move the visible area.

   • To change the character of the notehead, click **Select** in the **Notehead** section. The Symbol Selection dialog box appears where you can choose a new character.

   • To change the font of the existing character, click **Set Font** button in the Notehead section.

   • Click **Reset** in the **Stem Adjustments** section to remove stem adjustments and return stems to the default placement.

   • Use the up and down arrows for **Connection** (at the top) to move between notehead characters as they appear in the Stem Connections dialog box.

7. Once you have finished editing your stem connection, click **OK** to return to the Stem Connection dialog box.

8. Click **OK** to return to the Document Options, and click **OK** again to return to the score. Stems on notehead characters you edited will appear according to your settings in the Stem Connection Editor.

Editing Stems for a Selected Region

There are a number of ways to edit stem direction, placement, and visual definition for a selected region of your score. You can easily freeze stems up or down with the Selection Tool 🔲 . To do this, click the Selection Tool and highlight a region of measures. Choose **Utilities** > **Stem Directions** > **Up** or **Down**.

> **TIP:**
> To apply the Freeze Stem utility or any Utilities Menu function to a specific layer, choose **Show Active Layer Only** from the Document menu. Then, select the layer you want to edit. Now, changes with the Utilities Menu will apply only to the visible layer.

Defining Stem Settings for Individual Staves

Since Finale 2003 you have been able to edit stem placement, direction, and the visual definition for individual staves in Staff Attributes. Click the Staff Tool and double-click a staff to open the Staff Attributes dialog box. In the **Items to Display** section, click the **Stem Settings** button to open the Staff Stem Settings dialog box (see Figure 8.20). Here are some ways to edit stems for a staff in the Staff Stem Settings dialog box:

- In the **Stem Direction** section, define a default stem direction for notes in the staff. Note that if there is more than one layer in a measure, the stem direction settings will revert to those specified in Document Options-Layers.
- Uncheck **Show Beams** to remove all beams from a staff (used mostly for tab).
- Click the **Units** drop-down menu to change measurement units (Inches, EVPUs, Centimeters, etc.) for values in this dialog box.

To place stems directly above the staff or below the staff (as commonly used in tab notation):

1. Choose **Window** > **Score Manager**.
2. Click **Add Instrument** > **Tablature**, and add a tab staff.
3. Close the Score Manager.
4. Choose the Staff Tool and double-click a staff. The Staff Attributes dialog box appears.
5. Under **Items to Display**, check **Stems**.
6. Click **OK** twice to return to the score. Stems throughout the staff change to reflect settings you configured in the Staff Stem Settings dialog box. See "Tablature, Percussion, and Note Shapes Notation Styles" on page 210 for more details on tab notation.

Since the Staff Stem Settings are a staff attribute, you can create a new staff style and apply stem settings to any region of your score.

1. Choose the Staff Tool 🔳 .
2. Choose **Staff** > **Define Staff Styles**.
3. Click **New** at the top and enter a name in the **Available Styles** text box.

4. Click the **Stem Settings** button and make your custom settings.

5. Click **OK** twice to return to the score.

6. Highlight a region of your score, right/CONTROL click the highlighted area, and choose the staff style you created. See "Defining a New Staff Style" on page 209 for more information on staff styles.

Midline Stem Direction Plug-In

Usually, the stem direction is down for notes on the middle staff line. However, if the previous note's stem is up it is common to flip this stem for a cleaner look. With this plug-in, you can tell Finale to flip the stem on notes on the middle staff line based on the stem direction of the previous and following notes (see Figure 10.25). Click the Selection Tool and highlight a region of music. Choose **Plug-ins/** > **Note, Beam and Rest Editing** > **Midline Stem Direction**.

Figure 10.25

Use the Midline Stem Direction plug-in to edit the midline stem direction based on surrounding notes.

Changing the Default Midline Stem Direction

You can set the stem reversal (point in the staff where stems flip automatically) in the Staff Setup dialog box.

1. Choose **Window** > **Score Manager**.

2. Click the drop-down menu for **Staff**, and choose **Other**. The Staff Setup dialog box appears (see Figure 8.8).

3. In the Stem Reversal text box, enter the position, in steps, from the top staff line you want Finale to flip stems down (the default setting is -4, so notes on the middle line and above flip down by default). Enter -3 if you want all stems on the middle line to flip up automatically, and all notes on the third space and above to flip down.

4. Click **OK** and close the Score Manager to return to the score with the new stem reversal applied. Apply these settings to all desired staves, or create a staff style to apply them to any selected region.

Editing Stems Individually

Finale lets you edit stems individually in many ways. You can flip stem direction for any note with the Simple or Speedy Entry Tool, or you can modify the length and appearance of stems using several tools in the Special Tools Palette.

Use the Simple Entry Tool or Speedy Entry Tool to flip stems.

1. Click the Simple Entry Tool ♪ , and then CTRL/OPTION+click a note.
2. Press the L key to flip the stem (you may have to press it twice). To flip the stem back, simply press the L key again.
3. To edit the stem direction in Speedy Entry, click the Speedy Entry Tool ♪ and click a measure to open the Speedy frame. Move the cursor over an entry and press the L key to flip the stem direction.

While in Simple Entry, hold down the Shift key and press L to tell Finale to use the default stem direction for the specified note. Use CTRL/OPTION+L in Speedy Entry.

You can also change the stem direction for a number of individual notes with the Stem Direction Tool.

1. Click the Special Tools Tool .
2. Click the Stem Direction Tool ✳ in the Special Tools Palette.
3. Now, click a measure to see a handle above and below each note in the active layer.
4. Click the top handle to flip a stem up or the bottom handle to flip a stem down.

Changing the Stem Length and Horizontal Positioning

You can change the length and horizontal positioning of any stem with the Stem Length Tool.

1. Click the Stem Length Tool ⬆ in the Special Tools Palette, and then click a measure containing notes. You will see a handle above and below all the notes in the active layer.
2. Click and drag the handle to increase or decrease the length of the stem. You can also move the stem left or right relative to the note.
3. Use the arrow keys to nudge a selected handle to make fine adjustments. Hold down SHIFT to constrain to horizontal or vertical dragging.

Changing the Appearance and Hiding a Stem

You can change the appearance or hide a stem with the Custom Stem Tool.

1. Click the Custom Stem Tool ♫ in the Special Tools Palette, and then click a measure to display a handle on each stem.
2. Double-click a stem to open the Shape Selection dialog box where you can choose from a library of shapes to use for the stem.
3. To create your own shape, or replace the stem with a blank entry to hide it, click **Create** to open the Shape Designer. Here, use the various tools to design your own stem shape. If you want to hide the stem, leave this window blank.

4. Click **OK** and Select to return to the score with your new settings applied. To clear the custom stem edits selecting the stem's handle and press DELETE.

Editing Notes and Noteheads

There are many ways to edit notes and noteheads individually Here are special ways to edit a variety of properties of individual notes using the Special Tools.

Editing Noteheads and Note Positioning with the Special Tools

There are three Special Tools devoted to editing notes individually. You can use the Note Position Tool to reposition a note horizontally, the Notehead Position Tool to position a notehead, or the Note Shape Tool to change the character of a notehead individually.

To Manually Reposition Notes Horizontally

1. Click the Special Tools Tool .
2. From the Special Tools Palette, choose the Note Position Tool .
3. Specify the layer containing the notes you want to reposition (choose the layer as you would normally).
4. Click the measure containing the notes. Handles appear above the staff for each note in the measure.
5. Click and drag (or user the arrow keys to nudge) a handle to reposition its corresponding note horizontally.

NOTE:
You can also reposition individual notes horizontally by dragging them in the Speedy Frame. Use the Beat Chart (Measure Tool) to reposition the beat placement (See "The Beat Chart and Spacing with the Measure Tool" on page 248 for details).

To Reposition Noteheads Horizontally

1. Click the Special Tools Tool .
2. From the Special Tools Palette, choose the Notehead Position Tool .
3. Specify the layer containing the notes you want to change (choose the layer as you would normally).

4. Click the measure containing the notes. Handles appear by each notehead in the measure (in the active layer).

5. Click and drag (or user the arrow keys to nudge) a handle to reposition the noteheads horizontally.

To Change/Remove Notehead Characters Individually

1. Click the Special Tools Tool 🖪 .

2. From the Special Tools Palette, choose the Note Shape Tool 🖪 .

3. Specify the layer containing the notes you want to reposition (choose the layer as you would normally).

4. Click the measure containing the notes. Handles appear by each notehead in the measure (in the active layer).

5. Double-click a handle to open the Symbol Selection window where you can choose from the characters available in the current music font.

6. Double-click a character to use it for the selected note. If you want to hide the notehead, choose the blank character (# 32 in the Maestro font). For information on percussion notehead characters, see "Percussion Layouts" on page 212.

Editing Accidentals

I have already described how to enter accidentals with the Simple and Speedy Entry Tool. You can make a variety of changes to the positioning and appearance of accidentals for your entire document, or for individual entries. You can change the default character or positioning for accidentals throughout your document in the Document Options dialog box. Choose **Document** > **Document Options** and select **Accidentals**. The Accidentals options appear as shown in Figure 10.26.

Figure 10.26

Make document-wide settings for accidentals in the Accidentals category of the Document Options.

Use these options to adjust the positioning and character of accidentals throughout your document.

- Enter new values in the four available text boxes for positioning of accidentals relative to notes and to each other. Click the drop-down menu for **Units** to change the unit of measurement.
- Here, you can change the character of any accidental. Click the **Music Characters** drop-down menu and select the character you want to change. Then, click **Select** to the right to open the Symbol Selection dialog box where you can choose a new character for the accidental. Click **Select** to return to the Document Options.

If you would like to select a different font for your accidentals:

1. Click the Fonts category in the Document Options dialog box to display the font options.
2. Click the drop-down menu for **Notation** and choose **Accidentals**.
3. Click **Set Font** to the right to open the Font dialog box where you can choose a new font, size, and style for your accidentals.

Changing the Default Enharmonic Spelling

You can adjust the default spelling for pitches in the score that lie outside the key by using settings under the **Edit** (Mac: **Finale 2012** > **Preferences**) > **Enharmonic Spelling** submenu. These settings generally apply to music entered with a MIDI keyboard. If you want Finale to tend to use sharps while representing pitches in your score, from the **Edit/Finale 2012** > **Preferences** > **Enharmonic Spelling** submenu, choose **Favor Sharps**. Choose **Favor Flats** if you want Finale to tend to use flats to represent pitches.

Choose **Use Spelling Tables** to tell Finale to use a custom definition for enharmonic spelling as specified in the spelling tables.

Editing the Major and Minor Key Spelling Table

Use this table to define the automatic spelling of non-diatonic pitches in major and minor keys. From the **Edit/Finale 2012** > **Preferences** menu, choose **Enharmonic Spelling** > **Edit Major and Minor Key Spellings**. The Edit Major and Minor Key Spellings dialog box appears as shown in Figure 10.27.

Figure 10.27

Edit the spelling of non-diatonic pitches in the Edit Major and Minor Key Spellings dialog box.

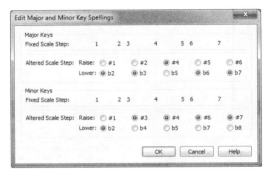

In this dialog box, choose whether to use a raised or lowered note to represent pitches between whole steps in a major or minor diatonic scale. In the key of C, for example, step 1 = C, step 2 = D, step 3 = E, etc. For example, in the key of C, to display the D flats instead of C sharps, choose b2 between 1 and 2. Finale will use the settings you specify in the Major or Minor spelling table depending on the mode (major or minor) of the key specified in the key signature dialog box.

If you are using a nonstandard key that is modal or chromatic, you may want to assign a spelling for each pitch in the chromatic scale. To do this, from the **Edit/Finale 2012** > **Preferences** menu, choose **Enharmonic Spelling** > **Edit Modal or Chromatic Key Spellings**. The Modal or Chromatic Key Spellings dialog box appears as shown in Figure 10.28.

Figure 10.28

Edit the spelling of non-diatonic pitches for modal or chromatic key signatures in the Edit Modal or Chromatic Key Spellings dialog box.

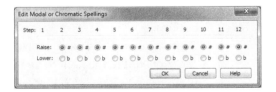

Here, choose the enharmonic spelling for each pitch of the chromatic scale. Click **OK** to return to the score. Notes entered with a MIDI keyboard will reflect the settings you specified in the spelling tables (be sure **Use Spelling Tables** is checked in the **Enharmonic Spelling** submenu if you want to use them).

Checking Accidentals

Occasionally, there may be an accidental visible at the conclusion of a tie that should be hidden. To check for and remove extraneous accidentals, run the Check Accidentals utility:

1. Select a region of the score (CTRL/CMD+A to Select All).
2. Choose **Utilities** > **Check Notation** > **Check Accidentals**. Extra accidentals in the selected region are removed.

Checking Ties

Occasionally ties across system breaks do not display properly. Also, ties sometimes do not play back correctly. If you experience either of these problems, run Check Ties:

1. Select a region of the score (CTRL/CMD+A to Select All).
2. Choose **Utilities** > **Check Notation** > **Check Ties**.

Positioning Accidentals Individually

You can manipulate the positioning of each accidental in your score individually with the Special Tools. Click the Special Tools Tool to display the Special Tools Palette (on Windows, choose **Window** > **Advanced Tools Palette** > **Special Tools Tool**). Click the Accidental Mover Tool in the Special Tools Palette . Now, click a measure containing notes with accidentals. You will see a handle on each accidental. Click and drag, or use the arrow keys to nudge accidentals horizontally.

If you are creating early music notation that requires musica ficta markings, click the Accidental Positioning Tool, context-click an accidental handle, and choose Edit (or double-click a handle). Set the size of the accidental (usually 75%) and check **Allow Vertical Positioning**." Click **OK** and return to the score. Click this accidental's handle and drag it up above the notehead.

> **TIP:**
> Use the Canonic Utilities plug-in (**Plug-ins/** ⚙ > **Scoring and Arranging**) to show accidentals on all notes. A handy tool for atonal music.

Editing Augmentation Dots and Ties

Like beams and stems, augmentation dots and ties can be positioned for an entire document or individually. To edit the default positioning and visual definition of augmentation dots, from the Document menu, choose Document Options and select Augmentation Dots. The Augmentation Dot options appear as shown in Figure 10.29.

Figure 10.29

Make document-wide settings for augmentation dots in the Augmentation Dots category of the Document Options.

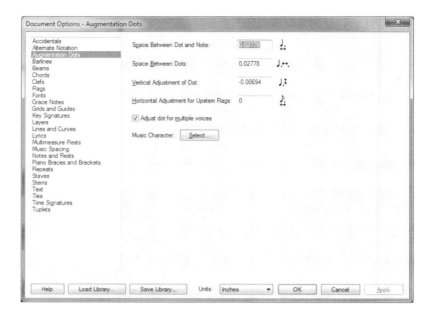

Use these options to adjust the positioning and character of augmentation dots throughout your document.

- Enter new values in the four available text boxes for positioning of augmentation dots relative to notes and to each other. Click the drop-down menu for **Units** to change the unit of measurement.
- To change the character of augmentation dots, click **Select** to open the Symbol Selection dialog box where you can choose a new character for your augmentation dots.

If you would like to select an augmentation dot character in a different font, click the Fonts category in the Document Options dialog box. Click the drop-down menu for **Notation** and choose **Augmentation Dot**. Then, click the Set Font button to the right to open the Font dialog box.

To edit the default positioning and visual definition of ties, choose **Document** > **Document Options** and select **Ties**. The Tie options appear as shown in Figure 10.30.

Figure 10.30

Make document-wide settings for ties in the Ties category of the Document Options.

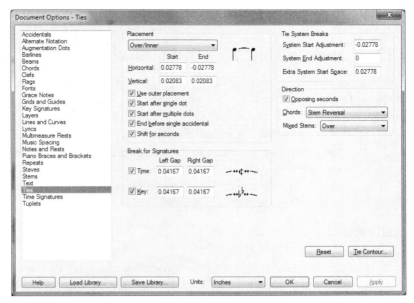

Use these options to define the default visual definition of ties:

- In the Placement section, click the drop-down menu and choose the type of tie you want to edit (depending on note placement). Look to the preview display on the right to see the selected tie style.
- Use the **Horizontal** and **Vertical** text boxes to enter a start and stop point for ties of the selected style. Click the drop-down menu for **Units** to change the unit of measurement.
- In the **Break for Signatures** section, specify the treatment of ties over meter and key changes. Use the text boxes to indicate the amount of space before and after the tie break.
- Click **Reset** to revert all settings in this box back to the defaults.
- Click **Tie Contour** button to open the Tie Contour dialog box where you can specify the precise shape of ties throughout your document.

Editing Augmentation Dots

You can edit augmentation dots individually with the Dot Tool.

1. Click the Special Tools Tool to display the Special Tools Palette (on Windows, choose **Window** > **Advanced Tools Palette** > **Special Tools Palette**).
2. Click the Dot Tool in the Special Tools Palette. Then, click a measure containing notes with dots. A handle appears next to each dot in the measure.
3. Click a handle and drag, or use the arrow keys to nudge augmentation dots.

4.   Hold down SHIFT to constrain dragging vertically or horizontally.

Adding and Editing Ties Individually

Use the Simple Entry Tool or Speedy Entry Tool to add or remove a tie between any two notes of the same pitch. To add or remove ties in Simple Entry.

1.   Click the Simple Entry Tool ♪ , and then CTRL/OPTION+click a note to select it.
2.   Press the T key to extend a tie to the next note or remove an existing tie or use the / key on the num pad.
3.   Hold down SHIFT and press T to extend or remove a tie to the previous note. Finale will automatically remove extra accidentals.

To add or remove a tie in Speedy Entry:

1.   Click the Speedy Entry Tool ♪ and click a measure to invoke the Speedy Frame.
2.   Move the cursor over a note and press the T key or the = key to extend a tie to the next note or remove an existing tie.
3.   Hold down SHIFT and press T to extend or remove a tie to the previous note.

You can edit the shape of ties individually with the Tie Tool. Click the Tie Tool 📄 in the Special Tools Palette.

Then, click a measure containing notes with ties. Three handles appear on each tie in the measure. Click a handle and drag, or use the arrow keys to nudge these handles to adjust the start point, end point, and contour (see Figure 10.31). Hold down the Shift key to constrain dragging vertically or horizontally.

Figure 10.31
Use the handles to edit ties with the Tie Tool.

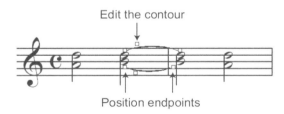

Double-click the Contour handle to activate an additional handle (see Figure 10.32) for greater control.

Figure 10.32
Use the additional hidden contour handle for precision adjustments.

11
Measure Numbers, Graphics, Layout, and Printing

And flying saucers with turnips. Yes, you might want to split this chapter up into a couple sessions. What do all these things have in common? Well, layout, parts and printing should generally be the last steps in your project as you are wrapping up your score. Measure numbers and graphics don't really fit anywhere else, and don't really deserve their own chapter, so here they are. By this point you are a hardened Finale virtuoso anyway and I know you can handle it.

So, this chapter will focus on techniques for finalizing the score for printing. You will learn how to edit measure numbers and define measure number regions, add graphics, finalize system/page layout, create and edit parts along side the full score, and print the score and parts. You will find that a number of techniques discussed in Chapter 10, such as alignment and positioning, come into play throughout the final stages of score development. Some of the following topics expand on concepts introduced in earlier chapters, such as page layout and printing.

Here's a summary of what you will learn in this chapter:

- How to edit measure numbers
- How to work with graphics
- How to manage page layout
- How to work with Linked Parts
- Techniques for printing

Measure Numbers

Measure numbers are an important element to any score. They can be added and manipulated with the Measure Tool ▦. By default, Finale places a measure number at the beginning of each system, though you can edit their frequency, positioning, and appearance individually, or for any region of your score.

You can begin numbering at any measure, or even create several measure number regions to number multiple movements within the same file.

To prepare for this section, open a new Default Document (**File** > **New** > **Default Document**). You will see a measure number at the beginning of each system.

TIP:
To add rehearsal letters or numbers, or measure number style rehearsal numbers, use expressions. See "Rehearsal Marks" on page 77.

Managing Measure Number Appearance

The default settings for measure numbers are stored in the Measure Number dialog box. Choose the Measure Tool . Then, choose **Measure** > **Edit Measure Number Regions**. The Measure Number dialog box appears as shown in Figure 11.1.

Figure 11.1

Edit the frequency, font, size, style, and positioning, and create measure number regions in the Measure Number dialog box.

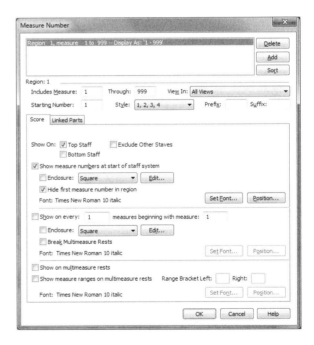

Make global changes to the appearance and positioning of measure numbers here, for both the score and all linked parts in the document. Click the **Linked Parts** tab to edit the appearance of linked parts, which include identical settings.

I had a relatively thorough explanation here that detailed the hierarchical nature of the three measure number definitions (each definition delineated by its own Font and Positioning button). Alas, it was axed by my technical editor for brevity. Therefore, let it simply be known that the higher definition generally overrides the lower in case of a conflict, although there are special circumstances where the lower definition can override the higher. Most of the time, it just works. See the "Measure Number dialog box" in the Finale User Manual for details.

Editing Measure Numbers in the Score

You can make a number of adjustments to measure numbers individually in the score. Click the Measure Tool to display handles on all measure numbers. Use the following techniques to make basic changes to measure numbers:

- Click and drag to adjust the positioning of a measure number manually. Hold down SHIFT to constrain to horizontal and vertical dragging.
- Select a measure number handle and press BACKSPACE/CLEAR to return a measure number to its original placement.
- Select a measure number handle and press Delete to hide a measure number.
- Right/CMD+click a measure number handle to open the Measure Number context menu where you can restore the default position, delete the measure number, or edit its enclosure.
- Double-click a measure number handle to edit its enclosure or add an enclosure.

When you double-click a measure number, the Enclosure Designer dialog box appears as shown in Figure 11.2.

Figure 11.2
Create or edit a measure number enclosure in the Enclosure Designer dialog box.

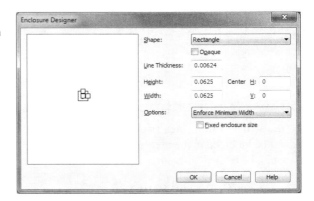

In the Enclosure Designer dialog box, click the **Shape** drop-down menu to choose an enclosure shape. Check **Opaque** to tell Finale to hide items behind the enclosure. Click and drag the handles in the preview window to resize or move the enclosure. Click **OK** to return to the score. The enclosure now surrounds the measure number you selected.

You can also use the Measure menu to edit and manage measure numbers in the score.

- Select one or more measure number handles, and choose **Measure** > **Edit Enclosure** to open the Enclosure Designer where you can define an enclosure for all selected measure numbers.
- To show measure numbers for every measure in a selected region of your score, highlight the region of measures and choose **Measure** > **Show Measure Numbers**. Measure numbers appear above all selected measures.
- Select one or more measure number handles, and choose **Measure** > **Hide Measure Numbers** to clear the selected measure numbers.
- Select one or more measure number handles, and choose **Measure** > **Restore Measure Number Defaults** to revert back to default settings for measure numbers as specified in the Measure Number dialog box.

Creating and Editing Measure Number Regions

All measure numbers in your score are organized by measure region. Choose the Measure Tool ▦ . Then, choose **Measure** > **Edit Measure Number Regions**. Notice the existing default entry at the top of this box, "Region 1, measure 1 to 999-Display As: '1-999'." This entry tells Finale to number measures 1-999 as 1-999.

This means each measure in the score is numbered consecutively for up to 999 measures. If each measure of your score consists of a valid musical measure, without interruption, the default measure number region will serve your purposes fine (for the first 999 measures).

However, the actual measures in your score may not always serve the purpose of a "real" measure. Your numbering may need to skip a hidden measure used as a placeholder, or begin from measure one within the document for a second movement, for example. You can resolve any such measure numbering problems by creating a new measure number region. Or, you could also skip individual measures within a region...

Skipping Measures (measure numbers)

For the following example, let's say measure 11 is hidden with the "Force hide staff" Staff Style and should not be included in the measure numbering. "Real" measures are those at the core of the Finale document and "defined" measures are those you assign deliberately.

1. Click the Measure Tool ▦ .
2. Double-click the measure to open the Measure Attributes dialog box.
3. Uncheck **Include in Measure Numbering**.
4. Click **OK**.

Measure Numbering for Multiple Movements

To start numbering at measure 1 for the second movement (and additional movements):

1. Click the Measure Tool.

2. Choose **Measure** > **Measure Numbers** > **Edit Measure Number Regions**. The Measure Number dialog box appears (see Figure 11.1).

3. Define the measures for the existing (first) region. Let's assume the first movement is 5 measures. Just below the region display window, for **Includes Measures**, enter the first and last "real" measure, "1" in the first box and "5" in the second.

4. For **Starting Number**, enter "1," (already set) since the first region begins at the first measure of the document.

5. For this demonstration, check (and enter) **Show On Every "1" Measures Beginning with Measure "1."**

6. Click **Add**. A new region appears in the region display window. It is selected by default.

7. Now, define the measures for the next movement, in this case 6-999 (the second region will extend to the end of the score). Just below the region display window, for **Includes Measures**, enter the first and last "real" measure of the second region. Finale's "real" measure 6 = our second movement's measure 1. So, enter "6" in the first box and "999" in the second.

8. For **Starting Number**, enter "1" (already chosen).

9. Click **OK**. Notice that measure 6 is now numbered as measure 1.

Use the above method to define as many measure number regions as you like.

TIP:
To tell Finale to display 'actual' measure numbers (those in the measure indicator at the bottom left of the screen in Scroll View) instead of defined measure numbers, choose **Edit** (Mac: **Finale 2012** > **Preferences**) menu, choose **Program Options**, and select **View**. Choose **Display Actual Measure Numbers** and click **OK**. Now, choose **View** > **Scroll View**. Finale now displays the "real" measure number.

TIP:
To show the full staff and group name at the beginning of a new movement, choose the Measure Tool, double-click the first measure of the movement, check **Show Full Staff & Group Names**, and click **OK**.

More Measure Number Settings

Edit each measure region independently in the Measure Number dialog box. Simply click the desired region in the region display window, and then apply settings for the region using the available options. You can edit each region without leaving the Measure Number dialog box. Here are some common ways to edit measure numbers for a region:

- If you would like to use a numbering convention other than standard measure numbers, such as letters or time, click the **Style** drop-down menu to choose a different format for your measure numbering. (Note that "letters" here do not behave like Finale's auto-sequencing rehearsal mark expressions. Every measure is re-lettered.)

- Check **Always Show on Top Staff** or check **Always Show on Bottom Staff** to show measure numbers on the top or bottom staff regardless of measure number settings in the Staff Attributes. These settings can be particularly useful if you plan to hide empty staves.
- To display measure number ranges for multimeasure rests, check **Show Measure Ranges on Mulitmeasure Rests**. In the Left and Right text boxes, enter the character to use (brackets, parentheses, etc.) to enclose the number ranges (see Figure 11.3). Assigning measure regions for multimeasure rests will apply to multimeasure rests both in the score and in any parts.

Figure 11.3

Measure regions on multimeasure rests

- To position measure numbers, click **Position.** The Position Measure Number dialog box appears. Be sure both Alignment and Justification are set to Center to center the measure number as shown in Figure 11.4. Click and drag the measure number in the preview window to specify the measure positioning, or enter specific values in the **H:** and **V:** text boxes.

Figure 11.4

Use the Position Measure Number dialog box to position measure numbers for a measure number region.

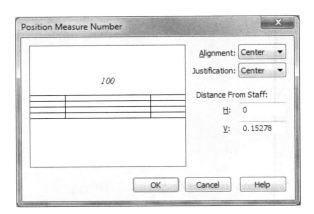

Show or Hide Measure Numbers on a Staff

You can show or hide measure numbers for a specific staff in the Staff Attributes. Click the Staff Tool and double-click a staff to open the Staff Attributes dialog box. In the **Items to Display** section, uncheck **Measure Numbers**. Click **OK** to return to the score.

> **NOTE:**
> Settings in the Measure Number dialog box override the **Display Measure Number** setting you assign in the Staff Attributes. If editing the Staff Attributes does not change the presence of measure numbers on the staff, edit the corresponding measure region in the Measure Number dialog box. Choose **Measure > Edit Measure Number Regions.** Uncheck the **Always Show** check boxes under **Positioning and Display.** Or, uncheck **Exclude Other Staves.**

Clear Measure Number Positioning

You can clear manual measure number positioning for any selected region of your score with the Clear Measure Number Positioning plug-in. Highlight a region of your score. Choose **Plug-ins/** ✂ > **Measures** > **Clear Measure # Positioning**. Measure numbers in the selected region return to their default placement.

Number Repeated Measures

If you have several consecutive measures that are identical, you may want to number them (independently from the measure numbering) to aid the performer. To do this, highlight a region of identical measures. Choose **Plug-ins/** ✂ > **Measures** > **Number Repeated Measures**. The repeated measures are now numbered consecutively. They are entered as measure expressions, so you can edit or delete them with the Expression Tool or Selection Tool.

Working with Graphics

Graphics are commonly used in Finale documents for figures in your score outside of music notation, such as logos. You'll want to use a separate graphic program to prepare an image to place into a Finale document. You also may need to save a page or excerpt of music from a Finale document as a graphic to import into a file in another program. Finale can place graphics in PDF, TIFF, EPS, JPEG, PNG, BMP, and GIF format (Windows users can also place WMF, and Macintosh users can also place PICT). Finale can export PDF, JPEG, PNG, TIFF, and EPS (and Macintosh users can also export PICT files). Use the Graphics Tool 🖼 to import or export a graphic.

To prepare for this section, open a new Default Document (**File** > **New** > **Default Document**). Then, click the Graphics Tool. (On Windows, choose **Window** > **Advanced Tools Palette**, and then click the Graphics Tool.)

> **NOTE:**
> Due to OS limitations, Finale does not support EPS export in Windows Vista or Windows 7. As of Finale 2012, this is not nearly as much of a problem, since you can now export PDFs for all your vector graphic needs (PDFs are better anyway).

Exporting a Graphic

You can export a portion of a page or an entire page from Finale as a graphic file. To export an entire page, you will need to be in Page View (**View** > **Page View**).

To export a rectangular section of a page:

1. Choose the Graphics Tool .
2. Double-click and drag to enclose the desired region. When you release the mouse button, a dashed rectangle should remain with pink editing handles.
3. For all, but especially upgrading users, note you achieved the art of creating a bounding box the first time you tried (no, it wasn't just you all those years). Also note you can click in the center of the box to drag it around and resize the box using those attractive hot pink handles. I invite you to pause for a moment to appreciate the little things in life...OK, moving on...
4. Choose **Graphics** > **Export Selection**. To export an entire page, or several pages, click the **Graphics** > **Export Pages**. After choosing Export Selection or Export Pages from the Graphics menu, the Export Pages/Selection dialog box appears as shown in Figure 11.5.

Figure 11.5

Choose properties for an exported graphic in the Export Pages/Export Selection dialog box.

5. From the **Type** drop-down menu, choose the format of the graphic you want to export. After you have chosen the file type, specify the pages you want to export. If you are exporting multiple pages, each page will be saved as a separate graphic file. Choose **Generate Names From** to tell Finale to name each graphic with the file name of the Finale document followed by a number (increasing by one for each successive page). If you are exporting a single page, choose Prompt for Each Name if you wish to name the file yourself. If you are exporting an EPS graphic, choose **Include TIFF Preview** if you want a preview of the graphic to display on-screen. Choose **Embed Fonts** if you plan to move the file to a computer that does not have fonts used in the graphic. If you are exporting a TIFF or PICT file, for example, click the drop-down menu for **Resolution** to choose a resolution for the graphic. 72 dpi is screen resolution; choose a higher resolution to export a sharper graphic file (like 300 or 600). Most inkjet printers print at 600 dpi or higher.
6. Click **OK**. Finale generates the graphics, or, if **Prompt for Each Name** is selected, the Save As window appears.
7. Windows users, if you are saving a PDF, in the Save As dialog box, you may see an **Additional Properties** button that allows you to enter PDF information, such as the

Title, Subject, and Author. You can also click the **Security** tab to pasword-protect your PDF file and apply encryption settings.

8.   Enter a filename, choose a location, and click **Save** to save the graphic.

Importing a Graphic

Importing, or "placing" graphics can be done in Page View or Scroll View. Use Page View to attach the graphic to the page, Scroll View to attach to a measure.

To import a graphic:

1.   With the Graphics Tool selected, double-click in the score. The Place Graphic/Open File window appears. On Windows, click the drop-down menu for **Files of Type** and choose the format of the file you want to import.

2.   Navigate to the file and double-click to open it. You return to the score with the graphic placed in the document.

Editing Placed Graphics

Click a graphic to reveal those nifty hot pink handles, then click and drag to move the graphic around or click and drag a handle to stretch it. To resize the graphic proportionally, SHIFT-drag one of the corner handles. Double-click the graphic to open the Graphic Attributes dialog box (see Figure 11.6) where you can make specific settings for positioning and appearance.

Figure 11.6

Position and scale graphics in the Graphic Attributes dialog box.

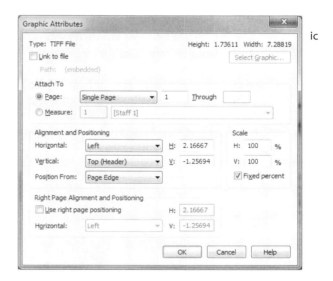

Here are some common ways to edit graphics in the Graphic Attributes dialog box:

- In the **Attach To** section, choose **Page** to place the graphic at a set location on the page. It will remain static relative to the page edge, or page margin (depending on the setting in the Alignment and Positioning section). With this option selected, all items in the **Alignment and Positioning** section become active. Specify specific horizontal and vertical placement for your graphic in this section.

- In the **Attach To** section, choose **Measure** to attach the graphic to a specific measure. Do this if you want the graphic to always reposition with a measure respectively. Specify the measure and staff in the text boxes to the right of this option.
- Scale the graphic by changing the percentage in the **Scale** section. 100% always equals the original size of the graphic. Check **Fixed Percent** if you want the graphic to remain the same size regardless of page resizing with the Resize Tool.

After you have finished editing the graphic, click **OK** to return to the score and review your changes.

Using Embedded vs. Referenced Graphics

Graphics placed in your Finale documents are embedded by default. This means they are stored within the file data and continue to appear if you, for example, move a file to a different computer. This was not always the case. In fact, embedded graphics were only introduced in Finale 2006. In Finale 2005 and earlier, graphics were always referenced using the path to their location on the local machine or network. Therefore, if you needed to move the file to a different computer, you were also required to move the graphic and, in some cases, reassign the graphics's path. Finale still offers this option which could be useful if you are trying to minimize the file size (or want to edit placed graphics in another application, for example). To do so:

1. Double-click the graphic or double-click the score to place a new graphic. The Graphic Attributes dialog box appears.
2. Check **Link to File,** navigate to the desired graphic and double-click to choose it.
3. Make any additional settings in this dialog box and click **OK.**

When you do this, Finale references graphic by using the path you specified when you initially placed the graphic, or the folder of the Finale file. Remember, this means that if you move the Finale file or graphic to a different folder, the association will be lost and the graphic will not appear in the document (just the file name of the missing graphic). Use **Graphics** > **Check Graphics** to see where Finale is expecting to find the graphics (See Figure 11.7).

Figure 11.7
Use the Check Graphics dialog box to view or change the path for referenced graphics.

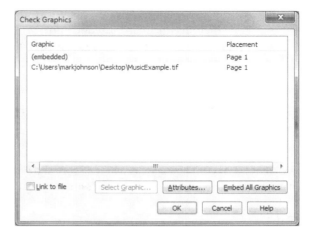

Missing graphics are marked with an * (asterisk). If you know where the graphic has been moved, or want to choose a new graphic, click **Select Graphic** to specify a new path.

TIP:
If you choose to reference graphics, to avoid breaking the association, store each graphic file in the same folder as its host Finale file. Then, if you ever move the Finale document, be sure to also move the associated graphic with the Finale file. Finale will always find a graphic if it exists in the same folder as the Finale document.

Page Layout

Chapter 2 covered the basics for editing the page layout. You learned how to edit system margins, the distance between staves, systems, and page margins. These basic layout concepts are important throughout the score production process, and can be quite adequate for smaller projects. However, there are several other options that can save you time while preparing the layout of a score. By devoting a little extra time for page layout after completing the entry process, you can produce a consistent, professional-looking score.

TIP:
If you're worried about mangling the layout of your score beyond repair, save a backup copy of the Finale document. In fact, you may want to save a separate version of your score specifically for the purpose of experimentation, especially if you are less familiar with this

Editing the Overall Page Format for Your Score or Parts

To decrease the amount of manual editing necessary in a score, you may want to define the overall page format, and then go back and make additional page layout changes. Page format includes:

- Page size and orientation
- Page margins (including left and right)
- System margins including a separate definition for the top system margin
- Page and system scaling

To define the overall format for a score (system margins, page margins, and spacing), use the Page Format for Score dialog box. Choose **Document** > **Page Format** > **Score** to open the Page Format for Score dialog box.

The exact same options are available for predefining the layout of linked parts. (Choose **Document** > **Page Format** > **Parts**). The Page Format for Score and Page Format for Parts dialog boxes appear as shown in Figure 11.8 (these two dialog boxes are identical in structure).

Figure 11.8

Use the Page Format for Score or Parts dialog box to define the layout for your score or linked parts.

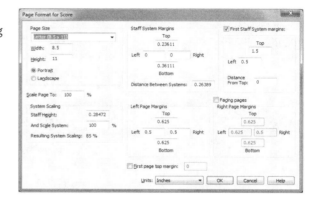

- Select the measurement unit you would like to use from the drop-down menu in the lower-right corner of this dialog box.
- At the top, in the **Page Size** section, choose the page size of the Finale document (any new page that is generated gets its dimensions here). Click the drop-down menu for a list of available choices. (Note that after setting up the page size, you will then need to select the actual size of the printed page in the Page Setup dialog box (**File** > **Printer Page Setup**). If you want to print one "Finale" page on one "physical" page, enter the same page size in both the Page Format for Score (or Page Size) and Page Setup dialog boxes.)
- Enter a page reduction for all items on the page in the **Scale Page To** text box. The page reduction can also be adjusted with the Resize Tool.
- For **System Scaling**, you can reduce or enlarge all systems in the document and their contents. Note that the values for **Staff Height** and **Scale System** are cumulative, so adjustments to either of these parameters will affect the overall system scaling. Finale calculates this value for you and displays it to the right of **Resulting System Scaling**.
- In the **Staff System Margins** section, enter specific value to control the system margins for the entire document. Here, you can also set the space between each system. Usually, the first system is indented to allow more space for the full staff name. You can define the top and left margin for the first staff system in the section to the right. First

check **First Staff System Margins**, then enter the top and left margin for the first staff system in the section below this check box.

- Under **Left Page Margins**, enter the space between page margins and the edge of the page. If you want to define separate page margins for odd numbered pages, check **Facing Pages** and then enter the margin values in the Right Page Margins section.

Once you have finished making changes to the Page Format for Score/Parts dialog box, click OK to return to the score. **If you made settings for the layout of your current score, you will need to redefine the pages for these settings to take effect. To apply these changes, click the Page Layout Tool and then from the Page Layout menu, choose Redefine Pages > All Pages.** Then click **OK**.

TIP:
To make broad-scale adjustments to the vertical spacing of systems, use Finale 2012's new Space Systems plug-in. Choose **Plug-ins** > **Scoring and Arranging** > **Space Systems**.

Hiding Empty Staves

Way back in Finale 2010 and earlier there was an old term, "optimization," that tended to confuse a lot of people. Fortunately, you don't need to worry about this draconian term, because all its purposes have been integrated into Finale 2012's more intuitive design. (For example, positioning staves in individual systems is now simple, as explained earlier under "Changing the Distance Between Staves (for printing)" on page 42). Because of these design changes, hiding empty staves in order to maximize page efficiency (see Figure 11.9) is one aspect of Finale that no longer requires much explanation.

Figure 11.9

A score before and after hiding empty staves. Notice the groups adjust accordingly.

To hide empty staves:

1. Choose the Staff Tool   .
2. Move to Page View (**View** > **Page View**).
3. Choose **Edit** > **Select All** (or press CTRL/CMD+A). (Or, select the staves/systems that include the staves you want to hide).
4. Choose **Staff** > **Hide Empty Staves**.

A dashed line appears representing 1 or more empty staves in a system. To show hidden staves, context click the handle and choose **Show All** (or an individual staff).

If Automatic Music Spacing nudges measures with notes into a system where the staff has been hidden, or if a measure with notes is moved across systems manually, Finale will display the staff automatically in that system. In other words, you can hide or show empty staves to your hearts content with absolutely no risk to life or limb (or notes being hidden unintentionally).

Hiding Staves with Notes

To hide a staff *with notes* (so that it plays back but doesn't show), you need to "force" the staff to hide:

1. Choose the Staff Tool   .
2. Double-click the staff you would like to hide. The Staff Attributes dialog box appears.
3. Check **Force Hide**, then **and Collapse** from the adjacent drop-down menu.

4. Click **OK**. The staff disappears from the score *and will also not appear in linked parts*. To hide the staff in the score only and not the part, you would choose **in Score Only (Collapse)** from the **Force Hide Staff** drop-down menu instead.

To show a "force hidden" staff:

1. Return to the Staff Attributes dialog box. (Double-click any staff with the Staff Tool selected).
2. At the top, after **Staff Attributes For**, choose the hidden staff. (The word "(hidden)" will appear next to its name).
3. Uncheck **Force Hide Staff**.
4. Click **OK**.

Cutaway Scores

Sometimes empty measures within systems are hidden from the score, as shown in Figure 11.10. This method of score formatting is known as a cutaway score.

Figure 11.10

Use the Hide Staff staff style to create cutaway scores.

Use the Force Hide Staff (Cutaway) staff style to hide any number of measures from a staff. To do this:

1. Click the Staff Tool.
2. Highlight the measure or measures you want to hide.
3. Context-click the highlighted area and choose **Force Hide Staff (Cutaway)** from the staff style context menu (or press H). The measure(s) disappear and the staff style is marked with a horizontal gray line.
4. Repeat these steps for all occasions where a measure needs to be hidden within a staff system.

Systems Per Page

To specify a certain number of systems to place on each page

1. Choose the Page Layout Tool .
2. Choose **Page Layout** > **Space Systems Evenly**. The Space Systems Evenly dialog box appears as shown in Figure 11.11.

Figure 11.11

Specify the number of systems per page in the Space Systems Evenly dialog box.

3. In the **Space Systems Evenly On** section, choose the page or pages you want to change.
4. In the **Distribute Systems** section, choose **Place _ Systems on Each Page**.
5. Click **OK**. Finale will place the number of systems you specified on the chosen pages provided there is room on the page. The systems will be spaced evenly as well. If there is not room on the page or if your music looks scrunched, try reducing the system scaling with the Resize Tool %.

Customizing Systems

In Chapter 2 you learned how to manually adjust system margins individually. You can also adjust margins for several systems at once. The following methods are particularly useful while editing the layout for parts, or scores with more than one system on a page.

Choose **Page Layout** > **Systems** > **Edit Margins**. The Edit System Margins dialog box appears as shown in Figure 11.12.

Figure 11.12

Use the Edit System Margins dialog box to edit margins of a selected region of systems.

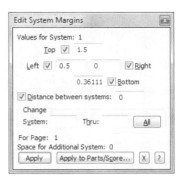

In the Edit System Margins dialog box:

- Whenever the Edit System Margins dialog box is open, you can click a system to see the values for that system. Enter new values in this box and click apply as many times as you like before closing the dialog box (or let it disappear when you switch tools).
- Check the box that corresponds to the margin or margins you want to edit (left, right, top, bottom). Then specify the new system margin value in the appropriate text box.
- Check **Distance Between Systems**, and enter a value to specify the distance between systems.
- In the **Change** section, specify a system range. (You can type 2 thru 0, for example, to indicate systems 2 through the end of the score.)
- Click **Apply** to see results without leaving the dialog box. (Also, pressing the ENTER or RETURN key is the same as clicking **Apply**.)
- The **Apply to Parts/Score** button is really handy if you want edit system margins in linked parts.

Customizing Pages

You can also edit page margins for a selected region of pages. Choose **Page Layout** > **Page Margins** > **Edit Page Margins**. The Edit Page Margins dialog box appears as shown in Figure 11.13.

Figure 11.13

Edit page margins for a region of pages in the Edit Page Margins dialog box.

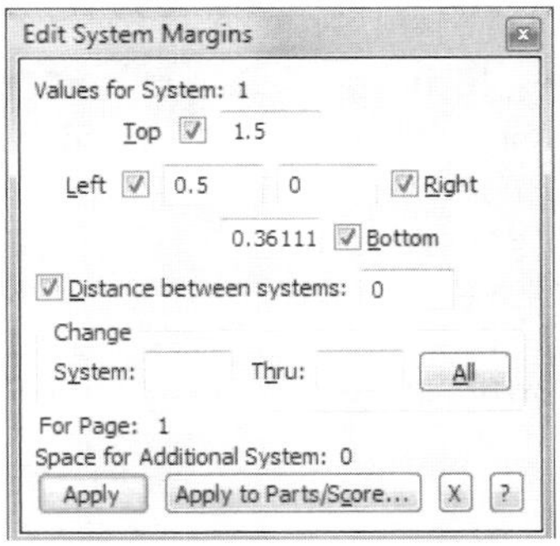

- Check the box that corresponds to the margin or margins you want to edit (left, right, top, bottom), and then enter a value.
- Specify the margins to edit in the **Change** section.
- Click **Apply** to update the page. Enter new values in this box and click apply as many times as you like before closing the dialog box. This dialog box can be open at the same time as the Edit Page Margins dialog box if desired.
- The **Apply to Parts/Score** button is helpful if you want edit page margins in linked parts.

Page Turns

To format a part for optimal page turns automatically, use the Smart Page Turns plug-in. This plug-in adds page breaks and adjusts the measure spacing to avoid difficult page turns. Choose **Plug-ins/** ✂ > **Scoring and Arranging** > **Smart Page Turns**. Here, you can specify the timing, choose whether the rests should appear at the end or beginning of the page, and even add warnings for quick page turns (e.g., "V.S."). If you need to format parts for a large ensemble, this plug-in can save you a lot of time. Experiment with the settings in this dialog box on one part until you have found the best settings, and then use the same settings for additional parts from the same score. (Note that the best settings will vary depending on the tempo, instrument type, and other factors). This plug-in does not work with linked parts, so you will need to extract parts into separate score documents before running this plug-in.

You can also set a system to always appear at the beginning of a page by assigning a Page Break.

To assign a page break:

1. Click the Page Layout Tool 🗐 .
2. For the system you want to assign to the beginning of the page, context-click the upper-left handle and choose **Insert Page Break**. Now, this system will always appear at the top of a page. Note that this system is still subject to moving between pages based on other page layout changes. (Context-click and choose **Delete Page Break** to restore.)

Splitting Measures Across Systems

With split measures, the first portion of a measure appears at the end of one system and the second portion at the beginning of the next, as shown in Figure 11.14.

Figure 11.14

Notice measure six extends across the system break

To split a measure across a system break without disturbing the measure numbering, use the Split Measure plug-in.

1. Make sure all notes have been entered in the measure you want to split.
2. Click the Selection Tool ![icon], then select the measure you want to split.
3. Choose **Plug-ins/** ![icon] > **Measures** > **Split Measure**. The Split Measure dialog box appears as shown in Figure 11.15.

Figure 11.15
Split measures across systems with the Split Measure plug-in.

4. In the text box, enter the desired last beat of the system. Make sure Move second part of split measure to next system is checked.
5. Click **OK**. You return to the score. The second part of the measure moves to the next system.
6. Use the Measure Tool ![icon] to change the barline style if necessary.

Printing Techniques

The final step to almost any project is generating the physical sheet music from your Finale document. In Chapter 2, you learned the basics for printing a document by configuring the Page Size and Page Setup dialog boxes (under "Page Size, Orientation, and Printing" on page 46). Here are a couple methods you can use to customize the page format, placing two-up on a single page, or printing half of a score on two pages if a printer doesn't support a large enough page size.

Printing 2-Up

You can easily place two pages of your Finale document in portrait orientation on a letter page in landscape orientation (see Figure 11.16).

Figure 11.16

Two-up printing

To do this:

1. Choose **File** > **Page Setup**. The Page Setup dialog box appears.
2. Set the size to **Letter** (or any preferred page size) and the orientation to **Landscape**. On Macintosh, be sure to keep the **Scale** percentage at 100%.
3. Click **OK**.
4. Choose **File** > **Print**. (On Mac, click the **General** pop-up menu and choose Finale 2012. The Finale print options appear.)
5. Check **2-up**, then choose the page range.
6. Check **Ignore Printer Margins for N-up printing** if you want to extend the music as close as possible to the page edges.
7. Click **Print** to print the document. Two pages appear side by side on a single sheet of paper.

Fitting a Score on Two Pages: Tile Pages

If your score is too large to fit on a paper size supported by your printer, you can, for example, print two 8.5 x 11 inch pages tiled so the full score appears on the two pages stacked horizontally. This way the score appears as if it were printed on tabloid size paper (11 x 17 inch).

NOTE:
Note you can use the **Fit to Page** command to print, for example, a tabloid score on letter-sized paper.

To print a score on tiled pages:

1. First, set the page size to **Tabloid**. Click the Page Layout Tool and choose **Page Layout** > **Page Size**. From the **Page Size** drop-down menu, choose **Tabloid (11 x 17)**. Then click **OK**.

2. Use the Page Layout Tool to customize the layout of systems to properly fit on this page size. You may want to use the Resize Tool to resize the page, or the Staff Tool to change the distance between staves.

3. Choose **File** > **Page Setup**. The Page Setup dialog box appears.

4. Set the orientation to landscape, the page size to 8.5 x 11 and click **OK**.

5. Choose **File** > **Print**. (On Mac, click the **General** pop-up menu and choose Finale 2012. The Finale print options appear.)

6. Check **Tile Pages**.

7. If you want the pages to overlap slightly, enter the margin of overlap in the **Tile Overlap** text box. Specify the overlap in the unit of measurement you have selected in the **Edit** (Mac: **Finale 2012** > **Preferences**) **Measurement Units** submenu. About 1/4 inch usually works well.

8. Choose the page range and print the document. Half of each system will appear on each 8.5 x 11 inch page. Stack the pages horizontally to view a full page of the score.

Batch Printing and Booklets

You can easily print in booklet format or print several documents at once (batch print) using the Finale-Script plug-in. Choose **Plug-ins/** > **Miscellaneous** > **FinaleScript Palette**. In the FinaleScript Palette, open the "Print Booklet" and "Batch Print" scripts for instructions. You can also batch print with the full version of TGTools. Choose **TGTools** > **Print Multiple Files**. See the TGTools User Manual for more information. The JW Booklet plug-in <jwmusic.nu/freeplugins> can also be used to print in booklet format.

> **TIP:**
> There is a good description of how to batch print and print booklets in the Finale 2012 User Manual. Search for "Booklets" and "Batch Printing".

12
Specific Projects and Composing with Finale

Kudos. In the last 11 chapters you have learned the fundamentals for efficiently producing a score, from starting a new document to the final printout. After having finally blazed a trail up the long-anticipated slope, you walk slowly as the unknown terrain materializes beyond the high mountain sagebrush. Much like Lewis and Clark peering over the Lemhi Pass, I'm afraid it's not all down-hill from here. But, you've come this far, and you've only begun to explore your capabilities. It's time to unleash the droves of widgets and doo dads that are essential for specific projects, and a catalyst for creativity. Yes, they are often scattered about the Plug-ins Menu, but don't be fooled, they are as vital to using Finale efficiently as horses to an early 19th century trans-continental expedition, or perhaps a walking stick to a scenic overlook, whatever the case may be.

In this chapter, you will learn a variety of techniques for notation of specific instruments, such as cross staff notation for a piano score, figured bass, and other common notation types. Some of Finale's most impressive features are particularly useful to arrangers and composers. If you plan to arrange with Finale, you will learn how to use valuable orchestration utilities. Explode a single staff of music into many, or easily compress any size score into a grand staff for a piano reduction. If you plan to compose with Finale, you can use the Composer Assistant, Auto Harmonizer, and other plug-ins to inspire/fuel the creative process.

Here's a summary of what you will learn in this chapter:

- Tricks for specific projects
- How to use Finale's Orchestration Tools
- How to use Finale's Creative Tools

Tricks for Specific Projects

It would be impossible to cover the endless number of notational styles possible in Finale. I have already discussed percussion notation and tablature (in Chapter 8), though there are a number of other common types of music notation made easy with Finale. These include cross-staff notation for piano, figured bass, chant, and notation for handbells and harp.

Cross-Staff Notation and Tricks for Piano Scores

Cross-staff notation appears often in keyboard music. It is a way of beaming notes placed across the right- and left-hand staff in a piano score, often with stems up and down on the same beam (see Figure 12.1).

Figure 12.1

Cross-staff notation

Prior to Finale 2004, creating this type of notation was a pain. Now, the TGTools Cross Staff plug-in included with Finale makes this easy. To create cross-staff notation:

1. In a grand staff, enter all notes into one staff. For this example the notes are entered in the top staff (see Figure 12.2).

Figure 12.2

To create cross-staff notation, first enter the notes into the same staff.

2. Choose the Selection Tool ![icon] .
3. Select the region containing the notes you want to move to the other staff.
4. Choose **Plug-ins/** ![icon] > **TGTools** > **Cross Staff**. The Cross Staff dialog box appears as shown in Figure 12.3.
5. In the Cross Staff dialog box, for "Split Point," enter the lowest pitch you want to appear in the top staff (C4 = Middle C). For "Pitches," choose whether you want to move all pitches, or pitches below or above the split point pitch, then select whether you want to move notes to the previous (above) or next (below) staff.

Figure 12.3

Specify the lowest note you want to appear in the top staff and other settings for cross-staff notes in the Cross Staff dialog box.

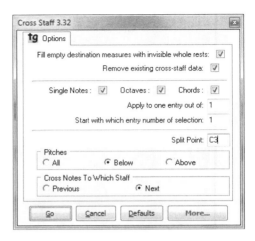

6. Click **Apply**. The specified notes move across the staff. The stems and beams adjust for you automatically (see Figure 12.4).

Figure 12.4
After clicking Apply, notes move across the staff automatically.

7. Now, you can simply highlight a region of measures with the Selection Tool and press ALT/OPTION+SHIFT+DOWN ARROW (or ALT/OPTION+SHIFT+UP ARROW) to move notes to the next or previous staff based on the settings you have already specified.
8. To flip the stems in the bass staff, select them with the Simple Entry Tool and press the L key twice.

NOTE:
After using the plug-in to create cross staff notation, notes moved to the other staff are still technically a part of their original staff. To edit them, use the Simple Entry Tool to select a note in the original staff and use the left and right arrow keys to move selection to the cross staff notes.

For complete control, you can also create cross-staff notation the "old fashioned" way using the Note Mover and Special Tools (Reverse Stem Tool, Beam Angle Tool, etc.). See "cross staff" in the Finale

2012 User Manual for details. But always try the plug-in before even thinking of using the Note Mover/ Special Tools method (the plug-in almost always does the trick).

Here are some other tips that will come in handy while working with piano scores.

- To begin a new piano document, use the Setup Wizard (**File** > **New** > **Document With Setup Wizard**). Then, on page 2, choose the Keyboards category and select Piano (or another keyboard instrument). You can also easily add a grand staff to your document with the Score Manager.
- To add a pedal marking to your score (as shown in Figure 12.5), use the Custom Line Tool. Click the Smart Shape Tool ✎, then CTRL/OPTION+click the Custom Line Tool ? in the Smart Shape Palette.
- (The Smart Line Style Selection dialog box appears). Choose the Pedal Custom Line of your choice and click **Select**. Now, simply double-click and drag to add the pedal marking.

Figure 12.5

Use the Custom Line Tool to create pedal markings. Finale includes several styles.

- You can add an 8va or 8vb marking with the Smart Shape Tool as well. With the Smart Shape Tool ✎ selected, choose the 8va/8vb Tool in the Smart Shape Palette. Double-click above the staff and drag to enter an 8va. Double-click below the staff and drag to create an 8vb (notice your cursor points to the staff the Smart Shape will be attached to). These indications will also apply to playback.
- Use the Articulation Tool 𝄒 to enter fingerings. With the Articulation Tool selected, hold down the fingering number and click an entry to add it to the score (the number keys 1 through 5 are preset fingering metatools).

Figured Bass and Harmonic Analysis

These topics are like peas in a pod with regards to how they are entered in Finale, so I've lumped both into one section, each focused on the task at hand, but each also including some information pertaining to both (because really, no one likes reading the same text twice). So consider this a two-fer–it's two numeral-based ways to indicate harmony fer the thought of one!

In Finale, figured bass and harmonic analysis are entered as lyrics using Finale 2012's new Finale Numerics font. This font was specially-designed with zero-width characters that allow for stacked characters, slashes, brackets, lines, and everything you will ever need to enter figured bass and harmonic analysis. Because of the nature of font characters and the way they are mapped to keystrokes, it will be easier to type-in figured bass on Mac than on Windows, but in either case, entering these is much easier now than it was in Finale 2011.

Whether you are entering harmonic analysis or figured bass, start with the following:

1. Choose the Lyrics tool . First, let's tell Finale not to do all the usual automatic stuff that makes entering lyrics easy (but figured bass/harmonic analysis messy).

2. Choose **Lyrics** > **Lyric Options** and uncheck **Use Smart Hyphens**. Click **Word Extensions,** uncheck **Use Word Extensions,** and click **OK** twice.

3. Now choose **Lyrics** > **Auto-Number** and ensure **Verse, Chorus,** and **Section** are unchecked. We don't need any extra numbers in there.

4. Choose **Lyrics** > **Type Into Score.** Now, select the Finale Numerics font, click the first note, and start typing. It sounds simple, but you may find this task curiously difficult. If so, try the following.

5. **Windows users:** Click **Lyrics** > **Lyrics Window.** In the Lyrics Window, choose **Text** > **Font.** Choose Finale Neric (between Finale Mallets and Finale Percussion). Click **OK.** Type the first character so it appears in the Lyrics Window. Click the (Click Assign) button and click the note that belongs to the figure. (This sort of 'locks in' the font–Finale tends to revert back to your default font if you don't do this). Then, click (Type Into Score) and click the next note to begin typing figures into the score. **Mac users:** Click the note to display a blinking cursor beneath the staff. Click **Text** > **Font** > **Finale Numerics.** Type the first character.

> **CAUTION:**
> If you press BACKSPACE/DELETE over the first Finale Numerics character, Finale will revert to the default font. Repeat step 5 to remedy.

Now, you're ready to start entering those numerals. Let's begin our two-fer with that integer-based, Baroque version of a chord chart.

More on Figured Bass

Figured bass (or basso continuo) originated in the 1600s as a method for notating accompaniments, and is basically a system of shorthand written beneath the bass part that indicates the chord to be played above it. Entering the figures in Finale is pretty straightforward. You can use Figure 12.6 as a basic guide. When you've entered a figure, press SPACEBAR to move to the next entry.

Figure 12.6

Use the Lyrics Tool with the Finale Numerics font to enter figured bass

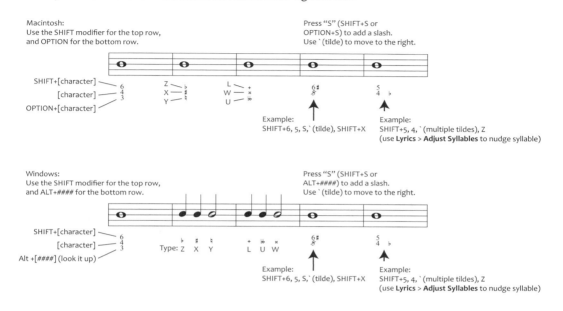

Tip:

There is a nice list of all the usual figured bass characters in the Finale User Manual under "Figured Bass." To see every single character in the font, refer to the Finale Numerics font on your system's Character Map/Viewer for a list of all the available characters. See "Adding characters using the Character Viewer/Map" on page 254.

And now, in case your studies summon you from the uproarious, harpsichord-laden continuo of the parlor, a word on buckling-down and drafting your harmonic analysis with icy precision.

More on Harmonic Analysis

Whether you are exploring secondary dominants in your first semester of music theory, or preparing Schenkerian analysis for your doctoral thesis, Finale offers just about all the functionality you'll ever need. Our exploration will be oriented more towards the former, but once you get the hang of it you'll be able to focus on identifying all those French augmented sixth chords rather than fiddling with Finale.

Type the roman numeral, then use the stackable zero-width characters for the inversions. For example, for "VI$_4^6$," type "VI (capital vi), SHIFT+6, 4, then press SPACEBAR to move to the next entry (see Figure 12.7). (See figure 12.6 for a description of the stackable characters.)

Figure 12.7

Use the Finale
Numerics
font to enter
harmonic analysis as
lyrics.

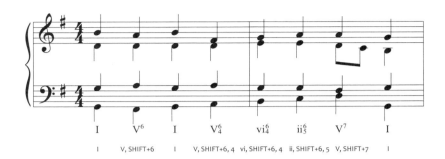

Here are some tips for entering harmonic analysis:

- If you have the choice, use a Macintosh for easier access to all the characters. (On Mac, easily enter third level using the OPTION key ("V, SHIFT+6, 5, OPTION+2" = V^6_2).
- Use SHIFT-S or S to add a slash ("V, SHIFT+6, SHIFT+S, 5" = V^6_5)
- Press ` (tilde) to move to the right under the same syllable ("V, SHIFT+6, 5, ` (tilde), SHIFT+S" = $V^{6\sharp}_5$).
- Use SHIFT+J or J for half diminished ($^\varnothing$ or $_\varnothing$).
- Use SHIFT+K or K for diminished ($^\circ$ or $_\circ$).
- Use SHIFT+L or L for a plus sign ($^+$ or $_+$).
- For full-size accidentals, "<" = ♭, ">" = ♯, and "n" = ♮ ("<", vii" = ♯vii).
- Use a / (slash) for modulations (III/VII).
- You can use | (vertical line) between pivot chords ($\underline{I}|V$). Use the \ (backslash) to add a larger pivot figure and then press DOWN ARROW to move the baseline down a bit to the second verse and begin adding numerals in the new key. Press UP ARROW to return to the original baseline in verse 1).

Tip:
There is a nice list of all the usual harmonic analysis characters in the Finale User Manual under "Harmonic Analysis." Again, to see every character in the font, refer to the Finale Numerics font on your system's Character Map/Viewer for a list of all the available characters. See "Adding characters using the Character Viewer/Map" on page 254.

Chant

There are a number of common techniques for producing chant in Finale. Generally, you will want to make some global adjustments first, like removing the time signature and barlines. To prepare a document for chant notation:

1. Choose **File > New > Default Document**.

2.   Choose the Selection Tool , and then press CTRL/CMD+A to select all.

3.   Choose **Utilities** > **Fit Measures** to open the Fit Measures dialog box.

4.   For **Lock Layout With _ Measure(s) per System**, enter "1."

5.   Click **OK**. There is now a single measure in every system. It is impossible to "eliminate" measures in Finale, so you can place a single measure on each system to give the appearance of a measureless document.

6.   Press CTRL/CMD+A to select all.

7.   Choose **Edit** > **Edit Measure Attributes**. The Measure Attributes dialog box appears.

8.   In the Measure Attributes, if you want to eliminate the barline at the end of each system, choose **Invisible** from the row of icons next to Barline. For Time Signature, choose **Always Hide**. Under **Position Notes** (at the bottom), check **Evenly Across Measure**.

9.   Click **OK**. You return to the score. Now, tell Finale to accommodate many notes in each measure/system with the Time Signature Tool .

10. Choose the Time Signature Tool and double-click the first system. The Time Signature dialog box appears.

11. After **Number Of Beats,** click the right arrow to select the number of beats you want to place in the first measure/system. For example, if you want 24 quarter notes in the first system, create a time signature of 24/4.

12. Click **OK**. You return to the score.

Now you have created what appears to be music without measures. If you intend to create chant notation in the future, save this document as a template to use later (and avoid having to repeat the previous steps). To do this, choose **File** > **Save As** (then, on Windows, for **Save As Type**, choose **Finale Template File**). Save the file to your Templates folder for use later. (Your templates are located in the Finale 2012/Music Files folder).

> **Tip:**
> If you are having trouble finding the "Finale 2012" folder, see page 5 of this book

Notes entered in the score will be spaced evenly across the system. You will probably want to turn off **Fill with Rests** (**Simple** > **Simple Entry Options** and **Speedy** > **Speedy Options**).

Here are some other helpful tips to use as you enter chant notation:

•   To remove stems from all notes in a staff, click the Staff Tool and double-click the chant staff. In the **Items to Display** section, uncheck **Stems**. Click **OK**. You return to the score with all stems removed from the selected staff.

- To position notes manually, choose the Measure Tool ▦ and click the lower handle on the right side of a staff to display the beat chart above the measure. Use the lower handle to position any note horizontally.
- As you enter lyrics into chant notation, you may want to enter more than one syllable under a note. To do this, use a "hard space." Type the first syllable, then type a hard space (Windows: ALT+0160 on the numeric pad; Mac: OPTION+Spacebar). Then type the second syllable and so on. You can also add these characters under the Lyrics Tool's Text menu.
- If you want to use tick barlines for chant, without setting one measure per system, choose the Measure Tool ▦ and highlight a region of your score (or press CTRL/CMD+A to Select All). Then, double-click the highlighted area to open the Measure Attributes dialog box. In the Barline row, choose **Tick** and click **OK**.
- Use the Note Shapes notation style to select shapes for pitches and/or note durations. With the Staff Tool ▦ selected, double-click a staff to open the Staff Attributes. Click the drop-down menu for Notation Style and choose Note Shapes. The Note Shapes dialog box appears. Choose the shapes you want to use for each scale degree and click OK back to the score. For more information on the Note Shapes notation style, see Chapter 8.

Mensurstriche Notation

Due to the absence of pulse in chant and other early notation, some reproductions of this music include barlines between staves rather than through them to offer a general sense of meter. This practice is known as mensurstriche notation. In Finale, mensurstriche barlines can be specified with the Staff Tool.

To create mensurstriche notation:

1. Begin with any document containing more than one staff.
2. Choose the Staff Tool ▦.
3. Select any number of desired staves.
4. Choose **Staff** > **Group and Bracket** > **Add**. The Group Attributes dialog box appears.
5. Click the drop-down menu for **Draw Barlines** and select **Between Staves (mensurstriche)**.
6. Make any other settings you would like to apply to the group and click **OK**. You return to the score with barlines extending between staves, and not through them.

Handbells

If you are creating a score for handbells, use the Create Handbells Used Chart plug-in.

To quickly add a handbells used chart at the beginning of your score:

1. Choose **Plug-ins/** ✂ > **TGTools** > **Create Handbells Used Chart**. The Create Handbells Used (see Figure 12.8).

Figure 12.8
Use the Create Handbells Used Chart plug-in to quickly add a handbells used chart at the beginning of your score.

2. Define your chart here using the available settings. Click **Go** to create the chart. These settings are relatively self explanatory. If there is a question, create the chart to preview. If you need to change something, undo (CTRL/CMD+Z) and reapply the plug-in.

Tremolos

Tremolo markings indicate a rapid succession of notes, usually on two different pitches (see Figure 12.9). The speed at which tremolos can be added drastically improved with the introduction of the Easy Tremolos plug-in.

Figure 12.9
There's a great plug-in for this.

1. Enter the two notes so they equal the full duration of the tremolo. For example, for a half-note tremolo, enter two quarter notes (one after the other in the same layer).
2. Choose the Selection Tool ![icon] .
3. Highlight the measure containing the notes you would like to convert to a tremolo.
4. Choose **Plug-ins/** ✂ > **TGTools** > **Easy Tremolos**. The Easy Tremolo dialog box appears as shown in Figure 12.10.

Figure 12.10

Use the Easy Tremolos dialog box to specify the visual appearance of the resulting tremolo.

5. In the text box, enter the total number of beams. If you check **Include Playback Notes**, Finale will enter hidden notes in layer four for playback. (Note that if you do not choose to add playback notes, Human Playback will playback the tremolo using its interpretation depending on the style chosen).
6. Click **Go**. The notes in the selected region convert to tremolo markings.

Feel free to adjust settings in the Easy Tremolo dialog box and apply them to the same selected region. The figure will update accordingly.

TIP:
If you add or delete notes in the same measure as a tremolo that was created with the Easy Tremolos plug-in, beaming may be lost on the tremolo. If this happens, simply run the plug-in on the region again to restore beaming.

Harmonics

Harmonics are notes manipulated to sound at a higher partial (in the harmonic series) of the fundamental pitch, and are most common in string notation. They are usually notated with a regular note on the fundamental pitch, and the secondary note above on the same stem (see Figure 12.11). This plug-in is designed to generate string harmonics from an interval of a third or fourth.

Figure 12.11

There's a great plug-in for this.

To create a harmonic:

1. Enter the fundamental pitch and the interval required for the desired harmonic on the same beat and in the same layer. Enter an interval of either a perfect fourth, major third, or minor third (intervals of a fourth will sound two octaves higher, an interval of a major third will sound two octaves and a major third higher, and an interval of a minor third will sound two octaves and a fifth higher than the fundamental).
2. Choose the Selection Tool .
3. Highlight the measure containing the notes.

4. Choose **Plug-ins/** ✂ > **TGTools** > **Easy Harmonics**. The Easy Harmonics dialog box appears as shown in Figure 12.12

Figure 12.12
Use the Easy Harmonics dialog box to specify the interval to look for.

5. Select the interval of the notes you want to convert to harmonics.
6. Click **Apply.** The notes in the selected region convert to harmonics. Play back the region to hear the resulting harmonic pitch. (The harmonic will play as notated with or without Human Playback).

Cadenzas

Cadenzas are solo passages with no barlines, and are usually notated with smaller than normal noteheads. There are several ways to create a cadenza passage in Finale. The most widely agreed upon method is to alter the time signature of a single measure (preserving the music spacing), enter the notes, and then use the Selection Tool to reduce the note size.

To create a cadenza:

1. Click the Time Signature Tool ⬛ , and then double-click the measure you want to enter the cadenza into. The Time Signature dialog box appears.
2. Change the time signature to accommodate the number of notes you want to enter in the cadenza passage. For example, if your cadenza is 48 eighth notes, define a time signature of 48/8. (Here, you could also use a time signature with a larger beam grouping like 24/4 or 12/2 so that not every single eighth note is flagged).
3. Click the **Options/More Choices** button to expand the dialog box.
4. Check **Use a Different Time Signature for Display**.
5. Set the time signature at the bottom to whatever you want to use for the display. For example, if the time signature for the measure previous to the cadenza is 3/4, define 3/4 here so there is no time change indicated on the cadenza measure.
6. In the **Measure Region** section, choose **Measure _ Through _** and enter the measure number for the cadenza in both entry fields (to define this time change for the cadenza measure only).
7. Click **OK** to return to the score.
8. Enter the notation into the measure and break or join beams as necessary using the slash (/) key.
9. Click the Selection Tool ⬛ , and then click the cadenza measure to highlight it.

10. Choose **Utilities** > **Change** > **Note Size.** Enter "75" and click **OK.**

Orchestration Tools

Whether you are composing a piece from scratch or copying from an existing handwritten score, Finale can be used as an excellent orchestration tool. Play an excerpt of music into one staff and explode it into many, or reduce large scores into a grand, or single, staff. You can even check for notes outside of an instrument's range, or tell Finale to search for occurrences of parallel motion in your score. Use the following techniques to save time while orchestrating.

Explode Music

While creating a score with several staves, you may want to enter many chord voicings into a single staff at once and then separate each voice into its own staff. To do this, use the Explode Music utility. This utility basically takes each note from chords entered in a single staff and delegates them into new staves or existing staves in the score. The result is an independent line of music in each staff consisting of a note from each original chord (see Figure 12.13).

Figure 12.13

Explode each note of a
chord into its own staff with
the Explode Music utility.

Here is a quick demonstration showing how to explode chords in one staff into independent voices on several staves.

1. Open a new Default Document (**File** > **New** > **Default Document**).
2. Enter some four-note chords into the first few measures (in a single layer).
3. Choose the Selection Tool ![selection tool icon].
4. Click just to the left of the staff to highlight the entire staff.
5. Choose **Utilities** > **Explode Music.** The Explode Music dialog box appears as shown in Figure 12.14.

Figure 12.14
Choose the number of new staves to create and where to put the extra notes while exploding music in the Explode Music dialog box.

6. You will want to create four new staves, so for Split Into, enter "4" (if it isn't there already). For **Place Music Into,** select **New Staves Added to Bottom of Score.**

7. Click **OK**. Finale adds four new staves to the score, with each voice in its own staff.

Now, make any additional edits to the new staves. Use the Score Manager to assign an instrument to each staff, which sets their transposition, staff name, clef, etc. You can use the Explode Music utility to explode music into up to eight staves.

Here are some ways to customize the results generated by exploding music while in the Explode Music dialog box:

- If your score already contains the staves you want to explode to, choose them from the **Existing Staves Starting With Staff** drop-down menu.
- If some of your chords contain extra notes, in other words, if some chords have more notes than the number of staves you're exploding to, you can tell Finale on which staff to place the extra notes. If you want Finale to put the extra notes into the bottom staff, in the **Extra Notes** section, select **Put in Bottom Staff**. If you want Finale to group the extra notes in the first staff, choose **Put in Top Staff**.
- If a chord contains fewer notes than the number of staves, you can use the **Top Down** and **Bottom Up** functions to add notes from the top staff down or from the bottom staff up. For example, if you explode to 4 staves with **Top Down** chosen, a 3-note chord will be dispersed among the top three staves and a rest will appear the fourth staff. With **Bottom Up** chosen, the rest would appear in the top staff and the three notes would be distributed among the bottom three staves.

TIP:
To isolate a specific layer for explosion, choose **Document** > **Show Active Layer Only**, and then choose the layer you want to explode.

Implode Music

You can also squeeze music from many staves into one with the Selection Tool's Implode Music utility. This utility takes notes from a region of selected staves and stacks them within a single staff as shown in Figure 12.15.

Figure 12.15

Use the Implode Music utility to consolidate notes in many staves into a single staff.

To implode notes from many staves into one:

1. Start with any document containing several staves, and a single line of music on two or more staves.

2. Choose the Selection Tool .

3. Highlight the region of measures you want to consolidate into a single staff.

4. Choose **Utilities** > **Implode Music**. The Implode Music dialog box appears as shown in Figure 12.16.

Figure 12.16

Choose a destination for the notes you want to implode, and edit their quantization in the Implode Music dialog box.

5. Here, choose whether you want to place the resulting notes in the top staff of the selected region or into a new staff added to the bottom of the score. Click the **Quant Settings** button to open the Quantization Settings dialog box (see Figure 4.3) where you can choose the smallest note value, and other parameters for your results.

6. Click **OK**. You return to the score. All notes from the selected region now appear in one staff.

Piano Reductions

Finale can generate a reduction of any number of staves automatically and place the results in a grand staff as shown in Figure 12.17.

Figure 12.17

Generate a piano reduction automatically with the Piano Reduction plug-in.

To create a piano reduction from any score:

1. Start with any document containing several staves with music.

2. Choose **Plug-ins/**  **> Scoring and Arranging > Piano Reduction**. The Piano Reduction dialog box appears as shown in Figure 12.18.

Figure 12.18

Select staves to include and a split point for your piano reduction in the Piano Reduction dialog box.

3. Here, highlight the staves you want to include in your reduction. Hold down the Shift key and click to select consecutive staves. Hold down the CTRL/CMD key and click to select non-consecutive staves. For **Split Point**, choose the lowest note you want to include on the right-hand staff of your piano reduction (60 = middle C).

4. Click **OK**. It may take a while for Finale to generate the reduction. When it's done, your reduction appears in a new grand staff added to the bottom of your score.

You will most likely need to edit the results of the generated piano reduction. Finale will sometimes need to shorten a note if it finds a shorter one on the same beat of a different staff. When this happens, try entering the note in a different layer.

TIP:
Finale will quantize to the smallest note duration while generating a piano reduction. If you want to create independent lines of music in the reduction, try using the **Move Layers** feature to distinguish voices in your staves before running the Piano Reduction plug-in. With the Selection Tool selected, highlight some music, then choose **Edit** > **Move/Copy Layers**. After creating the piano reduction, you may want to move the music back to its original layer on the staves above.

The Check Range Plug-In

While orchestrating, arranging, or composing, you may want to check over a region of your work to ensure all notes are within a playable range for the instrument. You can check for notes out of range, change them, or delete them with the Check Range plug-in.

To check a region of your score for notes out of range for an instrument, do the following:

1. To check range for the whole score, move to step 2. To check range for a staff or staves, click the Selection Tool, and then click to the left of the staff (SHIFT+click to the left of additional staves you want to check to select them).

2. Choose **Plug-ins/** > **Scoring and Arranging** > **Check Range**. The Check Range dialog box appears as shown in Figure 12.19.

Figure 12.19

Check your score for notes out of an instrument's range with the Check Range plug-in.

3. Look after **Staff Name:** at the top to see the staff you are currently checking. In the Instrument section, choose the instrument you are using for the current staff. Notice the **High Note** and **Low Note** fields update as you move between instruments. For **Range Class**, choose the skill level for the instrument range. You can also adjust the high and low pitches by using the up and down arrows, or by entering your own pitch manually.

4. Click **Check**. If Finale finds any notes out of range, the Note Out of Range dialog box appears as shown in Figure 12.20.

Figure 12.20
Erase or change out-of-range notes in the Note Out of Range dialog box.

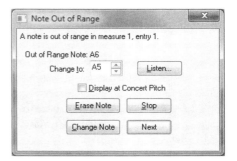

5. Click **Erase Note** to remove the note from the score. Click **Change Note** to change the note to the pitch specified in the **Change To:** field. Click **Stop** to return to the score.

If you are using an external MIDI device, like a MIDI keyboard, click the Listen button while checking the range (in either of the range checking dialog boxes) to specify the pitch by simply playing a note on your external MIDI device.

TIP:
To transpose any selected region of music, choose the Selection Tool, highlight the region, then choose **Utilities** > **Transpose**.

Find Parallel Motion

If you are composing or arranging a score and need to observe classical rules of voice leading, try running the Find Parallel Motion plug-in to find all occurrences of parallel motion in your score.

To check for parallel fifths or octaves:

1. Choose the Selection Tool .

2. Select a region of your score you want to check for parallel motion, or press CTRL/ CMD+A to Select All.

3. Choose **Plug-ins/** > **Scoring and Arranging** > **Find Parallel Motion.** The Find Parallel Motion dialog box appears as shown in Figure 12.21.

Figure 12.21
Use the Find Parallel Motion plug-in to find occurrences of parallel fifths and octaves in your score.

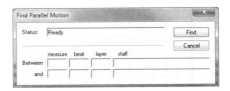

4. Click **Find**. Finale will search for parallel fifths and octaves in all staves, layers, and voices. Finale reports the measure, beat, layer, and staff in the two rows at the bottom of this dialog box.

5. Click **Find** again to move to the next occurrence or click Cancel to return to the score.

TIP:
If you're using this plug-in to quickly analyze a score for parallelism in a music theory homework assignment, be sure to learn the rules of parallel motion in traditional voice leading in case Finale isn't available in an upcoming exam.

Creative Tools

Many composers and arrangers prefer to use Finale throughout the process of writing an original score. Among the advantages of composing with Finale are the numerous plug-ins and other features designed to offer ideas and spark creativity. If you are looking to generate harmony for a melodic passage, Finale can offer a large number of suggestions for up to six parts with the Band in the Box Auto Harmonizer plug-in. If you are composing serial music, or a related genre, you can easily rearrange notes by inversion or retrograde with the Canonic Utilities. Use any of the following utilities to generate thousands of musical possibilities to choose from while creating a score.

Band-in-the-Box Auto Harmonizing

As questionable as it sounds, Finale can actually create a viable harmonic solution for up to six parts from any given melody. By choosing from an extensive collection of harmonization options, you can usually find one that works well. In practice, it is best to use the Auto Harmonizing plug-in for a basic harmonic outline and then edit the voice leading, spelling, and texture to your own taste. Use the following instructions to easily create a four-part saxophone arrangement from a simple melody.

1. Start by creating a new default document. Choose **New** > **Document with Setup Wizard**, and click **Next** to move to page 2. Here, choose the **Woodwinds** category and add a **Soprano, Alto, Tenor,** and **Baritone** saxophone. Click **Next, Next,** and **Finish** to create the new document with four saxophones.

2. Enter a simple melody with chord symbols like the example in Figure 12.21.

Figure 12.22

To prepare for running the Band-in-a-Box Auto Harmonizing plug-in, enter a melody with chord symbols.

3.   Choose the Selection Tool  and click to the left of the top staff to highlight the entire staff.

4.   Choose **Plug-ins/** ✂ > **Scoring and Arranging** > **Band-in-a-Box Auto Harmonizing**. The Band-in-a-Box Auto Harmonizing dialog box appears as shown in Figure 12.22.

Figure 12.23

Choose the type of harmonization you want to apply and where you want to place the generated notes in the Band-in-a-Box Harmonizing dialog box.

5.   Here, choose the number of parts and the type of harmonization. For this example, I used four parts and the "Super Brass" type of harmonization. In the **Place New Voices Into** section, choose the staves you want Finale to place the harmonization into. For this example, I chose the **Three Existing Staves** starting with the **Alto Sax** staff.

6.   Click **OK**. Finale generates the harmonization and places the resulting notes into the subsequent staves (see Figure 12.24).

Figure 12.24
Band-in-a-Box Auto Harmonizing results

After auto harmonizing, you may need to edit the enharmonic spelling of certain notes. Also, use the Simple Entry Tool to change any pitches to customize the harmonization to get the sound you're looking for. Press CTRL/CMD+Z to undo the harmonization and try one of the other harmonizing options available in the Band-in-a-Box Auto Harmonizing dialog box.

> **TIP:**
> To give your score a handwritten look (like the score in Figure 12.22, for example), choose the **Handwritten Style** Document Style on page 1 of the Document Setup Wizard.

Inversions, Retrogrades, and More: The Canonic Utilities

The Canonic Utilities plug-in is particularly useful if you are composing serial music. Invert or retrograde a portion of music easily with this plug-in. You can also add or remove accidentals and transpose the region while performing these tasks. To invert (flip the music upside-down), or retrograde (flip the music end-to-end), or both, do the following:

1.   Open a new Default Document (**File** > **New** > **Default Document**).
2.   Enter a series of notes into the first few measures like those shown in Figure 12.25, for example.

Figure 12.25
Invert or retrograde any passage such as this one with the Canonic Utilities plug-in.

3. Choose the Selection Tool  and highlight the region containing the notes you want to manipulate.

4. Choose **Plug-ins/** ✂ > **Scoring and Arranging** > **Canonic Utilities.** The Canonic Utilities dialog box appears as shown in Figure 12.26.

Figure 12.26

Choose the type of inversion or retrograde you want to apply to the selected region, and select a transposition, in the Canonic Utilities dialog box.

5. Here, choose the type of inversion from the drop-down menu at the top. For this example, select **Diatonic Mirror Inversion**. Click the **Retrograde** check box if you would also like to retrograde the selection (as in this example). You can also make additional settings for mirror inversions, transposition, and retrogrades by clicking the corresponding buttons on the right. Click **Verify Retrograde** to check the selection for invalid entries. You will not be able to retrograde music containing slurs, note expressions, or mirrored measures.

6. Click **OK**. Finale calculates the inversion and/or retrograde and adjusts the notes accordingly (see Figure 12.27).

Figure 12.27

Canonic Utilities results with retrograde applied.

13
Customizing Finale, Scanning, and Education Tips

Don't like Finale? Then change it! From conception, Finale has been designed to give you nearly unlimited control over the workings of the program. If there is something about the way Finale works that you don't like, you can probably tweak it. For example, you can tell Finale to always open a new lead sheet on startup, or nudge four pixels instead of one. You can even remove tools you don't use from certain palettes to save space or modify Finale's overall appearance. In many ways Finale adapts to your needs rather than the other way around, so you might as well take the red pill and deal with it, the payoffs really are worth it.

Scanning is a popular feature. Some purchase Finale for the sole purpose of transferring sheet music to a digital format. In this chapter, you will learn how to use Finale to produce the industry's best results while converting scanned files without having to purchase an entirely separate scanning program. You will also learn techniques for cleaning up files after conversion.

If you're a music educator, you can use one of Finale's education templates to create examples, worksheets, and quizzes. You can also create customized technique-building exercises for any sized ensemble in minutes with the Exercise Wizard.

Be sure to read the first sections of this chapter. Change/customize what you want and then feel free to skip what doesn't apply to you later on. No sense force feeding the brain any empty calories.

Here's a summary of what you will learn in this chapter:

- How to create custom documents
- How to customize Finale
- How to work with scanned files
- Tricks for music educators

Creating Custom Documents

Avoid the redundancy of adding the same libraries and making the same document settings for each new project. Do this by defining your own Document Styles or creating your own Finale templates.

Using Document Styles

As mentioned in Chapter 2, Document Styles are basically robust templates that can be used to easily replicate an existing document's settings and formatting whenever you start a new document with the Setup Wizard.

A Document Style's definition includes:

- Libraries (expressions, articulations, Smart Shapes, etc.)
- Page Format for Score and Page Format for Parts settings
- All document settings (Document Options dialog box, default music font, etc.)

Document Styles can be more convenient than templates because they can be mixed and matched with any orchestration/ensemble in the Setup Wizard. However, if your score contains an inconsistent page layout (varying system widths, etc.), you should create a template instead (described next).

To define a Document Style:

1. Open a file that includes the settings and formatting you would like to replicate in the future. Or, begin a new document, load/define libraries, and configure the document settings and page format according to your needs (see Chapters 2 and 11).
2. Save the file to the Finale 2012/Music Files/Document Styles folder.

That's it! Now, when you use the Setup Wizard (**File** > **New** > **Document with Setup Wizard**), this option will be available on the first page.

NOTE:
Finale doesn't allow you to apply a Document Style to an existing document, but you can create a new document with the Setup Wizard (defining the desired orchestration and Document Style), then use the Selection Tool to copy music from the existing document into the new one.

Creating Your Own Templates

As you have seen, Finale contains a variety of template files that you can use as a starting point for working on a specific type of project (**File** > **New** > **Document from Template**). When you open a template file, Finale opens a copy of the template as an untitled document, so you won't have to worry about overwriting it.

Although Document Styles are often sufficient, templates are necessary in some situations; for example, if you frequently use a document that includes systems of varying width - which Document Styles do not accommodate.

To create your own custom template:

1. Open any file. You might want to begin with a new Default Document, a new document with the Setup Wizard, or an existing template file.

2. Edit or load any desired libraries, edit the Page Format for Score, or make any other document-specific settings.

3. Choose **File** > **Save As**. The Save As window appears.

4. Navigate to the Finale 2012/Music Files/Templates folder (if you want to store this template along with the other Finale templates, though any location will work fine).

5. On Windows, from the **Save As Type** drop-down menu, choose **Finale Template File [*. FTM]**. On Macintosh, a template is a regular Finale Notation file.

6. Give your template file a unique name. You should now see your file name followed by the .ftm extension on Windows or a .mus extension on Mac.

7. Click **Save**.

8. Now, any time you want to use this template, choose **File** > **New** > **Document From Template**. Then double-click the file you created. A copy of the file will open as a new untitled document.

Customizing Finale

In addition to the basic program options described in Chapter 2, there are a number of other ways to customize the way Finale works both from within the Program Options dialog box and by using other tools Finale provides.

Customizing Finale with Program Options

Use the Program Options dialog box to customize a variety of default program settings that you have probably been using without even knowing it. For example, you can tell Finale to open all new files in Scroll View at any view percentage, use a different startup action (instead of starting the Launch window every time), or use the arrow keys to nudge five pixels instead of one. These, and many other program settings, are conveniently located in the Program Options dialog box.

Options for Opening New Documents

Choose **Edit** (Mac, **Finale 2012** > **Preferences**) > **Program Options** and select **New** from the list on the left. The New page of the Program Options dialog box allows you to customize settings for new or newly opened documents (see Figure 13.1).

Figure 13.1

Use the New page of the Program Options dialog box to specify a default file and the default view for all documents you open, including new documents.

Here are some ways to specify the way Finale treats new documents from the New page of the Program Options dialog box:

- In the **Default Document** text box, specify any template file to use for your Default Document in place of the Maestro Font Default file. For example, you can specify that Finale always use the **Handwritten Font Default** file as the Default Document. On Windows, click the **Browse** button to open a Windows Explorer window where you can navigate to the desired file. This is the file Finale will use when you open a new Default Document (**File** > **New** > **Default Document**). On Mac, just type the name of the file you want to use as your Default file. The file, however, must be located in the Finale 2012/Music Files/Default Files folder. If you leave the **Default Document** text field within the Program Options blank on Mac, Finale will automatically use the Maestro Font Default document.

- For **Default New Operation**, specify the result of opening a file using the CTRL/CMD+N keyboard shortcut by choosing **Setup Wizard** or **Default Document**.

- By default, every time you start Finale, you see the Launch window. You may want to tell Finale to open the Document Setup Wizard, a new default file, template, or other file during startup instead. If this is the case, from the **Startup Action** drop-down menu, choose what you want Finale to do when you first start the program. If you choose **New Document from Template**, at startup you will be prompted to choose a file from the Templates folder (as specified in the Templates field on the Folders page). If you choose **Open Document**, at startup you will be prompted to choose a file from your Music folder (as specified on the **Music** field of the Folders page).

- In the **New Document Windows** section, choose the view percentage and view (**Page**, **Scroll**, or **Studio View**) to use for all documents you open or create.

TIP:
For information on using Finale's AutoSave and Backup features on the Save page of the Program Options dialog box, see "Auto Save" on page 15.

View Options

Use the View page of the Program Options dialog box to customize the appearance of certain items. In the Program Options dialog box, choose the View category from the list on the left. The View page appears as shown in Figure 13.2.

Figure 13.2

Make settings for the appearance of certain items in the View page of the Program Options dialog box.

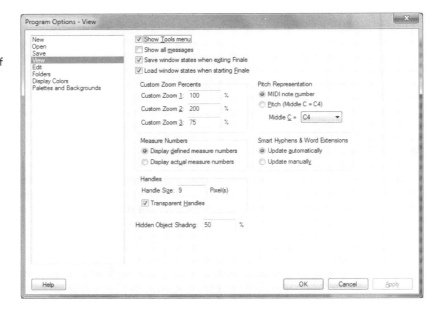

- The zoom percentages represent the size of the viewable area which can be selected under the **View** Menu They correspond to the CTRL/CMD+1, +2, and +3 view percentage keystrokes.

- For **Pitch Representation,** you can tell Finale to display pitches as MIDI Note Numbers (C = 60) or Pitches (C = C4). This representation of pitch crops up in a variety of places. For example, choose the HyperScribe Tool, and then choose **HyperScribe** > **Record Mode** > **Split Into Two Staves**. The split point representation (60 or C4, by default) will depend on this setting.

- If you are defining measure number regions, you may want to tell Finale to display the actual measure numbers beginning from the "real" measure one. To do this, after **Measure Numbers**, choose **Display Actual Measure Numbers**. Choose **Display Defined Measure Numbers** to go back to displaying measure regions as defined in the Measure

Number dialog box. In Scroll View the real measure numbers appear in the lower left of the Finale window (in the measure counter).

- In some situations, such as when working with the Special Tools, it is difficult to see Finale's transparent handles. Uncheck **Transparent Handles** to restore the handle appearance back to its old, Finale 2009 and earlier, opaqueness.

Undo Options, Dragging, and Nudging, etc.

You can adjust Finale's settings for dragging and nudging in the Edit page of the Program Options dialog box. Choose the Edit category from the list on the left of the Program Options dialog box to see the Edit page as shown in Figure 13.3.

Figure 13.3

Customize Finale's settings for dragging and nudging on the Edit page of the Program Options dialog box.

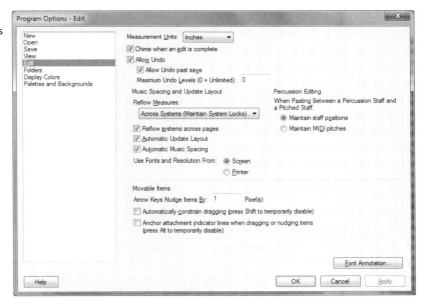

Here are some ways to edit Finale's treatment of Undo, dragging, and nudging in the Edit page of the Program Options:

- Finale records just about everything you do in your open file(s) in case you want it undone (CTRL/CMD+Z). Make sure **Allow Undo** is checked. You will want to keep the default settings, so you can undo any unwanted changes while working on the score. Also, make sure **Allow Undo Past Save** is checked to tell Finale to keep a record of your work so you can undo changes even after you have saved. To redo an Undo, press CTRL/CMD+Y. Note that the undo records are cleared after you close and reopen the file.

- In the **Movable Items** section, specify the number of pixels to nudge an item each time you press an arrow key.

- Check **Automatically Constrain Dragging** to tell Finale to always constrain to horizontal or vertical dragging (then press SHIFT to drag normally at any time).

Customizing Placement of Finale Files on Your Computer

I have touched on the Folders page of the Program Options a few times already. This page of the Program Options can be used to manage the placement of files used by Finale, or those you create. Choose Folders in the Program Options dialog box from the list on the left. See Figure 13.4.

Figure 13.4

Designate a folder for files used by Finale and those you create on the Folders page of the Program Options dialog box.

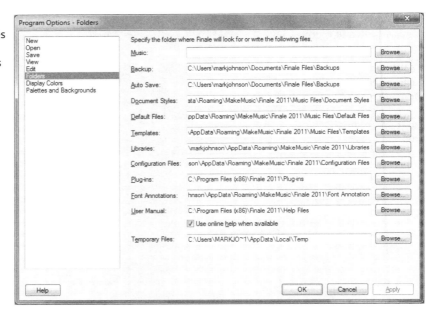

Use this page as a reference if you're looking for a specific file type used by Finale on your system. Or, select a folder to use for any of these file types by clicking the **Browse** button and choosing a path. On Mac, to specify a folder, click the check box or the **Select** button. For example, if you select the Finale 2012/Music Files/Templates/Band Templates folder for Templates, Finale will open this folder when you choose **File > New Document from Template**.

Customizing Finale's Display Colors

You can customize the color associated with any item, or turn off all display colors, in the Display Colors page of the Program Options dialog box. Choose Display Colors from the list on the left. You can also open this page from the View menu (**View > Select Display Colors**). The Display Colors options appear as shown in Figure 13.5.

Figure 13.5

Specify a color for any item, or turn off display colors altogether on the Display Colors page of the Program Options dialog box.

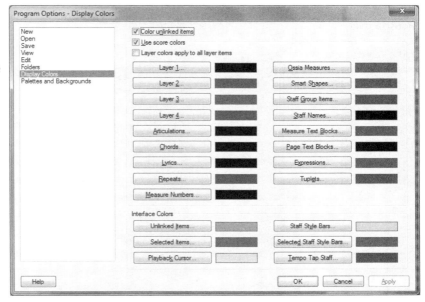

Click the item you want to customize to open the Color dialog box where you can choose a new color for the item. Check **Layer Color Apply to All Layer Items** if you want all articulations, note expressions, or other note-attached items to match the color of the layer to which they are attached. Uncheck **Use Score Colors** to tell Finale to use only black and white for display in the score.

TIP:
To print the display colors on a color printer as they appear on-screen, check **Print Display Colors** in the Print dialog box. On Mac, you will find this in the "Finale 2012" settings of the Print dialog.

Customizing Finale's General Appearance

Finale offers many options with regards to the general appearance. You can change the style to use for both palettes, backgrounds, and manuscript paper texture and make other palette settings. Choose Palettes and Backgrounds from the list on the left to display the Palettes and Backgrounds page as shown in Figure 13.6.

Figure 13.6

Choose a style for your palettes and backgrounds on the Palettes and Backgrounds page of the Program Options dialog box.

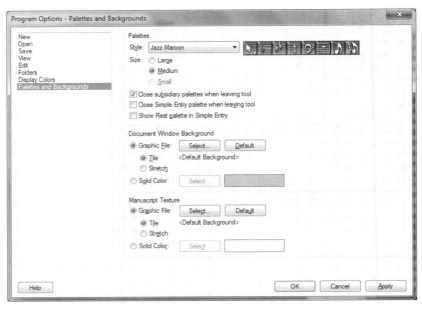

Here are some ways to customize the graphic style of tool palettes, and the background and manuscript graphics:

- Click the **Palettes** drop-down menu to choose from the several available palette styles. Choose **Traditional** if you want to revert back to the palettes as they existed in Finale 2002 or prior (you can save some screen real estate this way).

- Check **Close Subsidiary Palettes When Leaving Tool** if you want Finale to automatically remove palettes not associated with the selected tool. For example, with this option checked, Finale will display only the Smart Shape Palette when the Smart Shape Tool is selected. The following two check boxes allow you to make specific palette settings for the Simple Entry Tool palettes.

- In the **Document Window Background** section, you can set a color or graphic file to appear behind the page while working with Finale in Page View. Click the **Select** button to open one of Finale's background graphics, or navigate to your own graphic file to set it as the background.

- Choose **Solid Color** and click the **Select** button to the right to choose your favorite color for the background.

- In the **Manuscript Texture** section you can make similar settings to edit the graphic or color of the screen representation of the manuscript paper.

Customizing the Tool Palettes

If there are some tools you do not use at all, you may want to hide them from the tool palette to save space on your screen. You can do this with the Main Tool Palette, any of the secondary palettes, or the menu toolbars. Since this functionality is closely tied to the operating system, it works differently on Macintosh than on Windows.

TIP:
To display any tool palette, select it from the Window menu.

To customize your tool palettes on Windows:

1. Choose **Window** > **Customize Palettes** and then choose the palette you want to modify. The Customize Toolbar dialog box appears as shown in Figure 13.7.

Figure 13.7
Remove items from any palette using the Customize Toolbar dialog box.

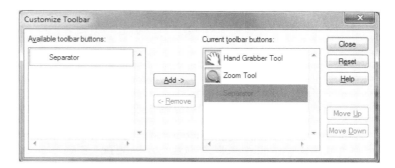

2. Choose any of the icons on the right and click **Remove** to remove it from the palette. After removing a palette icon, select it from the list on the left and click **Add** to place it back into the palette.

3. Select a palette icon on the left and click the **Move Up** or **Move Down** button to change the order of the palette icons. Click **Reset** at any time to restore the palette back to the default settings.

To customize your tool palettes on Macintosh:

1. While holding down the SHIFT key, click and drag a tool icon in the Main Tool Palette to move it to any location in the palette. You can do this with any Finale tool palette, but your changes to the Main Tool Palette can be retained from session to session if you program a Tool Set. Changes to the tool reordering on subsidiary palettes are lost when you quit Finale.

2. You can save the Main Tool Palette configuration to use at any time. SHIFT+click and drag the tool icons to the desired configuration. Then, hold down OPTION and choose **View** > **Program Tool Set** > **Tool Set 1**.

3. Choose **Master Tool Set** from the **Select Tool Set** submenu to use Finale's default palette settings.

4.   If you intend to resize the palette to hide certain icons, move the ones you want to keep to the left side of the palette. Click one of the icons you want to remain visible before resizing the palette. This way, Finale won't change the arrangement of icons as you resize.

5.   Click and drag the resize box at the lower-right corner of the palette to change the size and number of visible tools (see Figure 13.8).

Figure 13.8
Use the resize box on the lower right of any tool palette to change its shape and the number of visible tools.

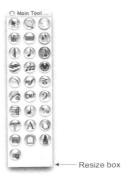

Menu Shortcuts (Windows only)

On Windows, you can map any menu selection to a keystroke using the TGTools Menu Shortcuts plug-in. This way, you can quickly access the dialog boxes you use often or easily activate and deactivate parameters.

To program a keystroke to any menu item:

1.   Choose **Plug-ins/** ✂ **> TGTools > Menu Shortcuts.** The Menu Shortcuts dialog box appears as shown in Figure 13.9.

Figure 13.9
Use the Menu Shortcuts dialog box to program keystrokes to any menu item for easy access.

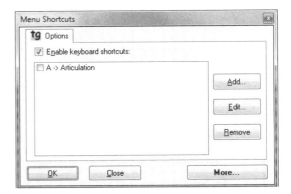

2. Check **Enable Keyboard Shortcuts**. For this example, program two menu shortcuts: one to toggle the **Display in Concert Pitch** setting, and one to open the Global Staff Attributes dialog box.

3. Click **Add** to open the Key Assignment dialog box where you can specify the key and menu item for your menu shortcut (see Figure 13.10).

Figure 13.10
Choose the keystroke and menu item for your menu shortcut in the Key Assignment dialog box.

4. Click the **Key** drop-down menu and choose the keystroke you want to use. For this example, choose the F4 key (in the future, you can select a modifier for any keystroke by checking CTRL, ALT, or SHIFT on the right for more options).

5. Under **Select Menu Command**, choose the menu from the first drop-down menu and the submenus in the following drop-down menus. For this example, choose **Document** from the top drop-down menu and **Display in Concert Pitch** from the second. You may need to use all four tiers for some menu items.

6. Click **OK** to return to the Menu Shortcuts dialog box.

7. Now, let's add another menu shortcut that opens a dialog box. Click **Add** again to open the Key Assignment dialog box.

8. Now, click the **Key** drop-down menu and choose the F3 key. (Or, click **Listen** and type the keystroke).

9. Under **Select Menu Command**, choose **Plug-ins/** ✂ from the top drop-down menu, **Scoring and Arranging** from the second drop-down menu, and **Global Staff Attributes** from the third.

10. Click **OK** twice to return to the score.

11. Now, to demonstrate these menu shortcuts at work, choose **File** > **New** > **Document With Setup Wizard**. Move to page 2 and add any transposing instrument (Horn in F, for example). Then click **Next, Next**, and **Finish** to open the new score. You might also want to enter some notes.

12. Press F4. Your score displays in concert pitch. Press the F4 key again to display the score in its transposed form. Now, pressing the F4 key does the same thing as choosing **Document** > **Display in Concert Pitch**.

13. Press F3. The Global Staff Attributes appears. Now pressing the F3 key does the same thing as choosing **Plug-ins/** ✂ > **Scoring and Arranging** > **Global Staff Attributes**.

Program as many keyboard shortcuts as you like in order to creatively improve efficiency while working on any project. The shortcuts you program will be available whenever you use Finale. To turn off Menu Shortcuts, uncheck Enable Keyboard Shortcuts in the Menu Shortcuts dialog box.

TIP:
For more options for keyboard shortcuts on Windows or Macintosh, you might investigate QuicKeys. Visit quickeys.com for more info.

Working with Scanned Files

Scanning in Finale has improved drastically over the years. In the past, this particular feature was a technical-support nightmare as scanning technology overall really wasn't ready for prime-time score recognition. Though there are still a number of limitations and problems with translating a scanned page of sheet music into Finale, you can produce far better results with SmartScore Lite, included in Finale 2012, than in older versions. In this section, you will learn tricks for getting the best possible results while translating a page (or pages) of sheet music into a Finale document.

Scanning Sheet Music

To use Finale's scanning features you will need a scanner and compatible scanning software. Most flatbed scanners will do the trick. Musitek, the company that produces the scanning software used by Finale (SmartScore Lite), offers their scanner recommendations at musitek.com/bundle.html. If you purchased Finale primarily for scanning, consider purchasing one of these scanners. (A higher-priced scanner does not translate to better Finale import). Do not try to use a hand scanner while scanning music intended for Finale. For best results, the goal is to create the cleanest possible gray scale graphic image of the page. You can acquire sheet music directly from your scanner. When you do this, Finale attempts to configure your scanning software to optimal settings automatically. Before you scan, note the following:

- The original document should be 16 staves or less.
- Do not expect quality results while translating handwritten scores, or poor-quality printed manuscripts. The cleaner the piece looks on the page, the better Finale will be able to translate it.
- Before scanning, the page should be aligned square with the plate of the scanner.

To acquire sheet music and translate it to a Finale file, do the following. (If you want to translate TIFF graphics that have already been scanned, skip to the next section).

1. Place the first page of sheet music on the bed of the scanner.
2. In Finale, choose **File** > **Scanning: SmartScore Lite** > **Scan and Import**. Click **OK** to dismiss the obligatory naggery. The SmartScore Lite 6 dialog box appears as shown in

Figure 13.11. Click the Preview button if you do not see the music. If you see the message, "Scanner not ready" make sure your scanner is turned on and properly installed.

Figure 13.11

Scan pages individually in the SmartScore Lite 6 dialog box.

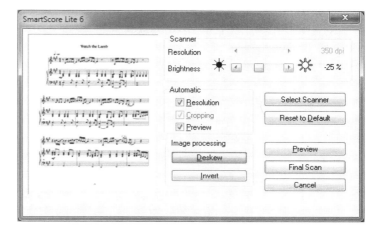

3. If the image is faded, use the Brightness slider to maximize the contrast.

4. Click **Scan** to scan the first page. When the scan is complete, Finale asks you if you want to scan another page. If you do, click **Yes**, place the next page of music in your scanner, and scan the next page. Keep doing this until you have scanned all pages of the score. After you have scanned all pages, when you are prompted to scan another page, click **No** and then **OK**. The SmartScore Lite dialog box appears.

5. Click **Add Files to List**. Here you see the files you just acquired from you scanner. (From here, you can also navigate to a folder containing existing scanned files). CTRL/CMD+click to select the files you want to translate. When you have chosen the desired files, click **Open**. The files you selected now appear listed in the middle of the SmartScore Lite dialog box as shown in Figure 13.12. Click a file name to see a preview of the file in the preview window on the left.

Figure 13.12

Prepare for scanning recognition in the SmartScore Lite dialog box.

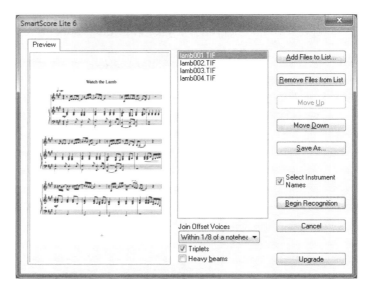

6. SmartScore Lite will translate each scanned image as a new page of the same Finale document if you have added several files to the list. Rearrange the file/page order by clicking the **Move Up** and **Move Down** buttons on the right.

7. Click **Begin Recognition**. The Instrument Name Assignments dialog box appears. Here, choose the staff names and transposition for each staff. This way, Finale will translate the music into the correct concert key and instrument transposition.

8. Click **OK**. Finale translates each file and opens the resulting document.

The raw results you get immediately after translation will depend on the image quality and complexity of the original sheet music. You may find somewhat of a mess after translating a staff with many voices and complex rhythms. Use the Simple or Speedy Entry Tool to edit any basic notation errors after translation (see Chapters 2 and 3 for information on editing with Simple and Speedy Entry).

Here are some more tricks for editing scanned files opened with SmartScore Lite:

- To improve the layout, start a new document with the Document Setup Wizard and then use the Selection Tool to copy the music from the scanned document file to the new document.

- Use the Selection Tool to reposition items throughout the score as necessary.

- You may find a variety of other changes necessary, for which you can find help throughout this book. If your results are poor (due to file complexity or image quality of the original score), evaluate the time necessary to fix the scanned score compared to entering the music from scratch with the Speedy Entry Tool or any of the other entry methods.

Scanning TIFF Files for Finale Import Manually

If you need to scan your music using a computer without Finale, you can scan the sheet music manually and then import the files from within the SmartScore Lite dialog box. Here are some guidelines to follow while scanning the sheet music. Consult your scanning program's user manual if you have trouble making any of these settings.

- SmartScore Lite accepts TIFF and bitmap files. Always scan in gray scale. Some scanners save TIFF files specific to their product line. If you find your scanning software is producing non-standard TIFF files, try using a gray scale bitmap file instead. Open the image in another graphics program and then save it in standard gray scale TIFF or bitmap format.
- Set the resolution of your scan to 300 or 350 dpi.
- Save your scan as an uncompressed TIFF file (without LZW compression).
- Scan each page and save it to a convenient place on your computer. Save each page as a separate file. You might try using a naming convention that relates to the page number (e.g., mypiece1.tif, mypiece2.tif, etc.).

After you have scanned and saved the music, open Finale. Choose **File** > **Scanning: SmartScore Lite** > **Import Existing TIFF File**. Now, follow the steps in the previous section, beginning with step 5.

Orchestrating Scanned Scores

Finale 2012 is able to identify transposing instrument staves while importing a scanned file (which wasn't always the case). But, the imported file may not include the appropriate group brackets or other score aspect, such as the desired Document Style. As mentioned earlier, to quickly apply this information to your scanned music, copy and insert the scanned results into a clean new file created with the Setup Wizard. To do this:

1. Scan and import the music into Finale. Then, create a new document with the same instrumentation.
2. Start the Setup Wizard (**File** > **New** > **Document with Setup Wizard**). Add the instruments in the same order they appear in the scanned file. Then, complete the Setup Wizard. (There is no need to set the time or key signature). See "Starting a Score with the Document Setup Wizard" on page 19 for more information regarding the Setup Wizard.
3. Return to the scanned file. You can select it from the Window Menu.
4. Choose the Selection Tool . Then press CTRL/CMD+A to Select All. Press CTRL/CMD+C to copy. Click **Edit** and ensure **Filter** is unchecked.
5. Return to the empty document you just setup (Window menu).
6. Press CTRL/CMD+A to Select All. Then, press CTRL/CMD+V to Paste. The music appears in your new document.

Tricks for Music Educators

Finale can make an excellent addition to a music educator's toolbox. Use Finale to create examples, quizzes, worksheets, or even custom exercises for warm-ups for your ensemble. Whether you are a music theory instructor or a band director, in this section you will learn how to effectively benefit from some of Finale's educational features.

Worksheets

Finale includes around 300 worksheets that cover everything from rhythm to pitch to instrumentation, and even jazz. You can find all of Finale's worksheets in the Finale 2012/Music Files/Worksheets folder. The answer key is located loose on the Finale 2012 DVD.

Tip:
If you are having trouble finding the "Finale 2012" folder, see page 5 of this book

Finale's Educational Templates

Finale 2012 offers several templates designed specifically for use in music-oriented classes for worksheets or quizzes. To use one of these, choose **File** > **New** > **Document From Template**. Then, open the Education Templates folder.

Two- and Four-Measure Examples

Finale's two- and four-measure templates can be used to create musical examples with descriptions or questions for music theory tests or quizzes (see Figure 13.13).

Figure 13.13

Use Finale's two- and four-measure example templates for music theory examples or questions.

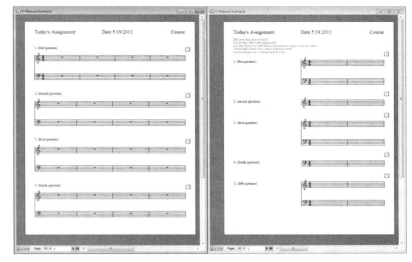

These documents are specialized in many ways. Courtesy key, clef and time changes have been turned off, so you won't see extra material at the end of your examples if you decide to change one of these items. The final barline has been removed, the page layout altered, and other minor modifications have been made. The "2 Measure Examples" file offers some suggestions for managing these files in an existing text block. To delete this text block, use the Text (or Selection) Tool. Here are some suggestions for creating musical examples or questions:

- There are two staves per system in both of these documents. Some staves in the two-measure example document have been hidden with a staff style. To hide or show any region of measures, click the Staff Tool. Gray lines appear above all hidden staves. To display the staff, click the gray line to highlight the hidden measures. Then, press DELETE to clear staff styles. Now, the two systems overlap. Click the Page Layout Tool ![icon], and then choose **Page Layout** > **Avoid Margin Collision**. Click and drag the middle of the overlapping system slightly to snap the systems to a more acceptable layout, then make fine adjustments accordingly.

- To insert a measure in an example, select the Selection Tool ![icon]. Click a measure to highlight it, then, choose **Edit** > **Insert Measure Stack**. Finale will insert a measure to the left of the highlighted one. To move a measure from system to system, highlight it with the Selection Tool and press CTRL/CMD+up or down arrow buttons on your keyboard. To add a measure to the end of your document, double-click the Measure Tool (pages added will appear in the same format as the first page by default).

- For the two-measure document, use the Page Layout Tool ![icon] to increase the overall width of the example. Click the Page Layout Tool, then click one of the system handles on the left. Press CTRL/CMD+A to select them all, then drag or nudge. Now, all of the left system margins will move in uniform.

- Use the Text Tool to edit any of the title information or the questions (double-click the handle to view the editing frame).
- Use Staff Styles to change any staff attributes (show/hide barlines, rests, etc).
- Use the Score Manager to change the transposition or number of staff lines.

You can also use the "Full System, No Barlines" template to create musical examples or questions (see Figure 13.14).

Figure 13.14

Use the "Blank Manuscript" template to create dictation and other types of examples that do not require a meter.

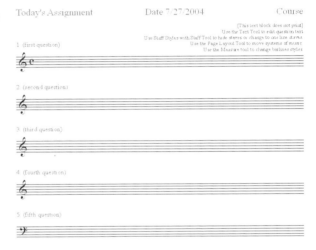

> **TIP:**
> Email your students a worksheet or musical example. They can open, print and playback, with Finale Reader, Finale's free notation software available for download at finalemusic.com/reader.

Manuscript Paper (staff paper)

You can print a page of manuscript paper from Finale containing staff lines only. To do this, open the "Blank Manuscript" template. Choose File > New > Document from Template. Then, open the Education Templates folder and double-click the file "Blank Manuscript." A page appears with blank staves and some text. Use the Text Tool (or Selection Tool) to delete any unwanted text. Use the Page Layout Tool to adjust the system spacing. Then print this document to produce a sheet of blank manuscript paper. Rename and save this file as a template for future use.

AlphaNotes plug-in

For a year or two, Finale has offered a Font, called "Finale AlphaNotes" that can be used to place letter names of notes on your noteheads (see Figure 13.15). While this has been fine and dandy, and somewhat accessible with a template, it has really come into its own in Finale 2012 with the accompanying Alpha-Notes plug-in. Using this plug-in Finale not only shows the diatonic pitch letters, but also accidentals, and can be applied to measure region.

Figure 13.15

Use the AlphaNotes plug-in to add pitch letters to noteheads for any score region.

To apply AlphaNotes to your music, select a region of music and choose **Plug-ins > Note, Beam, and Rest Editing > AlphaNotes.** Finale converts the notehead characters to Finale AlphaNote characters based on the concert pitch. If you change the pitch of any AlphaNotes notes, the character remains the same–reapply the plug-in to update. (Oh, and the AlphaNotes font includes more than just note letters ☺.)

TIP:
Use your system's Character Map/Viewer to see all Finale AlphaNotes characters. See "Adding characters using the Character Viewer/Map" on page 254.

The Exercise Wizard

If you are a music educator responsible for directing an instrumental ensemble, use Finale as a professional tool for enhancing your students' warm-up routine with customized technique-building exercises. Create scales, arpeggios, and twisters with custom articulations, in any key, transposed for any instrument. Best of all, this can be done in minutes (you can usually create a customized lesson faster than you can print the parts). You can see an example of a part generated by the Exercise Wizard in Figure 13.16.

Figure 13.16

Create customized lessons, such as this one, orchestrated for any ensemble with any number of performers.

A lesson can contain several different exercises occurring sequentially on the page. You can print or save the lesson for a single part or any combination of instruments (with any number of copies of a part for multiple persons in a section). Here, you will learn how to easily create, save, and print custom lessons.

There are two types of files you can produce with the Exercise Wizard:

- The first is a Lesson file (.LSN). This is basically a text file containing all of the settings you have made in an Exercise Wizard session. You can open a lesson file to launch the Exercise Wizard automatically and edit a collection of settings you have already made.
- The second type of file is the actual notation file (.MUS). Instead of printing directly from the Exercise Wizard, you can save a standard Finale file for each instrumental part to be viewed on-screen or stored and printed at a later time.

Exercise Wizard-Page 1

From the File menu, choose New > Exercise Wizard. Page 1 of the Exercise Wizard appears as shown in Figure 13.17.

Figure 13.17

Specify a title and the page size for your exercises on page 1 of the Exercise Wizard.

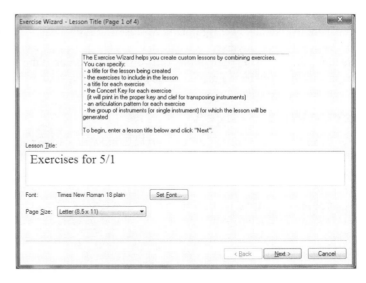

First, click the Set Font button and choose a font for the lesson title. Then enter the lesson title in the text box (this title will appear at the top of the printed page). From the Page Size drop-down menu, choose a page size for your exercises. Then, click the Next button to move to page 2.

Exercise Wizard-Page 2

On page 2, choose from hundreds of available exercises (see Figure 13.18).

Figure 13.18

Choose the type of exercises you want to include on page 2 of the Exercise Wizard.

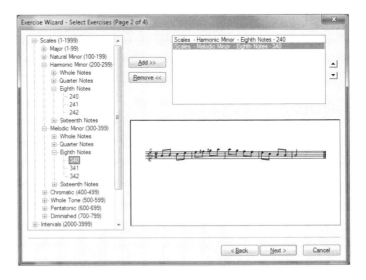

Click the plus sign (+) (Mac: triangle) to the left of any category to view and choose from items in the sub-categories. First choose the melodic structure, then scale type, interval, and note duration. The actual exercises will appear as a number (1-5571). Click a number to see a preview of the exercise in the preview window on the lower right. Double-click the exercise number (or click **Add**) to add the exercise to the lesson. Add as many exercises as you like. Select one of the exercises you have added and use the up and down arrows to the right of the list to change the order of the exercises as you want them to appear on the page. When you have finished adding and arranging your exercises, click **Next** to move to page 3.

Exercise Wizard-Page 3

Here you can enter an exercise title, concert key, and articulation pattern for each exercise (see Figure 13.19).

Figure 13.19

On page 3 of the Exercise Wizard, specify a title, concert key, and articulation pattern for each exercise.

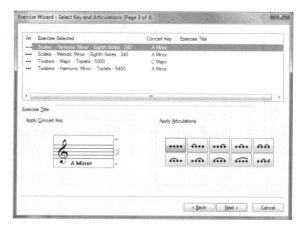

First, click the exercise you want to edit from the list at the top. Then, after Exercise Title, type a title for the selected exercise (the title will appear above the first measure of each exercise). In the **Apply Concert Key** section, use the up and down arrows in the scroll bar to modify the concert key. Under **Apply Articulations**, select an articulation pattern for the exercise. Click **Next** to move on to page 4.

Exercise Wizard-Page 4

On page 4 of the Exercise Wizard, choose the instruments you want to include in your lesson and number of instruments for each part (see Figure 13.20).

Figure 13.20

On page 4 of the Exercise Wizard, create an ensemble, then print or save your lesson.

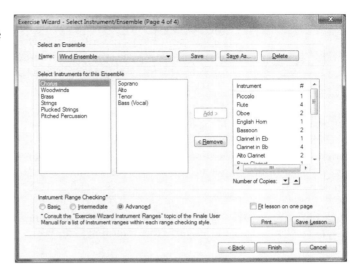

First, in the **Select an Ensemble** section, choose the instrumental ensemble that most closely matches the one you are instructing. Notice the instruments in the list on the right update to your selection. This is the master list of instruments for which you will be generating parts. Use the following methods to edit the instruments in your ensemble:

- Click to select an instrument you want to remove from the list on the right, and click **Remove** to clear it from the list.

- To add an instrument, choose the instrument type from the list on the far left, then double-click the desired instrument from the second column. Notice that the instrument appears in your ensemble list on the right.

- To add or remove the number of copies per part, click one of the instruments in your ensemble to select it. Then, click the up and down arrows for **Number of Copies**. Notice the number to the right of the instrument changes to reflect the number of copies for that part.

After you have created an ensemble, save it for the next time you create a custom set of exercises. To do this, in the Select an Ensemble section, click **Save As**. The Save Ensemble dialog box appears. Type a new name for your ensemble and click **OK**. Now, next time you create a lesson, this ensemble will be available from the **Name** drop-down menu.

Under Instrument Range Checking, choose a skill level for your ensemble. If the range of an exercise is too high or too low, Finale will transpose it an octave so all notes fit within a playable range for the selected skill level.

Check **Fit Lesson on One Page** to tell Finale to manipulate the page layout to fit the lesson on a single page. Finale will make adjustments up to a certain point but will still create more than one page if the layout becomes unreasonable.

CAUTION:
If you're just experimenting with this, remember that clicking **Print** will print a lesson for every instrument shown in the 3rd column. If you just want to test this out, create a small ensemble to save paper and ink.

Click **Print** to open the Print dialog box where you can immediately send the lesson to the printer. Finale will place the exercises in the order specified on each page and will also print the number of parts chosen for each instrument. Click **Save Lesson** to open the Save Lesson As dialog box where you can save the current configuration of settings for future use (choose **Lesson File**), or save the lesson files as standard Finale files to your computer (choose Notation File). Choose Both to save the lesson configuration and Finale files.

Click **Finish** to exit the Setup Wizard. If you have made changes to the current lesson, Finale will ask you if you want to save the lesson before returning to the score.

NOTE:
When you are ready to come back and edit a lesson you have already created, choose **File** > **Open**. Select **Lesson File** as the format. When you open a lesson file (.LSN), Finale will automatically launch the Exercise Wizard where you can make changes to the lesson.

14
Playback, Audio, and the MIDI Tool

Finale is a scorewriter if it is anything at all. Sure, you can use it to produce some killer recordings, but plenty of pro audio software products were designed specifically for that sort of thing. Finale was designed primarily to allow you to notate and print sheet music. So, if you don't need notes on a staff you are probably using the wrong product! But if you do, bonus, your score will sound great even before the premier.

Over the past few Finale versions, and in Finale 2012, emphasis has been directed to providing the highest-quality playback possible with the least amount of hassle. These improvements include Garritan Personal Orchestra sounds, the Garritan Aria Player, SmartMusic SoftSynth improvements, mixer controls, tempo control (TempoTap), greatly enhanced Human Playback, audio recording, synchronization with video, Save as Audio, integration of the Ambience Reverb plug-in, support for other VST/AU plug-ins, and finally, Finale 2012's new Score Manager. That's quite a list, but all these features were designed to make your music sound better and your life easier. Consequently, creating a live-performance-quality recording is not only possible; it's easy, as long as you use these tools correctly (and have a capable computer).

In this section you will first learn how to manage Finale's included sound libraries including Garritan instruments, and then integrate Human Playback to generate a realistic performance of your score with minimal effort. Then, you'll learn how to use Finale's playback features to spot-check any note or chord on the fly, play from any measure, or even isolate specific staves or layers for playback. Once the fundamentals are out of the way, you'll learn the other essentials; "conducting" the tempo, tweaking the balance, applying reverb, and saving as an audio file. Finally, you'll learn how to dig in and edit the MIDI data yourself, and even combine Human Playback's interpretation of the score with your own. You'll learn how to manipulate MIDI data for a single note or any selected region with the MIDI Tool, and define a variety of playback effects manually using expressions including volume, pitch bends, tempo, and MIDI controller data.

If you don't care about playback at all you can skip this chapter entirely.

Here's a summary of what you will learn in this chapter:

- How to use Finale's Instrument Sounds
- How to use Human Playback
- General playback techniques

- How to define playback with expressions
- How to use the MIDI Tool

Instrument Sound Setup

The way instrument sounds are handled in Finale 2012 is completely new, and very smart. If you were a zombie, and happened to stumble upon the computer keyboard, which in turn opened a new orchestral score, you would have superb playback (assuming enough random flailing of limbs somehow also resulted in note entry). Here, in a nutshell, is how it works: all sounds are part of Finale's *instrument* definition, as shown in the Score Manager. VST/Audio Units sounds are automatically assigned using *Sound Maps*. A Sound Map matches sound samples in a particular sound library (like Garritan sounds) to Finale's instruments as shown in the Score Manager (**Window** > **Score Manager**). Whenever you start a new score with the Setup Wizard, or add an instrument with the Score Manager, Finale uses Sound Maps to automatically load a sound for each instrument. This begs two questions: "how does Finale know which Sound Map you want to use?" and "what if the instrument added doesn't have a corresponding sound in the Sound Map?" Glad you asked. When you add an instrument, Finale attempts to use the Sound Map you have prioritized highest in the Sound Map Priority dialog box (**MIDI/Audio** > **Sound Map Priority**). If the highest Sound Map in the list does not include the instrument sound, Finale defers to the second Sound Map in the list, and so forth, until an appropriate sound is found and loaded. The magic Finale does behind the scenes (such as assigning channels and configuring the VST/Audio Units Banks & Effects dialog box) need not concern you in the slightest, or infringe upon the important notation tasks at hand.

Finale includes Sound Maps for the sound libraries installed with Finale and also those available for sale by MakeMusic. The ones included in the box/download that are ready for use are the Garritan Instruments for Finale and SmartMusic SoftSynth. Other Sound Maps include Garritan Jazz and Big Band (JABB), Garritan Personal Orchestra (full GPO), and Garritan World Instruments (see finalemusic.com for details). If you have installed a 3rd party VST/AU library of sounds, unfortunately, you will not be able to create your own Sound Map. But, you will be able to assign those sounds manually. See "Assigning 3rd Party VST/Audio Unit Sounds" on page 361.

When you open a score from an earlier Finale version, or open a template that uses 3rd party sounds, Finale 2012 does not alter the file's original sound assignments–Sound Maps are not applied automatically. In both cases, it's easy to benefit from Finale 2012's Sound Map intelligence without having to manually choose a Sound Map for each instrument. At any time, to automatically reassign sounds to all your score instruments based on the Sound Map priority you've selected, choose **MIDI/Audio** > **Reassign Playback Sounds**. This also comes in handy if you have reconfigured sound settings in the Score Manager manually and want to revert back to your Sound Map settings. Also, if you change the Sound Map priority, you will need to run this command to apply the updated sound assignments.

Sound Maps only apply to playback if you are using VST/Audio Units. If you are using MIDI for output, all the playback settings in the Score Manager will be different, and depend on your MIDI setup. Let's explore this distinction further...

MIDI vs. VST/Audio Units Playback

Here are descriptions of these two playback mechanisms; these can be found under the MIDI/Audio Menu.

- When **Play Finale through MIDI** is selected, Finale uses the instruments selected in the MIDI Setup dialog box for playback. This includes Finale's SmartMusic SoftSynth SoundFont based on the standard General MIDI sounds. If this option is selected, VST/ Audio Units are disabled in favor of SmartMusic SoftSynth and/or MIDI internal or external output devices.

- When **Play Finale through VST/Audio Units** is selected, Finale uses the instruments configured in the VST/Audio Units Banks & Effects dialog box for playback (usually set automatically using the Sound Maps assigned in the Score Manager). This may include Finale's Garritan instruments, the VST/AU SmartMusic SoftSynth library, or your own 3rd party sound library. If this option is selected, settings in the MIDI Setup dialog box/ Internal MIDI Setup dialog are not used.

Finale does not allow MIDI and VST/Audio Unit playback simultaneously. It's either one or the other. Also, the two mechanisms are handled quite differently. With VST/Audio Units, when you add instruments, Finale references Sound Maps, assigns channels, and loads banks intelligently without requiring hardly any work on your end. When playing Finale through MIDI, on the other hand, the output devices in the Score Manager reflect the devices you choose for output in the MIDI Setup dialog box, so those need to be configured by you first (see "Using the SmartMusic SoftSynth" on page 361 for setting up playing back through MIDI with the SmartMusic SoftSynth).

The basics for setting up Finale with any MIDI output device can be found in the "Setting up your MIDI System" section of the Finale User Manual. This next section describes Finale's integrated VST/Audio Unit sounds and how they can be handled with the Score Manager.

Working With Garritan Sounds

Finale's Garritan sounds are professionally recorded sound samples that offer the most realistic performance imaginable. Of course, this advancement comes at a price. Like any collection of VST/Audio Units sound samples, in order to get the most out of the Garritan sounds it is advisable to own a machine with a fast processor and lots of memory. In fact, the usefulness of Garritan sounds is directly proportional to the power of your computer. Finale 2012 recommends 1 GB of memory, but more is better. The memory necessary is also dependent on the size of the score, so if you only plan on working with brass quintets and SATB scores, the minimum requirements will work fine. If you work with full orchestral scores, obtain a lot of memory or use a sound other than Garritan (i.e. external MIDI or SmartMusic SoftSynth). While Finale applies Garritan sounds to new instruments automatically (see "Instrument Sound Setup" on page 358), you have complete control to change the configuration of your sound assignments with the Score Manager.

To manually assign Garritan sounds with the Score Manager:

1. Open any document or begin a new one. To use one of Finale's included examples, choose **File** > **Open,** then click the **Repertoire** shortcut and open a piece from Finale's Repertoire library.

2. Choose **MIDI/Audio** > **Play Finale Through VST/Audio Units**.

3. Choose **Window** > **Score Manager**. You can assign any of Finale's instruments to a sound without leaving the Score Manager. (To add or change instruments using the Score Manager, see "Adding, Removing, and Changing Instruments" on page 26.)

4. Under the **Device** column for the instrument you want to change, choose **Garritan Instruments for Finale** (see Figure 14.1). This Sound Map, installed with Finale, allows you to select any of the included Garritan sounds. If you have installed another sound library that MakeMusic offers (like full GPO or Garritan Jazz and Big Band), you can choose that Sound Map instead to choose from sounds in its library. (3rd party sound libraries do not have Sound Maps. See "Assigning 3rd Party VST/Audio Unit Sounds" on page 361 to load a 3rd party sound.) Finale's Sound Maps always appear at the top of this list.

5. Under the **Sound** column you'll see the default Garritan sound assigned to the instrument. You can click the drop-down menu and choose a new Garritan sound.

Figure 14.1

Use the Garritan Sound Map in the Score Manager to easily assign Finale's included Garritan sounds.

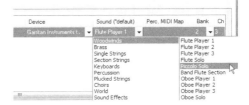

Finale assigns banks and channels automatically. If you'd like to view the Garritan Aria Player where the sounds are loaded, choose **MIDI/Audio** > **VST/Audio Units Banks & Effects**. Next to **Bank 1:(1-16)**, "ARIA Player" should be selected. Click the button to the right. The Garritan Aria Player appears as shown in Figure 14.2.

Figure 14.2

The Garritan instrument assignment is displayed in the Garritan Aria Player. The Garritan Aria Player can be used to modify many aspects of the instrument's performance.

If you click the **Controls** button on the right, you will see several dials and settings. These settings can generally be left alone. In fact, the most important role of the Aria Player is the ability to assign each Garritan sound to Finale instrument using identical channel assignments. And, since Finale does this automatically, there isn't much need to meddle here. Close the Garritan Aria Player window and the Score Manager to return to the score.

TIP:
For a thorough tutorial on using Garritan sounds with Finale, consult the "GPO and HP Tutorial" in the Finale User Manual. Choose **Help** > **User Manual**. Then, in the **Table of Contents** pane on the left, click **Finale Tutorials** and then **GPO and HP Tutorial.**

Now, click the Play button in the Playback Controls to play the document. (If the Playback Controls are not visible, select **Window** > **Playback Controls**.)

NOTE:
Finale's SmartMusic SoftSynth VST/AU General MIDI sound library is loaded directly, and does not require a separate player interface.

Using the SmartMusic SoftSynth

MakeMusic's *SmartMusic SoftSynth* is a high-quality General MIDI sound library that is available for both MIDI and VST/Audio Units playback. This device uses the 128 standard General MIDI sounds.

To use the SmartMusic SoftSynth:

1. If you would like to use SmartMusic SoftSynth with MIDI, choose **MIDI/Audio** > **Device Setup** > **MIDI Setup** (Mac: **MIDI/Internal Speaker Setup**).

2. Mac users, for **Playback Device**, choose **SmartMusic SoftSynth**. Windows users, for **MIDI Out**, choose **SmartMusic SoftSynth**. (Click **Show Advanced** to set additional MIDI banks). Click **OK**.

3. Choose **Window** > **Score Manager**.

4. Under the **Device** column, choose **SmartMusic SoftSynth**. For MIDI, the eight banks refer to the slots in the MIDI Setup dialog box. For VST/AU, the SmartMusicSoftSynth can be loaded into as many banks as desired. In any case, there are 128 different sounds available (16 channels in 8 banks).

Assigning 3rd Party VST/Audio Unit Sounds

If you are using a VST/AU sound library *not* offered by MakeMusic, you will unfortunately not be able to benefit from the automatic Sound Map functionality when adding or changing instruments. But, you can easily assign sounds from your library to Finale instruments using the Score Manager.

1. Choose **Window** > **Score Manager**.

2. Under the **Device** column for the instrument, choose your player (Aria, KontaktPlayer2, etc.). Finale automatically assigns the bank and channel. Note the channel listed under the **Channel** column for the instrument.

3. Under the **Sound** column, click **Edit Player**. The sound library's player opens.

4. Load the desired sound and set it to the corresponding channel listed for the instrument in the Score Manager. You can load additional sounds, assigning them to other Finale instruments the same way.

5. Close your player and the Score Manager and play the score. (Or, you can leave the player open as you play to review the interaction between the player and Finale).

TIP:
To apply effects to your VST/Audio Units sounds (like reverb settings with Finale's included Garritan Ambience, or other effects with your own plug-ins), use the VST/Audio Units Banks & Effects dialog box. (**MIDI/Audio** > **VST/Audio Units Banks & Effects.**)

Using External, Non-General MIDI Sounds

If you are using an external MIDI device (i.e. if **Play Finale Through MIDI** is selected under the MIDI/Audio menu), you can use any sound from that device by defining a new *Custom MIDI Sound* in the Score Manager. To create a Custom MIDI Sound for playback through an external device, see "Assigning external MIDI sounds in the Finale User Manual. (Custom MIDI Sounds are like Finale's MIDI "instruments" in 2011 and before).

NOTE:
Finale does not support simultaneous playback of Garritan sounds and external MIDI devices.

How to Use Human Playback

Using Human Playback (also called HP) isn't difficult. In fact, if you haven't changed any HP settings, all of your new files will play back using the Standard HP style. Here's how it works: when you click the Play button, Human Playback basically analyzes the entire score and adds its own MIDI data temporarily. This MIDI data is based on articulations, dynamics, and any other marking a performer would respond to during the performance. Although many of Finale's default articulations and expressions have included a default playback effect for years (such as key velocity), HP applies many types of MIDI controllers simultaneously to generate a realistic performance. After the performance, this temporary MIDI data is deleted. Of course, a live performer wouldn't sit down and play a new piece for the first time without evaluating the style of the music. (A Romantic piano concerto is performed differently than a Baroque one.) Because of this, HP allows you to specify the style of your piece. For example, if your Jazz Band score requires a swing feel, simply choose the Jazz style and the swing effect is applied automatically.

To specify the Human Playback style, choose **MIDI/Audio** > **Human Playback**, and then select the desired style (see Figure 14.3).

Figure 14.3

Choose a Human Playback style, create a new style, or turn off HP in the Playback Settings (Windows)/Playback Controls (Mac) or under the MIDI/Audio menu.

Click the Play button in the Playback Controls to review playback. The document plays back using HP's interpretation.

> **TIP:**
> HP has a repertoire of words it understands. For example, you can add an expression that contains the text "stretto" and HP will increase the tempo accordingly. For a list of text that HP understands, see "HP Dictionary" in the Finale 2012 User Manual.

It's important to remember that assigning a Human Playback Style in the Playback Settings/Playback Controls is like handing your score over to a performer. None of the MIDI data you have added yourself will be used, and the entire score will play back using Human Playback's interpretation. If you want to hear your own manually defined MIDI data for playback (as will be described later in this chapter), you have two options: You can either set Human Playback to None so no HP is applied, or you can specify types of MIDI data HP should use or incorporate in the Human Playback Preferences dialog box (see "Human Playback Preferences" on page 366).

Applying Human Playback to a Region

When you assign a Human Playback style, you resign to using the same HP style for the entire piece. If you want to apply HP to a specific region of your score, or use more than one HP style in the same score, you can do so with the Apply Human Playback (AHP) plug-in. Rather than temporarily adding MIDI data to your score, the Apply Human Playback plug-in actually adds the HP MIDI data to the selected region.

To apply a Human Playback to a region:

1. Choose **MIDI/Audio** > **Human Playback** > **None**. Since this plug-in actually adds MIDI data to your score, HP needs to be set to **None**. (Remember, if you choose an HP style, all existing MIDI data is ignored in favor of HP's interpretation during playback).

2. Choose the Selection Tool .

3. Select a region of measures.

4. Choose **Plug-ins** > **Playback**, and then **Apply Human Playback**. The Apply Human Playback dialog box appears as shown in Figure 14.4.

Figure 14.4
Specify a Human Playback Style or assign custom HP settings in the Apply Human Playback dialog box.

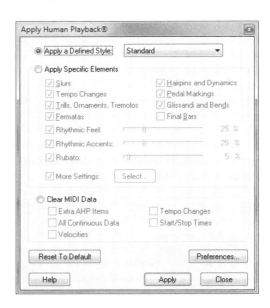

5. Here, you can choose an HP style, or, select **Apply Specific Elements** to specify precisely which items you want HP to incorporate or ignore. Select **Clear MIDI Data** to specify types of existing MIDI data to clear from the selected region.

> **NOTE:**
> To apply a Jazz style with swing, choose the **Jazz** style from the list at the top.

6. Click **Apply** to apply these settings to the selected region.

7. Click the Play button in the Playback Controls to review playback.

Now, you can follow the same steps to apply HP to other regions of your score. For some playback effects, like tremolos and trills, HP adds hidden notes to your score, so you may see a clutter of gray notes among your original notation. These apply to playback but will not print. (To hide these completely, choose **View** > **Show** and uncheck **Hidden Notes and Rests**). The MIDI data that the Apply HP plug-in adds to your score can be edited with the MIDI Tool like any MIDI data you add yourself. You will learn how to create and edit MIDI data manually later in this chapter.

Creating a Custom Human Playback Style

To make fine adjustments to existing HP styles:

1. From the Audio/MIDI Menu, choose Human Playback > Custom. The Human Playback Custom Style dialog box appears as shown in Figure 14.5.

Figure 14.5

Modify an existing Human Playback Style in the Human Playback Custom Style dialog box.

2. From the **Human Playback Style** drop-down menu, choose the style that most closely resembles the piece. When you do this, you see the dialog update to the settings for that style. (Note that changing the settings will not affect the existing style in any way.)

3. Use the options and sliders here to modify the resulting playback effect. Here is a quick description of some of the less-obvious parameters:

   - **Rhythmic Feel.** This slider controls the amount of rhythmic variance allowed from the designated time signature and tempo. Moving this slider to the right allows HP more freedom to make subtle stylistic adjustments to the rhythm (without making any changes to the global tempo).

- **Rhythmic Accents.** This slider controls the amount of dynamic accentuation that is allowed. Move the slider to the right to instruct HP to exaggerate dynamic changes it applies.

- **Interpret section.** Here, check items you want HP to recognize in its interpretation.

- **Mood slider.** This is the most nebulous parameter in HP. It affects many other HP settings, and no one really knows precisely how (except maybe Mr. Piechaud, who designed HP). Moving the slider to the right increases general chaos, or randomness, during playback.

- **Automatic Expression.** This option adds expressivo to held notes for sustaining instruments, and smooths attacks and releases for soft notes. The degree to which Automatic Expression is applied depends on the Mood slider.

- **Detection of Solo Instruments.** If you have a solo instrument in you score, or any solo sections, this box should be checked. HP finds solos in your score (sections marked with the text "solo"), and brings them out automatically.

- **Match Harmonic Cadences.** This feature keeps track of the harmonic progression and automatically slows the tempo slightly for cadences.

4. Click **OK** to return to the Playback Settings/Playback Controls. Notice "Custom... " now appears for Human Playback Style. You can choose **Custom** from this drop-down menu again to edit your custom style.

5. Click **OK**.

6. Click the Play button in the Playback Controls to review playback.

TIP:
To apply this custom style to a selected region, in the Apply Human Playback dialog box, under **Apply a Defined Style**, choose **File's Custom Style.**

Human Playback Preferences

You can apply additional settings to HP's interpretation, like the number of notes per second in trills, or length of Fermatas in the Human Playback Preferences dialog box. In fact, you can apply specific settings to each output device you intend to use. You can also use this dialog box to combine existing MIDI data with Human Playback's interpretation. Important: There are two HP Preferences dialog boxes that house the same parameters: one will affect standard HP (defined in the Playback Settings/Playback Controls) for the entire document; the other will affect HP applied with the Apply Human Playback plug-in.

To edit HP Preferences for standard HP, choose **MIDI/Audio** > **Human Playback** > **Human Playback Preferences**. The Human Playback Preferences dialog box appears as shown in Figure 14.6. (Changes you make here apply to regular HP and do not apply to HP data added to a region with the Apply Human Playback plug-in).

To edit HP Preferences for HP data added to regions of your score with the Apply Human Playback plug-in:

1. Choose **Audio/MIDI** > **Human Playback** > **None**.

2. Choose **Plug-ins** > **Playback**, and then **Apply Human Playback**. The Apply Human Playback dialog box appears.

3. Click **Preferences**. The Apply Human Playback Preferences dialog box appears (which looks the same as the Human Playback Preferences dialog, except for the word "Apply" in the title bar). Changes you make here apply to all regions of your score for which HP is applied with the Apply Human Playback plug-in, and do not apply to HP defined in the Playback Settings/Playback Controls.

Figure 14.6

Define global settings for HP in the Human Playback Preferences dialog box.

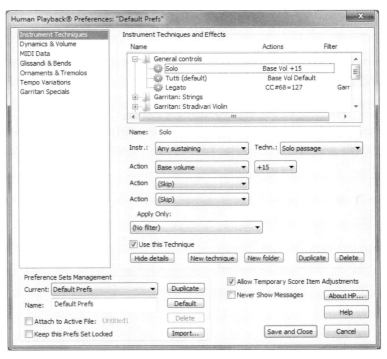

Detailed customization can be applied to Human Playback's interpretation of your score using these settings which are fully described in the Finale User Manual. Here is an overview of the seven available pages.

- **Instrument Techniques and Effects.** Use these settings to modify Human Playback's interpretation based on the needs of specific sound libraries. For example, you may wish to perform a tremolo differently using Garritan strings than SoftSynth strings. Human Playback's performance will differ depending on the instrument library used and its unique settings defined in this section.

- **Dynamics & Volume.** Use this page to customize Human Playback's interpretation of crescendos, diminuendos, and other dynamic effects for sustaining instruments (winds, strings, voice, etc.).
- **MIDI Data.** Human Playback allows you to trust it completely (Ignore), incorporate your own MIDI data (Incorporate), or use your own MIDI data exclusively (No HP Effect). Each of these options is available for Continuous Data, Velocity, Start/Stop Time, and Tempo. These settings are described in more detail later in this section.
- **Glissandi & Bends.** Here, you can define the granularity and shape of glissandos and the degree of pitch bend.
- **Ornaments & Tremolos.** Here you can define the frequency of trills, rolls and tremolos.
- **Tempo Variations.** HP uses this type of MIDI data for tempo changes (rit. or accel.) and other effects to interpret fermatas, breath marks, and other slight tempo variations.
- **Garritan Specials.** Use these settings to optimize Human Playback's interpretation when using Garritan sounds.

Later in this chapter, you'll learn how to add MIDI data to your score manually. If there is a type of playback effect you can't seem to get right using one of HP's options, you can apply the effect manually using the MIDI Tool , and then tell HP to use your manually defined MIDI data, or even incorporate it into HP's interpretation. This can also come in handy if you are using a score that already contains manually defined MIDI data that you want to use in combination with HP. Look at the four drop-down menus in the MIDI Data pane of the Human Playback Preferences dialog box (Figure 14.7).

Figure 14.7

Integrate your own MIDI Data with Human Playback's interpretation using the MIDI Data pane of the Human Playback Preferences.

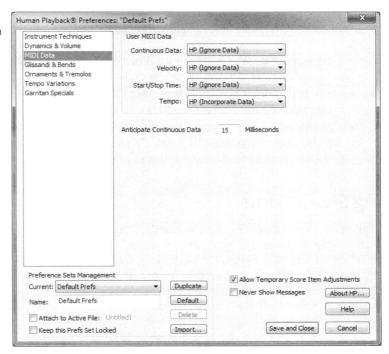

These are the four types of MIDI data you can meld with HP. Following is a list of the effects and how you can add them (select the MIDI Tool to display the MIDI Tool menu):

- **Volume.** HP uses this type of MIDI data for crescendos, diminuendos, and other dynamic effects for sustaining instruments (winds, strings, voice, etc.). Add this data using the Continuous Data option under the MIDI Tool menu.

- **Velocity.** (Also called "Key Velocity.) HP uses this type of MIDI data for crescendos, diminuendos, and other dynamic effects for non-sustaining instruments (piano, harp, etc.). This type of MIDI data affects the attack volume only. Add this data using the Key Velocity option under the MIDI Tool menu.

- **Start/Stop Time.** HP uses this type of MIDI data to create subtle changes to the duration of notes, for example, to overlap notes slightly for slurred passages. Add this data using the Note Durations option under the MIDI Tool menu.

- **Tempo.** HP uses this type of MIDI data for tempo changes (rit. or accel.) and other effects to interpret fermatas, breath marks, and other slight tempo variations. You can add tempo changes easily with TempoTap or by assigning expressions defined for a tempo change.

NOTE:
There is more information regarding the MIDI Tool later in this chapter.

HP offers 3 different settings for dealing with MIDI data, described below:

- **HP (Ignore Data).** Choose this option to ignore existing MIDI data in the score and use Human Playback's interpretation exclusively.
- **HP (Incorporate Data).** Choose this option to tell HP to recognize existing MIDI data of this type so that it influences HP's interpretation.
- **No HP Effect.** Choose this option to tell HP to use the MIDI data that exists in the score. If you choose this option for Velocity, for example, key velocity MIDI data you have applied yourself will be used instead of HP's interpretation.

Using SoundFonts

A SoundFont is a collection of instrument sounds (WAV files) that can be loaded by a soundcard or software program and triggered by MIDI controllers. You can use SoundFonts as your MIDI output device in Finale (with **Play Finale Through MIDI** selected under the MIDI/Audio menu). In fact, the SmartMusic SoftSynth SoundFont is ready for use when you first launch Finale. This is a General MIDI SoundFont, the same used in MakeMusic's intelligent accompaniment software, "SmartMusic." To use the SmartMusic SoundFont, see "Using the SmartMusic SoftSynth" on page 361.

General Playback Techniques

Now that you've learned how to manage Finale's Human Playback capabilities, let's move on to techniques you can use to review your score in progress. You have a great deal of control over the region of playback while working on a score. You can play back an entire document from the beginning (as you've already seen), easily start playback at any measure, or drag your mouse over a region to deliberately listen for specific chords (scrubbing playback). For any of these methods, you can isolate any number of staves and/or layers using the instrument list, or even specify a staff or the full score for playback on the spot while scrubbing. In this section, you will learn how to make the most of Finale's playback versatility to spot-check a score in progress, or generate a quality MIDI performance.

Playback Controls

You can use the Playback Controls to manage the basics for playing back your score. If you do not see the Playback Controls on your screen, from the Window menu, choose Playback Controls. They appear on your screen as shown in Figure 14.8.

Figure 14.8

Start, pause, stop, record, or specify the measure to start playback with the Playback Controls.

To use the Playback Controls:

- Click ▶ to begin playback at the measure specified in the counter box `1| 1|0000`. Playback will start at measure 1 by default. To use the counter on Windows, click ●. Then, under **Always Start At**, choose **Current Counter Setting** and click **OK** (or **Left-most Measure**). On Macintosh, click ▦ to display the advanced options. After **Play From,** choose the lower radio button. Now, on Mac or Win, enter a measure number in the counter box to specify a start point for playback (or **Leftmost Measure**). **Leftmost Measure** means playback will always begin at the leftmost visible measure on the screen. (Kami, my technical editor and wife, notes that **Leftmost Measure** is her "favorite option," so it's the real deal.)

- Click ■ to stop playback.

- Click ‖ to pause playback. Then use the ◀◀ and ▶▶ buttons to advance to a specific measure. Click ▶ again to resume playback.

- Click ⏮ on the left to move to the beginning of the piece for playback. Click ⏭ on the right to move to the end of the piece.

- You can click ● to automatically select the HyperScribe Tool ✍ and begin recording into the first measure of the staff specified for recording in the Score Manager. Though, you don't need to use the Record button. Instead, just the select HyperScribe Tool and click the measure you want to record into (see "Real-Time Entry: Hyper-Scribe" on page 88 for more information on HyperScribe).

- You can choose a tempo for playback in the Playback Controls. On Windows, click ♩▦ and select the main beat. On Macintosh, click ▦ on the left side of the Playback Controls to expand the settings, the click ♩▦ and select the main beat. Then, enter the number of beats per minute in the text box to the right. Note that tempo markings defined for playback in your score will override this setting.

You can make a number of other settings for playback in the Playback Settings dialog box (Windows) or the expanded Playback Controls (Mac). On Mac, click ▦ to expand the Playback Controls; on Windows, click ●. You will now see additional playback settings as shown in Figure 14.9. Use these settings to adjust the start point for playback, change the base key velocity, or set swing playback.

Figure 14.9

Use the Playback Settings (Windows)/expanded Playback Controls (Mac) to make a variety of settings for playback.

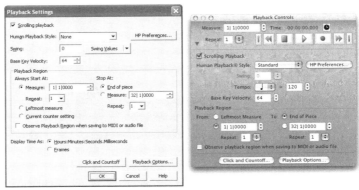

Windows   Macintosh

Here are some common ways to manage playback with these settings:

- Make sure **Scrolling Playback** is checked. With this setting, Finale always scans the music for changes and then plays back with a scrolling bar.
- In the **Playback Region** section, as mentioned earlier, **Leftmost Measure** is the best. It works in any view, and is probably what you want to use at all times (really).
- The **Base Key Velocity** is basically the default dynamic level. This is set at 64 by default to give you the optimal amount of contrast as you enter dynamic expressions and MIDI data that adjust the key velocity throughout the piece.
- If HP is set to None, Jazz, Reggae, Rock, or Samba, you can easily set swing playback here. Choose the type of swing playback you want from the Swing Values (Mac: Swing) option. Click the arrow to choose Light, Standard, Heavy, or Dotted Eighth, Sixteenth from the menu to set swing playback. This setting applies to the entire document.

Defining Regions for Playback

Though the Playback Controls can be adequate for general playback, if you really want more efficiency while reviewing a score in progress, you may want to begin playback at a specific measure on the page, or play back a specific staff of your score. Following are ways to quickly isolate specific regions for playback.

Spacebar-Click Playback

Here are ways to easily specify a particular measure for playback using the SPACEBAR+click method. After starting playback with the following methods, click anywhere in the score to stop playback.

NOTE:
Human Playback defined in the Playback Settings/Playback Controls is not applied when using the SPACEBAR+Click method to start playback.

- Macintosh users: Press SPACEBAR (the Playback Controls must be open), to begin playback at the measure specified in the counter box. Press SPACEBAR again to pause.
- To play back starting at any visible measure, hold down SPACEBAR and click the desired measure (with the Playback Controls closed on Mac). (Show or hide the Playback Controls by choosing **Window** > **Playback Controls**).
- To play back the contents of a single staff starting at any visible measure, SHIFT+SPACEBAR+click the staff in the desired measure.
- If you are using a staff set, SPACEBAR+click on a staff to play back the visible staves.
- If you are using a staff set, SPACEBAR+click between two staves to play back all visible and hidden staves (see "Customizing Staff Viewing: Staff Sets" on page 184 for more information on creating staff sets in Scroll View).
- To begin playback starting with measure one, SPACEBAR+click to the left of the staff

Scrubbing Playback

Listen to notes in your score as you drag by using the Scrubbing Playback feature. (This is called "Audio Spot-Check" in the Finale manual.) This is the fastest way to play back a small portion of your score for review.

- CTRL+SPACEBAR (Mac: OPTION+SPACEBAR) and drag (without clicking the mouse button) over a region of music to hear music in all staves. (On Mac, make sure to press OPTION before SPACEBAR to scrub).
- CTRL+SHIFT+SPACEBAR (Mac: OPTION+SHIFT+SPACEBAR) and drag over a staff to hear music in that staff only.

Recorded Versus Notated Playback

If you recorded a performance into Finale with HyperScribe, and Human Playback is set to **None** in the Playback Settings/Playback Controls, Finale plays the score back as you performed it, including all of the subtleties that go along with your recorded performance. This performance data includes key velocities, note durations, start times for each note, and continuous data you have specified in the Record Continuous Data dialog box. You can tell Finale to play back a score as recorded, or precisely as it appears in the notation. Choose **Document** > **Playback/Record Options**. The Playback/Record Options dialog box appears as shown in Figure 14.10.

Figure 14.10

Tell Finale to play back a score as recorded or as notated in the Playback/Record Options dialog box.

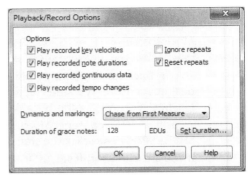

To tell Finale to play the score as notated (without the nuances of your recorded performance), in the **Options** section, uncheck the **Play Recorded Key Velocities** and **Play Recorded Note Durations**. Uncheck **Play Recorded Continuous Data** if you want playback to ignore continuous data (such as sustain pedal) as well. Then click **OK** to return to the score and play back the document to review your changes.

NOTE:
To specify the type of Continuous MIDI data you want to record in a HyperScribe session, choose **HyperScribe** > **Record Continuous Data**. Refer back to "Real-Time Entry: HyperScribe" on page 88 for details.

The Mixer and Staff Controls

Finale's Mixer and Staff Controls offer convenient sliders and dials that can be used to adjust playback effects on the fly (see Figure 14.11). You might use these staff sliders, for example, to adjust the volume of individual staves to perfect the overall balance.

Figure 14.11

Use the Mixer and Staff Controls to adjust volume, panning, and other playback effects in real-time.

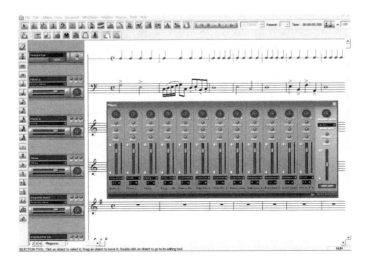

The Staff Controls, Mixer, and even the Score Manager, are dynamically linked. For example, a change to the volume of a particular staff will be reflected in all three of these places. These controls are pretty self-explanatory, so there's not much need to dwell on them. Here are a few things you should know.

- The Staff Controls are available in Studio View (**View** > **Studio View**).
- Choose **Window** > **Mixer** to open the Mixer.
- The Mixer settings apply to Channels, not the instruments themselves. Therefore, changes to a staff will also apply to all other staves assigned to the same MIDI channel. It is always recommended to assign a unique MIDI channel to each staff (which is usually only an issue with older files).
- Mixer settings are saved with the file.
- Mixer settings apply to saved Audio Files and SmartMusic Accompaniments (.SMP files).

"Conducting" the Tempo with TempoTap

The history of defining tempo changes in Finale is long, storied, and fraught with such unsavory terms as "executable shapes." It's much easier now:

To define a ritardando or accelerando (or any tempo change):

1. Click the HyperScribe Tool .
2. Choose **View** > **Studio View**. The TempoTap staff appears above the instrument staves.
3. Click a measure in the TempoTap staff to display the green TempoTap cursor to the left of it. Finale is now waiting for you to start conducting the tempo.
4. Tap the tempo on the SPACEBAR or any note on your MIDI keyboard. When you are done, click the score with your mouse. The Last Recorded Tempo dialog box appears as shown in Figure 14.12.

Figure 14.12
This dialog box displays the tempo reached at the conclusion of a TempoTap session (and a sprightly one at that).

5. Click **OK**. Your tempo changes have been applied to the score. Repeat these steps if necessary. The "Last Recorded Tempo" value is applied to the subsequent measures until it reaches additional tempo change data.

Fixing Percussion Playback

If you have opened a file created before Finale 2010 when Finale's percussion mechanisms were overhauled, especially a *really old* file, there is a chance your percussion notes require an overhaul as well. These specimens have a characteristic orange hue and make silly, unfamiliar sounds. If this is the case, you can transpose your existing notes to the appropriate Note Type to remedy. Then, if necessary, update the percussion layout to restore the original staff positions. You may need to do this for every percussion instrument in your score. (Don't worry, it's not that hard.)

TIP:
You may be able to automatically clean up all your percussion notes in one fell swoop. Try choosing **Document > Data Check > Reconvert Percussion Note Types**. Also, you can choose **MIDI/Audio > Reassign Playback Sounds** to reconfigure all your instrument sounds using Finale's Sound Maps, which also ensures Percussion MIDI Maps are properly assigned to instruments. See "Instrument Sound Setup" on page 358.

To assign percussion notes to Note Types:

1. Choose the Selection Tool .

2. Select a region that includes the percussion notes you want to change. Then, choose **Utilities > Transpose Percussion Notes**. The Transpose Percussion Note Types dialog box appears, which shows the MIDI note number of the selected percussion instrument.

3. Select the note (or MIDI note number) from the list, click the **Change Selected Note To** drop-down menu, and choose the desired Note Type, in this case "Claves." (See Figure 14.13.)

Figure 14.13

Use the Transpose Percussion Note Types dialog box to assign your percussion instruments to the correct sound.

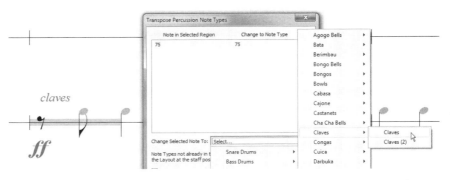

4. Click **OK**. If the Note Type is in the current percussion layout selected for the staff, it may shift staff positions, which we'll fix next. (If the Note Type is *not* in the staff's percussion layout, a new percussion layout will be created with the Note Type set to

the staff position of the original note, and you can repeat steps 1-4 for the next percussion instrument.)

5. Choose **Window** > **Score Manager**.

6. Select the percussion instrument (the staff) in the Score Manager, and click the **Settings** button next to **Notation Style: Percussion** and click **Edit**. The Percussion Layout Designer appears.

7. Scroll down and select the same Note Type you selected earlier, then, on the right, drag the notes to the correct staff position.

8. Click **OK** and **Select** to return to the score. Close the Score Manager. Repeat these steps for other percussion instruments as necessary.

NOTE:
If you would like to use an external MIDI device with a non-General MIDI percussion sound, you will need to define a custom Percussion MIDI Map. See "To setup an external MIDI device for percussion input & playback" in the Finale User Manual.

Using Mute and Solo

If you don't need all staves playing, you can turn some off using the Score Manager's *Mute* function. You can even turn off individual layers and other aspects of instruments. Or, you can *Solo* an instrument to silence all others (or, specifically, all others that are not also set to Solo).

1. Choose **Window** > **Score Manager**.

2. Click **Customize View** and ensure **Mute & Solo** is checked.

3. Notice the column labeled **M**. This is the **Mute** column. To remove an instrument from playback, click its box under the **M** column. Now, during playback, the staff will remain silent.

4. Designate a solo instrument under the **S** column. To designate a solo instrument (and mute all other instruments), click its box under the **S** column. Now, only the solo instrument will play during playback. Feel free to choose as many solo instruments as you like. Finale will play all instruments set to solo.

5. Now, click the arrow to the left of an instrument Name to expand and display more options for that instrument. You now see options for layers, expressions, and chords as shown in Figure 14.14. Use the **M** and **S** columns to mute or solo any layer within a staff. You can also mute or solo the staff's expressions and chord symbols here.

Figure 14.14

Mute or solo layers, expressions, and chord symbols in the Instrument List.

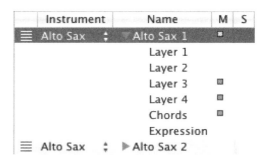

Defining Playback with Expressions

Human Playback is capable of interpreting dynamic markings, tempo changes and other markings that apply to playback automatically. For example, enter an expression with the text "rit." and HP knows it is supposed to slow the tempo. Add an expression with the text "cresc." and HP will gradually increase the dynamic level. If you decide to set HP to None and define playback for your score manually, or if you have set the Human Playback Preferences to use or incorporate existing MIDI data, expressions can be a good way to define these playback effects. Also, in some cases, such as changing the playback instrument mid-score, expressions are well suited to define the playback effect.

You can define a variety of playback effects in your score with expressions including dynamics, tempo, and the playback instrument. You can apply a playback effect to your score without displaying an expression marking. You can edit the playback effect of any existing expression or define your own playback effect. In this section, you will learn a variety of ways to edit the MIDI performance of your score using the Expression Tool .

> **NOTE:**
> For specific information on creating, assigning, and editing expressions, see "Entering Expressions" on page 75.

Dynamics

As a general rule, use HP (or the Apply Human Playback plug-in) to incorporate dynamics during playback. And then if, for example, a forte section isn't coming through, you might think about using a fortissimo instead. Believe it or not, HP can be used this way to discover the appropriate balance for your ensemble. However, to apply a dynamic level manually, you can assign a specific key velocity to an expression. Here's how:

1. Click the Expression Tool ![mf].
2. Double-click a measure to open the Expression Selection dialog box.
3. Click the **Dynamics** category and select an existing expression, then click **Edit**. (Or, to create your own new expression, click **Create**.) The Text Expression Designer dialog box appears.

4. Edit the text box as necessary. Then, click the **Playback** tab.

5. For **Type,** choose **Key Velocity.**

6. For **Effect,** enter the new key velocity, 0-127 (0 =silent, 127 = loudest). (See Figure 14.15.) Note that these changes apply to all occurrences of this expression in your score.

Figure 14.15

Use the Playback tab in the Text Expression Designer dialog box to specify a playback effect for the expression.

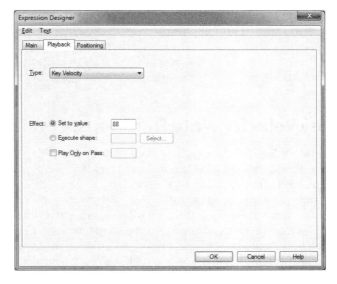

7. Click **OK,** then **Assign** to return to the score. Play the region for review. Finale will use this key velocity for the staff until it reaches another key velocity change.

Using the MIDI Tool

The remainder of this chapter describes advanced techniques for defining playback effects manually. If you are satisfied with Human Playback's results, and do not care to manipulate MIDI playback data manually, skip ahead to Chapter 15.

The MIDI Tool is a powerful way to manipulate playback in Finale. Alter the key velocity and duration of notes for any selected region, or number of selected notes. Or, apply continuous data to a region. Use the MIDI Tool window for a visual display of the MIDI data as you fine-tune changes to the playback. I won't cover every feature of the MIDI Tool, but the following instructions include concepts you can use as a foundation for exploring the thousands of possibilities for creating a custom MIDI performance.

CAUTION:
IMPORTANT! To hear your manually defined playback effects, either set Human Playback to **None** in the Playback Settings/Playback Controls or choose **Incorporate** or **No HP Effect** for that type of MIDI data in the MIDI Data pane of the Human Playback Preferences dialog box. A Human Playback Style selected in the Playback Settings/Playback Controls overrides all manually defined MIDI data by default. To learn how to incorporate MIDI data you define with the MIDI Tool with Human Playback's interpretation, refer back to "Human Playback Preferences" earlier in this chapter.

Key Velocity, Note Durations, Continuous Data, and Tempo

The MIDI Tool's framework is split into four sections: Key Velocity (how hard a key is struck as if it were played on a MIDI keyboard), Note Durations, Continuous Data, and Tempo. Windows users, choose **Window** > **Advanced Tools Palette**. Click the MIDI Tool, and then choose the MIDI Tool menu. Whenever you are using the MIDI Tool, you can choose which type of MIDI data you want to edit from the four items at the top of this menu. Key Velocity and Note Durations are somewhat self-explanatory. Tempo refers to tempo changes, ritardando/accelerando. Continuous data encompasses everything from pitch bends and patch changes to more than one hundred types of MIDI controller data, including sustain, panning, volume, and many others. You can manipulate Key Velocity, Note Durations, and Continuous Data in several ways as shown lower in the MIDI Tool menu (Set to, Scale, Add, Percent Alter, etc.).

Here are general steps you can take to edit MIDI data for a region of your score.

Key Velocity (Crescendo Example)

For this example, you'll scale the key velocity over two measures of eighth notes to create a crescendo effect. To prepare for these steps, open a new Default Document and add eighth notes into the first two measures. (To hear the effects, HP must be set to **None**. Choose **MIDI/Audio** > **Human Playback** > **None**.)

1. Click the MIDI Tool . Highlight the first two measures.
2. Choose **MIDI Tool** > **Key Velocities**.
3. Choose **MIDI Tool** > **Scale**. The Scale dialog box appears as shown in Figure 14.16.

Figure 14.16

Specify the opening and closing values for MIDI data applied to a selected region in the Scale dialog box.

4. In the first text box, enter the key velocity for the first note in the region. Try 64. In the second text box, enter the value for the final note in the region. Try 120. These values can be anywhere from 0 to 127. In this case 0 is silent, 127 is very loud.

5. Click **OK**.

Play back the region. Notice the crescendo effect. You just told Finale to evenly scale the key velocities for the selected region. Now, if you want to set all notes in the selected region to the same key velocity, from the MIDI Tool menu, choose **Set To**. To change by percent, choose **Percent Alter** (note that using Percent Alter after the previous example will retain the crescendo). Use the various menu items (Scale, Add, Etc.) to manipulate the key velocity of the selected region as you wish.

TIP:
To remove all MIDI playback data from a region, select the region with the MIDI Tool, then choose **MIDI Tool > Clear**. The type of MIDI data selected under the MIDI Tool menu will be cleared.

Note Durations (Start Time Example)

You can alter the start and stop times for any region of notes with the MIDI Tool as well. For this example, enter two measures of quarter notes into your scratch document. Let's say you want notes in the second of these measures to anticipate the beat by a sixteenth note. To do this with the MIDI Tool:

1. Click the MIDI Tool ⬤ . Highlight the second of the 2 measures.

2. Choose **MIDI Tool > Note Durations**.

3. Choose **MIDI Tool > Add**. The Add dialog box appears as shown in Figure 14.17.

Figure 14.17
Edit the start or stop times for a region of notes in the Note Durations > Add dialog box.

4. Enter "-256" in the text box. This setting is in EDUs. There are 1024 EDUs in a quarter note, so 256 EDUs equals a sixteenth. It's negative because you want the notes to play prior to their original placement. Any time you edit note durations in the MIDI Tool by entering a value, you will be using EDUs. (See Table 1.2 "Measurement Units" on page 13).

5. Click **OK**.

Play the region. Notice the second measure of quarter notes anticipates the beat by a sixteenth note. You can use the same basic procedure to change the start time, stop time, or overall duration of notes for a selected region. Percent alter can be very handy for note durations.

Continuous Data (Continuous Crescendo Example)

Continuous Data is somewhat different than Key Velocity and Note Duration data. Continuous Data applies not only to the MIDI "Note On" and "Note Off" signals, but to the entire duration of sustained pitches. For example, to enforce a crescendo or pitch bend on a single sustained pitch, you would need to apply Continuous Data to the region.

To prepare for the following steps, add any sustaining instrument with the Score Manager (like Trumpet in C). Enter a whole note in the first measure. Use the following steps to apply a crescendo to the whole note. (To hear the effects, HP must be set to **None**. Choose **MIDI/Audio** > **Human Playback** > **None**.)

1. Click the MIDI Tool ⊛ .
2. Choose **MIDI Tool** > **Continuous Data.** The View Continuous Data dialog box appears as shown in Figure 14.18.

Figure 14.18

Choose the type of continuous data you want to apply to your score in the View Continuous Data dialog box.

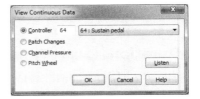

3. Choose **Controller** > **Controller 7, Volume.**
4. Click **OK.**
5. Click to highlight the first measure.
6. Choose **MIDI Tool** > **Scale.** The Scale dialog box appears.
7. Scale Continuous Data from 40 to 120 in increments of 1.
8. Click **OK.**

Play the region and notice the change in volume. To see a graphical representation of this Continuous Data, double-click the measure to open the MIDI Tool Window.

The MIDI Tool (Split) Window

Instead of editing your MIDI data directly in the score, you can use a separate window to view and edit MIDI data on a graph. When you double-click any measure with the MIDI Tool selected, the MIDI Tool Window will appear. This window takes up the top half of the screen on Windows, and opens as a moveable window on Macintosh (See Figure 14.19).

Figure 14.19

View MIDI data applied to a region of your score, or edit MIDI data
in the MIDI Tool Window.

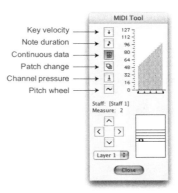

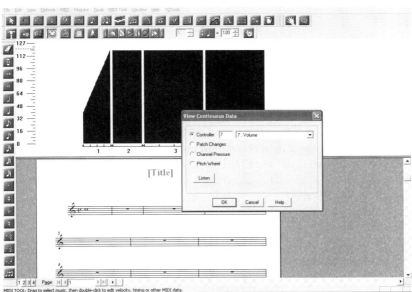

The shaded (Mac) or black (Windows) area indicates continuous data applied to the measures. You can
use the MIDI Tool Window to view or edit Key Velocities, Note Durations, Continuous Data, or Tempo.

Macintosh: Editing MIDI Data in the MIDI Window

In your scratch document, enter four quarter notes into a measure. Then, choose the MIDI Tool and
double-click the measure containing the four quarter notes to open the MIDI Tool Window. To edit the
MIDI data for this region, first choose the type of MIDI data from the icons on the left (see Figure 14.20),
or choose from the MIDI Tool menu. If you choose Continuous Data, choose the type of Continuous
Data from the View Continuous Data dialog box and click **OK**. Then, click and drag in the MIDI display

portion (upper right) to select the region you want to edit as shown in Figure 14.20. The selected region will be highlighted in blue.

Figure 14.20

Click and drag in the MIDI display portion of the MIDI Tool Window to select the region you want to edit.

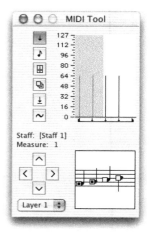

If you want to highlight more than one non-consecutive region in the graph area, SHIFT+click and drag. If you are editing Key Velocities or Note Durations, you can also highlight the handles to select individual notes in the measure display portion at the bottom (SHIFT+click to select non-consecutive notes). Now, choose **MIDI Tool** > the type of modification (**Set to**, **Scale**, **Add**, etc.). Enter the desired value and click **OK**. The MIDI display portion of the MIDI Tool Window updates to display your changes.

To navigate in the MIDI Tool Window:

- Use the arrows to the left of the measure display portion to navigate to the desired measure or staff. Notice the Staff and Measure indicator above the arrows shows the exact measure you are currently viewing.
- Click the layer select pop-up menu in the lower left to choose the layer you want to edit.
- Choose **MIDI Tool** > **Show Selected Notes** to isolate the selected notes in the MIDI display portion of the MIDI Tool Window.

To play back the region without leaving the MIDI Tool Window, choose **MIDI Tool** > **Play**. Click anywhere to stop.

Windows: Editing MIDI Data in the MIDI Split Window

In your scratch document, enter four quarter notes into a measure. Move to Scroll View (Scroll View tends to be more convenient while using the MIDI Split Window (see Figure 14.21), though both views will work). Choose the MIDI Tool and double-click the measure containing the four quarter notes to open the MIDI Tool Split Window. It will appear on the top half of your screen and display MIDI data for several measures. To edit the MIDI data for this region, first choose the type of MIDI data from the MIDI Tool menu.

Figure 14.21
Click and drag to enclose the notes or region you want to edit in the MIDI Tool Split Window.

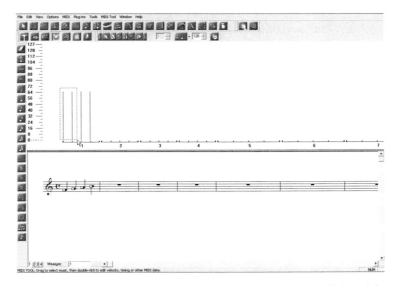

If you want to highlight more than one non-consecutive region in the graph area, SHIFT+click and drag. If you are editing Key Velocities or Note Durations, you can also highlight the handles to select individual notes in the staff below the Split Window (SHIFT+click to select non-consecutive notes). Now, choose **MIDI Tool** > the type of modification (**Set to**, **Scale**, **Add**, etc.). Enter the desired value and click **OK**. The MIDI display portion of the MIDI Tool Window updates to display your changes.

To navigate in the MIDI Tool Split Window:

- Use the scroll bar on the bottom to move horizontally through your score. Use the scroll bar on the right to move up or down between staves.
- Use the layer select buttons on the lower left of your screen as you would normally to switch layers.
- Choose **MIDI Tool** > **Show Selected Notes** to isolate the selected notes in the MIDI Tool Split Window.

To playback the region without leaving the MIDI Tool Window, choose **MIDI Tool** > **Play**.

Copying MIDI Data

You can copy MIDI data from one region and apply it to any other region of your score with the MIDI Tool. This feature works just like drag-copying with the Selection Tool. To copy MIDI data:

1. (On Windows, choose **Window** > **Advanced Tools Palette**). Click the MIDI Tool .

2. Highlight a region of your score containing MIDI data you want to copy.

3. Choose **MIDI Tool** > [the type of MIDI data you want to copy].

4. Choose **MIDI Tool** > **Dragging Copies MIDI Data.**

5. Click and drag the highlighted region to the destination region. If the destination region is out of view, CTRL/OPTION+click the first measure of the destination region.

6. Enter the number of times you want to copy the MIDI data. For example, if you are copying a single measure and want to apply the same MIDI data to the next five measures, enter "5" here.

Adding Audio

It turns out vocal syllables are rather difficult to synthesize or sample properly for use in a sound bank, and, realistic pitched text recognition just isn't feasible quite yet either. So, Finale is limited in this regard...it can't sing your aria for you. But, if you can sing, you can record your own vocal track. If not, import an audio file from someone who can. We'll explain both these scenarios in this section, and yes, this does apply to any type of recording, including your own inventive sound effects.

Recording Audio

To record audio, make sure Finale can hear you though your computer's microphone, add an audio track, set the countoff and metronome click, and start recording. Here's how:

1. Choose **MIDI/Audio** > **Device Setup** > **Audio Setup.** The Audio Setup dialog box appears.

2. For **Mic Source,** indicate the sound card or device associated with your microphone. When Finale hears a signal you will see activity in the Input Meter. Sing or play into the microphone at full volume. Adjust the Mic Level so that the signal is strong, but not into the red zone at the top.

3. Then select the desired reverb effect (**Reverb Type** > **Large Hall, Medium Room,** etc.) and click **OK** to return to the score.

4. Click the HyperScribe Tool ![icon]. You will be recording over a metronome click, so we'll set that up first.

5. Choose **MIDI/Audio** > **Click and Countoff.** The Click and Countoff dialog box appears. The Measures setting in the upper right is the number of countoff measures; change this to 1 if you want to. Use the default setting (with the internal metronome click).

6. Click **OK.**

7. Choose **View** > **Studio View.**

8. Choose **MIDI/Audio** > **Audio Track** > **Add Audio Track.** The audio track appears above the top staff.

9. Use headphones so the microphone doesn't pick up the click.

10. Click the measure you would like to start recording, listen to the countoff measure(s) and begin recording. When you are done, click the score. The audio representation appears within the audio track.

TIP:
Finale's Audio Track can only support one recording session. Any existing material in the audio track will be deleted if you record again into the same track. For greater control, use an audio editor (e.g. Wavelab or Sonar) to record at the same tempo and then load the Audio file.

Importing Audio (loading audio)

Finale can load a single audio file into any document as long as the file is in WAV, MP3, or AIFF format.

To import/load audio:

1. Identify the measure and beat you want the audio file to begin within the Finale score. If you do not want it to enter directly on a beat, note the beat prior to the desired entry point. Refer to the measure counter [1|1|0000] in the Playback Controls to identify a precise moment.

2. In your audio recording product, crop the part of the audio file you need and save it in its own file. (This is easier than entering "Start in Clip" and "End in Clip" values).

3. Move to Studio View. (**View** > **Studio View**).

4. Choose **MIDI/Audio** > **Audio Track** > **Add Audio Track** (if you haven't already). The audio track appears above the top staff.

5. Choose **MIDI/Audio** > **Audio Track** > **Load Audio**. The Audio Clip Attributes dialog box appears as shown in Figure 14.22.

Figure 14.22
Use the Audio Clip Attributes to position the audio clip where desired within the score.

Audio Clip Attributes	
Path:	W:\Finale_Doc\Mark's Folder\mus\fanfare2.wav Select...
File Type:	WAVE
File Length:	00:00:26.792
File Format:	16-bit Integer (Little Endian), Stereo, 44100.0 Hz
Start in Score:	1| 1|0000 Repeat: 1
Start in Clip:	00:00:00.000
End in Clip:	00:00:26.792 Set to End
Display Unit:	⊙ Time
	○ Samples

OK   Cancel   Help

6. For **Start in Score**, enter the desired entrance point (if not at the beginning).

7. If you do not have access to audio editing software, and cropping the needed portion wasn't possible, specify the portion of the audio clip you want to play using the **Start in Clip** and **End in Clip** settings. You might need to experiment with this setting to get it right.

8. Click **OK**. The audio representation appears in Finale's audio track. Playback the score to hear the results.

You can edit the placement of the audio file at any time. Choose **MIDI/Audio** > **Audio Track** > **Audio Clip Attributes**.

15
Finale, the Web and Other Programs

It's already the last chapter and it seems like we've only begun. Finale is really a behemoth of a program, and I hope I've been able to shrink it down for you a bit. There is plenty more to discuss, but it looks like we are running out of pages and all this Finale talk has got me thinking about my own compositions–the musical ones. After all, that's really why we do this; it's why I've written this book and why you read it. We are all contributing in some way; taking the smallest seeds of creativity and bringing them to life; flooding the world with the beautiful, unique, bold, or downright mysterious. You certainly have something in mind that I couldn't possibly imagine. If my descriptions of Finale's cogs, wheels and pulleys have helped bring something from your imagination into reality, that is truly my reward. May your dynamics align, your beams feather, and your alternate noteheads grow ripe with poetry! Oh, but first finish this chapter because there is still more stuff you should know.

Here's a summary of what you will learn in this chapter:

- How to share files online
- How to transfer music between programs
- How to enhance Finale with FinaleScript and third-party plug-ins

Sharing Files Online

There are two ways to post a Finale file on the Web. If you want to share your sheet music over the Web without playback capabilities, you can convert a Finale file into PDF format. Secondly, you can simply post a file in Finale format so that others can open it in Finale or any of the Finale Notation products. Visitors who don't own Finale can always download a free product called Finale Reader, which is capable of opening and playing and printing any Finale file. In this section, you will learn how to use the above methods to integrate Finale with the Web.

Finale Reader (it's free!)

You may want to transfer a Finale file over your website or by email with the intention of allowing those who receive the file the capability to print or play it back. Recipients of the file may not own Finale (or its most recent version). That's okay. Tell them to download Finale Reader.

In the Finale Family of notation products, Reader is MakeMusic's infant, and it offers a considerable amount of power considering the price (free). Finale Reader can be downloaded at finalemusic.com/reader.

Finale NotePad (it's cheap!)

You may want to transfer a Finale file over your website or by e-mail with the intention of allowing those who receive the file full access to print, save, or even make minor changes to the file. You may be a music educator sending a musical example or homework to your students. If this is the case, recipients of the file may not own Finale (or its most recent version). That's okay. Tell them to download Finale NotePad.

In the Finale Family of notation products, NotePad is MakeMusic's toddler, and it offers a considerable amount of power considering the price (about $10). Here are some of NotePad's features:

- Open, save, and print any Finale file. That includes any file created in any version of Finale, Finale Allegro, Finale PrintMusic, Finale Guitar, or Finale NotePad. You can also create new files from scratch with up to eight staves.

- Using Simple Entry, edit or create notation.

- Transpose to any key.

- Add basic elements to your score, including articulations, expressions, lyrics, text blocks, slurs, and hairpins.

- Create basic sheet music using a very limited set of score editing tools.

To download Finale Notepad, visit MakeMusic's Web site at finalemusic.com/notepad.

Saving as a PDF File

The PDF file format is great for transferring files over the Web or by email. PDF files can be opened using Adobe Reader (available for free at Adobe's website, adobe.com) or, on Macintosh, PDFs can also be opened with Preview.

There are two ways to save a PDF file from Finale. You can either export a graphic (page or selected region) and choose PDF as the format in the Export Pages/Selection dialog box (see "Exporting a Graphic" on page 296). Or, you can use a PDF print driver to 'print' to a PDF file. When you print to PDF, you have the advantage of many additional features, particularly printing the score and parts in one print session

To save a Finale file in PDF format on Macintosh:

1. Choose **File** > **Print**. If the Page Setup dialog box appears, set up the page size and layout as you would normally. Click **OK**.

2. In the Select Score and Parts for Printing dialog box, check the appropriate boxes and click **OK**.

3. The Print dialog box appears. Click **PDF** > **Save as PDF**.

4. Enter a name, specify a location, and click **OK**.

To save a Finale file in PDF format on Windows of the currently visible score/part:

1. Choose **File** > **Save as PDF**.

2. Name the file, set any **Additional Properties**, choose a destination, and click **Save**.

To print to PDF, which allows you to create a PDF of you score and parts simultaneously:

NOTE:
If you are using Windows, printing to PDF is not included with your operating system. To print to PDF, you will need to purchase some sort of PDF generation tool like Adobe Distiller <adobe.com> or the less costly PDF995 <pdf995.com>.

1. First set up the Adobe Distiller/Adobe PDF/PDF995 as a printer. Installation of these products may accomplish this automatically. See your Adobe Acrobat instruction manual for instructions on how to do this.

2. Choose **File** > **Print**. In the Print dialog, click the **Setup** button.

3. Click the **Printer/Name** drop-down menu and choose **Adobe PDF** or **PDF995**. Then click **OK** to return to the Print dialog box.

4. Select the score/parts you want to print.

5. Click **OK**.

6. The **Save As** dialog box appears. Name the file, choose a destination, and click **Save** to create the PDF file.

Transferring Music Between Programs

You may want to take a file you have created in a MIDI sequencer (such as Sonar or Cubase) and open it in Finale to generate sheet music, or even copy excerpts of music back and forth between these programs using the MIDI clipboard. In this section, you will learn how to do this. I'll also explain a method for opening new Finale files in earlier versions of Finale (as far back as Finale 2000!) and how to convert a Finale file into MP3 or WAV format for online sharing or to be burned to a CD.

MIDI Files

If you want to use a MIDI sequencer program to open a Finale file, you could save it from Finale as a MIDI file. To do this, choose **File** > **Save As**. On Windows, for **Save As Type**, choose **MIDI File**; on Macintosh, for **Format**, choose **Standard MIDI File**. Enter a file name and click **Save**. You will then see the Export MIDI File Options dialog box as shown in Figure 15.1.

Figure 15.1

The Export MIDI File Options dialog box

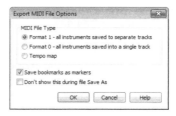

You will probably want to choose **Format-1**, which will designate your staves into tracks. This is by far the most common MIDI file format. If you want to place all of your music into one track, choose **Format-0**. Click **OK** to save as a MIDI file.

To open a file from a MIDI sequencer in Finale, first save the file in Standard MIDI format from the sequencer. Then, in Finale, choose **File** > **Open**. On Windows, for **Files of Type**, choose **MIDI File**, (on Mac, choose **Standard MIDI File** from the Enable pop-up menu), then double-click the MIDI file and you will see the Import MIDI File Options dialog box as shown in Figure 15.2.

Figure 15.2

The Import MIDI File Options dialog box

In this dialog box, you can tell Finale how to interpret the MIDI file. Make any desired changes and click **OK** to open the MIDI file into a Finale document. You may need to adjust the quantization settings to accommodate smaller rhythmic durations. Click **Quant Settings** to do this. (See "Quantization" in the Finale User Manual for details).

Backwards Compatibility and MusicXML

Many programs, such as Microsoft Word, allow you to save documents so that they are compatible with earlier versions of their software. For example, you can save a document from Microsoft Word 2011 in Word 2007 format. This makes the program "backward compatible." Finale does not support backward compatibility, so files created in Finale 2012 cannot be opened directly in Finale 2011 or any earlier version of Finale. But...

MusicXML is a universal music notation language that can be used to transfer scores between a variety of different programs, including different Finale versions, even to earlier ones. Unlike MIDI files, the Music XML format does retain text and musical symbols. You can use the Recordare's Dolet plug-in to export and import files in MusicXML format.

NOTE:
Though files created in newer versions of Finale cannot be opened in any older version (except with MusicXML), the latest version of Finale will open any Finale file created in any earlier version.

To transfer a file backward to an older Finale version:

1.   Open the Finale file you want to export.
2.   Choose **File > MusicXML > Export**. The Export MusicXML dialog box appears as shown in Figure 15.3.

Figure 15.3

Specify a path for your MusicXML file in the Export MusicXML dialog box.

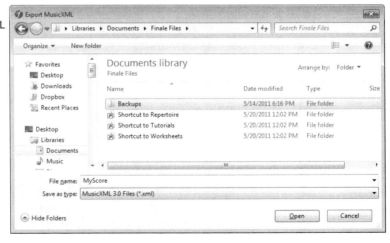

3.   Name and save your file.
4.   Now, open the older version of Finale. If you are importing the file in Finale 2005 or earlier, first download the Dolet for Finale plug-in. See the following note for details.

5. In Finale 2006 through Finale 2012, choose **File** > **MusicXML** > **Import**. Then, choose the desired file and click **Open**, and you're done.

NOTE:
The full version of their Dolet plug-in is compatible with Finale versions back to Finale 2000 (as a plug-in). Use the Dolet plug-in to import the file in Finale 2000 through 2005. A 30-day full-featured demo version of the Dolet plug-in is available at recordare.com/finale. Be sure to save the original file in MusicXML 1.0 (instead of 1.1) anytime you intend to move the file to Finale 2005 or earlier.

After importing the MusicXML file, you may need to make some changes since the music is essentially dropped into an empty Finale document.

Here are some suggestions for editing files imported from MusicXML:

*   Choose **Window** > **Score Manager** and click the **File Info** tab. Here, enter the title, composer, copyright, and description. Then use text inserts to put this info into your document. Select the Text Tool, double-click on your file and choose **Text** > **Inserts** > **Title**, etc.

*   Use the Page Layout Tool to edit the layout of the document (see Chapters 2 and 11 for more information on laying out the page)

*   If you have more than one staff in your document, you may have to respace your staves. Click the Staff Tool, and then, choose **Staff** > **Respace Staves**. Enter a percentage or value to restore your staff spacing back to that of the original document.

*   You will find that your score reverts to the default fonts. To specify a new music font, choose **Document** > **Set Default Music Font**. Then, to change other fonts, choose **Document** > **Document Options** and select **Fonts**.

Saving As an MP3, WAV, or AIFF File

To save as an MP3 or WAV/AIFF file:

NOTE:
MP3 is only available if **Play Finale Through MIDI** is selected in the MIDI/Audio menu

1. First, you will want to preview how the audio file will sound. Finale can use either SmartMusic SoftSynth or VST/AU sounds (depending on the option selected under the MIDI/Audio menu). See Chapter 14 for details.

2. Play back the score. Note that Finale will also use the Human Playback style selected in the Playback Settings/Playback Controls while generating the audio file. Refer back to "How to Use Human Playback" on page 362 for more info. Now, save the file.

3.   Choose **File** > **Export to Audio File**. The Save As Audio File dialog box appears as shown in Figure 15.4.

Figure 15.4

Specify whether you want to save as an MP3 or WAV/AIFF file in the Save As Audio File dialog box.

4.   Name the file, and then for Windows users choose **WAV**. Mac users, choose **AIFF** if you intend to burn the file to a recordable CD; otherwise, choose MP3.

5.   Specify a location and click **Save**.

That's all there is to it. What you heard during Finale playback has been converted to a file you can play back just like any other digital audio file. If you created a WAV or AIFF file you intend to burn to a CD, follow the instructions that came with your CD-writing software to do so.

Saving a Finale File as a SmartMusic Accompaniment

The SmartMusic intelligent accompaniment program is MakeMusic's rising star product. With this application, you can play your solo along with, for example, a full symphony orchestra that actually follows your spontaneous tempo changes while you play. You can also control the accompaniment by pressing a foot pedal to resume after a fermata, caesura, or the like. With a library of thousands of accompaniments, all readily available, it is becoming increasingly popular among music students and educators. It can accompany brass, woodwind, string, and vocal performers (see smartmusic.com for details). For our purposes, its most exciting feature is the ability to perform custom accompaniments created with Finale!

NOTE:
To use SmartMusic Studio accompaniments created from Finale, you need to first subscribe to SmartMusic Studio at smartmusic.com.

You can create a full-featured SmartMusic accompaniment with Finale 2012. You can even define markings such as rehearsal letters, pauses, and repeats using SmartMusic Performance Markers. To export your file as a SmartMusic Accompaniment, choose **File** > **Export to SmartMusic**.

For complete information regarding preparation and exporting of Finale files for SmartMusic, and how to create a file for SmartMusic assessment, go to the Finale User Manual and refer to the "SmartMusic" topic.

NOTE:
To preview how a Finale File will sound as a SmartMusic Accompaniment, play using SmartMusic SoftSynth (see "Using the SmartMusic SoftSynth" on page 361). Human Playback settings are also retained when you save a file as a SmartMusic Accompaniment.

Supplementing Finale with Third-Party Plug-Ins and FinaleScript

Finale offers anyone with programming experience in C or C++ (and their own development tools) the ability to create Finale plug-ins. In this way, code-savvy users can produce their own Finale "features" for use in their work. A number of third-party plug-in developers have created a large amount of helpful utilities and even sell their plug-ins to users anxious to get the very most out of Finale. Many professional engravers rely on third-party plug-ins in their Finale work, and any Finale user can easily benefit from them. This section offers just a taste of the power 3rd party plug-ins can provide.

NOTE:
All 3rd party developers can choose whether or not to update their plug-ins for compatability with Finale 2012. As of the printing of this book, the status of 2012-compatible 3rd party plug-ins is unknown.

As much as developing your own plug-in can increase efficiency, you don't need to be a programmer to automate complex or tedious procedures. Introduced in Finale 2004, FinaleScript allows you to specify a sequence of commands that can be applied to one or many documents. In this section, you will learn how to incorporate the available third-party plug-ins into your Finale repertoire, and how to create your own time-saving scripts using the FinaleScript plug-in.

NOTE:
If you are a programmer interested in Finale plug-in development, you can download the Plug-in Development Kit (PDK) from MakeMusic's download page (visit finalemusic.com, and then click Downloads to run a search for "pdk"). Note that MakeMusic's technical support department specializes in the Finale program itself and does not answer questions specific to plug-in development. Visit the PDK Users Forum, also available from MakeMusic's Web site, to interact with other plug-in developers (forum.makemusic.com).

TGTools

The TGTools plug-in set is a collection of supplemental plug-ins created by third-party plug-in developer Tobias Giesen. You have already seen a limited version of his plug-ins under Finale's Plug-ins menu

(**Plug-ins**> **TGTools**). These have been included with the Finale package since version 2002. The full version of TGTools offers many additional features including utilities for expression management, music spacing, lyrics, playback, and more (over 60 commands total). To purchase TGTools, or to download a demo version, visit tgtools.de. A full-featured 30-day demo is available. If you haven't installed this demo already, do so now. In this section I'll show you an example of one of the TGTools plug-ins in this section. For complete information on TGTools, download the PDF Manual available at tgtools.de.

After you have installed TGTools, you will see a TGTools menu item at the top of your screen. Under this menu you can find all of the TGTools utilities (see Figure 15.5).

Figure 15.5
After installation, you will see the TGTools menu on the top of your screen where you can access all of the TGTools plug-ins.

You can use TGTools to manipulate entries, selected regions, or your entire document. Most commands will require selection of a region of measures with the Selection Tool. Feel free to experiment with the TGTools commands. Any change to your score can be undone by pressing CTRL/CMD+Z.

Smart Explosion of Multi-Part Staves

Often, while creating a score, several parts in an instrumental section are entered on a single staff to minimize the number of staves necessary in the system. This works well for the full score, but such staves can be confusing to the performers while reading the extracted part. You can use the Smart Explosion of Extracted Parts plug-in to "explode" a staff containing multiple voices into two or more independent parts. This plug-in will even recognize keywords such as "tutti" or "a2" to intelligently place the correct notes into the generated staves (see Figure 15.6). This is a more comprehensive utility than the Process Extracted Parts plug-in available in the standard Finale 2012 TGTools package.

Figure 15.6

Use the Smart Explosion of Multi-Part Staves plug-in to generate two or more parts from a single staff.

To explode a multi-part staff into two or more parts, each on its own staff:

1. Open any document containing a staff containing multiple parts. The staff can display the voices in the form of different layers, the same layer, or using voice 2. (Note this does not work with linked parts. In order to use this plug-in, first extract the part (**File** > **Extract Parts**)).

2. Choose **Edit** (Mac: **Finale 2012/Preferences**) > **Program Options** and select the **View** category. Make sure **Show Defined Measure Numbers** is selected. Click **OK** to return to the score.

3. Choose **Document** > **Show Active Layer Only (ensure it** is turned off).

4. Choose the Selection Tool 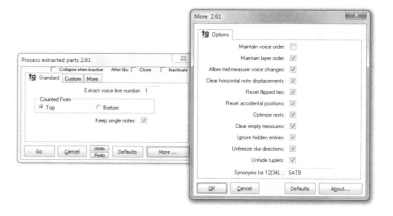, and click to the left of the staff to highlight it (or select any region of the staff you would like to explode).

5. Choose **TGTools** > **Parts** > **Smart Explosion of Multi-Part Staves**. The Smart Explosion of Multi-Part Staves dialog box appears as shown in Figure 15.7.

Figure 15.7

Choose from a number of settings for your exploded parts in the Smart Explosion of Multi-Part Staves dialog box.

6. The default settings here will work fine. Click **Go**. A dialog appears telling you not to touch the mouse or keyboard while the plug-in is working. Click **OK** and wait until things settle down. When a dialog pops up, click **OK.**

Your parts are now neatly separated into individual staves. To undo these changes, you'll have to undo several times (**View** > **Undo/Redo lists** > **TG Smart Explosion of Multi-Part Staves** and everything above, and then click **OK**). You can find more detailed information regarding exploding parts and even entire groups at once in the TGTools User Manual PDF (available at tgtools.de).

The Patterson Plug-In Collection

Robert Patterson is a third-party plug-in developer whose work appears both in supplemental plug-ins you can download from his website, robertgpatterson.com, and within the Finale program itself. Patterson Beams is also one of Robert's creations and has shipped with Finale since version 2002 (you can find more information on Patterson Beams under "Patterson Beams Plug-In" on page 274). The plug-ins offered at his Web site are free of charge for 30 days and can be activated with a single, modest registration fee.

You can find a complete description of all plug-ins included in the Patterson Collection in the User Help section of the Patterson Plug-in collection Web site. I recommend reading the user help for each plug-in before putting it to use as you will find a wealth of valuable information.

Staff Sets

Staff Sets are already one of those awesome features no one seems to know about, and they have been a part of Finale for ages.

"Customizing Staff Viewing: Staff Sets" on page 184 explained how to define specific staves for viewing in Scroll View using Staff Sets. The Patterson Staff Sets plug-in expands this concept to offer additional features for staff viewing including defining a view percentage for each staff set. With this plug-in, you can also save settings for each staff set you define allowing you to define an unlimited number of Staff Sets (instead of the eight offered in Finale proper).

Before going through the following steps, make sure the plug-in file "StaffSet" (Windows: with the extension .fxt) exists in your Finale 2012/Plug-ins folder.

To define staff sets with the Patterson Staff Sets plug-in:

1. Move to Scroll View (**View** > **Scroll View**).
2. Choose **Plug-ins/** > **Staff Sets.** The Staff Sets dialog box appears as shown in Figure 15.8.

Figure 15.8
Define staves to include in a staff set and a desired view percentage in the Staff Sets dialog box.

3. Select the staves you want to include in the staff set. CTRL/CMD+click the desired staves.

4. Check **Set View Percentage,** and choose a desired view percentage.

5. For **Use Finale Staff Set,** choose the staff set (1-8) you want to define. Note that you can define several staff sets for each Finale staff set by choosing the **Save Settings** option (see the User Help Web site for details).

6. Click **OK.** You return to the score with the selected staves isolated on the screen.

Staff Sets you define in the Staff Sets plug-in will be accessible from the View menu (**View** > **Select Staff Set**). To view all staves, choose **View** > **Select Staff Sets** > **All Staves**.

FinaleScript

FinaleScript is Finale's most customizable and, arguably, most powerful plug-in. It is a tool that allows you to specify a list of commands and apply them to the score, or to many documents, with a single click. In the body of these scripts, you can call tools, menu items, dialog box commands, and even other plug-ins. Perform operations like creating a score from parts, or transfer all or some document options to other documents The reach of this plug-in is really limited only by the commands available and your own imagination. Now, let's investigate the potential of FinaleScript.

1. Choose **Plug-ins/** ✕ > **FinaleScript,** and then **FinaleScript Palette.** The FinaleScript Palette appears as shown in Figure 15.9.

Figure 15.9

The FinaleScript Palette includes several example scripts.

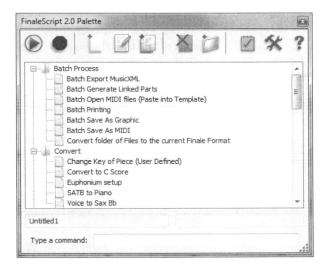

2. Finale includes many useful scripts already. You'll find these convenient resources to reference as you design your own scripts. Double-click one of the scripts to open the FinaleScript Editor. The // characters at the beginning of each line indicate a comment. When you write your own scripts, any time you want to leave a note to yourself, just type // and then your comment. Click **Cancel** to return to the FinaleScript Palette. Click the question mark icon ❓ to see a list of FinaleScript commands.

3. Notice the text field at the bottom of the FinaleScript Palette. You can enter any of the FinaleScript commands here. Enter "new default doc" and press ENTER. Finale opens a new Default Document.

4. Type the following and, after each command, press ENTER: "add staff," "select 1 11," "fit measures 3." You just added a staff, selected measure 1 through 11, then fit those measures to 3 per system. This text field can be a good way to test a command to see if it will work. Most commands are intuitive and can be applied several ways. For example, to select the Selection Tool, you can type "selection tool" or "selection".

TIP:
You can access any menu item in FinaleScript. Type "menu item "menu item name"" (with the name of the menu item in quotes). For example, to apply **Display in Concert Pitch**, type the following: menu item "display in concert pitch".

Instead of typing commands one after the other, write a script to apply them all at once. A script is just a list of commands like the ones you just entered that FinaleScript applies in the order written. Now, to demonstrate FinaleScript's capabilities, let's create a simple script designed for a unique scenario. Let's pretend the rhythm guitarist in our "Peter, Paul and Larry" tribute band contracted malaria and we need to produce a chord chart for Larry's 16 year old son who will be subbing for Larry during the evening's performance, which begins in one hour. The band is known for taking requests, so a chord chart is required for about 100 tunes. We have all the scores in Finale, but they are piano and vocal with no chords. We could open each file and apply the Chord Analysis plug-in, but that would take a lot of mousing around. FinaleScript to the rescue! Instead, you can create a script to analyze the music, add the chords, remove extra staves, and even apply rhythmic notation, converting all the scores into rudimentary chord charts. Here's how:

1. Copy the files to a new folder on your hard drive. You will be batch processing these copies of the files.

2. In Finale, choose **File** > **Open** and select one of the duplicate files in the folder you just created.

3. Click the New Script icon ⁺ . An "untitled" script appears in the list.

4. Click the Script Editor button ✎ . The FinaleScript Editor dialog box appears (see Figure 15.10). For the **Script Name**, enter "Change piano and voice to chord chart."

Figure 15.10

Type a list of commands in the FinaleScript Editor dialog box.

5. Type the following:

    process folder
    staff tool
    select staff 1
    menu item "staff/delete staves and r*"
    select all
    plug-in "chord analysis"
    click radio "all notes"
    click ok
    select staff 2
    menu item "staff/delete staves and r*"
    select all
    apply staff style "rhythmic notation"
    menu item "file/save"

TIP:
FinaleScript commands are not case sensitive. You need not capitalize unless you are specifying text to be added to the score.

6. Click **Save and Close.** You return to the FinaleScript Palette with the script you just created selected. Note an * (asterisk) can be used to abbreviate, such as in the "Delete Staves and Reposition" command used in this script.

7. Click to run the script. A flurry of activity ensues including selection, disappearing staves, dialogs being configured, files saved and opened, and so forth. (The "process folder" command applies the script to all files in the same folder as the open file). The Report button is blinking; click it to view a report on the script you just ran. Now, let's print all the files using another pre-configured script.

8. Open the **Batch Process** folder and double-click "Batch Printing." Click **Run Script** to print all files in the folder (as an alternative to the green play button).

Notice the above example script includes some dialog box commands. You can apply any dialog box command, but sometimes there are multiple "Select" or "Edit" buttons in the same dialog box. Fortunately, FinaleScript allows you to specify any button by identifying its proximity to static text using the "near" command. The * (asterisk) can be used to abbreviate long command names (e.g. you can type "(F Up P5)*" instead of "(F Up P5, Add 1 Sharp)").

When you save a script, you will be able to use it in future Finale sessions. Like Finale's existing scripts, those you create yourself can be edited at any time in the FinaleScript editor.

After creating and running a new script, the rest is a matter of familiarizing yourself with the available commands. Use the existing scripts as models. You'll notice that several commands have attributes. For example, you can type "first clef treble" to change the opening clef to treble clef. Typing "first clef bass" changes it to a bass clef. You can find a full list of all FinaleScript commands and their attributes in the "FinaleScript Plug-in" topic of the Finale 2012 User Manual. (Just click the Help button ? in the upper right corner of the FinaleScript Palette).

TIP:
Visit the FinaleScript forum to get helpful advise from other Finale users experienced with FinaleScript. Go to forum.makemusic.com forum and then go to the "FinaleScript" public forum.

The Next Finale Trailblazer Guide

Well, that about wraps it up. If you actually read this cover to cover, congratulations, you are now an official Finale Trailblazer! (That's way better than a mere 'power user'). I'd love to hear your comments and especially any suggestions for the next version. Please feel free to send me your thoughts at mark@penelopepress.com. (For those of you whose comments have helped improve this update, thank you!) Oh, and if this book happened to inspire or contribute to any original works, please send those too! I'd love to listen.

Happy scoring! ☺

-Mark

Index

Index

Index

Index

Index

Index

Index

Index

Index

Index

Index

Index

Index

trill extensions 156
trills 156
triplets. *See* tuplets
tuplets
    changing en masse 240
    entering with Simple Entry 52
    Speedy Entry 64
two-bar repeats 207
Type Into Score (lyrics) 105

U

Unicode 253
updating the layout 246
URL. *See* Hyperlink
User Manual 2

V

verse numbers 113
videos. *See* QuickStart Videos
viewing
    several score regions at once 187
views
    default view 11
    Page View 10
    Scroll View 9
    Studio View 9
VST 359

W

Wave (saving as) 394
WMF 295
word extensions. *See* Smart Word Extensions and Hyphens
worksheets 348

Z

Zooming 11